THE LIFE OF
FATHER DE SMET, S.J.

This book* is a

Loyola

request

reprint

THE LIFE OF
FATHER DE SMET, S.J.

(1801-1873)

By E. LAVEILLE, S.J.

AUTHORIZED TRANSLATION BY MARIAN LINDSAY

INTRODUCTION BY CHARLES COPPENS, S.J.

LOYOLA UNIVERSITY PRESS
Chicago 60657

© 1981, LOYOLA UNIVERSITY PRESS

A Loyola Request Reprint*

ISBN 0-8294-0372-8

Original copyright, 1915, by P.J. KENEDY & SONS

CONTENTS

CONTENTS

CHAPTER V

THE POTAWATOMI MISSION (1838–1839)

CHAPTER VI

THE FLATHEADS. FIRST JOURNEY TO THE ROCKY MOUNTAINS (1840)

CHAPTER VII

SECOND JOURNEY TO THE MOUNTAINS—ST. MARY'S MISSION (1841–1842)

CONTENTS

CHAPTER XII

THIRD VOYAGE TO EUROPE—PUBLICATION OF THE "LET-
TERS"—VISIT TO THE SIOUX (1847–1848)

CHAPTER XIII

FATHER DE SMET, ASSISTANT TO THE VICE-PROVINCIAL AND
PROCURATOR GENERAL OF MISSOURI (1849)

CHAPTER XIV

THE FORT LARAMIE COUNCIL (1851)

CHAPTER XV

THE YEARS OF TRIAL (1848–1855)

CHAPTER XVI

PROGRESS MADE BY CATHOLICISM IN THE UNITED STATES— FATHER DE SMET'S APOSTOLATE IN ST. LOUIS—THE "KNOW-NOTHINGS" (1849–1858)

CHAPTER XVII

EXPEDITION AGAINST THE MORMONS—PACIFICATION OF OREGON—CONDITION OF THE MISSIONS (1858–1859)

CONTENTS

CHAPTER XVIII

FAMILY INTERCOURSE—JOURNEYS TO EUROPE (1853–1860)

CHAPTER XIX

THE WAR OF SECESSION (1861–1865)

CHAPTER XX

A TOUR OF THE MISSIONS (1862–1863)

CHAPTER XXI

THE REVOLT OF THE SIOUX—FATHER DE SMET'S JOURNEY OF PACIFICATION (1864)

CHAPTER XXII

SEVENTH JOURNEY TO EUROPE—LAST JOURNEY TO THE MOUNTAINS (1865–1866)

CHAPTER XXIII

SECOND JOURNEY OF PACIFICATION (1867)

CHAPTER XXIV

SITTING BULL'S CAMP (1868)

CHAPTER XXV

FATHER DE SMET'S LAST LABORS—GRANT'S PEACE POLICY
(1869–1872)

CHAPTER XXVI

FATHER DE SMET'S LAST VOYAGE TO EUROPE—HIS RETREAT
IN ST. LOUIS—HIS RELIGIOUS VIRTUES—HIS DEATH
(1872–1873)

INTRODUCTION

ONE of the brightest glories of the Catholic Church shines forth in the zeal she has ever displayed for the propagation of the Gospel. From the time when Christ said to His Apostles: ",Go ye into the whole world and preach the Gospel to every creature," they and their successors, the missionaries of every age, have bravely carried on the sacred task entrusted to them, without any interruption whatsoever; and they are seen to-day as they have been seen all along, in every known portion of the earth, extending the kingdom of Christ, and preparing numberless souls for the enjoyment of heavenly bliss.

In the United States in particular the Church has nobly performed this divine mission. She has sent her heroic sons, bishops and priests, in large numbers to every tribe of the aboriginal population, baptizing, teaching, and civilizing its scattered millions, successful in converting and sanctifying large portions of them, notwithstanding the active opposition of false religionists.

Many of the most glowing pages of the great Protestant historian of the United States, George Bancroft, contain magnificent descriptions of the devoted labors of our Catholic missionaries, whose wonderful exploits he narrates with all the brilliancy and interest which attach to the writings of Prescott in his records of the Conquest of Mexico by Hernando Cortez. But every Christian feels, while reading such works, how far the sacred purpose and the self-sacrifice of the missionaries among the Indians surpass in nobility the dauntless courage of the steel-clad warriors.

It is gratifying to see that the learned world, even outside of the Catholic Church, has shown a high appreciation of the gigantic labors of our missionaries, as is evidenced by the publication in this country of a most expensive work, in seventy-three large octavo volumes, styled "The Jesuit Relations and Allied Documents," edited by Reuben Gold Thwaites. But, though this valuable collection is found on the shelves of nearly all the great libraries in the United States, its volumes are not frequently seen in the hands of the general reader, Catholic or Protestant. To enlighten him on the grandeur of our missions and missionaries, we need briefer and more popular works, which, while conveying the same information, afford more impressive and interesting reading, and communicate desirable knowledge in the charming language of lighter literature.

That is the secret of the popularity of a Prescott in his volumes on Mexico and Peru, and of a Washington Irving in his lives of Washington and Columbus. The same is an attractive quality of the life of Father De Smet, by Father E. Laveille, S. J., of which the present volume is a translation.

The French original was received in Belgium and France with marked enthusiasm. In three months the first edition was exhausted. The Belgian *Messenger of the Sacred Heart* said of it: "In the history of the Catholic apostolate few careers have been so glorious as that of the Reverend Father De Smet. We rejoice that the author has given us a clear, definite history of the man and his work." The French journal *La Croix* stated: "The life of Father De Smet reads like a novel, but one so realistic, so thrilling with interest, that you cannot tear yourself away from it."

The appreciation of the book by *Le Bien Public* calls for a more extended quotation. It says: "From the moment that you have cut its first pages you will not lay it aside until you have read the whole volume. And all along his career you will follow the hero, the apostle of the Rocky Mountains, with a passionate interest, with an ever-growing admiration, as when Fenimore Cooper, Mayne Reid, and Daniel Defoe first charmed your youthful imagination. Especially, this reading will strengthen your faith and your hope; it will show you in its divine splendor the civilizing influence of religion, transforming by a miracle of grace savage natures and raising up saints among them."

But it is not only in Father De Smet's native country that this book has been received with warm approbation. Our own able paper, *America*, has noticed its appearance in these terms: "The work seems to have been carefully and lovingly done. There is a frank enthusiasm and sympathy in the narrative which carry the reader on with growing interest; and the citations from letters and documents are very well chosen out of such a wealth of matter as lay at the biographer's command. His treatment seems full and candid, and he has been at pains to gather matter not only from the published sources, but from unpublished sources and manuscripts as well."

What has added much to the interest of the story and the reliability of the events narrated is the fact that the author had at his disposal a vast amount of material to select from. There is probably not a single one, among the numerous holy and able men whose names grace the annals of the American missions, on whose labors such copious information exists as on those of the subject of this biography. In particular I may mention that most remarkable work in which two Protestant gentlemen, Messrs. Hiram Martin Chittenden, Major, Corps of Engineers, U. S. A., and Alfred Talbot Richardson, struck by the extraordinary greatness of Father De Smet's achievements, have filled four large volumes with accounts drawn from the original sources of his life, letters, and extensive travels.

Still the book of Father Laveille is far from being a mere abridgment of even so rich a collection of original documents; it is an artistically written biography, making us familiar with the special traits of his hero's exalted character and his tenderly human personality, and at the same time citing authentic documents for every important statement, as will appear to every reader of this volume. A scion of that sturdy Belgic race, the records of whose bravery go back to the Commentaries of Cæsar, Father De Smet proved himself in every way worthy of his noble ancestry, and by his extraordinary achievements added further glory to his country. In recognition of this the prime minister of Belgium, Charles Rogier, in 1865 conferred on him the cross of a Knight of the Order of Leopold; and his fellow-citizens, since his death, have erected a statue to his honor in his native town of Termonde.

From his boyhood the future missionary gave signs of remarkable endowments. His bodily strength and his youthful daring gained for him among his playmates the sobriquet of Samson. Among those who had known him in his prime there was a tradition to the effect that, when at the age of twenty he was about to embark for America, and a bosom friend asked him for a memento, he took a copper coin out of his pocket, and biting it in two, handed him one half, as a characteristic remembrance of his herculean chum.

At that time young De Smet and eight companions, all aspirants to the missionary career, were leaving their native land without the permission of their parents; as the Holy Child Jesus had left His Blessed Mother and St. Joseph to be about His heavenly Father's business. Their reason was that they had no doubt of their holy vocation, and they well knew that permission to follow it would have been refused; their future flight would have become impossible once their parents had learned of their design. They felt convinced, besides, that the plan, when successfully executed, would bring a holy pride to the members of their pious families.

Shortly after they had reached the Jesuit novitiate in Maryland, an earnest request of Mgr. Rosati, then Bishop of Louisiana, arrived there, asking for several Jesuits to come and work in his extensive Western diocese. Two Fathers were given him, together with some of the young men who had lately come from Europe, Peter De Smet among them, who were to go and establish a new novitiate in the Far West. They were delighted with the prospect of thus coming into the closer vicinity of the Indian tribes, among which they eagerly desired to spend their zealous lives. They traversed the country, mostly on foot, for a distance of some fifteen hundred miles, till they came to the little town of Florissant, near the confluence of the Mississippi and the Missouri rivers. There in a couple of log huts they established the new novitiate, a center of future Jesuit activity for the Western States.

They felled the trees of the forest primeval—a welcome

task to the sturdy young Belgians—and in a few months built a solid edifice. But it was done amid the pangs of poverty and all manner of privations. There, on October 10, 1823, the six novices were allowed to pronounce their first religious vows, and make their consecration to the Lord lifelong and irrevocable. From that humble beginning has grown up the Jesuit Province of Missouri, which counts to-day 397 priests, 306 scholastics, 174 lay Brothers, a total of 877 members. Very soon a school was opened for Indian boys, with seven or eight tribes represented among its pupils. While teaching these, the young religious pursued their philosophical and theological studies; and on September 23, 1827, the holy priesthood was conferred on Peter John De Smet and some of his companions.

Then his missionary work began in right earnest, to be continued during forty-three years. The graphic account of these labors is given in the present volume. Here we read of numerous visits to Indian tribes and the fruitful work done among them; of the missionary's travels in unexplored regions of our continent; of his voyages to and from Europe; of his exertions in favor of the Indians with the Government and with army officials of the United States; and of the services he rendered to the administration at Washington by aiding it to secure treaties of peace with the outraged savages. He traversed the Atlantic Ocean in the course of his missionary labors as many as nineteen times, and traveled by land, it is said, over 87,000 leagues, mostly before railroads had been multiplied in America, while large portions of the regions he chiefly frequented were pathless forests or deserts. The little band at Florissant had received a number of accessions, some very talented men, when, in 1828, they undertook, at the earnest request of Bishop Rosati, to establish a college at St. Louis. It opened with forty boys, boarders and day scholars; and four years later there were 150 students, a large proportion of whom were Protestants. Father De Smet was treasurer, disciplinarian, and Professor of English. The college soon became a University.

The rapid expansion of Jesuit enterprise, which had then fairly begun, required liberal supplies of money and of new recruits; and Father De Smet was the man in the hands of Providence to procure both. This was the purpose of his frequent voyages to Europe. Each time he secured a number of candidates for the Society of Jesus, in various colleges and seminaries of Belgium and Holland, where his name was held in deepest veneration. One of his associates in St. Louis University has commented on these European travels as follows: "It is true that, in common with his companions, he lent his robust frame and gigantic strength to lay the foundation of the Society in the West. But he built up his Province much more efficiently by the resources and the members that he procured for it on the other side of the waters. When he pleaded in his native Flanders on behalf of the Indian missions, or of the growing Church in the New World, he was certain to meet with a favorable hearing. The wealthy opened their purses to contribute from their abundance, and the fervid youths in the colleges and seminaries listened with burning cheek and throbbing heart, until they had resolved to follow him and to spend themselves in the service of the Church among the Indians or among the equally destitute whites beyond the sea.

"It was thus that in the beginning we received so large an influx of those sturdy Flemings, whose panegyric St. Francis Xavier himself has left written. Strong and muscular in body, frank and open in character, ready to accommodate themselves to the customs of their adopted country, remarkable for their practical good sense and gifted with more than ordinary facility for acquiring a knowledge of English, they formed in those early days the thews and sinews, the bone and marrow, of the Missouri Province."

Further on the same authority adds: "Father De Smet rendered no less important services to his Province and to the whole Society in this country by bringing it prominently and favorably before the public. His merits were unquestionably of a superior order, and everywhere inspired admiration and respect, as well among Americans as among Europeans. With the prestige of a great name, with a presence that was imposing in his prime and venerable in his declining years, with an artless simplicity united to a dignity of bearing which always maintained the respect due to the priestly character, with winsome manners and great conversational powers, he was at home in every circle. When he wished, he soon commanded the interest and attention of the company and became the center of attraction. His hearers were won by the charm that he could throw around the simplest anecdotes of his missionary tours, and listened for hours at a time, not from mere deference for his person, but from genuine appreciation of his recital.

"Yet it was chiefly his extensive correspondence and other written papers that showed his rare talent for narration and description. Though most of them seem to have been intended for private communication, and written on the spur of the moment, they are deservedly admired by all judicious critics, and form no inconsiderable addition to the literature of the day. His published writings treat of the missions and their wants, the Church and its actual standing, the zealous lives and edifying deaths of many of our members; and a great variety of other subjects bearing upon the interests of religion. Among his manuscripts are literary Albums, highly appreciated by those who have ever glanced at them, as well as biographical sketches of our departed Fathers and Brothers, creditable alike to the virtue of the deceased and to the assiduous devotedness of the compiler, who spent his leisure moments in collecting materials for the edification of future generations.

"All his writings are remarkable for an ease and naïveté highly in keeping with his own character. Many of them display an uncommon amount of information that could scarcely have been acquired except by personal observation, and reveal to the unbiased reader the secret activity and energy of his mind. Much as he himself traveled, his writings have traveled still more, and have kindled in many a generous soul the love of a religious life. Even boys are fascinated by the romance of his Indian tales, and feel a sort of unaccountable attraction for the exploits of a missionary life, not unlike that usually awakened in them by books of adventure.

"These literary labors, added to his reputation, obtained for him an immense and influential circle of acquaintances.

The learned and the wealthy, the politician and the statesman, courted his friendship and bowed before him as before a superior."

But the principal charm of the volume here presented to the reader lies in the graphic sketches of the missionary's travels and labors among the Indians. Of these it would be vain to attempt a general outline. Their beauties sparkle on every page; the whole book must be read to realize the magnificence of the scenery described, the grandeur of the achievements performed, the aroma of the virtues practiced and the noble sentiments exhibited, not only by the missionary himself and his heroic associates, but also by many of the red-skinned warriors and their wives and children, when once their wild natures had been subdued by the gospel of peace and their souls sanctified by the waters of baptism.

Father De Smet loved his Indians warmly, not only because so good a man necessarily pitied their benighted condition and longed to make them children of God, but also because he found in large numbers of them truly noble characters, as unselfish and sincere and faithful to their friends as they were brave and fearless in battle. He found them also hospitable to strangers, and compassionate to all unfortunates who were not their traditional enemies. They were far less savage, he used to say, than those whites who, in trading with them, would cheat them out of their furs and horses, and give them trifles or fire-water in exchange.

The Indians, on their part, revered and warmly loved the Black Robe—Father De Smet and any of his associates—in whom they knew they could always confide. He, as they often expressed it, was the only white man that did not speak with a forked tongue.

That was the reason why they trusted him as mediator between them and the civil and military authorities of the United States. Thus he succeeded on various occasions in preventing a bloody revenge on their part, when they had been grievously wronged, and in obtaining from the supreme Government a proper protection for their rights.

It cruelly tore his heart when, notwithstanding all his efforts to protect the red men, he saw them, as he often did, grievously outraged in their dearest interests; as when whole tribes, evangelized for many years by Catholic missionaries and partly converted to the Faith, were arbitrarily handed over by the Government to the care of some Protestant sects. Another sad disappointment would come to him and to his fellow-laborers when, as happened in 1850 at the Flathead mission, the Indians themselves would rebel against God, and plunge into terrible excesses of drunkenness and bloodshed, thus undoing in a few days all the success achieved by many years of devoted labors.

So great a work as that carried on by so many missionaries of the regular and secular clergy in the United States, was, of course, exposed to painful reverses, sometimes of an almost discouraging kind; but the successes obtained immensely surpassed the disappointments. Besides the countless souls saved and sanctified among the Indians, large numbers of the former missions have since developed into flourishing parishes and even dioceses, the whites gradually replacing the ever-retiring sons of the wilderness. We may mention here one among many examples.

The Jesuit Fathers had settled the tribe of the Potawatomies at the mission of St. Mary's, Kansas. Instead of the few scattered log huts of the early settlement, one sees there now some eight or ten large college buildings of solid rock and brick; instead of the frame chapel, there is now a large brick parish church in the town close by, and there is the elegant stone chapel, the Immaculata, for the college students. The rough prairie grass has made room for smooth lawns and bright beds of flowers, set with evergreen trees and adorned with statuary. One of the students' dormitories, the Loyola Hall, contains one hundred and fifty-six private rooms. In these not only are lodged boys and young men from many States in the Union during the school year, but during the summer vacations there assemble in them priests and laymen to sanctify themselves in the Spiritual Exercises of St. Ignatius. Thus the modest Indian mission of former times has become a beacon-light of religion, literature, science, and civilization generally for all the Middle West of the United States.

Nor is it forgotten at such places that the seed of this rich harvest was first sown by Father De Smet and his brethren. Thus St. Mary's, Kansas, on the fiftieth anniversary of its foundation, held a solemn celebration in commemoration of the event; and, in August, 1915, the mission among the Sioux Indians of South Dakota solemnized the seventy-fifth anniversary of the arrival of Father De Smet in that region by a numerous and enthusiastic session of an Indian Congress.

CHARLES COPPENS, S. J.

THE LIFE OF
FATHER DE SMET, S.J.

CHAPTER I

CHILDHOOD—YOUTH—DEPARTURE FOR AMERICA
(1801–1821)

Termonde—The Family—"Honest De Smet"—The Parish Priest of
Heusden — Peter's Birth — His Childhood — "Samson" — His First
Studies—Beirvelde, St. Nicolas, Alost, Mechlin—His Vocation—Father
Nerinckx—Young De Smet with Eight Companions Leaves Secretly
for America—His Brother Charles is Sent to Find Him—The Police of
King William—Arrival at Georgetown.

THE intimate charm of the old Flemish towns has
been vaunted in story and song. Termonde, although not so interesting as "Bruges-la-Morte," possesses
a certain picturesqueness of its own and more than one
heroic legend adorns its annals. Situated at the confluence of the Dender and the Schelde in the midst of a
plain, Termonde offers exceptional advantages for military
defence. Fortified at the beginning of the fourteenth
century, it has withstood many sieges at the hands of the
English, French, and Spaniards; in 1667 the brave burghers
of the place forced an army commanded by Louis XIV
himself to retreat.[1]

[1] It was at night while the King was celebrating his anticipated victory
that the defenders of the town pierced the Schelde dikes in several places
and opened the sluices of the Dender. Instantly the surrounding country
and the French camp were inundated. Louis XIV, warned in time by a
miller, fled, crying, "Cursed city—would that I could take you with an
army of ducks!"—(Chronicken van Vlaenderen, Vol. iv, p. 737.)

Translator's Note: History repeated itself on Sept. 7, 1914, when the
German Army in its operations against the Allies in Belgium laid siege to
Termonde with a force of twenty thousand troops. A garrison of six
thousand Belgian soldiers defended the city for six hours and when forced
to evacuate opened the dikes of the Schelde. The resulting inundation
obliged the Germans also to abandon the situation.

To-day Termonde boasts of a population of ten thousand inhabitants. It is surrounded by a moat, and this, with the sinuous canals and their ceaseless and silent traffic winding through the town, gives it the appearance of a Venice of the North. One finds considerable commercial activity there and it is also the seat of an important garrison, but these aspects of modern life have not stifled a proper respect for the traditions and monuments of the past. The imposing cathedral with its fine wainscoting, its paintings by Flemish masters, its time-honored Virgin; the town-hall where the municipal council were accustomed to take the oath of office in defence of liberty; the ancient belfry whence the joyful notes of the chimes are wafted over the city; the statues of Our Lady at the street corners; the silent monasteries veiled in mist, and the "beguinage" with its white cells grouped around the little church—all this reminds one of the Flanders of other times, with its busy life, proud independence, and solid faith.

The De Smet family was one that gloried in preserving intact its heritage of old customs and manners, and for three centuries strength of character and exemplary Christian living have been transmitted with the name from father to son. When John De Smet, grandfather of our missionary, lay dying, he summoned Joost, his youngest son, and, like the patriarchs of old, gave him a solemn blessing. That scene left an enduring impression upon the young man, who in after life would often describe it to his own children.

Joost De Smet was born December 18, 1736, at St. Amand-lez-Puers in the province of Antwerp. On January 15, 1761, he married Jeanne Marie Duerinck of Termonde, or rather its environs, a fact which doubtless decided them to live in Termonde. Joost was a ship-owner and resided in the Rue de l'Escaut,[2] in a large house which to-day is still standing. Through his untiring energy and his genius for business he amassed a fortune that enabled him to provide his numerous children with

---

[2] Rue de l'Escaut has recently been renamed Franz-Courtens.

Translator's Note: It is doubtful if this house is still standing, owing to the severe bombardment by German artillery in the operations against Termonde on or about Sept. 7, 1914.

honorable positions in life. His honesty was so proverbial that he was known as "honest De Smet." He gave generously in support of all good works and on two occasions came to the assistance of relatives who were in financial difficulties and thus saved the honor of the name.

When in 1792 Dumouriez requested the Belgians to select provisional representatives from each "commune" Joost De Smet was one of eighteen citizens elected by the city of Termonde.

The plans of Dumouriez apparently contemplated that the provisional representatives were to superintend and carry out the public policies, and guard the rights of the people until a constitution was established to replace the Austrian régime, and that the form of government thus adopted by them was in no wise to be interfered with.[3] We know how the decree of December 15th shattered every hope that was founded upon the moderation and disinterestedness of Dumouriez[4]; how, upon his own admission, this act proved that the Convention had sent an army only to despoil and tyrannize over the Belgians[5]; and with what universal protestation this decree was received by the entire country. At Termonde Joost De Smet and his colleagues steadfastly refused to accept a decision which was a brutal violation of the rights they had sworn to defend. Nor did they permit the insistence of the commissioners of the Convention to coerce them, even when that body held out threats of military execution. Some weeks later when the people of Termonde, at the "Assemblée Primaire" in the cathedral of Notre Dame, were called upon to choose between the existing régime or annexation to the French Republic, the ship-owner declared himself uncompromisingly on the side of adhering to the ancient constitution.[6]

[3] Cf. "Proclamation of General Dumouriez to the People of Belgium," Nov. 3, 1792.

[4] This decree, destined to prepare the way for annexing Belgium to France, was the work of the Deputy Cambon. After promising the Belgians "peace, support, fraternity, liberty, and equality," the Convention reduced them to a state of dependence and treated them as outlaws. Cf. Namèche, "Cours d'Histoire Nationale," Vol. xxvii, p. 327, et seq.

[5] See "Mémoires du Dumouriez," London, 1794, Book I, Chaps. iii and viii.

[6] Cf. "Register of the Resolutions of the Magistrate of the city of Ter-

Of Joost's marriage with Jeanne Marie Duerinck seven children were born. The eldest, Jean Baptiste, became a priest and had the honor and privilege of confessing his faith during the French Revolution. Being vicar of Sleydinge, near Eecloo, in 1797 he refused to take the civil oath required by the Directory, and, in consequence, was condemned to be deported to Guiana. For a time he succeeded in hiding himself in his parish, but finally was arrested a year later, was sent to the prison at Ghent, and thence to the Isle of Ré, where he remained for upward of twelve months, serving as a nurse in the military hospital of the garrison. He was ransomed finally by his father,[7] and, upon his return to Belgium, assumed with great ardor the functions of vicar of Sleydinge. In 1804 he was appointed parish priest at Heusden, near Ghent, and here the saintly Abbé remained for four years until his death, which was one altogether in keeping with the admirable tenor of his life. On the feast of Corpus Christi, June 19, 1808, in his forty-sixth year, while preaching an eloquent sermon on the love of Jesus Christ in the Blessed Sacrament, he faltered suddenly and sank to the floor. His parishioners rushed to his aid, but before they reached him he had passed away.[8]

Joost De Smet lost his first wife after thirty years of married life, and eventually contracted a second marriage with a certain Marie Jeanne Buydens, a native of the village of d'Acren-Saint-Gereon in Hainaut. Although there was great disparity in the ages of this couple, the second wife being at the time twenty and the husband fifty-six years of age, the union was not less happy or prolific than the former one. Marie Buydens became the mother of nine children, and Joost De Smet realized, in fact, the fruits of that paternal benediction which

monde," published by Jean Broeckaert in the Annals of the Archeological Society of Termonde, 1900, pp. 290–300.

[7] Joost De Smet at the same time ransomed J. B. Peeters, who was the dean of Laerne.

[8] Cf. Van Baveghem "Het Martelaarsboeck der belgische geestelijkheid ten tijde der fransche omwenteling," Ghent, 1875; p. 249. The memory of Father Jean De Smet is still venerated in his former parish. On Sept. 29, 1868, a monument was erected in the church at Heusden as a memorial to him.

had made so lasting an impression on him years before.[9]

Among the children of the second marriage mention must be made of Rosalie, Charles, and Francis, for their names will occur often during the course of this narrative. Rosalie De Smet married, in 1830, Charles Van Mossevelde, a man who was prominent in the business and politics of Termonde. Charles and Francis became lawyers and both attained distinction.

Peter, the future apostle of the Rocky Mountains, was born on January 30, 1801, a few moments before his twin sister, Colette Aldegonde. The twins were baptized the same day in the church of Our Lady, by Father Ringoot, the parish priest. Baptiste Rollier, their brother-in-law, stood sponsor for both children, the godmother being their sister-in-law, Colette De Saegher.

Peter's childhood was passed under the vigilant eyes of his father and Marie Buydens, and to him, who some day

[9] The following are the names of Joost De Smet's children by his first wife, Jeanne Marie Duerinck:

  Jean Baptiste, born Jan. 4, 1762, died June 19, 1808, curate of Heusden.
  Jeanne Catherine, born Aug. 1, 1763, died Sept. 27, 1769.
  Joost, born April 12, 1765, died in childhood.
  Isabelle Françoise, born May 16, 1767, died May 21, 1831, wife of
    Jean Baptiste Rollier.
  Joseph Antoine, born Sept. 11, 1769, died Sept. 18, 1769.
  Marie Therese, born March 8, 1771, died June 22, 1858.
  Joost Joseph, born Jan. 13, 1775, died March 31, 1817, married Colette
    De Saegher.

Children by his second wife, Marie Jeanne Buydens:
  Jeanne Marie, born Nov. 12, 1793, died Dec. 8, 1796.
  Colette, born May 24, 1795, died Dec. 13, 1796.
  Rosalie, born Nov. 7, 1796, died Oct. 26, 1875, married Charles Van
    Mossevelde.
  Charles, born Sept. 20, 1798, died Nov. 3, 1860, Counselor of the
    Court of Appeals of Ghent. Married Marie Liénart.
  Pierre Jean (Peter), born Jan. 30, 1801, died May 23, 1873. Missionary.
  Colette Aldegonde, born Jan. 30, 1801, died Aug. 15, 1807.
  Francis, born May 15, 1803, died April 28, 1878. Justice of the Peace
    at Ghent. Married Jeanne Catherine Rollier.
  Marie Jeanne, born Aug. 20, 1805, died about 1830. Married to
    Frederic Jean Lutens.
  Jean, born Feb. 11, 1807, died Feb. 3, 1813.

The family record states that Joost De Smet had twenty-two children. Several by his first wife must have died in infancy when an epidemic of smallpox was raging in Termonde.

was to win an entire people over to Jesus Christ, was given the privilege of growing to manhood in the atmosphere of that ardent faith which is engendered by religious persecution. "The lessons of piety taught me in childhood," he said in after life, "were the seeds of that desire, which I conceived and afterward executed by God's grace, to give myself without reserve to His service." [10]

The ship-owner possessed in a rare degree those qualities required by the head of a family. His portrait, still in the possession of his descendants, gives one the impression of a singularly energetic man, one perhaps even hard. [11] It seems, in fact, that this authority was exercised with a certain rigor; but this severity, inseparable from true discipline and training, was neither excessive nor arbitrary—if the hand was firm the heart was kind. He was treated with a sort of religious respect by his household; his wishes and his orders were accepted without question, and scrupulously obeyed. He whose life we are relating eulogized his father in these words: "He seemed to take God for his model in the training of his children." [12]

Less, however, is known about the character of Marie Buydens. She exercised a certain authority in the household and directed most successfully the education of her children. She died at the age of forty-seven, shortly before the departure for America of Peter, the future missionary. [13] Her son cherished always the tenderest memories of his mother and, in his letters, speaks of her with great veneration.

The boyhood of Peter gave ample promise of the disposition which, in the years of his maturity, so ably fitted him for the rôle he was destined by Providence to fill. "From childhood," writes his brother Francis, "he was endowed with a strong and vigorous constitution; he was hardy, adventurous, and indifferent to danger, and yet withal of a nature at once affectionate, gentle, and generous." [14]

[10] To his sister Rosalie, Florissant, Feb. 10, 1828.
[11] This portrait is, to-day, the property of M. Paul De Smet, judge of the Court of Appeals at Ghent.
[12] Letter to his family, Amsterdam, Aug. 2, 1821.
[13] Sept. 19, 1819.
[14] Letter to Father Deynoodt, Dec. 23, 1873.

As a boy he had a pronounced taste for games and athletics. The more violent and dangerous, the more they seemed to appeal to him. Frequently was he seen climbing a tree and then rapidly descending by swinging from one limb to another, but more often could he be found hazarding a long leap between the numerous boats that were brought almost to the door of his father's house by a small arm of the Schelde. On one of these occasions a false step precipitated him in the water and almost cost him his life, but the following day found him undismayed at this favorite pastime. Every morning Peter would relate to his family the dreams he had during the night, and these were always about ships, sea voyages, and shipwrecks. His father was often wont to exclaim: "God preserve him! He will be either a soldier or a great traveler; he will never remain at home."

And finally we come to his school-days, which had their beginning in a certain free school of Termonde, conducted by a lay teacher named Delauneau. Whatever aptitude for learning he might have displayed it was not such as made him conspicuous, but in agility and physical strength he was without an equal. His deeds of prowess were likened to those of the judge of Israel, the conqueror of the Philistines, and he was accordingly dubbed "Samson" by his companions, a name which was applied to him in every school that he attended. His sister Rosalie, who was four years his senior, retained a vivid recollection of his heroic childhood. Sixty years afterward she wrote: "he was a sort of Hercules, the terror of his class, highspirited, a fighter, and always in trouble." [15] It must be said, however, in Peter's defence, that when he fought, it was usually either to uphold the honor of his side or else assist some fellow-student too weak to defend himself.

The course of events so shaped themselves in time that he was given an opportunity, on a certain occasion, to employ his splendid strength in the service of religion. It happened that during a kermess a traveling show erected booths in front of the church, and at the hour for High Mass proceeded to parade about in grotesque fashion ac-

[15] Related by M. Leon Van Mossevelde in a letter to Father Deynoodt, Dec. 1, 1873.

companied by the music of trombones.   However amusing
the spectacle, the good people of Termonde preferred to
assist at Mass, and the mountebanks, angered by this
seeming indifference, sought to annoy the congregation
during the entire time of the service by making distracting
noises on their brass instruments.   On coming out of
church, Peter called several comrades to his side and led
an attack upon the booths.   At once the parade was disorganized and the music ceased braying.   The players were
disconcerted by this sudden attack, and, failing to gather
any assurance from the attitude of the bystanders, fled
without offering further resistance.   They removed their
paraphernalia under cover of darkness.

Encouraged by this success, young De Smet dreamed of
more brilliant conquests.   The Napoleonic wars were in
progress at this time and Peter listened with avidity to
the tales recounted by the veterans who had marched
through Europe with the conquering army.   The glory of
it all haunted the boy's mind.   To defend a barricade or
engage in a skirmish with the young element of the neighborhood was too tame an affair; henceforth nothing short
of major tactics for him.   In imagination he had the
Austrians and Russians encamped in the near-by villages
about Termonde and the young men of these communities
were to impersonate the hostile forces.

It later years, when an old missionary, he loved to
recount one of these expeditions in which his star for an
instant waned.   It was on a fine morning about the year
1812 or 1813, when, having assembled the school-boys
of several neighborhoods, he announced that they would
attack the "Russians" occupying the village of Grembergen.   The proposal was enthusiastically received, and
the "army" of about a hundred would-be warriors marched
gayly forth.   The "Russians," however, doubtless upon
the information of their spies, were in a state of prepared-
ness and rushed upon the invaders.   An encounter took
place and after a passage at arms amid some hillocks of
sand, the youths of Grembergen fell back upon their
village hotly pursued by the "French," who forced the
issue a second time, with greater fury, in the square near
the church.   That it happened to be Sunday was an

unfortunate circumstance, but that the hour of battle happened to coincide with the hour of Mass was still more so. Hearing the enraged cries of the combatants, and seeing their fellow-townsmen vanquished and seeking asylum in the church, the peasant congregation sallied forth, armed with pitchforks and sticks, and threw themselves into the mêlée. This turned the tide of victory and forced "General" De Smet to lead his tattered and bruised forces in retreat.

Rumors of this expedition, doubtless noticed on account of its early morning start, came to the ears of Joost De Smet, who at once set out in search of his son. As he was leaving the outskirts of Termonde Peter was entering, his "army" in complete rout. The ship-builder, wishing to add another cruel lesson to that of defeat, deprived the youthful general of his pocket-money for ten days, which meant, in other words, confinement to the house. Seclusion, however, is sometimes a bad counselor. One day, during this confinement, while his mother was engaged in sewing, Peter cleverly got possession of her scissors and cut out all the pockets of his coat and then took care to leave it where she could see what he had done. Marie Buydens reported this to her husband, who, in turn, summoned his culprit son and with severity demanded, "What is the reason that you cut out your pockets?" to which the youth responded, "What need have I for pockets since I have nothing to put in them?"

Although on occasions Peter was swayed by the impulses of his ardent nature he gave indications, day by day, that his was also a generous nature and one imbued with filial devotion. He had now reached his twelfth year and was preparing for his first communion. The time was at hand when the development of his rare qualities of heart must be rounded out and fixed by a careful cultivation of his intellect.

At Beirvelde, near Ghent, there was a large school which enjoyed the patronage of the best families. It was to this institution that Joost De Smet decided to send his son for the twofold purpose of completing his studies and experiencing the benefits of discipline. Accordingly, about the year 1814, Peter left the paternal roof, thereafter to return only for a few weeks' vacation every year.   His life at boarding-school contrasted greatly with the life he had been accustomed to lead at home, but there was little question as to his powers of adaptability when recreation hours came around.   At these times he was entirely in his element and was the life and soul of every game.   Here, as formerly, his unusual physical strength commanded for him the respect of his companions, although he was among the very youngest of the school.   On the occasion of holidays, instead of taking his place in the diligence with the rest of his comrades bound for Termonde, Peter, staff in hand, would make the journey on foot, arriving at his father's house by nightfall.

After a year or two passed at Beirvelde he entered the Preparatory Seminary of St. Nicolas, where he began his Latin studies, but did not long remain here, for in 1818 we find him at the college of Alost.[16]   We wonder at the frequent changes from one school to another and we find a partial answer in a certain letter written by his brother Francis: "He could not remain very long anywhere."[17] Peter was of a roving disposition, a fact to which the principal events of his life attest, and his letters tell us that of St. Nicolas he retained the most pleasant recollections.   In later years he often returned there and was always received with open arms and accorded enthusiastic interest on behalf of his missionary work.

His entry into the student life at Alost was marked by an episode that won for him at once a firm place in the respect of the student body.   The existence of bitter animosity between the Flemish and Walloon* boys led to frequent and violent quarrels.   The first time that young De Smet appeared at recreation he was accosted in a rude and insulting manner by a Walloon several years

[16] The college of Alost, opened by the Jesuits in 1620, was at that time conducted by the priests of the diocese of Ghent. Canon Van Crombrugghe, who later founded the Josephites, and the Ladies of Mary, was then in charge. The Jesuits did not return to Alost until 1831.

[17] Letter to Father Deynoodt, Dec. 22, 1873.

* *Translator's Note:* The Walloons are a mixed Italic, Teutonic, Celtic people in southeastern Belgium and parts adjacent. "The Walloons are descended from the ancient Gallic Belgi, with an admixture of Roman elements." (Encyc. Brit., 11th Ed.)

older and much bigger than himself.   In a flash Peter had
the aggressor down, and, doubling him up, carried him
bodily to a pool of water near by.   The bully shouted
and kicked, but "Samson" held him as with muscles of
steel, nor did he let go until he had immersed him two
or three times in the water, to the great amusement of
the spectators.

As a scholar, however, our hero was not so conspicuous;
his standing as such was at all times creditable, but not
unusually so, although he seems to have distinguished himself in mathematics.

From the college at Alost Peter went to the Preparatory
Seminary at Mechlin.[18]   There, it seems, his intellect was
judged more solid than brilliant.   His former companions
all agree that he was gifted with sound judgment and
that it was evident he would one day be a man of action.
If the future missionary lacked a passion for study it would
appear that, in his own way, he was a conscientious worker,
for one of his classmates, in alluding to that period of
Peter's life, said, "he was always writing."[19]

At recreation-time Peter was in his true element, first
in every foot-race, the most expert at ball and other games.
For sheer display of strength he would sometimes extend
his arms, setting his muscles rigid, and the united efforts
of his playmates could not bend them.   Dr. Cranincx,
afterward professor at the University of Louvain, recalled
with pleasure how many were the times that he had seen
Peter lifted up and carried on the shoulders of his comrades amidst enthusiastic applause.   The kind heart,
the cheerful disposition, and the straightforwardness which
had made Peter De Smet so well liked at Alost and at
St. Nicolas won for him an equal popularity at the
seminary at Mechlin.   He formed friendships there which

[18] The Preparatory Seminary or the archiepiscopal college of Mechlin was
at that time in the Rue St. Jean, in the house now occupied * by the Sisters
of Mary.   The Superior, Father Verlooy, a former Oratorian, was a man
of wide experience and eminent virtue.   His imposing personality commanded the respect of his pupils, and so great was his eloquence as a preacher
that the powerful impressions created by his Sunday sermons were remembered half a century later.

* *Translator's Note:* It is doubtful whether a vestige of this building has
been left standing after the devastating operations of the army of invasion.

[19] Abbé de Viron.

neither time nor distance could efface, and of these the most notable were with Dr. Cranincx and Monseigneur De Ram, who later became rector of the University of Louvain.*

A natural question comes up here as to what vocation Peter was destined to follow. The assertion has been made by one of his comrades[20] that the future missionary was at this time contemplating the life of a Trappist monk, but it seems unlikely that such was the case when we consider his adventurous spirit and how ill adapted it would have been to the limitations and restraints of monastic life. At all events, he soon began to entertain other designs, and at twenty years of age, in his second year at Mechlin, he encountered in Father Nerinckx, a missionary from Kentucky, the influence which was to decide his career.

Charles Nerinckx was born October 2, 1761, in the village of Herffelingen in Brabant. His ordination took place in 1785, after which he was appointed vicar of the cathedral of Mechlin, and later curate of Everberg-Meerbeke near Louvain. His work in this parish was attended with splendid success, but suffered a serious interruption when the Revolutionary authorities issued a warrant for his arrest. With this hanging over his head he was forced to leave his parish, seeking refuge in the hospital of Termonde, and there taking up the duties of the former chaplain, who had just been deported to the Isle of Ré. This post he continued to hold for several years, amid constant danger of being discovered by agents of the Republic. Caution obliged him to say Mass at two o'clock in the morning, after which he would spend the rest of the day in hiding. His enforced seclusion and the consequent leisure gave him opportunities for literary work which he improved by writing several treatises upon Theology, Sacred History, and Canon Law. When circumstances permitted, he would steal out of his hiding-place to visit the

* *Translator's Note:* The University of Louvain was practically destroyed by fire and demolition when the city of Louvain was captured and sacked by the Germans in their march toward Paris, Aug. 26, 1914.
[20] Abbé Jongmans.

sick and the prisoners of war held in Termonde, and at times he even found a way of secretly entering Everberg, where he brought religious encouragement to his abandoned parishioners.

This circumscribed missionary work, however, far from satisfied his ardent nature, and in 1804 he left Belgium and sought a vaster field of action in the United States. After a terrible crossing in a ship which he afterward described as "a floating hell," Father Nerinckx arrived in Baltimore. Bishop Carroll, at that time the only Catholic Bishop in America, received the missionary most cordially, accepted his offer of service, and sent him to join Father Badin, the priest who a few years previously had founded the Kentucky Mission. The priests of this mission had for the theater of their activities a territory larger than the whole of France, and here for twenty years Father Nerinckx labored with indefatigable zeal, consecrating his health, strength, and energy to the work of evangelization. He traversed Kentucky from one end to the other; at times in depths of winter through ice and snow; at times again through the torrid heats of summer. To ford a river or to swim it were alike to him, and he would oftentimes traverse twenty-five or thirty miles on horseback to say Mass, fasting from food till three or four o'clock in the afternoon. With his own hands he built a house for himself at a cost of $6.50. His was a rude apostolate, filled with terrifying hardships. As the number of Christians increased he built churches in proportion, until ten had been erected, as well as a number of chapels. He founded the congregation of the Sisters of Loretto, a congregation which soon established religious institutions in all parts of the continent, for the purpose of instructing children in their religion and also for taking care of orphans.

In 1808 the Bishopric of the See of New Orleans was offered to Father Nerinckx, but he declined the honor, saying, "Bonitatem et disciplinam et scientiam docendus, docere non valeo." [21] Bishop Spalding has said of him, "He was a learned, humble priest, content to hide his

---

[21] "I have need myself to acquire virtue, wisdom, and knowledge, and am not capable of teaching it to others."

knowledge and to bury himself among men who did not know even the meaning of the word 'learning.'" [22]

Charles Nerinckx returned to Belgium in 1817 to raise funds and to procure active assistants. He made a second visit to his native land in 1821 for the same purpose. Upon the occasion of the latter he remarked: "How can it be that Napoleon found millions of men ready to sacrifice their lives to ravage a nation and aid him to conquer the world, while I cannot find a handful of devoted men to save an entire people and extend the reign of God?" Before departing from America in 1817 Father Nerinckx stopped at Georgetown, where Father Anthony Kohlmann, then Superior of the Maryland Province, asked him to bring back a large reinforcement of Belgian novices. This he bent himself to with great ardor, for his sympathies lay very strongly with the Society of Jesus. Five young men returned with him to enter the novitiate.

His second voyage was even more successful in this respect, as will be seen. After his arrival in Belgium the missionary spent several days at Mechlin, where he had many friends. The seminarists received him warmly, and listened with lively interest to all he told them about the immense country, where, for lack of priests, thousands of Catholics were forgetting God and abandoning their religion. He told them particularly about Kentucky and the flourishing Christian communities he had founded there; described the state of ignorance in which the Western Indian tribes were languishing; and concluded by speaking of the Society of Jesus, that had just been re-established in America by Pius VII. This Society had important houses in the United States, where young novices received solid religious and ascetic training, and were wisely directed and fitted for every kind of apostolic work.

These discourses created a profound impression, and during his visit a goodly number of seminarists, including Peter De Smet, offered to accompany Father Nerinckx back to America. He, however, counseled them not to be precipitate. It was his wish that they take time for

[22] See "The Life of Rev. Charles Nerinckx," by Rt. Rev. Camillus Maes, Cincinnati, 1879.

sober reflection, but notwithstanding this it seems that their choice was instantly and definitely taken.[23] In a letter young De Smet wrote his father before embarking he spoke of his project as conceived long before.[24] The future proved that the youthful apostles were not obeying a passing impulse.

Father Nerinckx, after a thorough examination of all the applicants, selected nine to return with him to America. From the Preparatory Seminary only two were chosen, and these were Peter De Smet and Joost Van Assche, of St. Amand-lez-Puers. Of the applicants from the college but five were taken: Felix Verreydt, of Diest; Francis De Maillet, of Brussels; John Smedts, of Rotselaer; John Anthony Elet, of St. Amand-lez-Puers; and Van Horzig, of Hoogstraeten. A priest, Father Veulemans, and a young professor of the Preparatory Seminary, Peter Verhaegen, of Haeght, completed the personnel of the band.

The enterprise was not lacking in difficulties. The first one encountered was the opposition of the parents and families of the young missionaries. They seemed unable to reconcile themselves to the irrevocable separation—the prospect of loss being too sudden and immediate to be softened by sober reflection.

After due consideration the young men decided to leave Belgium without saying good-by to their families—a heroic resolution which to us hardly seems compatible with true filial devotion. It must be borne in mind, however, that they were driven by cogent reasons, a fact indicated by the words of Peter De Smet in a subsequent letter: "To have asked the consent of our parents would have been to court a certain and absolute refusal."[25] Thus, rather than jeopardize a well-defined vocation it appeared advisable to limit the leave-taking to farewell letters written before sailing. Whatever attitude this

[23] One of these young men, Joost Van Assche, had offered himself to Father Nerinckx in 1817. He was refused then on account of his age, but not only did he hold to his intention, but he communicated his desire to be a missionary to John Elet, and their example influenced others. Cf. the *St. Louis Times*, June 27, 1877. Chittenden-Richardson: "Father De Smet's Life and Travels," p. 11.

[24] Letter written from Texel Island, Aug. 7, 1821.

[25] From a letter of Father De Smet, written toward the end of his life.

course of action would seem to indicate, it is beyond doubt that all of the young men were fully aware of the great sacrifice that was being imposed upon their parents. That Peter De Smet had a poignant realization of this we know from his relatives, who tell us that to the end of his days the memory of his departure remained like an open wound. But, on the other hand, we are also told that he was never beset with any misgivings, because he always felt that he had obeyed an imperative call of duty.

All preparations were carried on with great secrecy. Dr. Cranincx tells us how he became the unwitting accomplice of Peter De Smet, who at that time occupied the bed next to his in the seminary dormitory. Young De Smet had packed the greater part of his books and clothing when he discovered that his trunk would not hold everything. His eye then fell upon his friend's trunk—"Cranincx," said he, "would you lend me your trunk to send away some books?" "Willingly," replied the doctor; whereupon Peter, taking him at his word, piled in the rest of his belongings and sent them off to the ship.

After leaving the seminary the young men remained hidden for a time in a neighboring house [26] whence they departed to join Father Nerinckx in Amsterdam. They could not call on their families for funds, and being able to realize but small sums from the sale of what few and insignificant trifles they possessed, some of them sought the assistance of friends to defray traveling expenses. Others of the party, however, preferred to seek help from strangers, and to this end relied upon the generosity of such as they could interest along the way through Holland. Among their benefactors in this cause mention must be made of Father Verlooy, Superior of the Preparatory Seminary, and Mr. Pierre De Nef, of Turnhout, a personal friend of Father Nerinckx and a well-known patron of foreign missions.

Before leaving Belgium Peter De Smet returned to St. Nicolas to take leave of his old teachers and also

[26] This house was situated at the corner of the Rue St. Jean and the Rue des Vaches. It was a tobacco-shop, and the sign above the door read: Het Schip.

his friend and counselor, Father Van Boxelaere, then a professor at the Preparatory Seminary. A few days later, at Mechlin, he joined John Baptiste Smedts, John Anthony Elet, and Joost Van Assche, who were to proceed with him to Amsterdam. They sailed July 24, 1821, and were accompanied as far as Contich by Monseigneur De Ram, an intimate friend of Peter's. When the moment of final separation arrived Monseigneur De Ram asked young De Smet to give him some souvenir or token of remembrance, and Peter, taking from his pocket a penny, bent it in two with his teeth and gave it to his friend; then the vessel started for Antwerp.

Having surmounted the difficulty of parental opposition, the young missionaries were very soon brought face to face with an obstacle of a different character. Belgium was at that period a part of the kingdom of the Low Countries and "the hostility of Protestant Holland toward Catholics, and especially foreign missionaries, manifested itself in various ways; sometimes through measures taken against them by the government and sometimes by the fanatical antagonism of the favorites of King William. . . . Among other formalities the law required all travelers to show their passports upon entering a town. Those who could not do so were detained in prison until they could be examined and state the object of their journey." [27]

The four fugitives, however, who had set out from Mechlin were successful in evading the watchful eye of the police. A friend from Antwerp, Father John Buelens, who was in the secret of their departure, procured for them the necessary money for the voyage without their having to again enter a town. But once in Holland, even greater prudence had to be exercised. Before arriving at any town the young men would leave the diligence and, armed with walking-sticks, mingle with the crowd on foot. This ruse carried out with assurance passed them through the gates without attracting the attention of the authorities. Peter De Smet and his companions reached Amsterdam on July 26th, where Father Nerinckx had arranged

[27] From Father De Smet's manuscripts.

accommodations for them. Here also their meager funds for the voyage were substantially added to through the generosity of certain Catholic families interested in American missions. [28]

Before long the nine young men were assembled at their meeting-place and in a few days were to set sail. The chance of their being detected seemed very slight in this large city where so many strangers foregathered amid much coming and going, and Peter was much buoyed up by the propitious beginning and the nearness of departure, but an unlooked-for incident which befell him almost disorganized his plans as well as those of his companions. Despite all precautions taken by the fugitives, news of their project had spread abroad in Belgium and their respective families were at their wits' end for some means to stay their departure.

Joost De Smet, we know, was capable of a sacrifice, and in other circumstances might have considered it an honor to pledge to God the flower of his offspring, but being aware of his son's impulsive and somewhat fanciful disposition, and making due allowance for lofty motives, he could not but question the prudence of his decision. He felt that the boy had acted precipitately. The voyage appeared to him merely the beginning of an adventurous career that would end badly. There seemed but one proper course open to him and he accordingly dispatched his son Charles, armed with parental authority and instructions to bring back the runaway by force if necessary. Charles duly arrived in Amsterdam, went to the City Hall for information as to his brother's whereabouts and after vain enquiries proceeded forth upon a random search. Faring up one street and down another, interrogating a stranger or a native from time to time, he seemed to make no headway—and then the much-to-be-desired result came to pass. Suddenly and without warning while crossing a bridge he came face to face with Peter. The latter, in no wise disconcerted, was minded to settle the whole question upon the spot—but Charles did not consider the place propitious for an interview and prevailed upon Peter to

[28] Father De Smet was particularly grateful all his life to the Roothaan, Van Has, Van Damme, and Koedijk families.

DEPARTURE FOR AMERICA 19

conduct him to the rendezvous of the conspirators—nothing more or less than a garret which he was sharing with his three companions.

Charles lost no time in setting forth the object of his mission, but, knowing his brother's character too well to try to intimidate him, he made an appeal to the kindness of his heart. He described to Peter the anguish into which their loved ones at home had been plunged by the prospect of his departure. He pictured the home bereft of its mother; their lonely father in his eighty-fifth year, whom the shock of separation would probably hasten to his end. How could he have the heart to leave without seeing them all once more? Were Peter truly heeding God's call to a foreign mission no one would oppose his real vocation. Was it not possible to wait a few years and mature his plans, comfort his father's declining years and remain at home until he had closed his eyes in death? Peter listened to his brother's appeal without once interrupting. He was deeply moved while hearing of the grief of his family, but so inflexible was his resolution that he not only never wavered, but vouchsafed a reply so eloquent with sound reason and earnestness that Charles, instead of opposing him, actually ended by placing a large sum of money at his disposal.

Amsterdam now could no longer shelter them in complete security, so the fugitives forsook their garret to go aboard the ship which was to carry them a portion of the way, the captain being already won over to their cause. July 31st saw them on their way down the Zuider Zee, but before the anchor was weighed Peter, as a last proof of his filial devotion and as a consolation to his bereaved family, addressed a farewell epistle to his father. "It seems needless to assure you of the tender love I bear you," he wrote. "Believe me, I love you deeply, although the sorrow I am about to cause you may lead you to doubt my affection. The religion to which you are so sincerely attached will dry your tears and fill your heart with joy. How is it possible that you are inconsolable because one of your children is giving himself to God's service and putting into practice the lessons you have taught? . . . It would have been my greatest happiness to spend this short life with you, but God calls me and I must obey. Every day we say to God, 'Thy will be done on earth'—well—to-day our hearts must echo these words which our lips pronounce. May the submission of our will to God's designs render us capable of every sacrifice!" After again protesting the deep affection he bore him whom he called "the best of fathers" he reassured his family in the following words: "We are embarking with confidence, encouraged by the captain's kindness, the sturdiness of the ship, which is quite new, and yet chiefly by our trust and faith in the providence of Him who never abandons His own."

On the evening of August 2d the ship reached Texel Island. The young missionaries were hospitably received into a Catholic household recommended to them by their friends in Amsterdam. Here Father Nerinckx joined them, as he had come by a different route to avoid suspicion. He even lodged under a different roof on account of the disquieting rumors that the police were in pursuit under orders to arrest and prevent them from continuing the voyage. Twelve days of irksome suspense were passed here awaiting the arrival of the ship that was to finally take the little party to America, and yet Peter De Smet's letters show us that he at least felt no apprehension. "God be praised!" he writes to his father, "we have all arrived at Texel in good health after making a passage down the Zuider Zee, and we now hope to land safely at Philadelphia. I wish I could describe to you how pleasant the voyage has been. At night the roaring of the waves as they splashed on the decks and the clattering of the rigging reminded one of the chimes at Termonde. Nothing, however, prevents me from sleeping like a dormouse, nor yet from singing in the morning like a young nightingale. But at times I weep, though God the Supreme Comforter dries my tears by permitting me a glimpse of the great reward. 'I have called you,' He says, 'who can resist?' It was a bitter trial that I felt deterred from telling you of my departure and my future plans, and to be obliged to leave without your blessing has caused me cruel suffering. I was convinced that you would never consent to my departure, and for this reason and upon the advice of a wise and disinterested man, I decided to leave without seeing you. Conquer your sorrow, my dear father, and say to yourself the All-Powerful has decided this affair. . . . The voyage to Philadelphia is no more hazardous than a trip to Sac-a-Houblon to play a game of cards. We cross the ocean with the same feeling of security that the children of Israel experienced during their passage through the Red Sea."

The half-grave tone of this letter might give the impression that Peter De Smet never realized how great a sacrifice he imposed upon his family. In reality he was haunted by the knowledge. Thinking that their parish priest could better than himself persuade his father to consent to his departure, he wrote a touching letter in Latin, begging him to visit and console his father. The separation caused Peter intense suffering. He wrote to Father Van Boxelaere on August 10th, saying: "Charles tried to prevent our departure, but reason and religion soon won him over to our side. He wept bitter tears and I wept with him; for what could be more heartrending than to leave the old father I love tenderly, sisters and brothers who are dear to me, friends and the good things of life? But God calls me and I must obey." He continues in this grave strain, which supposes a knowledge of life rare at his age: "O Vanity of vanities! How strong are the ties of earthly things? Should it be God's will that I return to Europe, I wonder if those who are now so saddened by my departure will greet me with joy? Man changes and so easily forms new ties and habits and we occupy such a small place even in the hearts of our friends!"

These letters are the beginning of a correspondence that lasted fifty years, and shows not the least trace of indifference or diminished affection for his family. Could Joost De Smet have known through these letters the sentiments that animated his son at that time, he would have understood how he was obeying an impulse that had little to do with love of adventure. But unfortunately these letters never reached their destination [29] and not even the account given by Charles of his interview with

---

[29] These letters, written in Flemish, were seven in number. They had been given to Father Buelens of Antwerp, and only after his death in 1868 were they by chance found among his papers.

Peter could mitigate the bitterness of the old ship-builder. It required actual results in missionary work and the first letters he received from America to finally convince him that his son had obeyed a divine call.

The vessel so anxiously awaited at Texel arrived at length. She was an American brig called the *Columbia*. Dutch law required that officials should visit every ship and examine all passports, a provision that somewhat complicated the embarkation of our young men. Fortunately for them, some Amsterdam friends who accompanied them succeeded in securing the cooperation of the captain, and the arrangements were made whereby the missionaries were not to go aboard in the regular way, but were to be picked up from a fishing-boat after the ship had put to sea. The *Columbia* weighed anchor at night and, accordingly, a short distance out hove to and took the fugitives aboard, to their unfeigned joy and relief. Henceforth there was nothing to fear, and they could send from a distance their felicitations to the police of King William. The day of their sailing was August 15th, the feast of the Assumption. The date was of good omen, and to Peter De Smet it partook of a privilege that he was enabled to begin his career under the protection of the Queen of heaven.

The *Columbia* encountered heavy weather in the North Sea and our missionary tells us that he, like the majority of the passengers, "paid tribute to inexorable Neptune," but on the whole the crossing was not altogether bad. The nine young men were given over to visions of themselves in the performance of their apostolic work and the accomplishment of great things in the future. Father Nerinckx kept their zeal and enthusiasm aroused with anticipation of a wonderful harvest of souls. This was, for the embryo missionaries, the beginning of their apprenticeship to the ministry, and the older missionary did not fail to strengthen his vivid recitals of life and color with lessons drawn from his experience and the inspiring example of his own upright life. Austerity was the dominant note in his régime, but it neither alarmed the ardent neophytes nor abated their zeal.

When the *Columbia* finally entered the Delaware River

and went to her moorings at Philadelphia she had been
forty-two days out from Texel Island. The young Belgians were totally unprepared for the wonders that were
revealed in their first glimpse of the Quaker City. They
had imagined America to be a country devoid of any save
the most rudimentary marks of civilization, and instead
they beheld a city which in area and population, in point
of architecture, public buildings, and the number of
churches, surpassed many of the cities of Europe. It
took no great lapse of time, however, to teach them that
their view of Philadelphia comprehended but a very small
part of America and at the same time a very large portion
of its civilization. If that part of the United States on
the Atlantic seaboard were a land of "the strenuous life,"
there lay, indeed, beyond the Alleghany Mountains an
immense territory the inhabitants of which were living "in
darkness and the shadow of death."

From Philadelphia the missionaries went to Baltimore,
where Archbishop Maréchal received them most cordially.
Here Father Nerinckx left the little band and took up once
more his work in Kentucky. "We parted from him,"
wrote Peter De Smet, "filled with veneration and esteem
for his character both as a priest and as a man. The wise
counsels he never tired of giving us, and the example of
his virtue which we were privileged to behold during a
journey of forty-two days, will ever remain fresh in the
memories of his young companions."[30]

Father Veulemans and young Van Horzig, who had
come over to be associated with the missions directed by the
secular clergy, remained in Baltimore and placed themselves
at the service of the Archbishop.[31] The others, seven
in number, tarried but one day and then proceeded to
Georgetown, where they presented themselves to Father
Kohlmann, the Superior of the Jesuits in the United States.
This priest was so impressed with the solidity of the vocations
which could overcome obstacles and face such trials, that
he received the young men with open arms and afterward
sent them to Whitemarsh to enter upon their novitiates.

[30] Selected Letters, 2d series, p. 250.
[31] Father Van Horzig died in Washington, D. C., after having labored zealously for many years as parish priest of St. Peter's.

CHAPTER II

The Jesuits in New France and Maryland—Bishop Carroll—Whitemarsh—
Father Van Quickenborne—Peter De Smet at the Novitiate—De-
parture for Missouri—"A Floating Monastery"—Florissant—Madam
Duchesne—"Samson," Architect and Carpenter—First Vows.

THE American Missions, from their very beginning, attracted great numbers from the Society of Jesus. Jesuits were the early explorers of New France and gave to it its first martyrs. "The history of their labors," says a Protestant writer, "is connected with the origin of every celebrated town in the annals of French America: not a cape was turned, nor a river entered, but a Jesuit led the way."[1] While Fathers Jogues, de Brébeuf, and Lalemant shed their blood upon the shores of the St. Lawrence, Father Marquette in a bark canoe explored the course of the Mississippi as far as the Arkansas. Like their confrères of France, the English Jesuits, who in 1634 came to Maryland with Lord Baltimore, were not only missionaries of a heroic type, but were possessed of a genius for civilizing. "We have not come to make war," said Fathers White and Altham to the Indians, "but to teach you the law of grace and love, and to live with you as brothers." They spread the light of Christianity from the Great Lakes to the Gulf of Mexico. At their recital of the sufferings of Christ, the Abenaki, the Iroquois, the Hurons, the Illinois, and the Natchez put aside their ferocity, buried the tomahawk, and felled the most beautiful trees of the forest to build "prayer lodges." The day came when fanaticism undertook to undo the work of the mis-

[1] Bancroft's "History of the United States," Boston, 1852, Vol. xi, p. 122.

sionaries. The Catholics of Maryland saw their goods, their laws, their churches, their schools, and their children taken from them. The Indian congregations were slaughtered—the Jesuits themselves, through a brief of Clement XIV, were dispersed.

In 1776 the War of Independence liberated the American Colonies from England's yoke of oppression. Soon after the war Washington addressed these words to the Catholics of the Original States of the Union: ". . . may the members of your society in America, animated alone by the pure spirit of Christianity, and still conducting themselves as faithful subjects of our Government, enjoy every temporal and spiritual felicity."[2] An era of peace was then inaugurated, and Catholics, profiting by the change, petitioned the Pope to make Baltimore an episcopal see.

On August 15, 1790, in the private chapel of an English manor house, John Carroll, the newly-elected Bishop, was consecrated. He belonged to the Society of Jesus, and was a native of Maryland, where his family had fought valiantly for liberty. The Bishop of the United States at that time presided over a diocese fifteen hundred leagues long by eight hundred leagues wide, containing a population of forty thousand Catholics and from three to four million Protestants. His clergy numbered some thirty, several of whom had belonged, like himself, to the Society of Jesus.

It was not long ere the Revolution and religious persecution in France and Belgium caused the immigration to America of many missionaries well qualified for hardships, and whose fidelity to duty was paramount to a love of the fatherland. The Sulpicians undertook the establishment and direction of a large seminary, and among these priests were eminent men, of whom several became Bishops. Bishop Carroll, however, was longing to see the Jesuits re-established in his diocese, and on May 25, 1803, he wrote to Father Gruber, Superior of the Jesuits in Russia: "From the letters of many of our faithful we have learned with joy that, by a miracle, as it were, the Society has been saved and exists still in Russia. We know the Sovereign

[2] Rupp, "History of the Religious Denominations of the United States," p. 165.

Pontiff recognizes it and that he has issued a brief which authorizes your Paternity to readmit those who formerly belonged to the institution.   Nearly all our old Fathers entreat to be allowed to renew the vows they made to God when in the Society.   They ask to end their days within its fold and consecrate their declining years to building it up in this country should such be the will of God."

The good Bishop did not write in vain.   Father Gruber replied, granting the desired permission, and the former Jesuits of America were restored to their previous status. Father Molyneux was appointed Superior with authority to receive novices.   In 1806, at Georgetown, Bishop Carroll opened the first college of the restored Society.   It proved a success from the start, and in 1815, a few months before the death of its founder, it was granted the title and charter of a university.[3]

The novitiate was at first an annex of the college, but later on the Fathers were able to secure for it a more retired location.   The Jesuits for some time had been proprietors of a large plantation at Whitemarsh.   Situated as it was, twenty-four miles from Georgetown, in a salubrious district, surrounded by vineyards, prairies, and forests, with a large and commodious house upon it, it lent itself easily to the requirements of a novitiate.   The novices were transferred there in the spring of 1819.

It was October 6, 1821, when Peter De Smet and his companions arrived at Whitemarsh.   Father Van Quickenborne of heroic memory, a native of Belgium also, was Master of Novices at the time.   He had been born in the village of Peteghem in the diocese of Ghent on January 21, 1788, and in 1812 received his ordination as a secular priest.   Following this came his appointment as a professor at the Preparatory Seminary of Roulers and later that of vicar of St. Denis near Courtrai.   When the Jesuits opened a novitiate at Rumbeke [4] the young priest

[3] Cf. John Gilmary Shea, "History of Georgetown College." Washington, 1891, Chap. iv.
[4] Concerning the novitiate of Rumbeke, see "Life of Father Hélias d'Huddeghem," by A. Lebrocquy, S. J., Ghent, 1878; Chap. ii.

sought admission to the Society. This was granted and he had no sooner completed his noviceship than he obtained permission from the Father-General to devote his activities to the missions in America. Father Van Quickenborne arrived in Maryland at the close of the year 1817, and in 1819 was placed in charge of the novices at Whitemarsh. Archbishop Maréchal said of him: "Father Van Quickenborne is a saint. The only fault I can find with him is that he neglects his health."[5]

Superior and Master of Novices, Father Van Quickenborne was at the same time farmer, carpenter, and mason. He managed the plantation and the negroes that worked it; and the two churches, one for the novitiate and the other at Annapolis, eighteen miles away, were the products of his own skill and supervision. Endowed with prodigious energy, he also found time to travel through a vast extent of country, laboring as a missionary among Catholics and Protestants alike. Every fortnight he went to Annapolis to say Mass. He regularly visited the sick and the poor and devoted a portion of his time to the instruction and encouragement of the negroes, whose cause he espoused. He possessed the true spirit of a missionary, and his zealous soul was rewarded with the satisfaction of numerous conversions. His view of life is aptly shown by a comment which he was wont to utter frequently: "How consoling it is to work with the angels for the happiness and salvation of men!" In order that the novices might better comprehend and share his elation he would announce a holiday and give them a repast whenever a hundredth convert was added to his flock.

At such times as Father Van Quickenborne was called away by the exigencies of his missionary work, his place was filled by his assistant, Father Peter Timmermans. This priest was a Belgian, a native of Turnhout in the province of Antwerp. He was twenty-nine years of age and had come out to America, a priest, with Father Nerinckx in 1817. His virtuous character was an inspiring association for Father Van Quickenborne, and his premature death removed from the society of the novices an influence

---

[5] Letter to Mr. De Theux, Nov. 22, 1821.

which caused his memory to be deeply venerated by them.[6]

The following letter gives an account of Father De Smet's entrance into the novitiate: "You suffered deeply," he wrote his family, "when I left you without a word of farewell. Grieve no longer—God was calling me and I had to follow Him. . . . If you only knew how happy I am in the place where God has deigned to place me! Far from the tumult of the city and sheltered from the corrupting influence of the world my life passes in serene and tranquil days. Here is the beginning of that golden age I used to dream about when reading Virgil's Pastorals. My time is spent in serving God, imploring His mercy for the remission of my sins, begging for grace to persevere, and praying for your happiness."[7] Time served not to cool his ardor. The vigilant repression of an inflammable temper, the long retreats, the minutiæ of religious routine, unceasing labor, and the interior work of the soul striving for self-mastery were all doubtless vexations to his ardent nature, yet in the observance of the rules of his Society he was never known to relax.

Letters written by him at that time throw considerable light on his moral attitude and the character of his piety. It does not seem that he was taken up by the speculative study of virtue, but rather that he sought after practicality according to the maxim of Bossuet: "Woe to sterile knowledge that leads not to love and betrays itself." His simple, sincere piety was neither strained nor studied. Prayer, to Father De Smet, like study, was a means of preparing for action and of rendering it fruitful. He prayed to the Blessed Virgin with an abandonment and confidence almost childlike in its simplicity, begging her to bless his missionary career. Together with some of

[6] "We never speak of Father Timmermans," wrote Joost Van Assche some time later, "without expressing our admiration for his great humility, his obedience, piety, and exact observance of the rules. One word from his Superior was sufficient and he would go forth no matter where and without a penny in his pocket. However numerous his occupations, he found time every day to visit the Blessed Sacrament. Before starting out on a mission he would prostrate himself before the altar, and when he returned, no matter how wet and cold he might be, he would get off his horse, greet us, and go straightway to the chapel." (Letter to Mr. De Nef, Dec. 4, 1825.)

[7] Whitemarsh, Oct. 18, 1821.

his fellow-workers he became an apostle of the Rosary in the country about Whitemarsh, and he was to learn later that for every Rosary distributed by his band the reward was one Protestant converted to Catholicity.[8] Peter De Smet's happy nature, which in Belgium had won him the affection of his schoolmates, was still evident in the Jesuit novice. His uprightness, rare common sense, and great delicacy of feeling were admired and appreciated; his characteristic virtue—simplicity—was at this time already manifesting itself—"that candor of soul which seeks virtue, duty, and God alone."[9]

The Society of Jesus was for him "the tenderest of mothers, giving happiness to all who seek refuge within her fold,"[10] but not, however, to an extent that eclipsed his affection for his family. The irregularity of the foreign mails left Peter two years without news from Belgium. "Your silence," he wrote his father, "is a great sorrow to me. I am unable to discover the reason of it. I imagine that perhaps the letters in which I endeavored to justify my course of action have displeased you. Alas! dear father, is it then so reprehensible a thing for one to obey the voice of God?"[11]

Eventually, however, the long-awaited letters arrived: "I have received three of your letters with the money which you have had the goodness to send me. I was beginning to despair of hearing from you when they came to hand. Nothing could so rejoice my heart as your submission to God's will. He wishes me to be in America not only to labor for my own salvation, but, should I prove worthy, for the salvation of others as well."

"I can never forget," wrote his father, "that you left without telling me"—words which Peter could not read without weeping. "Dear father," he writes again, "God alone knows what it cost me to leave you as I did; but after all was I not right? Reflect for a moment and I am sure, considering the circumstances, you will not condemn me. Had I told you of my departure and gone to say good-by to you, what would you not have done to prevent my going, or at least to persuade me to

---

[8] Whitemarsh, Dec. 27, 1822.
[9] St. Francis de Sales.
[10] Letter of Aug. 26, 1823.
[11] *Ibid.*

wait for a few years? I foresaw everything and feared the urgent promptings of human nature, which so often triumph when we expose ourselves to their assaults. I should not have been the first who, through yielding to the tears and insistence of parents and friends, stepped aside from his vocation. . . . Was it not my duty to trample on my natural affections, rather than expose myself to the loss of that happiness I came to seek in this distant land? I have already been abundantly compensated for all I sacrificed to acquire it." [12]

Peter De Smet had been eighteen months at Whitemarsh novitiate when an unforeseen circumstance brought him in touch with the field of his future apostolate. For some time past Bishop Dubourg of New Orleans had urged the Jesuits to found a mission for the Indian tribes in Missouri. [13] At the beginning of 1823 he renewed his entreaties and, this time, to Father Charles Neale, who had succeeded Father Kohlmann as Provincial of the Maryland Province, he offered by way of a gift to the Society a large and productive farm near the village of Florissant, sixteen miles from St. Louis. Economic conditions at Whitemarsh had come to such a pass as to make Bishop Dubourg's offer seem providential. Improper rotation of crops—wheat and tobacco having been the only alternates for years—had so impoverished the soil of the plantation that revenues sufficient to maintain the institution were no longer possible, and as the Maryland Province was too poor to support the twenty young novices, a plan was already under consideration for the removal of the novitiate to a more favorable region.

Father Neale gladly accepted Bishop Dubourg's offer and thereupon appointed Father Van Quickenborne Superior of the new mission. Father Timmermans was selected to accompany him, and also given authority to

[12] Letter of Dec. 8, 1823.

[13] Born in St. Domingo in 1776, William Dubourg was ordained priest in Paris, and afterward joined the Society of St. Sulpice. In 1796 he came to America. Bishop Carroll appointed him head of Georgetown College, and later on he founded St. Mary's College at Baltimore. In 1815 he was made Bishop of New Orleans. He labored zealously in his diocese, which comprised nearly the whole of the basin of the Mississippi from the mouth of the river to St. Louis and beyond into the Indian country.

take with him those novices who showed special fitness and natural inclination for Indian missionary work. Father Van Quickenborne announced the project to his community and without a moment's hesitation seven Flemish novices volunteered. Nothing, they said, could give them greater happiness than to consecrate their lives to the education and salvation of the Indians; for this purpose they had come to America and they were gratified to be the first called. The Master of Novices, being satisfied as to their earnestness, accepted their offer to accompany him to Missouri. Three lay Brothers also formed part of the band: Brothers Peter De Meyer of Grammont, Henry Reiselman of Amsterdam, and Charles Strahan of Maryland. To complete the efficiency of the personnel the Superior chose from among the negroes attached to the plantation three families to work the farm at Florissant.

Peter De Smet, his fondest dream realized, wrote to his family at Termonde: "For some time past Bishop Dubourg of New Orleans has wanted the missionaries of the Society of Jesus to begin the conversion of the Indians, large numbers of them being idolaters and still larger numbers being without laws or religion. He has now obtained twelve of us—eleven Belgians and one American. I thank God I am one of those chosen. . . . Pray for me and my companions that God may deign to bless our enterprise."[14] Bishop Dubourg asked Father Van Quickenborne how he would accomplish the journey, as, much to his regret, he was not in a position to furnish him with funds for that purpose. "Don't worry," was the cheerful reply, "we will go on foot and beg our food; all my little band are of one mind as to this."[15]

April 11th was the day appointed for their departure, and the missionaries started at sunrise, arriving by nightfall at Baltimore where the final preparations for the trip were to be made. Father Van Quickenborne hired two wagons, each drawn by six horses, to transport the baggage to Wheeling on the Ohio River. He had also a light

[14] Baltimore, April 12, 1823.
[15] Letter of Bishop Dubourg to his brother, Georgetown, March 17, 1823. (Annals of the Propagation of the Faith, Vol. i, No. 5, p. 41.)

wagon brought from Whitemarsh in which the missionaries could travel in case illness or excessive fatigue rendered any of them incapable of continuing on foot. When they started off with that simple and inadequate equipment to open a mission to savages fifteen hundred miles distant, our young men little dreamed they were going to found in the center of the United States a new province of the Society of Jesus; that at St. Louis they would establish a flourishing university; that they would erect numerous colleges, and that their missions would extend from the Gulf of Mexico to the Great Lakes, Canada, and even to the shores of the Pacific.

On April 14th they left Baltimore and started on the journey across the Alleghanies. The novices with the lay Brothers, staff in hand, led the procession on foot. Except on rare occasions they cooked their own food, and at night sought shelter within the outhouses of some farm or in an abandoned cabin. Father De Smet tells us in his journal that "the Catholic families who were without a resident priest would try to detain them; the Protestants in general looked upon them as young adventurers of fortune and would offer them inducements to remain in the neighborhood." This roving life in no way interfered with the ascetic training of the novices. Arriving at Conewago two days in advance of Fathers Van Quickenborne and Timmermans, they employed the intervening time in transcribing Father Plowden's instructions upon religious perfection, a work they had been obliged to abandon upon leaving Whitemarsh.[16]

After a march of eighteen days the young Jesuits arrived at Wheeling. Their resources were inadequate for the purchase of a boat, so the Superior, by way of a makeshift, procured two scows which he caused to be lashed together. On one he placed the negroes and the baggage; the missionaries occupied the other, and thus they committed themselves to the current of the Ohio. The beautiful river flowed between densely forested banks with only here and there a cluster of miserable huts. The

[16] Father Percy Plowden (1672–1745), "Practical Methods of Performing the Ordinary Actions of a Religious Life with Fervor of Spirit." London, 1718.

present cities of Cincinnati, Louisville, and Madison were then but small villages. The expedition traveled day and night, only stopping to procure provisions. The religious exercises for the novices were continued on board. A bell was rung every morning for rising, meditation, and examination of conscience. Mass was said every day and the boat was, in fact, a floating monastery.

The usual dangers and difficulties which were features of the river navigation at that time beset the party. Violent wind-storms took their craft beyond their control and falling trees toppling into the stream from the eroded banks, as well as sunken snags, were a frequent menace.[17] Steering so unwieldy a craft was at best difficult, but floating brushwood made the task of the pilot quite arduous. Brother Strahan, on whom this responsibility rested, was kept unceasingly on the alert to avoid the steamboats which traveled up and down the river.

At Louisville the voyagers encountered the famous falls of the Ohio. In order to safely make the passage of the rapids it was necessary to lighten cargo, and to this end all of the party except Joost Van Assche went ashore, loading the baggage into carts. Joost Van Assche alone was permitted to remain aboard with the local pilot to whose skill the craft was entrusted for shooting the rapids. The band was to be reunited and to embark again some miles below the falls, where, as it happened, a pleasant surprise was awaiting them. They were destined at their point of rendezvous to meet no less a person than their venerated and beloved friend, Father Nerinckx. The old missionary was conducting a community of the Sisters of Loretto who were leaving Kentucky for Missouri. He was moved to tears by the happy and unexpected meeting, for, realizing that his span of years was nearly done, it brought comfort to his zealous soul to know that

---

[17] "Trees that topple into the stream when the current washes away the sustaining earth about the roots, float for some time until the roots or limbs catch on the bottom and hold them fast against the current. In the course of months and years the action of the swift-flowing water sharpens the trunk and branches and they go by the name of 'snags.' Frequently these are hidden beneath the surface, and woe to any steamer that strikes one of them, for they will rip the hull in the twinkling of an eye." (Jules Leclercq, "Un été en Amérique." Paris, 1877, p. 166.)

the apostolic work which he had begun would be perpetuated by such worthy and ardent men. "Your work will be arduous," he told them, "but never forget God and He will not forget you." To the very close of his life Father Nerinckx followed with interest the missionary and religious careers of these young men, and it so happened that only a few days before his death he went to Florissant to visit them and encourage them in their work.

The two flatboats, having made a safe passage through the rapids, joined the missionaries who were awaiting them at Portland. The horses and the wagon and all the impedimenta were reembarked and the voyage continued on down the Ohio. From Louisville to Shawneetown the voyage was devoid of incident, but from here on a modification of travel was necessary because, though only a few days from St. Louis, the boats could not get up the Mississippi and the party was obliged to complete the journey on foot. Father Van Quickenborne sent the baggage on a steamboat bound for St. Louis, and the missionaries took their way overland through Illinois.

The prairies were inundated by spring rains and they were obliged to tramp one hundred and eighty miles through marshes, often up to the waist in water, seldom finding shelter in farm or inn. Night would overtake them with no better quarters than the floor of some barn or empty stable, and the singing and biting of mosquitoes made sleep an impossibility. At length, however, on Saturday, May 31st, the travelers came in sight of St. Louis. They were exhausted, Father De Smet tells us, having descended nearly the whole length of the Ohio River, and having covered more than four hundred miles on foot since leaving Whitemarsh six weeks before. Did the sight of the Mississippi's broad expanse, as it lay before them, recall to their memory the splendors of *Meschacebé*, "The Father of Waters," spoken of by Châteaubriand? It is more probable that their thoughts were only for those brave pioneers of religion who had already evangelized that country, and that they were thanking God for having called them to take up again, after a lapse of more than a century, the work of salvation which religious persecution had suddenly arrested.

The population of St. Louis at that time numbered four or five thousand. The new-comers were cordially received at the Catholic academy lately erected by Bishop Dubourg. The next day being the feast of Corpus Christi, to the Father Superior was given the honor of carrying the Blessed Sacrament in the procession, and this was, in fact, the first time in the history of the town that a Jesuit had lifted up the monstrance to the gaze of the faithful.

The evening of the same day Father Van Quickenborne, impatient to reach his post, mounted a horse and set out in company with Charles de la Croix, a former native of Ghent and a missionary of six years' residence in Missouri. Three days later, on June 3d, he was joined at Florissant by his young traveling companions.[18]

The village of Florissant, also known at the time as St. Ferdinand, was situated about sixteen miles from St. Louis, and at no great distance from the confluence of the Missouri and Mississippi rivers. At that time it boasted about four hundred inhabitants, and concerning the country surrounding it a traveler who visited there at the beginning of the last century remarked, "No words can describe its beauty and fertility."[19] In spring and summer the undulating floor of the valley was a sea of verdure extending to the borders of vast forests of red, black, and white oak, walnut, maple, and trees of every species. In 1823 not a single habitation was to be seen as the eye swept the verdant expanse of the surrounding country. The soil of the district was of inexhaustible richness and fertility, and such land as was under cultivation produced each year enormous crops. Florissant was regarded as the granary of St. Louis and the wheat grown there was renowned throughout Missouri, whence it was conveyed by water to the markets of Lower Louisiana.

The house of the Jesuit Mission was about one and a half miles from Florissant and stood upon an eminence. The situation commanded a fine view of the country lying spread before it like a panorama, with Florissant nestling

---

[18] The account of this journey is taken from Father Hill's interesting book, "Historical Sketch of the St. Louis University," Chap. ii, St. Louis, 1879.

[19] H. M. Breckenridge, "Views of Louisiana," Book ii, Chap. ii.

in the valley, the roofs of the houses peeping here and there through the trees. To the west lay St. Charles, with its low-roofed buildings rising in tiers on the bluffs of the Missouri River, and to the north sinuous white cliffs crowned with forests marked the course of the Mississippi River above Alton.

However inspiring was this location, the buildings themselves left much to be desired. The main structure was an affair of one room about eight or nine yards wide, surmounted by a gable roof pitched so low that a man could not stand upright in the attic beneath it. A short distance away stood two huts, each about twenty feet square, and this group of three buildings was all their accommodation. If comforts there were, they were very few; the walls were of logs placed one upon the other, the intervening cracks being plastered up with mud. The roof consisted of large shingles,* which for lack of nails were held in place by strips of wood laid crosswise. The doors were made of rough, hand-hewn slabs, and were fastened by means of a wooden latch which was lifted by a string that hung outside. The windows were mere openings, without glass, having shutters that fastened in a manner similar to the doors.

The missionaries proceeded at once to make themselves at home. The dark and stuffy attic became the dormitory of the novices, and its floor, softened by a buffalo robe or a handful of straw, served as their bed. The ground floor was divided by a curtain which separated the chapel from the bedroom occupied by the Superior and his assistant. One of the two outhouses, which in a former day had served successively as a chicken-house and then a pig-pen, was transformed into a study for the novices and also a community refectory. The other outhouses were used as a shelter for plows and farm implements, and as a kitchen and sleeping-quarters for servants.

The long journey had exhausted their modest financial resources and in a short while the community felt the

---

* *Translator's Note:* The shingles referred to were in all probability what were commonly known in this part of the country as "clapboards." These differed from shingles, being made of oak generally, and being longer, wider, and thicker.

bite of poverty. The farm, it is true, comprised about three hundred acres, all agricultural land, but it had to be cleared, plowed, and planted with no help other than the three idle negroes. The labor was arduous and was followed by a protracted period of waiting for the first crop yield. Scant clothing and an inadequate diet of corn and bacon failed, however, to call forth a complaint. "Far from complaining," wrote Bishop Dubourg, "they thanked God for giving them such a truly apostolic beginning." [20]

The courageous Bishop himself gave them an example of perfect trust in Providence: "I wished to be prudent and have money in hand before seeking for missionaries, and behold, the men came before the money! Thus does God disconcert the plans laid by our poor human prudence. . . . Could I refuse the services of this holy band of apostles under the cowardly pretext that I did not know where to find means to feed them? God sent them to me and He will not let them starve. Moreover, never have I felt such entire confidence and peace as in this enterprise, which I feel to be above and beyond my own powers and strength to accomplish." [21] The good Bishop's trust did not go unrewarded. About that time the Society for the Propagation of the Faith sent him a sum of money which he hastened to divide with the missionaries, and in addition to this, Providence seemed to help them in other practical ways.

The Ladies of the Sacred Heart had then been established some three years in Florissant. Madam Duchesne, a woman celebrated for her virtues and renowned for the religious houses which she had founded, was the Superior at the time, and while her community was, in fact, quite poor itself and had but scant means of support, the order of its charity was heroic. They conducted a small school and had enrolled several postulants. The arrival of the Jesuit Fathers redoubled the self-sacrificing devotion of these good women. "Believing that this special mission had been confided to her, Madam Duchesne conserved

[20] To his brother, Aug. 6, 1823. (Annals of the Propagation of the Faith, Vol. i, No. 5, p. 41.)
[21] To his brother, March 17, 1823. (Annals of the Propagation of the Faith, Vol. i, No. 5, p. 39.)

her resources for the new-comers. Not content with begging alms from the well-to-do families of St. Louis, she also deprived herself of her own belongings, kitchen utensils, linen, bedding, and other essentials, as well as provisions; and whenever she heard that the missionaries were in want she would assemble the nuns and, intimating that she had rather divined the Fathers' needy condition than been told of it, because they never made their wants known, she would let her tears plead the cause of her protégés. This was always followed by a unanimous resolution to practice greater self-denial. The nuns devoted a portion of every evening to making and mending clothing for the missionaries. On one occasion, having received a donation of five dollars for her convent, the Mother Superior turned it over to her poorer neighbors, and in commenting upon it when writing to Madam Barat she said: 'We shall be a little Providence to others, even as God is to us.'" [22]

Thanks to the heroic charity of these nuns, the missionaries were able to eke out an endurable existence amidst the hardships of the early days of the novitiate, and ere long Father Van Quickenborne took steps to enlarge the house, adding a wing and a second story to the main building and also porches running the entire length. July 31st, the feast of St. Ignatius, was chosen for the beginning of the work. The only building-stone procurable had to be quarried from the river-banks, and the trees from which the timbers and boards were to be hewn were selected from a small island in the Missouri River not far from the novitiate. Father Van Quickenborne and his novices fell to their task with energy, and it was not long before the ground was covered with huge oak logs of many years' growth. The hewing and shaping of the timbers was all done on the spot where the trees were felled so as to facilitate transportation. While engaged on this work an accident occurred which revealed Father Van Quickenborne's indomitable will and resolution. One of the novices who was assisting him in squaring up a timber, for lack of skill permitted the axe to glance, striking the Superior on the foot. The blood gushed from

[22] Bishop Baunard, "Life of Madam Duchesne," p. 303.

the wound, but the priest would not desist from work till overcome by faintness; only the weakness from loss of blood compelled him to be seated and to permit his foot to be bandaged with a handkerchief. When the time arrived to return to the novitiate nothing would do but Father Van Quickenborne must trudge the several miles on his wounded foot. On the way, however, the pain became so excruciating that he was obliged to mount a horse. For several days he was confined to bed with a high fever, but at the first sign of improvement he returned to his work.

It was necessary for him to ride horseback, and this circumstance gave rise to another accident. In certain places the river-banks proved to be very marshy, and Father Van Quickenborne suddenly found that his horse had sunk into one of these treacherous bog-holes and was mired to the shoulders. He, fortunately, was able to dismount upon firm ground, but every effort to extricate the poor animal was futile, and he had the pain of seeing his mount perish before his eyes.[23] * These misfortunes, however, were to the laborers but a part of the day's work, and their ardor was unabated. On the island, which was now transformed into a lumber-yard, the axe, saw, and plane were plied incessantly, and it was not long before the work of dressing was finished and the last beam had been hauled up the hill upon which the novitiate stood. Nor was the gathering of the timber and its preparation attended to with more than sufficient dispatch, for the following night the island was washed away by a sudden freshet in the Missouri.

The building operations went on apace, and no member of the little colony lent himself to the work with greater enthusiasm than Father De Smet. His skill and herculean strength enabled him to do the work of three men. As late as a few years ago the remains of a hut built of enormous logs, one above the other and cemented with mud, were still to be seen at the novitiate, the work of "Samson," who was both architect and builder. His notes tell

---

[23] Cf. Father De Smet, Selected Letters, 2d series, p. 174.

* *Translator's Note:* This bog-hole was in all likelihood nothing more or less than one of the beds of quicksand which are quite common in the Missouri River, especially near sloughs formed by islands or on sand-bars.

us how every man labored at this arduous task with great enthusiasm: "most joyfully and pleasantly."

A truly remarkable thing is to be noted in the fact that none of these hardships and engrossing labors were permitted to interfere with the routine and regular spiritual exercises of the novitiate.[24] It bespeaks the great strength of soul of Father Van Quickenborne and his associates that the spiritual practices peculiar to the community life of the Society were not in any wise permitted to lapse or be abbreviated under the stress of pressing and necessary material occupations.

The enlargement of the house was finally accomplished and the little household more comfortably lodged; but added space and new walls had not shut out the gnawing wolf of poverty. The hard experience of the past months had taxed to the limit the endurance of Francis De Maillet and Charles Strahan, and they withdrew from the Society. These defections from the ranks served only to strengthen the tenacity of Peter De Smet. In one of his letters to his father he said: "I am in good health, contented, and happy in our little hut. . . . You are convinced, I feel sure, that the greatest happiness man can know here below is to serve God, love Him with his whole soul, abandoning himself to the Divine Will; rejoice that your son has left the world and sought refuge in religion, where he is sheltered from the dangers that would have beset his path had he not followed his vocation."[25]

The two years which had now passed since our young men entered the novitiate at Whitemarsh were deemed to be a sufficient term of probation, and on October 10, 1823, the six Florissant novices made their first vows. Concerning the happiness which he felt on this occasion Peter De Smet wrote to his family: "I have had the honor of consecrating myself to God by vows which to me will be indissoluble bonds. I have given myself completely to His service, making thereby an irrevocable and absolute gift. It only now remains for me to sanctify myself in this state and remain faithful all the days of my life. Pray for me that I may persevere."[26]

[24] "Nothing of the spiritual exercises was meanwhile neglected."
[25] Letter of Dec. 8, 1823.   [26] *Ibid.*

CHAPTER III

THE SCHOLASTICATE—PRIESTHOOD—FIRST LABORS
(1823–1830)

Father Van Quickenborne at once Superior, Professor, Parish Priest at
Florissant, and Chaplain of the Sacred Heart Convent—Father De
Theux—Peter De Smet's Studies—Confidence Reposed in Him by His
Superiors—His Taste for Natural Science—The Priesthood—Joost De
Smet's Death — The Third Year — Beginning of Apostolic Work—
Florissant, St. Charles, etc.—The "Indian College"—The Plan for a
"Reduction"—Circumstances Preventing Its Accomplishment.

TWO days after pronouncing their vows the young
missionaries entered upon the studies that were to
prepare them for the priesthood, and, owing to the fact
that most of them had finished the "humanities" before
leaving Belgium, the course was opened with the study of
philosophy. A lack of text-books confronted the students,
and Peter De Smet wrote to his father asking that the
necessary ones be sent out. In addition to being Master
of Novices Father Van Quickenborne assumed the rôle
of Professor of Philosophy, and Peter Verhaegen, who had
begun his ecclesiastical studies at Mechlin, became his
assistant. The course was necessarily of a summary character, because a detailed knowledge of systems was not
as important to the future missionaries as a careful preparation in theology and a proper training and maturing of
their minds. The circumstances of the times called for the
earliest possible ordination of new priests.

On May 31, 1824, Father Timmermans succumbed to
"the hardships he endured during his missionary work;
the travel through arid and flooded districts; the lodging
in dilapidated huts and the sleeping on the ground; the
diet of water and salt pork."[1] He was only thirty-five

[1] Letter to Madam Duchesne, Baunard, *op. cit.*, p. 311.

years of age and was the first Jesuit to die in Missouri. Two months later the missionaries lost Father Nerinckx. The old priest had but just come to St. Louis, intending to devote the remaining years of his life to the poor and the Indians. With this object in view he had asked Bishop Rosati, coadjutor to Mgr. Dubourg, to give him the most neglected mission in his diocese. After visiting the Sisters of Loretto, who had established themselves the previous year at Barrens, he went to his friends at Florissant in order that he might take a long-needed rest. This visit was destined to be Father Nerinckx's farewell, for following it, a few days later, the intrepid missionary died at St. Genevieve in his sixty-third year, worn out by the fatigues of his laborious ministry.

Father Van Quickenborne was now the sole remaining priest at the Florissant Mission, where he filled the offices of Superior, professor, parish priest, and chaplain to the Ladies of the Sacred Heart. "Although weak in health," wrote Madam Duchesne, "he looked after four parishes and other remote missions across the river. On Sundays he said two Masses, preached three times in the morning, taught catechism, and heard confessions in the intervals between religious exercises."[2] No constitution, however robust, could withstand the exactions of such a routine, and, moreover, the training of the scholastics and the direction of their studies required his constant presence. This finally compelled Father Van Quickenborne to ask his Superiors for an assistant.

On August 20, 1824, Peter De Smet wrote to his father: "I have finished my course in philosophy, and when the vacations are over I expect to begin theology—we are daily expecting professors from Rome." The expected professors never came, but Providence bestowed upon the new mission another remarkable Belgian who was destined to leave behind him a reputation for sanctity. This was Theodore De Theux of Meylandt, born on January 24, 1789, at Liège. After taking his degree brilliantly at the seminary of Namur, he became, in 1812, the vicar of St. Nicolas in his native town.

The hospitals at Liège were at that time overcrowded

---

[2] Florissant, June 10, 1824.

with Spanish prisoners who had been deported by Napoleon, and a malignant fever raging in their midst was decimating their numbers daily. Abbé De Theux, that he might hear the confessions of the stricken Spaniards, lent himself with diligence to the acquiring of their language, but before he made any progress in it he himself fell a victim to the scourge, and was compelled to return to his home. The disease was so contagious that in a few weeks two of his brothers and four servants had died of it. The young priest was at the point of death, but the designs of Providence seemed to contemplate reserving him for other work.

He was appointed professor of Dogma and Sacred Scripture at Liège in 1815, and presided at the opening of the new seminary, where he happened to meet Father Nerinckx, and experienced the call which added him to the ranks of American missionaries. In April, 1816, he left Belgium without again seeing his parents, and was received into the novitiate of the Society of Jesus by Father Grassi, Superior of the Maryland Province in America. Almost immediately following his reception into the Society he was given the chair of philosophy in Georgetown University, was appointed preacher to the students, and soon thereafter became head of the Georgetown parish and mission. "Such," wrote Archbishop Maréchal, "is the fervor of his piety, the immensity of his zeal, and his great charity, that numerous Protestants attended his instructions and afterward embraced the Catholic Faith."[3] To those who remonstrated with Father De Theux for his excessive labors he replied, "It is for this that I became a Jesuit."

Father De Theux had been eight years in Maryland when his Superior, Father Dzierozynski, sent him to join Father Van Quickenborne in Missouri. Upon his arrival at Florissant in October, 1825, he was struck with the poverty and needs of the mission, but, far from being dismayed, he remarked, "The Apostles were only twelve in number when they undertook the conversion of the world; our successors will finish the work we have been unable to accomplish."[4]

[3] Letter to Mr. De Theux, Nov. 22, 1821.
[4] Letter to his mother, Feb. 3, 1826.

Father Van Quickenborne had by this time been appointed Vicar General of Upper Louisiana,[5] a position which did not, however, abolish his ministry in Florissant and the surrounding country, and Father De Theux relieved him of the theological training of the young religious. Father De Theux's previous studies and his experience in Georgetown facilitated this work for him, and though time was wanting in which to thoroughly develop his course of instruction, he made it his aim, through solid and practical teaching, to prepare his students for a fruitful apostolate, not only among the Indians, but also in the field of Protestantism.

Having already studied theology for a year under Father Van Quickenborne, Peter De Smet followed only a two years' course under the direction of Father De Theux. At Florissant, as at Mechlin, the solid quality of his mind and the sureness of his judgment won him the entire confidence of his Superior. "For several years," he writes later on, "I enjoyed the happiness of living with Father De Theux in a miserable little hut, and at his express wish I became his monitor. It was agreed between us that twice a week he should question me upon the faults and defects I had observed in him. He begged me never to spare him, nor consider his feelings, saying he would be most grateful for this service, and would often pray for me. I observed him carefully in the performance of his spiritual exercises, in his class of theology, at table, and at recreation, and never discovered the least failure in duty. He was grieved that I did not correct him—so to quiet the good priest I would mention some trifling imperfection, a mere nothing, which he thanked me for. I feel sure he prayed for me."[6]

Innumerable were the unpleasant circumstances and incidents which conspired to render the studies of the scholastics burdensome, but Peter De Smet took everything in good part. "Thank God!" he writes, "I am wonderfully well. I have suffered with the heat, it is true, but then we have other advantages of which you are deprived. In Flanders I had often to be bled—a custom of the country, and an operation which there required a doctor. It is done here, gratis, by gnats, mosquitoes, fleas, ticks, and flies. They are so obliging! It is far easier to kill them than to try to dissuade them from rendering this service."[7]

During vacation young De Smet collected minerals, plants, and the insects peculiar to the country, thereby acquiring so thorough a knowledge of natural science that his name came to be known among scientific men. He collected not only to satisfy his own curiosity and his thirst for knowledge, but also to send specimens to his family and the benefactors of the missions. "I have read with pleasure," he writes his brother Charles, "that you have an extended knowledge of foreign trees and plants, and I am only waiting to know what specimens you want before sending you some from my own collection. I have gathered near here every interesting specimen that is not to be found in Flanders. These I will send you at the first opportunity. . . . I know several travelers who often pass through the Indian country, and you shall have your share in everything I receive."[8] He further tells about a consignment of insects, birds, and snakes, and refers to the fact that he had made a collection of reptiles of "every species in the State of Missouri." Madam De Theux, the mother of his theology teacher, received a collection of some two hundred insects, as well as of the different seeds peculiar to the locality. A similar collection was forwarded to the Jesuits in Rome.

The care of souls, however, remained the all-absorbing interest of these pioneer priests: "A mission territory some three thousand leagues in circumference and one devoid of ministers of the Gospel has been confided to our care. Pray and have prayers and Masses said for us and for the unfortunate people scattered through this wilderness who are waiting on our ministration."[9] "The misery of so many souls deprived of the light and consolation of true religion saddens my heart. Since I am not in a position

[7] To his father, St. Ferdinand, Aug. 20, 1824.
[8] Feb. 10, 1828.   [9] To his father, Dec. 8, 1823.

to labor among them, the thought of their condition spurs me on and urges me to beseech heaven in their behalf. I beg you, my dear father and my sisters and brothers, to add your supplications to mine.   Our united prayers cannot fail to obtain what should be the desire of every good Catholic—the conversion of sinners, and the return of our erring brothers to the fold."[10]

The time for his ordination was now approaching. Having finished the course in philosophy, Peter De Smet received the tonsure and minor orders from Bishop Rosati. In a letter to his father under date of May 7, 1827, he says: "We shall pass our examinations in logic, metaphysics, natural philosophy, and theology in July, after which, in all probability, we shall be ordained.   Pray for me." On September 23d of the same year, in the parish church at Florissant, Bishop Rosati conferred Holy Orders upon young De Smet and his three companions, John Elet, Joost Van Assche, and Felix Verreydt.[11]   The following day, the feast of Our Lady of Mercy, Father De Smet celebrated his first Mass.

The father of our missionary was not destined to realize here on earth the joy and satisfaction of knowing that his son had become a priest, for seven months before, in his ninety-first year, he passed away in the bosom of his loving and devoted family.[12]   Peter could never free himself from the feeling that his father cherished a certain resentment against him because of his departure from home.   "In reading over the letters you wrote me three or four years ago I experience an inexpressible joy when I perceive that you are completely resigned to the will of God, and note the sentiments you entertain in my regard, but when I consider that these letters are the only ones I have received from home, and that I am in complete ignorance of all that is happening to you, I am weighed down with sadness."[13]

The irregularity of sailings and mails at that period would account for the silence of De Smet senior.   There

[10] April 29, 1824.
[11] John Baptiste Smedts and Peter Verhaegen had been ordained the previous year.
[12] Joost De Smet died Feb. 15, 1827.
[13] To his father, May 7, 1827.

exists, however, a touching proof of the affection which Joost De Smet felt for his son. Not long before his death he sat for a portrait, in which he is seen holding in his hand a letter from Peter, a pose he insisted upon taking. When the missionary returned to Belgium he often stood before that venerated image and there read the assurance of his pardon.

Having completed their studies for the priesthood, the young religious now passed from the status of scholastics to probationers, as it were. Despite the fact that the mission was in need of active ministers of the Gospel, Father Van Quickenborne would not curtail the course prescribed by St. Ignatius by omitting the "third year," and he even took upon himself the duties of instructor. With appealing eloquence he preached to these young men the principles of self-abnegation, and instilled into them the love of Christ. He exhorted them to apostolic zeal with such burning words that the lapse of thirty years could not efface them from the memory of Father De Smet: "The salvation of souls was the one thought, desire, and longing of his life. . . . He communicated his devouring zeal to others and one felt carried away by his words. Those who could not materially aid him in his work were moved to pray for his success."[14]

In addition to the lectures of the Superior the young priests now added the practical work of ministry by frequently visiting the Catholics living in the neighborhood of Florissant. Touching upon his early experiences in a letter to his sister Rosalie, Father De Smet says: "Numerous difficulties confront us who are working for the evangelization of this country. In this part of America there are few churches. We are obliged oftentimes to say Mass in a roofless hut, with the congregation exposed to heat, cold, and inclement weather. In winter the altar is often covered with snow, and in summer it streams with wax from the candles melted by the excessive heat. Another great difficulty is the scattered population. By far the smaller percentage of the Catholics live in the settlements, the majority being dispersed throughout the wilder-

[14] Selected Letters, 3d series, p. 178.

ness sometimes at a distance of fifteen or twenty miles from one another. We are obliged to seek them like lost sheep, often at the peril of our lives. Sometimes we spend the night in the woods, exposed to the attacks of the wolves, which are quite numerous in these parts, or we may sojourn in a hut where a fire is our only light, and our clothes the only bed-covering. We cross rivers on horseback, or on the trunk of a fallen tree, or in a bark canoe. Again and again we eat our first meal at six o'clock in the evening, and oftentimes are obliged to postpone even this one till the following day. Hardships of this character, however, reduce *embonpoint*, and we are all in excellent health, a fact that astonishes the Americans. We tell them it is the Belgian blood in our veins. There is much talk about black and yellow fever and chills and fever, but as for myself, thank God! I have not fallen a victim to any of these maladies and am always the same Peter." The letter concludes with an appeal to the generosity of the clergy and Catholics of Termonde: "I know, dear sister, that you enjoy a game of lotto with Mlle. X. . . . Give the winnings to our poor missions."[15]

The exercises of the "third year" were concluded July 31, 1828, and from that time forward the needs of the mission were not so great. Before beginning the work of converting the Indians, the Catholics were sought out and drawn away from Protestant influences. The Protestant ministers were endeavoring in every way to interfere with the work of the Jesuits. Catholicism was represented by them as a collection of absurd doctrines, and this attitude was backed up by gross calumnies about the Jesuits. In addressing the ignorant classes these preachers were wont to paint the Jesuits as monsters with hoofs and horns, and when the first priest came among the people of this locality he was scrutinized as a curiosity. It did not take long, however, to dispel these false impressions and win the misguided ones to the faith.

Prior to the founding of the college in St. Louis the Jesuits had two principal centers of activity: Florissant and St. Charles. When they came to Florissant they

[15] Florissant, Feb. 16, 1828. (Translated from the Flemish.)

found a Belgian priest, Father Charles de la Croix,[16] in charge of the parish. This man's faith and piety had caused Bishop Dubourg to regard him as his principal auxiliary, and the Bishop used to call him "his good angel." When, eventually, physical exhaustion compelled Father de la Croix to quit his post, the parish was turned over to Father Van Quickenborne, who from 1828 on had as his assistants Fathers De Theux and Elet.

The ardent zeal, the charity, and the forceful, convincing words of these priests deeply moved Catholics and Protestants alike, and enthusiasm spread. Retreats were preached by the missionaries, attracting the villagers to the church at first, and afterward bringing them to the holy table. Madam Duchesne, who witnessed these marvels, was lost in admiration: "These Fathers," she remarked, "seem capable of converting an entire kingdom."

St. Charles, situated on the left bank of the Missouri River, some ten miles above Florissant, numbered in population about one hundred Catholic families, all more or less poor. From contributions which he had begged Father Van Quickenborne was enabled to replace the barnlike building that served this community for a church, by a stone structure, which was looked upon as the most imposing in that region. The parish was ministered to by Father Verhaegen first, and later by Fathers Smedts and Verreydt, with the same success that their fellow-priests had already attained at Florissant.

From these two main centers the missionaries extended their apostolic work unto the surrounding country. Father Van Quickenborne, writing in 1829, says: "The St. Charles church had three smaller churches attached to it. These

[16] Born in 1792 at Hoorebeke-St.-Corneille in Eastern Flanders, Charles de la Croix was one of those valiant seminarists of Ghent who were forced into Napoleon's army. Ordained priest by Bishop Dubourg in 1817, he followed the missionary bishop to America. His first appointment was that of parish priest at Barrens, going later on to Florissant. He had begun the conversion of the Osage Indians when he was stricken down by a severe illness. After a sojourn in Belgium, where he remained some time, he was called to the pastorate of St. Michael's in Louisiana in 1829. He remained five years longer in America, and returned to Ghent, where he became Canon of the Cathedral and Secretary General of the Society for the Propagation of the Faith. Thence, until his death in 1869, he labored for the cause of the missions.

the Fathers visited once a month to celebrate Mass,[17] and also called upon six other stations about one hundred and forty-two miles distant. These latter places were only recently established, and when, two years ago, I visited them for the first time there were but seven Catholics to be found. The mission priest, on his latest visit to these stations, gave thirty-two communions and also converted several Protestants. To-day the Catholics there number one hundred and eighty souls."[18]

Although he was at that time in charge of the "Indian College," of which we will speak later on, Father De Smet tells us he often went to assist his companions in the different mission posts.[19] No one rejoiced more than he in the progress Catholicism was making. "It seems," he writes, "that the National Synod of the Bishops of America that sat last October, has thrown the Protestant ministers into a state of panic.[20] Before that event the progress our religion was making no doubt alarmed them, but now they have abandoned all restraint, and in their alarm give vent to a bitterness and hatred which betrays itself in atrocious calumnies spread abroad against everything Catholic. One can hardly repress a smile when reading their periodicals: 'The terrible Inquisition is being born again in this beautiful land of liberty, and instruments of torture and the gallows will soon be erected upon the ruins of Protestantism.' *Despotism, Jesuitism*—such are the names applied to the government of the Church. . . . The National Synod is condemned as a work of Satan and is every imaginable abomination. . . . 'The standard of the beast with ten horns (thus they designate the Sovereign Pontiff) is being waved from one end of the Republic to the other, and rivers of blood will soon inundate the land.'

"By having recourse to the basest calumnies, the

---

[17] These villages were Dardenne, Hancock Prairie, and Portage des Sioux.
[18] Letter to Mr. De Nef, May 30, 1829.
[19] "From 1827 to 1833 I was attached to the missions at St. Charles, Portage, Dardenne, St. Ferdinand, etc." (Itinerary manuscript.)
[20] This was the first Provincial Council of Baltimore, held Oct. 1, 1829, presided over by Archbishop Whitfield. The assembled bishops deliberated upon means of extending the Faith and combating "the spirit of indifference which, under the specious name of liberalism, tends to confound truth with error, representing all religions as equally good." (See pastoral letter of the Archbishop of Baltimore in "L'Ami de la Religion," Dec. 16, 1829.)

Protestants endeavor to terrify good people, but, God be praised! the people are beginning to mistrust these prophets. They are investigating the situation for themselves, and cease to put faith in the worn-out stories of our enemies. We shall soon have the joy of seeing prejudices vanish one by one, and truth triumph." [21]

The kind services rendered the Fathers upon their arrival in Florissant by the Ladies of the Sacred Heart were not forgotten, and in gratitude the Jesuits offered themselves as chaplains to the community. Father Van Quickenborne became their spiritual director. He was a stern man, brief in conversation, and knew but one road—that of humility and renunciation. The Mother Superior, no less than the nuns, was conducted along a thorny path. One day the good Mother, moved by the poverty of the Fathers, sent them a cooked dinner. Father Van Quickenborne returned it with the curt remark that he had not asked any alms of Madam Duchesne. Such rigor as this can be applied only to strong souls, but that it was to the liking of the Superior and her heroic companions is evidenced in her correspondence with Madam Barat. "Truly," she writes, "it would be very bad taste on my part to complain, when I am favored and upheld by so many friends of God. The guidance of these holy men is so uplifting that I delight more in our poverty-stricken country life than I should in that of a well-endowed convent in town."

The esteem felt by Madam Duchesne for the Jesuit Fathers was evinced even in a greater degree by the interest she showed in their work. On occasions when they went forth to visit their outlying congregations she would with celerity and generosity equip them with vestments, altar linen, sacred vessels; also money, cooking-utensils, and even the horse belonging to the convent. Indignant at the thought of the money which the Protestants were raising to oppose the work of the missionaries, she exclaimed, sublimely: "Could my flesh be converted into money, I would give it willingly to help our missions!" [22] From this time dates the religious friendship between Madam Duchesne and Father De Smet. Appreciating

[21] To his sister Rosalie, Feb. 1, 1830.
[22] "Histoire de Mme. Duchesne," Baunard, pp. 306 et seq.

his zeal and initiative, she never ceased to pray for the success of his work and encourage him in every way. He in return venerated her, and was grateful to her to the end of his life.

The Indians, meanwhile, were not overlooked. Dispossessed of their lands and driven west by the whites, they now found refuge and support in the Catholic Church. A considerable number of them, whose fathers had been instructed and baptized by the Jesuits, were well-disposed toward Catholicity. Protestant ministers made repeated attempts to gain their confidence, but were always coldly received.[23] "What had they to do," asked the Indians, "with married preachers, men who wore no crucifix, and said no rosary? They wanted only the Black Robes to teach them how to serve God. They even went so far as to appeal to the President of the United States, asking that the married ministers might be recalled and Catholic priests sent in their place."[24]

In 1823 a deputation of the Indians of Missouri came to St. Louis, and had an interview with the Governor. They also saw the pastor of the Cathedral, begged that missionaries be sent among them, and promised that any priests who should come would be accorded the very best treatment. The following year a family of Iroquois or Algonquins journeyed to Florissant to have their children baptized. On another occasion the head of a family brought the dead body of his son, wrapped in a buffalo robe, to a priest, asking to have it interred in consecrated ground.

The all-absorbing desire of the missionaries was to go at once to the Indians. The scarcity of priests, however, made it impossible for them to found new missions, so in 1824 they decided to open a school in Florissant where the children of the various tribes could be instructed, baptize, and brought up in the Catholic faith. In addition to the fact that the United States Government granted a subsidy to this school, it offered to the Jesuits a further

[23] "Each sect desired the conversion of the Indians as a proof of the divinity of their particular doctrine." (Letter of Father Van Quickenborne to Mr. De Nef, May 30, 1829.)

[24] Letter of Father De Smet to his father, Aug. 20, 1824.

advantage, in that, while the scholastics were awaiting ordination, they could study the language and habits of the Indians. It was further hoped that the Indian pupils would eventually be of assistance as interpreters and catechists. The Ladies of the Sacred Heart shortly afterward opened a similar school for Indian girls.

Father Van Quickenborne built a frame school-building of two stories and about forty foot frontage adjoining the mission house, and it was not long before the Indian children began to arrive, some being sent by Catholic families in St. Louis, others by superintendents of the tribes in Missouri, a few being brought by their own parents. Two months after the opening of the school Peter De Smet writes: "Already two chiefs of the Ayonais have brought their children to us for instruction. One of the chieftains, in giving his children to the Superior, said, 'Black Robe, this one is an orphan boy; the others have lost a mother whom they loved tenderly; in you they will find both father and mother. By teaching them to know the Master of life you will be giving them every good.'" Father De Smet describes this chief as "a giant in stature, tawny of skin, hair and face daubed with vermilion after the manner of savages.[25] His ears were pierced with many holes, and from his head hung two tin tubes in the form of a cross filled with feathers of different colors. His clothes consisted of a green shirt and knee-breeches of doe-skin, attached to which were the tails of wildcats that flapped about his legs as he walked." In the same letter Father De Smet goes on to say, "The children are very attentive at the instructions. They are being prepared for baptism, and we hope they will one day be apostles to their respective tribes. Many more children are on their way to our school, and if we had the means we could accommodate about eighty pupils."[26]

Before long the children that congregated at the school

[25] It is an abuse of the word to speak of the "redskins" of America. "None among the peoples of the New World have red skin, unless painted, which often happens. Even the reddish tinge of the skin resembling that of the Ethiopian is found only among half-breeds. In America one sees people of various shades of yellow from brownish to yellow, and even paler."—Deniker, "Les Races et les Peuples de la Terre," Paris, 1900, p. 593.

[26] Letter to his father, Aug. 20, 1824.

represented seven or eight different tribes. They were taught writing and English. The older ones were instructed in agriculture, and in order to incite them to take up the manual labor inseparable from this study, it was necessary for the Fathers to join in the plowing and spading of the soil, as the savage regards this as menial work, and hence beneath his dignity.[27]

The day came when the Catholic families of St. Louis in default of a college sent their children to the mission school. At first the scholastics of Florissant taught the young Indians, and Father De Smet was at the head of this department. After the "third year," however, he seems to have been left quite alone. No human motive could have persuaded him to seek this particular phase of the work, for those who know the idleness, the unsteadiness, and the revolting filth of the Indians, know also that constant contact with these gross natures requires a heroic charity of which God alone can judge the price.[28] But nothing deterred this man, who, upon his arrival in St. Louis, wrote to his father: "To suffer and die for the salvation of souls is the sole ambition of a true missionary." [29]

The Indian children grew and prospered, and while at Florissant contracted industrious habits and learned pious practices. When, however, this part of their education

[27] The presence of the children was a means of reaching the parents. "A short time ago," writes Joost Van Assche, "a party of about thirty Indians came to visit us. One of them, seeing his son carrying a bucket of water, asked him had he become a slave—they call those who work, slaves—but after three days, seeing that the children were well treated, the Indians suffered a change of mind and spoke quite otherwise. During their visit they entirely consumed one of our biggest beeves and nearly all our potatoes. The day the caravan arrived one of the Indians said he wished to take away his son, who seemed quite willing to go. Before leaving the father made the boy recite his prayers and other things he knew perfectly. He then in my presence said to him: 'My son, I will not take you with me. You have everything here that is good for you. You pray night and morning to the Master of life while we are roaming the woods like wild beasts. Remain here, and I will come soon again to see you." (Letter to Mr. De Nef, Dec. 4, 1825.)

[28] "We pray fervently for the conversion of the Indians, and to obtain laborers in the missionary field," wrote Madam Duchesne, "but they must be men who have died to all things, for every feature about the work is against human nature. Faith only, and the love of Christ suffering, can support a soul in such labor." (June 10, 1824.)

[29] Aug. 26, 1823.

was finished, there was no alternative but to send them back to their tribes, there to be deprived of religious help, and exposed, in their own families, to gross superstition and revolting immorality. To meet this situation the Jesuits formulated a plan whereby, instead of returning home, the young men upon leaving school should marry the Christian girls of their tribes—girls who had been educated by the nuns of the Sacred Heart. Each family was to receive a certain allotment of land, and thus the newly-baptized, under the vigilant eyes of the missionaries, would found a Christian village, the first foundation serving as a model for others.[30] This plan met with the approval of President Jackson and also that of Very Rev. John Roothaan, General of the Society of Jesus,[31] but two obstacles were encountered which rendered it impracticable.

The first difficulty grew out of the limited resources of the Florissant mission, which in 1827 barely sufficed to feed thirty pupils, and which could not be expanded or stretched so far as to purchase the six thousand acres of land necessary for the project.[32] The second difficulty was found in the unstable character of the Indians, and still more in the land-grabbing policy of the United States Government. When the Osages consented to cede their Missouri lands to the Government and retire to Indian Territory, they took away with them the greater number of the children at the mission. From this time on the number of scholars, never exceeding forty, decreased steadily.

This train of circumstances forced the Fathers, in 1830, to close their school. Providence was calling them to labor in other fields. They continued striving by every means, nevertheless, to follow and convert the Indians who were constantly moving further and further west,

[30] In a letter to Mr. De Nef (May 30, 1829) Father Van Quickenborne set forth this project, and its advantages. This letter, almost in its entirety, is to be found in the Annals of the Propagation of the Faith, Vol. iv, p. 583.

[31] Cf. The Woodstock Letters, Vol. xxv, p. 354.

[32] The Government which had approved the scheme should have supported it, but Father Van Quickenborne hardly hoped for this: "The expense for one year exceeded 1,600 francs ($320) and the Government paid only 400 francs ($80). . . . For many reasons I think it is not to our interest to ask for their cooperation." (Letter cited.)

and Father Van Quickenborne, at the price of great difficulty and inexpressible hardships, started new missions
among the tribes.

As to Father De Smet, he was the last to leave his
beloved school, where, to the end, he had the satisfaction
of seeing the children docile to his directions and attentive
to the lessons he taught them. He had learned their
language and come to understand their habits. Later,
when he was in the Rocky Mountains and in Oregon, and
again became instructor to the Indians, he needed but to
recall to memory the customs and organization of the
Florissant school.

CHAPTER IV

UPON the west bank of the Mississippi, twenty miles below the mouth of the Missouri River, and in the center of an immense plain extending from the Great Lakes to the Gulf of Mexico and from the Alleghanies to the Rocky Mountains, stands the city of St. Louis, "the Queen of the West," as it has long been called by Americans.

Few cities equal it in its commercial and agricultural advantages. A network of streams, whose navigable waters total some thirty thousand miles, formed by the tributaries of the Mississippi, makes St. Louis the center of the whole Mississippi basin. The Missouri, the Arkansas, the Illinois, the Ohio, and the Wisconsin rivers flow through States abounding in wheat, coal, minerals, and timber of every variety. This river system waters a land that is exceeded in fertility by no country in the world.

Founded in 1764 by French colonists from Louisiana, St. Louis was at that time an outpost from which trappers penetrated into the wilderness to trade with the Indians, and to hunt the beaver and the bison, returning after each expedition to place their furs in its market, which was a dominant factor in the raw fur trade of the world.

St. Louis, with Louisiana, was ceded to the United States by Napoleon in 1803, and soon thereafter began the settling up of the rich country that to-day forms the State of Missouri. Through concessions of land and the granting of immunities, the Government encouraged immigration, and the population increased rapidly. When the Jesuits arrived in Missouri, St. Louis was entering upon a development destined to make it one of the first cities of the New World.[1] In 1822 the town was granted a municipal charter, and four years later (1826) it became the seat of a Bishopric independent of the See of New Orleans.[2] The population of Missouri, which for the greater part was Catholic in the beginning, began to feel the influence of Protestantism, as exemplified by Methodists, Quakers, Anabaptists, and Presbyterians, all of whom had their ministers, preachers, and schools, and to offset this influence a Catholic college was badly needed for those of good faith, who were thrown into contact with the dissenters.[3]

Before returning to France Bishop Dubourg offered the Jesuits a large tract of land just outside the city limits, and Bishop Rosati's first act, when he became Bishop of St. Louis, was to renew the offer made by his predecessor.

The main object of the Jesuits in coming to Missouri had been the evangelization of the Indians; but a ministry to the whites seemed to offer at that time an opportunity for more abundant and lasting good. Father Van Quickenborne submitted the proposition to Father Dzierozynski,

[1] In 1820 St. Louis had about 5,000 inhabitants; in 1850, 80,000, and the census of to-day credits it with over 700,000.

[2] Overcome by the fatigues and difficulties of administration, Bishop Dubourg returned to France in 1826, where, as Archbishop of Besançon, he died in 1833. Bishop De Neckère, a Belgian, succeeded him at New Orleans, and Bishop Rosati, who since 1823 had acted as Coadjutor at St. Louis, became titular Bishop of that city in 1827.

Joseph Rosati was born in 1790 at Sora in the kingdom of Naples. He joined the congregation of St. Lazarus and early in life consecrated himself to the American Missions. This worthy man created the diocese of St. Louis, which he administered for sixteen years, during which time he honored with his constant friendship the Fathers of the Society of Jesus.

[3] A former college, confided by Bishop Dubourg to some secular priests, had not prospered.

who, regarding it favorably, confided to the Superior at Florissant the foundation of the new college. Money being an important factor in the project, Father Van Quickenborne was obliged to raise what he could by subscription from the people of St. Louis. His efforts in this direction were rewarded by the collection of $3,000, which was but half of the sum required; for the balance he trusted to a beneficent Providence.

In the autumn of 1828 work was begun under his direction and that of Father Verhaegen. Father De Smet often laid aside the duties of his professorship and for a change of occupation went to St. Louis to help in the construction work. With his own hands he cut stone, carried bricks, and directed the sanitary arrangements. In less than a year the building was finished and Father Verhaegen was appointed Rector, with Fathers De Theux and Elet as directors of the institution. The college opened November 2, 1829, with forty pupils, including both dayscholars and boarders, and from that time on the attendance grew constantly. Three months later Father De Smet writes: "There are already more than one hundred scholars at the St. Louis College, the greater part of them being Protestants, and many of these coming from a distance of more than four hundred leagues."[4] This rapid growth called for a corresponding increase in the faculty, and in 1830 the school at Florissant was closed and Father De Smet sent to St. Louis, where he filled the offices of Procurator, Prefect of Studies, and Professor of English.

"Our establishment continues to prosper," he writes to his sister. "We have more than one hundred and fifty pupils, of whom half are Protestants. You can picture me in the midst of this mischievous band, making deafening noises at recreation, and leading me a merry dance when it gets the opportunity. In spite of all this, however, we have every reason to be satisfied, since the greater number behave well, and make rapid progress in their studies."[5] It was evident that Father De Smet regretted the separation from his little savages at Florissant, but his

[4] Letter to his sister Rosalie, Feb. 1, 1830.
[5] St. Louis, May 9, 1832.

kindness and good spirits soon won the affection of his
new pupils, many of whom remembered him in after-life,
and contributed to his missions.

In 1831, Father Roothaan, General of the Jesuits, deeming the future of the Missouri Mission assured, detached it
from the Maryland Province to which it had hitherto
belonged.   Father De Theux was appointed Superior, and
Father Van Quickenborne, happy to be relieved of authority, left at once for the west to consecrate his remaining
years to the conversion of the Indian tribes.   In conjunction with these changes, the Provincial sent to St. Louis
from Georgetown three other Belgians, one of whom was
Father James Van de Velde, the future Bishop of Natchez.[6]
Every year saw an increase in the number of scholars
attending the college and eventually it became necessary
to add a new building to the original group.   On December
28, 1832, the State of Missouri bestowed upon the college
the title and charter of a University, where letters, science,
medicine, law, and theology [7] were taught, and from that
time on the establishment became one of the leading intellectual centers of the United States.

The success achieved by the Fathers was not confined to
the activities of the class-room alone; they became equally
celebrated as preachers.   Being without a church of their
own, the pulpit at the cathedral was offered to them every
Sunday, and to the congregations gathering there they
preached sometimes in French and sometimes in English.
The Protestants were not slow in denouncing the "papist
invasion of the Mississippi valley," and, as it were, to
offset this, the Jesuits added the apostolate of the pen
to that of the spoken word, by taking over the direction
of "The Shepherd of the Valley," a newspaper founded
by Bishop Rosati.[8]   This organ defended Catholicism

[6] Arriving in America with Father Nerinckx in 1817, Father Van de Velde
soon became famous as an orator and a distinguished humanist.

[7] The courses of law and medicine were given by outside professors.

[8] Father Verhaegen, justly proud of his work, gives the benefactors of
the mission an account of the things achieved: "We Belgians, who came here
ignorant of English, now write in this language and have succeeded in reaching Protestants, who read our paper eagerly.   They find in it the truth
they boast of seeking, and are finally convinced.   It has an immense circu-
lation, and accomplishes much good.   Thus we not only labor to form the
hearts of our pupils, who will revive piety in their own homes, but from our

against Protestant attacks, and brought about many conversions.

Fanatical religious opposition was, however, the least of the trials that beset the missionaries at this time. A great disaster fell upon the community in the shape of a terrific cyclone that devastated the valley of the Mississippi. The college was all but demolished, the pupils and the professors barely escaping with their lives. Then came an epidemic of cholera, that claimed more than two hundred victims a day, and forced the institution to close its doors for three months. Three of the professors broke down in health from overwork brought about by these conditions, and their classes had to be cared for by the other already overburdened teachers. "But," writes the Rector, "in spite of all these difficulties that confront us daily we walk *erecto capite*."[9]

The limitations and embarrassments of poverty were, perhaps, not less difficult to bear than the other misfortunes.[10] Father De Smet, as Procurator, bore the brunt of the impoverished exchequer. "You will be surprised," he writes to his sister, "that I am Father Procurator, that is, steward of the college—I, who in Flanders could not keep a penny in my pocket! I am general purchaser, and it is no easy task, especially in this college, with money as scarce as it is. My cash-box is as empty and smooth as the palm of my hand, and yet from every side I am besieged for this thing and that, and, lacking the means to satisfy these demands, am called stingy."[11] Nor did poverty and want settle themselves upon the Jesuits only in St. Louis; Father De Theux had great difficulty in securing sufficient means to feed the novices, and Father

college we preach, so to speak, to every part of the West." (Letter to Mr. De Nef, May 26, 1833.)

[9] Letter to Mr. De Nef, May 26, 1833.

[10] In alluding to the title of University recently bestowed upon the college, Father Verhaegen wrote: "In according us the distinction bestowed on no other institution in Missouri, the Legislature gives public and unequivocal proof of the importance of our institution, and the esteem in which it is held. But it is a title without endowment, and one, moreover, that imposes upon us the necessity of proving ourselves worthy of the esteem we enjoy. The day school being free, the revenues from the boarders, which must meet the running expenses of the house, are insufficient to permit us to extend our work, and accomplish all the good we could do in our position." (Letter cited.)   [11] May 9, 1832.

Kenny, after sojourning at the mission as a visitor, tells us that the houses at Florissant and at St. Charles were "miserably poor."[12]

The Catholics of Missouri, for the most part of Canadian and Irish origin, had already made such great sacrifices to build the college that nothing more could be asked of them. Money was an absolute necessity. Additional missionaries were also needed, and these considerations, in conjunction with the fact that the Fathers were anxious to have their Missouri Province united with the Belgian Province of the Society, moved them to make an appeal to Belgium. Father De Smet was chosen for this mission. The privations he had suffered at Florissant, and his unremitting labor in St. Louis, had begun to tell on his robust constitution, so that, even had the dire needs of his community not required him to take this journey, his health would have demanded some such relaxation.

Father De Smet left St. Louis toward the end of September, 1833, and spent some time en route at Georgetown. The second Council of Baltimore was about to take place, and as the question of the Indian Missions would come before it, he wished to know the result of its deliberations before sailing. The Council advocated the policy of officially confiding this field of missionary work to the Jesuits, and, in the hope of soon being able to take up his ministrations to the Indians, he left at once to plead their cause with his compatriots.

He landed at Havre in the winter of 1834, going at once to see Father Van Lil, the Belgian Provincial residing then at Ghent. From there he wrote to his brother Charles: "After this long absence I am pining to see you and embrace you. For three years I have had no news of my family: please, I beg you, tell me all that has happened and all about each one. Where is my dear brother Francis, and where are my dear sisters Rosalie and Jeannette? and tell me if my sisters Rollier and Therese are in good health, etc."[13] A few days later he arrived in Termonde, and after an absence of fourteen years beheld again his

[12] Letter to Mr. De Nef, Nov. 7, 1832.
[13] Ghent, Oost-Eecloo, Jan. 6, 1834.

old home and the places that had witnessed his childish feats of valor. The father's chair by the fireside was vacant, but, despite this sorrow, he had much cause for rejoicing, for he was united to his brothers and sisters by ties of the tenderest affection. Although his eldest sister Rosalie had married Charles Van Mossevelde, the younger children still called her "mother." Charles and Francis occupied honorable positions in the magistracy, and the other members of the family were equally prosperous and happy. God had blessed their marriages, and charming children smiled from the cradle and climbed upon Uncle Peter's knee. The gladness of home-coming did not, however, render the missionary oblivious of his adopted family beyond the seas, and after a few days' rest he set out upon his journey through Belgium.

Father De Smet's first visits were to the parents of his associates to bring them news of the absent ones in America. He told them of their labors and successes, and made them appreciate the honor of having a son or a brother among the apostles of the New World. He then sought out the benefactors, to give them an account of the progress made by the missionaries in Missouri. To Mr. Peter De Nef of Turnhout, more than to any one else, did the missionaries owe a debt of gratitude. Concerning this worthy man a word is not out of place.

He was born in 1774 of a humble family of farmers, and after a brilliant school career entered upon commercial life. His business prospered beyond his most sanguine hopes, and he was moved to devote his fortune to the cause of religion and good works. Seeing the clergy decimated by the Revolution, he opened a school in his own house in which young men could be prepared for the priesthood and the missionary field. Instruction was free, Mr. De Nef himself teaching some of the classes. So great was the success of his undertaking that, eventually, he had to provide enlarged accommodations for the institution.[14] The school gave a complete course in the humanities, and in 1830 numbered one hundred and eighty pupils.

[14] The school was transferred to Rue d'Herenthals, and later became the well-known college now under the direction of the Fathers of the Society of Jesus.

By reason of the fact that he was appointed Commissioner of the district of Turnhout, also member of Congress and later on Deputy of the House of Representatives, Mr. De Nef was compelled to give up his classes. He confided them to the priests of the diocese of Mechlin, reserving to himself the management of the institution. The assumption of these distinguished offices did not, however, prevent this intrepid worker from carrying on the active management of a linen textile factory and a large wine business. These prosperous and varied industries enabled him to maintain the college, clothe and feed poor students, and endow the missions in a generous way. "For the benefit of the missions," he writes to Father De Theux, "I have formed an association with my honorable friends, Messrs. De Boey, Le Paige, and Proost, of Antwerp, the object of which is to invest in the securities of different countries. Should any losses result they are to be assumed by us entirely, but a large portion of any profits that may accrue is to be given to our beloved missions."[15]

Not content with furnishing the money, this extraordinary benefactor provided even the men. Over five hundred priests received their first instructions in his establishment, and among this number many consecrated their lives to the missions and became brave and indefatigable workers in the United States. The Superiors of the Society of Jesus left to "Father" De Nef, as he was called, the choosing of those who were to be sent to the American Missions. In addition to his regular pupils he often accepted seminarists and priests from Holland as well as Belgium, and not infrequently he undertook to furnish lay Brothers to the missions.[16] Father De Smet's

[15] Turnhout, Aug. 23, 1832.

To one of his friends who had sent him a generous donation for his enterprise he replied: "I rejoice in the Lord for the good use you make of your fortune. As for myself, I am persuaded that I would fail in my first duty, if, in my position, I did not do all in my power to further the cause of our holy religion. Unhappy would I be if I did not obey the voice of God, and, unmindful of the honor, should refuse to be His instrument. Should I fail in this respect, I would forever reproach myself for my cowardly negligence." (To Chevalier de Donnea de Grand Aaz, March 27, 1830.)

[16] Never was he so happy as when he could announce the arrival of new recruits. "Following the instructions given to me by your predecessors," he writes to Father De Theux, "I have admitted several young men who will be received into the Society of Jesus in America. I know their

account of the use that had been made of the generous donations was very gratifying to Mr. De Nef. He gave the good priest a large sum of money and promised to send priests for the extension of the work in Missouri.

Following these first visits, which were made through motives of kindness and a sense of obligation, Father De Smet set out upon the unpleasant task of begging. He was most cordially received by the Archbishop of Mechlin. "I have obtained," he writes, "many things for the missions, among others a silver gilt chalice and two pictures. Several people are collecting books, vestments, and such articles as are needed for the altar."[17]

At Louvain he met his friend and colleague, the Abbé De Ram, who, although but thirty years of age, was then the rector of the Catholic University. From Liège he writes: "I have succeeded very well here."[18] Bishop Van Bommel had not forgotten the services rendered to the diocese by the Superior in Missouri, and had given generously to the mission. Madam De Theux also was instrumental in interesting a number of people in the work over which her son presided.

Father De Smet's next move was to Namur, from where he reports: "I have visited more than fifty families and have been most successful. I shall proceed next to Mons, then to Tournai, and on to Brussels."[19] In a letter written to his brother from Nivelles, he says: "When I left Termonde I thought I could easily canvass Belgium and complete my business in a fortnight, but here I am, after six weeks of traveling, with only about a fourth of my work accomplished. I hope, however, to be able to spend a few days with you and to rest from my travels. I am more fatigued now than I was after my voyage from America."[20]

sterling qualities, and have been struck with the fortitude which they have shown in abandoning parents, friends, country, and a life of ease, to face every kind of hardship and privation with the sole object of winning men to God. I rejoice in sending them to you, and I am confident that our poor Americans and Indians will find in them support and consolation. We lose them now only to find them again in heaven, surrounded by blessed souls saved through their labors." (Letter, Oct. 16, 1833.)

[17] Letter to Francis De Smet, Louvain, Feb. 27, 1834.
[18] Liège, March 9, 1834.
[19] Namur, March 14th.   [20] March 24th.

When writing, later on, to his brother, he tells us how his trials and labors were now and then rewarded by some unlooked-for piece of good fortune: "I expected to be with you before Easter, but Providence intervened to prevent it. An affair of small importance that could be settled in an hour called me to Enghien. There, by chance, I met a certain priest, and in conversation we got around to the subject of books. He pointed out a house where he thought I could procure some, and when we called to broach the subject I received a donation of nothing less than the entire library: Baronius in 22 volumes in folio; The Bollandists in 40 volumes, all the Councils, Moreri's large dictionary, a history of the Church, a large number of the Fathers of the Church, and several other works."[21]   The books were piled into the diligence and brought to Brussels that same evening, and in a few months were adorning the shelves of the library in St. Louis.

Upon leaving Brussels Father De Smet visited successively Erps-Querbs, Aerschot, Montaigu, Diest, Santhoven, and Antwerp, all of which responded to his call for aid, the last-named city giving more than six hundred dollars. From Antwerp Father De Smet went to France by way of Lille and Arras. A gentleman from Bruges traveling in the same carriage with him offered to pay the expenses of his journey if he would go as far as Paris. The good priest did not accept the offer, however, as his desire to be with his family outweighed the attractions of the great capital. His longing to see Amiens did, nevertheless, cause him to visit that place and call at the college of St. Acheul, the institution which the Jesuits were forced to leave after the Ordinance of 1828. There again he came across an opportunity to acquire something valuable for the St. Louis College; "I have bought," he writes, "a complete physical science cabinet, including a collection of minerals, for 3,500 francs [$700], the original price of which was more than 15,000 francs [$3,000]."[22]

His return to Belgium was by way of Courtrai, and the

---

[21] To Francis De Smet, Brussels, March 31, 1834.

It is probable that these books came from the convent of the Augustinians at Enghien.

[22] Amiens, May 22d.

hot weather and the long journey exhausted his strength. He was taken with a fever and, upon the advice of the Provincial, wrote to Father De Theux for permission to remain some time longer with his family. Rest with him did not mean idleness. He exchanged many letters with Father Van Lil relative to putting the missions under the direction of the Belgian Province. "It is," he says, "the consensus of opinion, among those familiar with the situation, that this is the most certain way to assure the future of the mission." This idea, however, was carried out only after a fashion. The Belgian Province, which counted only one hundred and fifty religious, was barely able to support itself, and the mission was to continue under the direction of the General, the Belgians being pledged, as it were, to assist with money, and to send to St. Louis any young men who manifested a desire to go to foreign missions.

Summer, meanwhile, was drawing to a close. Father De Smet's health was not yet reestablished, and Father Van Lil insisted that he remain longer, but the missionary, in his desire to take up his labors in America, disregarded these considerations and decided to start. His party was made up of the five young men promised by Mr. De Nef, among whom were Peter Verheyden of Termonde and Charles Huet of Courtrai, his future companions in the Rocky Mountains. The latter part of October saw them on the way to Antwerp to make preparations for the voyage. Their baggage numbered some fifty boxes and chests, the contents of which included sacred vessels, vestments, pictures, books, and instruments of physical science. In addition to these effects Father De Smet carried $8,000 in money, a fair return for his ten months of labor in Belgium.

His family expected he would come back to Termonde to say farewell, but this hope was dispelled by the following lines: "Dear brothers and sisters, contrary to my wishes, you have been informed that the end of my stay is at hand. Please forgive me for not telling you myself. As to returning to Termonde, it is quite impossible; time is wanting. You must pray for me during the voyage and I will write at once upon my arrival. A thousand kisses to little Charlie.[23]   Take good care of him: he will be the pride of the family.   Have courage—as for me, I will not fail."[24]

Whatever regrets this hurried departure may have engendered, we are of the opinion that, in his heart, Father De Smet was relieved at being spared a painful leave-taking.

The brig *Agenoria* sailed from Antwerp November 1st, with the missionaries on board.   "We embarked," they wrote, "under the protection of the heavenly court and the special auspices of the Mother of God.   Under her safe guidance neither wind nor waves can affright us"[25]—an assurance of protection of which they were to stand in need to brave the trials that awaited them.

Six days later, while waiting at Deal on the English coast, Father De Smet wrote his family the following letter: "I must make an effort to send you a line to tell you of the dreadful situation I am in.   You know already that we sailed on the feast of All Saints and several days later left Flushing in our wake.   The North Sea was very stormy, and for three days we were in great danger. Thank God the brig did not perish, but the rolling and tossing occasioned me such seasickness that my companions asked the captain to put me ashore at Deal.   I am in bed, attended by two physicians, who leave me neither night nor day.   They give me hope that the rupture caused by retching can be cured, but only at the price of great care.   My other malady,[26] on account of which Father Van Lil counseled me to remain in Belgium, has been greatly aggravated by over-excitement and inflammation.

"The captain put in here for two days to await an improvement in my condition, but, hearing from the physicians that I would not be able to travel for a fortnight, or perhaps a month, he squared away this morning, and

---

[23] Charles De Smet, then four years of age, son of Francis De Smet, and nephew of the missionary.

[24] Antwerp, Oct. 30, 1834.

[25] To Mr. De Nef, from the harbor of Flushing, Nov. 3, 1834.

[26] This was a sort of eczema from which Father De Smet had long been a sufferer, and it never entirely left him.

to my great regret left me separated from my companions. If I continue to improve I shall continue on my journey, sailing from Liverpool. Should the physicians, however, advise against it, I will be with you again in a month from now. This delay is an overwhelming disappointment, but I resign myself to it, for God has His own designs in all that happens. Do not be uneasy about me. God will not abandon me. Three days ago I despaired of being able to stand on my feet, and I have not yet done so, it is true, for I still have to be carried, but the hope of doing this has sprung up anew. I should like to write you at length, but I am not able to do more now. To-morrow I will try again. Good-by." [27]

The other missionaries continued their voyage under the guidance of Peter Verheyden. Adverse winds detained the vessel a month off the coast of Newfoundland, and they did not reach New York until December 23d, fifty days after their departure from Belgium.

As soon as his condition permitted, Father De Smet had himself removed to a neighboring village, one near Deal, where living was much less expensive. "Thank God," he wrote, "I am a little better. . . . I have had the good fortune to fall into the hands of an excellent physician. I am up now and can walk, although with great difficulty." [28]

Three days later he went to London, where he met the Abbé John Nerinckx, a brother of the missionary. [29] "That good priest," he writes, "procured me comfortable lodgings

[27] Deal, Nov. 9, 1834.
The following lines written by Peter Verheyden give us some idea of the virtue of our missionary:
"I proposed to Father De Smet that I remain and nurse him. He thanked me, saying that his sorrow would be insupportable if through any fault of his our enterprise came to naught. He frequently asked us if we were discouraged by this trial, and if we would persevere in our holy vocation. We assured him of our ardent desire to work for the glory of God in the land where he had labored with the sweat of his brow, and which he longed so to see again. This seemed to calm and reassure him. I wrote to the Provincial in Belgium to tell him of our affliction and our difficulties. Father De Smet found two expressions in my letter which offended his humility, and he wished me to change them, but I must admit that I did not yield to his importunities." (Extract from a letter of Peter Verheyden to his family, New York, Dec. 26, 1834.)
[28] To Charles De Smet, Nov. 11, 1834.
[29] The Abbé John Nerinckx had succeeded the Abbé Carron, in 1815, as director of Catholic Works at Somerstown.

and a good doctor. He rarely leaves me. The doctor says I must abandon all idea of returning to America; that it is a question of life and death. I am on a strict diet, and he promises me that in eight or ten days I shall be well enough to journey to Belgium.

"My physical pains are equaled only by my mental worries. From the time I became unable to walk until I met Father Nerinckx I was in a condition of depression and complete discouragement. That kind old man, by his untiring care and goodness, has cheered and consoled me and I shall never forget him."[30]

Father De Smet, with the return of his strength, began to fret at his detention in Europe: "Did the doctor and our Fathers in London with whom I stayed not forbid it, and were my life not in danger, I would go to Liverpool and endeavor to join my companions in America. I have done nothing but think of them and sigh for them since I was taken ill."[31]

At last, on November 24th, he was permitted to set out for Belgium. He could not leave London, however, without purchasing presents for "his little friends," as he called his nieces and nephews; "I have bought something for Sylvia and Elmira[32] that will amuse them. I am not going to tell you now what it is, as I wish the gift to be a surprise, but it is something beautiful that will give them pleasure. I have seen many things that would delight little Charles, but they are too cumbersome to carry with me. It will cheer me if I can leave to-morrow. I would like so much to bring him a magic lantern."[33]

Thus the invalid forgot his sufferings in thinking of the happiness of others. His simple and upright soul felt greatly drawn to children. At Florissant he consecrated to them the first labors of his apostolate, and to the end of his life children brightened and solaced the fatigues of his missionary labors.

Upon his return to Belgium Father De Smet was condemned to a long convalescence. The physician gave him

[30] To Francis De Smet, from London, Nov. 14, 1834.
[31] To Charles De Smet, from London, Nov. 23, 1834.
[32] Daughters of Charles De Smet.
[33] To Charles De Smet, from London, Nov. 24, 1834.

no hope of being able to return to America, and the idea of becoming a charge upon the Society rankled within him. While in London he had thought of becoming a secular priest in the diocese of Ghent, and he had even approached his Superior concerning the matter.

Would it not have been better to ask to be received into the Belgian community and remain in the Society? Assuredly he would have been well received, but Father De Smet was a born missionary, and his training in Missouri had ill-prepared him for the ministry of parochial teaching and preaching. Prematurely aged by illness, and feeling that at thirty-four years his career had been blighted, our missionary succumbed to utter discouragement.

On May 8, 1835, permission was granted to Father De Smet to sever his connection with the Society of Jesus,[34] and also immediately afterward he abandoned the idea of becoming a secular priest at Ghent. Although his health debarred him from undertaking regular work, Father De Smet had no wish to remain idle, and so offered his services to the Orphanage, and to the Carmelites of Termonde, as well.

The religious in charge of the Orphanage, knowing Father De Smet to be an experienced administrator, accepted gladly the offer of his services, confiding to him their books and the management of their business affairs. That he faithfully and conscientiously discharged this duty for nearly two years is fully attested by the books of the community.

To the daughters of St. Teresa, Father De Smet rendered still greater services. The Bishop of Ghent appointed him spiritual director of the Carmelites, with faculties for preaching and hearing confession. For some time past, these nuns, with the approval of their Mother Provincial, had been nurturing the idea of restoring the ancient Carmel of Alost which had been suppressed in the time of Joseph II. The Prioress opened the question with Father De Smet, and he gave his approval to the project and promised his assistance.

---

[34] The archives of the Society show "ill-health" as the sole reason for his withdrawal: *Petrus De Smet, scholasticus sacerdos, dimissus 8 maii, 1835, Gandavi, ob valetudinem. Postea reassumptus.*

Father De Smet, accompanied by another Jesuit, Father
Peter De Vos, went to Alost to look about for a building for
the Order.   The old convent of the Annonciades, although
mutilated by numerous changes, could be utilized to
shelter the community in the event that nothing better
was to be had, and it was accordingly bought.   Hearing
that the Poor Clares intended to establish themselves in
the same city, the Carmelites wished immediate possession
of the property, but owing to the fact that the principal
part of the building was under rental to a schoolmaster
they could not move in until the incumbent had made due
provision to house his own institution elsewhere.   Father
De Smet, in the mean time, through the good offices of some
charitably inclined person, secured an apartment containing a kitchen and two rooms.   One of the rooms served
as a chapel and the other as a dormitory—a very humble beginning, but one in keeping with St. Teresa's first
foundations.

The Carmelites arrived in Alost, August 1, 1836.   We
read in the accounts of the foundation that "they were
accompanied by Father De Smet, the chosen instrument
of God for the negotiation of the affair."[35]   Poverty dogged
the early footsteps of this enterprise.   No furnishings for
the building were to be had, and often no bread.   Father
De Smet, aided by the Jesuits, succeeded finally in interesting the people of Alost in the new community.   "These
are angels you have in your midst," he said to them,
and from that time on the nuns were recipients of kindness and generosity that endured for more than sixty
years.[36]

Missouri and the mission enterprises were, however, a
perennial theme in the mind of Father De Smet.   Aided
by Mr. De Nef, he organized in Belgium an aid-association
for the furtherance of the Indian Missions, and on September 23, 1835, he accompanied to Antwerp seven missionaries bound for America.   In the hope of further cultivating
missionary vocations, our good priest began a correspondence with the Superiors of the Holland seminaries in

[35] Archives of the Carmelites of Alost.
[36] Cf. De Potter and Broeckaert, "Geschiedenis der stad Aalst," Vol.
iii, p. 376.

Bois-le-Duc and in Breda, and assisted Father Van Lil in preparing some young men who were to leave in 1836.

Father De Smet's former fellow-missionaries, knowing the circumstances that compelled him to remain in Belgium, continued to consider him as one of themselves, especially so in view of the fact that he acted as intermediary between the missionaries and their benefactors.[37] Had the Fathers in St. Louis an affair to transact or a package to send, it was through Father De Smet that they communicated with the Belgian Jesuits.[38] Father Verhaegen, who succeeded Father De Theux as Superior of the missions, likewise counted upon Father De Smet to bring about the much-desired union of Missouri with the Belgian Province.[39]

The missionaries longed for Father De Smet's return[40] and he himself felt that he must go back to them.[41] Gradually his health returned. Being spiritual director of a community and only of indirect assistance to the missions, constituted a career that could not for long satisfy his active and energetic nature. He reproached himself, moreover, for having left the Society, considering it an act of weakness, nay, almost a fault. "I could not," he writes, "find peace and interior satisfaction save in fulfilling my duty."[42] And now was it not his duty to return

[37] On Jan. 7, 1836, Father De Theux wrote to Mr. De Nef: "You see by Father Verheyden's letter to Father De Smet that I begged him to tell you all about us and our doings."

[38] "Not long ago we sent Father De Smet a box containing petrified wood, stalactites, crystals, fossils, and shells. I hope our Fathers have received their share. If, in return, they could send us some Belgian and Swiss curios, etc., we would be most thankful." (Letter of Father Hélias d'Huddeghem to his family, St. Louis, Dec. 3, 1835.)

[39] "I trust you will do all in your power to further the success of the affairs I have confided to kind Father De Smet. It means in many ways the happiness of those who labor here in the Lord's vineyard." (Letter of Father Verhaegen to Mr. De Nef, St. Louis, July 10, 1837.)

[40] "*Ex litteris recenter Roma acceptis, magno gaudio intelleximus apud vos novam pro nobis parari expeditionem. Illius ducem futurum P. De Smet exixe speramus.*" (Letter of Father Verhaegen to Mr. De Nef, St. Louis, Sept. 17, 1836.)

[41] "During the years that Father De Smet directed our community, he often asked us to pray that God would restore his health and permit him to return to the Indians." (Letter of Rev. Mother Marie Gonzaga, Prioress of the Carmelites of Termonde, to Father Deynoodt, April 3, 1878.)

[42] To Francis De Smet, New York, Dec. 26, 1837.

6

to Missouri, beg to be readmitted t. the Society of Jesus, and to take up once more his chosen labors? It was not possible to join the missionaries who left Belgium in the autumn of 1836. His weak condition obliged him to defer his departure to the following year.

Mistrusting his strength to resist the tears and supplications of his family, Father De Smet again concealed from them his intention to return to America. He left Termonde in September, 1837, and with four missionaries remained some time in Paris before embarking from Havre. Again he suffered a relapse, which once more put to the test his fortitude and determination to return to the missions.

Hardly had the missionaries arrived in Paris when he was taken down with a violent fever, which for eight days kept him in a very precarious condition. "The eve of our departure for Havre," writes Arnold Damen, one of Father De Smet's companions, "he was desperately ill. Two physicians of note declared that if he sailed he would not live three days. It was an agonizing decision; both for us who saw ourselves forced to make a journey of six thousand miles alone, and for the good Father, consumed with a desire to return to America. A second time the Provincial consulted the doctors: again their verdict was against his departure. Finally they agreed that he might accompany us as far as Havre. The poor invalid made that journey with us, lamenting all the time that he could not join his mission and at last coming to a decision to return to Belgium.

"Then an inspiration came to us to storm heaven, and implore the intercession of St. Philomena. Father De Smet and Father Gleizal, a French priest who accompanied us, said three Masses for this intention; the others received holy communion. The Fathers promised nine Masses and we a novena if the saint obtained for our invalid the strength to make the crossing.

"The day of departure arrived, and found us without hope. Father De Smet accompanied us to the boat, said good-by, and returned to the city. We sailed out of the harbor, and were already at sea when we saw a little skiff making for our ship. It was Father De Smet coming to join us! Transports of joy dispelled our fears and anxieties. He alone remained calm—his faith had been rewarded. The seasickness from which Father De Smet suffered during the voyage was as nothing compared to his previous sufferings."[43]

When about to leave Europe, Father De Smet announced his departure to his family: "I am sending you a hurried line, for I have only a moment. . . . After long and mature reflection I have decided to make a second trip to Missouri. I hope to hear from you often, and I promise to give you news of myself. . . . A thousand embraces for my little Charles. I take him with me in my heart. Good-by for two or three years."[44]

Having sailed from Havre September 26th, the missionaries landed in New York just a month later to the day, and an overland journey of three weeks more found them in St. Louis. They were welcomed in a manner that compensated for the fatigues and trials which they had lately undergone. The unmistakable evidences of joy occasioned by his return manifested to Father De Smet how greatly he had been missed.

Three days later the new arrivals went to St. Stanislaus' novitiate, near Florissant. Father Verhaegen, Superior of the mission at the time, was also Master of Novices, and on November 29th he readmitted Father De Smet into the Society of Jesus.

In the happiness that was now his by virtue of possessing that which he had sought at the price of many trials and much suffering, he wished to console his family by explaining his departure: "I hope that the sorrow and vexation my hasty departure occasioned you has been entirely forgotten, and that you will not reproach me for concealing it from you. I had not the courage to say good-by. Whenever I found myself in your midst, I wavered in my resolutions and my duty to God. The sight of your children, of Charles, Sylvia, Elmira, and the little Rosalie tore my heart, and I rebelled at the thought that I was about to leave these dear creatures. But God willed it:

[43] Account of the voyage sent to Mr. De Nef, Florissant, Dec. 28, 1837.
[44] To Francis De Smet, Havre, Sept. 25, 1837.

we must submit.   He will recompense us for the sacrifices
we make for love of Him.   I am waiting impatiently for
news from you, and trust you will not disappoint me.
You have given me too many proofs of your affection
for me ever to doubt it and I hope you will keep me always
in your heart." [45]

[45] St. Stanislaus, Dec. 26, 1837.

CHAPTER V

THE POTAWATOMI MISSION (1838–1839)

Progress Made by the Jesuits in Missouri—Father Van Quickenborne's Apostolate to the Indians—His Death—Fathers De Smet and Verreydt are Sent to Open a Mission for the Potawatomies at Council Bluffs—First Journey on the Missouri—A Dinner at the Otoes—The Disposition of the Indians—Their Conversion will be "a Work of God"—The Missionaries' First Successes—Loneliness and Privations—Father De Smet Effects a Reconciliation between the Sioux and the Potawatomies—Whiskey—"What Could One Do with Two Thousand Drunken Indians?"—Father De Smet's Journey to St. Louis—He is Replaced at Council Bluffs by Father Christian Hoecken.

FATHER DE SMET, upon his return to Missouri, was amazed at the improvements and the progress that had been made during his absence. In four years the population of St. Louis had increased from 7,000 to 15,000 inhabitants. The success of the University was assured. Father Elet, through his wise and intelligent direction, aided by Father Van de Velde's renowned classes, attracted numerous pupils to the University, many of them from Louisiana. A library containing several thousand volumes, a complete physical-science cabinet, and a chemical laboratory facilitated the work of the preachers and professors.

Although Florissant and St. Charles were still in dire need, their hardships had been somewhat ameliorated by the Belgian contributions. The novitiate had been enlarged by connecting the Indian college with the main building. The churches, now vastly improved in construction and decoration, gave a better impression of the Catholic religion. Copies of Flemish masters covered the bare walls, and spoke to the missionaries of their far-off land, recalling to the faithful the touching mysteries of the lives of our blessed Lord and His holy Mother.

With regard to the Indians, the results that had been

obtained were satisfactory and consoling. The appeal of the American Bishops, to confide the Indian Missions to the Jesuits, had been granted by Rome, and the Fathers of the Missouri Province would now be the first to prove themselves worthy of the confidence of the heads of the Church. Congress had just set apart a territory on the banks of the Arkansas exclusively for the Indians, where native tribes scattered throughout the United States would be united under Government supervision, and upon this there followed a series of willing or forced migrations, assembling to the west of Missouri nearly 200,000 Indians.

It was to these tribes that Father Van Quickenborne consecrated his labors and remaining strength. Having been relieved of his post of authority at Florissant, he was free at last to devote himself to a work that had been the dream of his life, and for the past six years he had labored for the conversion of the Indians with all the energy of his ardent nature. To reach the wandering tribes that were often at war with each other, this intrepid missionary endured unspeakable fatigues and faced innumerable dangers. More than once he owed his life to the direct intervention of Providence.[1]

After making many conversions among the Osages and the Iowas, Father Van Quickenborne went in 1836 to the Kickapoos, inhabiting that part of Northern Kansas situated upon the right bank of the Missouri. Father Christian Hoecken, a Hollander, and three lay Brothers,

---

[1] The Woodstock Letters, Vol. xxiv, p. 37; Vol. xxv, p. 357.

"In the first excursions made by Fathers Van Quickenborne and Christian Hoecken, they were often lost for days at a time, and would traverse the immense prairies in every direction in a vain endeavor to discover their whereabouts. These plains resembled a vast sea; as far as the eye could reach one beheld nothing but a limitless sketch of green pasture and blue sky: deer, chamois, and roebuck were plentiful; prairie-chicken and other wild game abounded. Wolves and bears creeping from their lairs to eat sheep terrified both man and beast. But even in such straits they were not abandoned by divine Providence. At nightfall the Fathers would often throw the reins on the horse's neck, letting him take his own direction, and before long would find themselves in sight of some habitation. Once an immense and strange dog sprang in front of their horses, and, making a path through the high grass, brought them to the home of a Catholic, where they rested and were refreshed, and, to their great consolation and that of their host, they celebrated the Divine Mysteries." (Letter of Father Hélias d'Huddeghem to his family, St. Louis, Dec. 17, 1836.)

accompanied him. In a few months he established there a flourishing mission and was about to go to the neighboring tribes, when physical exhaustion obliged him to abandon his work. He retired to Portage des Sioux near Florissant. As the pastor of a small Christian community, he hoped (with the help of a lay Brother) to be able to rest and regain his strength. "But," says Father De Smet, "who could restrain his ardent zeal?" He began at once to make plans for the erection of a church; undertook the conversion of several Protestant families, and was absorbed in his work when he fell ill with an attack of bilious fever that carried him off in a few days.

The man of God remained calm and resigned to the end. He received the Last Sacraments with profound piety, and fearlessly saw his last hour approach. "Pray for me," he said to those around him. These were his last words. He died without a struggle, August 17, 1837,[2] having not yet attained his fiftieth year. The young religious trained by Father Van Quickenborne hastened to claim their heritage and undertake his work.

Father Verreydt joined Father Hoecken at the Kickapoo Mission. These Indians, being unreliable, rebellious against authority, and, moreover, thieving and addicted to drink, had disappointed the hopes of the missionaries. In 1838 they began to leave Missouri in order to lead a nomad life far from Government supervision. The Fathers, seeing they had very little influence with this tribe, were rejoiced at receiving a delegation of Potawatomies who came to ask for a Black Robe for their tribe. This tribe had recently been brought from Michigan on the

[2] Selected Letters, 2d Series, p. 183.
"You heard some months ago of Father Van Quickenborne's death. Now comes the news that great favors have been obtained at his tomb. A Sacred Heart nun at St. Charles, a victim of consumption and given up by the physicians, went with the other nuns and young pupils to pray at his grave. After praying fervently they returned in procession, reciting prayers. The nun (Mme. Eulalie) was instantly cured, and from that time on enjoyed perfect health.
"The undertaker who had charge of Father Van Quickenborne's funeral told me, that although the body was kept three days during the excessive heat of summer, and was transported during the day from the parish of St. Francis at Portage des Sioux to St. Charles, there was no unpleasant odor and it appeared fresher and handsomer than in life." (Letter of Father Hélias d'Huddeghem to his family, St. Louis, Dec. 8, 1837.)

Missouri, near the mouth of the Nebraska River. Their camp was situated at Council Bluffs, just opposite the present city of Omaha. Father Verreydt, accompanied by Brother Mazelli, had previously visited the Potawatomies in the summer of 1838 with the idea of establishing a mission among them.[3]

Since his return from Belgium Father De Smet occupied the post of minister at the Florissant novitiate. His health was now completely restored and with it his former vigor returned. The object of his life continued to be the conversion of the Indians.

On January 26, 1838, he wrote to the Carmelites of Termonde: "New priests are to be added to the Potawatomi Mission, and my Superior, Father Verhaegen, gives me hope that I will be sent. How happy I would be could I spend myself for the salvation of so many souls, who are lost because they have never known truth! My good Sisters, I beg you to pray for this intention. Implore the divine Pastor to deign to look upon the most unworthy of His servants, who longs to work for His glory. I tremble when I think of the great qualities an apostolate to the Indians demands. We must make men before making Christians, and such work requires unlimited patience and solid virtue, and you know what I am. Nevertheless, I am not discouraged. God's strength is greater than my weakness, and He can bring forth from stones children of Abraham."[4]

Zeal for the salvation of souls, and profound humility (God could not resist his supplications) were the distinguishing traits of our missionary, and a few weeks later he was appointed to the Potawatomi Mission. Father De Smet left St. Louis May 10th, Father Verreydt and Brother Mazelli joining him at Leavenworth. In going up the Missouri he greatly admired the vast river, dotted

---

[3] Father Hoecken remained some time longer, endeavoring to convert the Kickapoos.

[4] If any one fancies that Father De Smet exaggerated, let him read his letters to Father De Theux: "As for myself, in my opinion, to come to America to teach in a college or to be a missionary to the whites, is child's play in comparison to the Indian Mission. I see so many difficulties in this work that, did I not know that our divine Lord is all-powerful, I should regard the enterprise as a great folly." (To Mr. De Nef, St. Stanislaus, July 9, 1835.)

with its many islands; the villages that rose one above the other on its banks, the towering rocks, the caves, the forests, and the immense prairies, all of which lent infinite variety to the aspect. But the scenic beauty failed to render agreeable a journey fraught with many dangers.

"I would rather cross the ocean," he writes, "than ascend the Missouri River. The current is so swift that in order to get up the river the boat must be heavily loaded and the steam at full pressure. Hence, the traveler is in imminent danger of being shot up into the air by an explosion, and coming down perhaps in bits. Added to this, we run upon sand-bars every day—a dangerous proceeding. Lastly, the river bristles with snags which tear a boat open, and are the terror of pilots and travelers. More than once we were in great peril from them."[5]

Crowds of Indians came to the landing to greet the missionaries, and wherever the boat stopped for fuel the priests went ashore to visit the different villages. The chief of the Iowas, an old pupil of Father De Smet's at Florissant, wished to keep him with his tribe. An Indian convert, eighty-four years of age, prepared himself for death by confession, shedding, meanwhile, tears of repentance. Everywhere they were most cordially received.

The visit to the Otoes enabled Father De Smet to initiate himself in the ways of the savage. The following lines give us an idea of his impressions:

"The village is composed of several large mud huts, each containing about ten families, and several buffalo-hide tents reeking with vermin. The women slave for the men, and appear most miserable. Some are blind, others have only one eye, and all appear extremely dirty. Their dress consists of a skirt of deer-skin to the knee, with tunic, garters, and shoes of the same hide. The whole costume is greasy and black, as though they had wiped their hands on it for a century. Both men and women wear bracelets of polished metal, and five or six strings of china or glass beads around the neck.

"I was ushered into the large hut of the chief or king. The queen placed a cushion of deer-skin shiny with grease upon a still greasier cane mat, and made me signs to be seated. She then presented me with a roughtly-cut wooden plate which I think had not seen water since it was made, and served me on it a dish of disgusting appearance, cooked by herself. Opposite me a dozen wolf-dogs, seated on their haunches, eyed my plate. They seemed to envy me my happiness, and showed willingness to aid me in disposing of the food.

"I was hungry, I admit; but my stomach revolted at the sight of that mysterious stew. I said to myself, 'No airs now, you are not in Belgium, begin your apprenticeship. When in Rome, do as the Romans do.' I took a spoonful of the mess and found it delicious. It was a *fricassée* of buffalo tongue, mixed with bear's grease and the flour of wild sweet potatoes. I evinced my appreciation of the princess' hospitality by rubbing my stomach as a sign of satisfaction, and returned the plate to her much cleaner than when she gave it to me."[6]

The missionaries arrived at the Potawatomi camp May 31st. Nearly two thousand Indians, painted in every conceivable way, came to the landing. Father De Smet and his companions repaired at once to the tent of the great chief, a half-breed called William Caldwell, renowned for his prowess and his victories over the whites. The missionaries were cordially received and promised protection. The chief then offered them three tents near his. Colonel Kearny, representing the Government, put an abandoned fort at the disposition of the missionaries. There they celebrated Mass and assembled the neophytes, until a wooden church was erected in honor of St. Joseph, patron of the mission. The Indians at first received them coldly,[7] but soon the missionaries got into touch with them, and Father De Smet was then able to discover their tastes and aptitudes, and the needs of their tribe.

[6] To Father Verhaegen, Council Bluffs, June, 1838.

[7] "We were far from finding here the four or five hundred fervent Catholics they told us about in St. Louis. Of the 2,000 Potawatomies that came to the landing not one of them seemed to know why we had come, and appeared quite indifferent. Out of thirty half-breed families, only two came to shake hands with us. Very few had been baptized, and all of them are profoundly ignorant of the truths of our religion. They do not even know how to make the Sign of the Cross, nor say the Our Father and Hail Mary, and this accounts, I think, for the great reserve they maintained toward us." (Letter to Father Verhaegen, June, 1838.)

"Imagine numerous huts or tents constructed of up-right poles covered with tree bark, buffalo hides, canvas, straw, and grass; dreary of aspect, and pitched pell-mell, with no regard to order or symmetry, and you have some idea of an Indian village."[8]   In these holes, for such they are, 3,000 savages lead a miserable existence. The women do all the rough work, while the men pass their time in playing cards and smoking the calumet; their sole occupation being war or hunting.

"For the most part, these Indians are content with a little dried beef and a pap made of pounded roasted corn. They are sober, less from virtue than necessity.   When food is plentiful, either at home or abroad, they plunge their hands into the boiling pot and eat like ravenous wolves, and when filled, lie down and sleep.   Their sole possessions are a few horses that graze at large on waste land.   At his birth an Indian is enveloped in rags, and during infancy left under a buffalo hide.   He is brought up in idleness, and abhors work.   He has no desire to change or ameliorate his condition.   Any Indian who would aspire to a greater degree of comfort, or to increase his fortune through his own efforts, would be the object of general hatred and jealousy.   Moreover, all his posses-sions would be pillaged and confiscated."[9]

And yet the Indians had redeeming qualities: "The Potawatomies are gentle and peaceful.   There is neither rank nor privilege among them.   The chief has no revenue save that which he procures with his lance, arrow, and rifle.   His horse is his throne.   He must be braver than his subjects; the first to attack, and the last to leave the field.   In the division of spoils, he shares equally with the others.   The greater number of the Indians can converse intelligently upon things that concern them.   They like to joke and listen to chaff, they never dispute or lose their temper, and never interrupt any one.   If the affair under discussion is serious, the Indian reflects before speaking, or defers his reply until the next day.   They know no blasphemous words, and often years pass without an angry word being spoken.   But when drunk—and now they

[8] Letter of Father De Smet to the Father General, Dec. 1, 1838.
[9] Letter of Father De Smet to Father Verhaegen, June, 1838.

get drink in large quantities—all the good qualities of the Indian disappear, and he no longer resembles man; one must flee from him. Their cries and howls are terrible; they fall upon each other, biting noses and ears, mutilating each other in a horrible manner. Since our arrival, four Otoes and three Potawatomies have been killed in these drunken orgies."[10]

Besides idleness and drunkenness, the missionaries had to combat prejudice and abolish polygamy and superstitious practices. They had to master a difficult language and undertake the still more difficult task of trying to domesticate men accustomed to a wandering life, who complained if obliged to stay three months in the same place.

Father De Smet said: "It is a work of God," and such indeed it was. He begged earnestly the prayers of his Superiors and friends. To the Carmelites of Termonde he wrote: "Here I have been for three months in the midst of the Indians. If it is your prayers that have obtained this favor for me, I beg you to ask that I may have courage, humility, fervor, patience, and the other virtues which make a good missionary."[11]

Success soon crowned his efforts. Before the close of 1838 Father De Smet was able to write: "A great number of Indians have asked to be instructed. We have opened a school, but, for the want of a large hut, we can only receive thirty children. Twice a day instructions are given to those preparing for baptism. We have already administered the Sacrament to one hundred and eighteen Indians; one hundred and five of this number I had the consolation of baptizing myself.

"The feast of the Assumption will long be remembered by the Potawatomies. The church in which Mass was said was perhaps the poorest in the world. Twelve neophytes, who three months before had no knowledge of God's laws, chanted the Mass in a most edifying manner. Father Verreydt preached upon devotion to the Blessed

[10] Letter to the Father General, Dec. 1, 1838. (Annals of the Propagation of the Faith, Vol. xi, p. 484.)
[11] Nov. 7, 1838.

Virgin. I followed with an instruction upon the necessity of baptism. I explained its ceremonies, and then administered the Sacrament to twenty adults, among whom was the wife of the great chief.

"After Mass I blessed four marriages. In the evening we visited the newly-converted families, who had all assembled and were thanking God for the graces received during the day, and now these good people traverse the country to induce their friends and relatives to be instructed and share their happiness. Several Indian women, whose relatives, being still pagan, refused to receive us, dragged themselves a distance of two or three miles to ask for baptism before dying."[12]

The good dispositions evinced by the Indians encouraged Father De Smet to exert himself to the utmost in their behalf. "Often," he writes, "I visited the Indians in their huts either as missionary, when they seemed disposed to listen to me, or in the capacity of a physician to minister to their sick. When I find a child in danger whose parents are ill-disposed toward religion, I take out my bottles and recommend certain medicines. I begin by rubbing the child with camphor; then taking water, I baptize it before their unsuspecting eyes, and thus open heaven to the innocent soul."[13]

The shiftlessness and filth of the Indians often occasioned epidemics; some tribes had as many as a thousand sick, and at such times the missionaries were dreadfully overworked. Each day Father De Smet visited a new village, carrying remedies and words of encouragement to the victims of the plague. His charity bore fruit in new conversions. Writing to his brother, he says: "I have baptized nearly two hundred Indians, and we now have three hundred converts. I can truthfully say they are all fervent Christians. Their greatest happiness is to assist at daily Mass and instruction, and receive holy communion. Several chiefs and their families have embraced the faith. I baptized an old man a hundred and ten years of age."[14]

[12] Letter to the Father General, Dec. 1, 1838.
[13] Letter to the Mother Superior of the Orphanage at Termonde.
[14] To Francis De Smet, May 30, 1839.

Protestant ministers tried to compete with the Catholic priests; but between a salaried official who distributed tracts to inquisitive members of the tribe, and the missionary, devoted body and soul to their interests, the Indians did not hesitate to make a choice.[15]   They refused the most alluring offers from Protestants and came from all directions to ask for a Black Robe to show them the way to heaven.[16]

One day three chiefs of the Pawnee-Loups came to beg the Jesuits to visit their tribe.   Noticing that the priests made the Sign of the Cross before eating, they, upon their return, instituted this practice in all the Indian villages.   This delegation was followed by the chiefs of the Omahas, accompanied by forty warriors, who, making their followers a sign to wait, approached the missionary and executed the dance of friendship.[17]

Father De Smet thanked God for the success that crowned his labors, and expressed his gratitude to his Superiors for appointing him to this mission.   "We suffer, of course, many privations in this far distant country; but God will never be outdone in generosity.   He rewards a hundredfold the smallest sacrifices we make for Him, and if our trials are heavy, our consolations are very great.   I thank God every day for having sent me to this country."[18]

The little community at Council Bluffs suffered many privations.   To the fatigues of the ministry was added the anxiety of providing for their daily existence.   Brother

---

[15] "After five years' residence with the Otoes, the Protestant minister has not yet baptized one person, and the greater part of the Protestant missionaries who overrun the Indian Territory make no better showing." (Letter of Father De Smet to Father Verhaegen, June, 1838.)

[16] "The Protestant ministers pay the chiefs to come and act as interpreters in their churches.   Some give as much as a hundred dollars, four beeves, etc."   (Letter of Father Hélias d'Huddeghem to his family, June 29, 1837.)

[17] "They all manifested great affection for us, and invited us to smoke the pipe of peace with them.   Pictures representing Our Lord's passion, and our explanation of the meaning of the crucifix, seemed to interest them greatly.   They begged me to go at once to baptize their children, presenting me at the same time with a beautiful beaver skin for a tobacco-pouch.   In return, I gave them rosaries for the children, and presented each one of them with a copper crucifix.   They kissed the crucifixes respectfully, put them around their necks, and appeared most grateful for the gifts.   When leaving, the Indians embraced me most cordially."   (Letter to the Father General, Dec. 1, 1838.)

[18] *Ibid.*

Mazelli, in his capacity of physician and surgeon, was in constant attendance upon the sick. Fathers Verreydt and De Smet chopped wood, cooked the meals, and mended their clothes. The distance from St. Louis, and the difficulty of communication interfered greatly with obtaining food-supplies. The mission was often without the necessities of life.

In the spring of 1839 their distress was extreme, their whole nourishment for weeks consisting of acorns and wild roots. At last, on April 20th, the provision-boat was sighted. Father De Smet hurriedly departed with two carts to get the mission supply. A cruel disappointment awaited them. At the moment of landing, the boat, striking a snag, was wrecked. The missionary arrived in time to see it sink before his eyes. A saw, a plow, a pair of boots, and some wine were all that was saved. But even this disaster did not disturb Father De Smet's habitual serenity. "Providence," he said, "is still kind to us. The plow has enabled us to sow a good crop of corn. Thanks to the saw, we can now build a better house and enlarge our church, which is too small; and with the boots I can tramp the prairies and woods without fear of being bitten by snakes. The wine permits us to offer to God the sacrifice of the Mass, a happiness we have long been deprived of. We returned courageously to our acorns and roots until May 30th."[19]

Great as may have been the hardships of poverty, loneliness, however, was still harder to bear. The missionaries had news from St. Louis only two or three times a year, and Father De Smet's sensitive nature suffered cruelly from this isolation. On December 18, 1839, he wrote to Father Peter De Vos, his friend of Alost, now Master of Novices in Missouri: "Your letter of last July reached me the beginning of the month. I had begun to fear that you also had put off your reply to the Greek Calendar. Can you believe it? although I have written numerous letters since June to our Fathers and brothers who are so dear to me, in reply, I have had, not counting your letter, exactly five lines. Would that I could hold the post responsible for this!

"We who are at the end of the world, far from friends

[19] To Francis De Smet, July 30, 1839.

and fellow-priests, in the midst of strangers and infidels, suffering privations, and daily witnessing revolting scenes, look forward to letters as a real treat.   If you only knew the joy they bring, I am sure every one of you would give us this consolation and support, for after reading our letters we are fired with renewed zeal."

With equal joy did our missionary receive news of his relatives and friends in Belgium.   "Your long and delightful letter," he writes to his brother, "enclosing a little one from my friend Charles, reached me the beginning of June.   It gave me such pleasure, that I read it over several times, not wishing to lose a word." [20]

To induce his family to write often, he continually gave them details of his life at Council Bluffs, recounting the habits and customs of the Indians, and the progress the mission had made.   His open and cheerful letters betray not only his strength of soul, but his unalterable attachment to his family.   "When I think of what my life was with you during four years, I often smile at my present condition.   My only shelter is a little hut fourteen feet square, constructed of trunks of fallen trees covered with a rough shingle roof that protects me from neither snow nor rain. The other night, during a downpour, I was obliged to open my umbrella to protect my face from the rain that fell on it and awakened me.   My furniture consists of a cross, a small table, a bench, and a pile of books.   A piece of meat, or some herbs and wild roots, washed down by a glass of fresh spring water, is about my only food. My garden is the immense forest of Châteaubriand, 'old as the earth which bore it,' bordering the largest river in the world;   the huge prairie resembles a vast sea, where gazelle, deer, roebuck, buffalo, and the bison graze at large.

"My gun is my constant companion.   One must go about armed to defend one's life from the red bear and the starved wolves that prowl about here.   Our situation is rendered even more precarious by the war that is going on between the Indians.   Bands of Otoes, Pawnees, and Sioux roam in every direction seeking scalps, and every day we get fresh news of their atrocities." [21]

[20] To Francis De Smet, July 30, 1839.
[21] Letter to Francis De Smet, May 30, 1839.

But in this barbarous community, the missionary devised means of being reminded of the dear ones at home: "Among the converts was the wife of the great chief and I named her Rosalie. There were already many named Francis, Charles, Anthony, Peter, Jeannette, Marie, Sophie, and Teresa. All those I have baptized are named after some member of my family and after friends." [22]

Father De Smet became a child again in replying to a letter from little Charles, his favorite nephew: "When I walk through the prairies and see the beautiful flowers, I often say to myself: 'If Charles, Sylvia, Elmira, Clemence, and little Rosalie were here, what exquisite bouquets they would make for mother and father! I have a roebuck with big horns, a deer, and a tame bear that follows me everywhere on the prairies and is as quiet and gentle as your little Fidele. Were you with your uncle and did your legs get tired, hop! hop! you and Sylvia would be upon the bear's back; and Clemence and Elmira upon the roebuck! Little Rosalie would mount the little deer, and we would all trot home together!" [23]

Although of a sensitive nature, Father De Smet was in no sense a weak man. No fatigue disheartened him, no danger held him back when the interests of the mission were in question. For two years the Potawatomies lived in constant apprehension of being attacked by their terrible and threatening neighbors, the Sioux of the Missouri. Recently two men of their tribe had been massacred, and the future of the mission was endangered so long as there was danger of these murderous incursions, which in a few hours converted a populous settlement into a field of carnage and death.

The missionary resolved to go to the enemy armed only with faith; to speak to them in the name of God and ask for peace. On April 29, 1839, he left the camp and took passage on a steamboat that was going up the Missouri River. On board he found two Europeans he had known in St. Louis, Mr. Nicollet and Mr. Geyer, who were being

[22] To Francis De Smet, Sept. 11, 1838.
[23] July 30, 1839.

sent by the Government at Washington upon a scientific exploration to the Indian country.

Low water, contrary winds, sand-bars, and numerous snags forced the boat to proceed slowly and with great caution. Every time it landed for fuel, Father De Smet accompanied Mr. Geyer in his search for plants and minerals. "I was proud," he writes, "to be able to enrich his herbarium with several specimens that might have escaped his notice. This study has great attraction for me, and the hours I have spent tramping over hill and dale with a friend are among the most agreeable of my life." [24] Mr. Nicollet, knowing Father De Smet's trustworthiness, left him his instruments for measuring heights and making observations, as they would be of great service to the missionary in working on his map of Missouri. [25]

The conquest of a soul, however, meant more to the missionary than the greatest discoveries. While aboard the boat Father De Smet instructed and baptized a mother and her three children. He also heard the confessions of many Canadians who were going to the Rocky Mountains. Twelve days after his departure from Council Bluffs, he arrived at the mouth of the Vermilion, where the Sioux were encamped. He parted with his friends with great regret. Alone, and unarmed, he was going to plead the cause of the Potawatomies, with an enemy who had sworn to exterminate them.

Providence, who destined our missionary to be an apostle of peace in the United States, crowned with success his first negotiations. Faithful to the law of hospitality, the Indians accorded him a reception that augured well. "Upon my arrival," he writes, "the chief and the warriors, some Yanktons of the Sioux nation, invited me to a feast. I found them seated in a circle in a large tent made of buffalo hide, their chins resting on their knees, a position my corpulence forbade me assume. I seated myself, crossing my legs tailor fashion. Each one received upon a wooden plate a huge piece of venison. Those who could

[24] To Francis De Smet, May 30, 1839.
[25] Cf. Chittenden-Richardson, pp. 1549 and 1552, two letters of Mr. Nicollet to Father De Smet. One sees how highly the learned geographer valued the missionary's contributions.

not consume all their portion were allowed to take away what was left. This I did, and I found myself with two days' rations."[26]

The repast finished, the missionary stated the object of his mission: he had come to conclude a lasting peace between the Sioux and the Potawatomies. The conditions of the peace pact were immediately under discussion. Father De Smet's forceful reasoning and his charm of manner soon dispelled the grievances that had caused the separation of the two peoples. The Sioux agreed to bury the hatchet, and swore to "cover the dead," by sending presents to the children of their victims, and to smoke with them the pipe of peace. Profiting by such dispositions, the missionary spoke to them about religion, and that evening gave an instruction upon the principal articles of the Creed. The following day he administered baptism to a few of the tribe and blessed several marriages.

After sowing the first seeds of faith in this tribe, he hastened back to Council Bluffs to tell the Potawatomies of the result of his negotiations. This time his only means of transportation was a primitive canoe, the trunk of a tree scooped out in the form of a boat, and in this frail bark he descended one of the most dangerous rivers in the world. Happily he had with him two skilled pilots who knew the whereabouts of the rocks that abound in the Missouri. The boat shot like an arrow into the current, covered the immense distance, and brought the missionary back safe and sound to his dear Potawatomies. No army had accompanied him, and without combat or bloodshed he returned victorious, his hands filled with the benedictions of peace. The Potawatomies greeted him as the father and saviour of their nation.

But it was far easier to cope with the ferocity of the Indian than to uproot his passion for intoxicating liquors. "The Government," writes Father De Smet, "pays the Potawatomies $50,000 annually for the land that was taken from them. With the payment of this money has come a following of thieves, drunkards, gamblers, counterfeiters; in a word, the dregs of the United States.

[26] To the Superior of the Orphanage at Termonde, July 1, 1839.

They exploit the Indians and furnish them with quantities of whiskey.[27]

"So long as he has a penny the Indian will drink and gamble. Their passion for drink is so inconceivable one must see it to believe it: it affects them like the bite of a tarantula. Instantly their blood is excited and like fire in their veins; they are mad with thirst for it, and, obtaining it, clamor for more! more! until, consumed with 'firewater,' they fall down dead drunk. Regaining their their senses, their first cry is for *whiskey! whiskey! whiskey!* as though life and death depended upon getting it.

"Under the influence of liquor their passions lead them into the grossest excesses, beginning with songs of joy and ending with howls and screams. Disputes and quarrels follow, then stabbing and head-smashing; finally, murder is the crowning crime of these abominable orgies. The ground is strewn with the dead, and the living are horribly mutilated. With a drunken Indian about, no one is safe, and many times my own life has been in danger." [28]

The Government, it is true, prohibited the introduction of whiskey into the Indian Territory under penalty of the law, but no agent respected the law, and brandy arrived in cargoes.[29] Indignant at the breach of the law, Father De Smet, with one stroke of a hatchet, broke open a cask destined for the Indians, and, not content with such measures, he wrote a strong letter to the Government at Washington denouncing this abuse as being both criminal and illegal. But apparently little heed was given in high places to these complaints; and a few unworthy Americans looked on with satisfaction at the self-destruction of a race they detested, and the whites, undisturbed, continued their odious traffic.

After two such orgies the mission seemed doomed. "What could one do with two thousand drunken Indians? Where would it end? Who can say? For with the yearly

[27] Letter of Father De Smet to Mr. Charles Van Mossevelde, Sept. 18, 1839.
[28] Letter to Francis De Smet, Oct. 29, 1839.
[29] One reads with interest Father De Smet's journal from May 10 to Oct. 15, 1839. Chittenden-Richardson, p. 171–178.

arrival of the money, the same blackguards would return, and the same scene be enacted."[30]

But, however dark the future appeared, the missionaries determined not to desert their post. More than ever did they endeavor to win these wild natures through kindness. They had at least the consolation of opening heaven to a large number of children. "I have often remarked," says Father De Smet, "that many of the children seem to await baptism before winging their flight to heaven, for they die almost immediately after receiving the Sacrament."[31] Among adults, conversions were becoming more rare; at times even some of the neophytes fell into habits of vice that desolated the mission. The greater number, however, remained faithful; they continued to follow the instructions, and even became monthly communicants. The neighboring tribes, especially the Omahas, were now clamoring for the Black Robes.

Seeing what good he could still accomplish, our missionary took heart. After writing to Father De Vos, "I do not dare advise any one to come here,"[32] he rejoiced to hear that many novices wished to share his labors. "My heart bounded so with joy, that had my arms not been tightly crossed, I believe it would have burst forth; this news, I feel sure, has caused equal joy to the angel guardians of our poor Indians. The tribe, for this, assembled to sing canticles of thanksgiving to the Most High." Nevertheless, he advises the Master of Novices "to drill these young soldiers of Christ after the rigorous methods of our holy founder, St. Ignatius. Such training will make them of great service in this country. A rusty gun or a dull sword is of little use here."[33]

In 1840 another famine threatened to increase the hardships and difficulties of the mission. Provisions were running low, and the looked-for succor did not arrive. Father De Smet offered to go himself to St. Louis to get supplies. He left Council Bluffs February 13th, and in spite of the state of his health, was quite decided to return to his dear Indians as soon as possible. The intense cold

[30] Letter to Mr. Charles Van Mossevelde, Sept. 18, 1839.
[31] Letter to Father De Vos, Dec. 18, 1839.   [32] *Ibid.*
[33] To Father De Vos, Council Bluffs, Feb. 10, 1840.

had suspended navigation, so he was obliged to travel on foot, then on horseback, and at times in a cart, a distance of nine hundred miles[34] with no other companion save his guide.

The winter, he tells us, was a severe one. "I suffered greatly during the journey, often sleeping in the open, in deep snow, with only two blankets for covering. A bitter north wind froze my cheeks and one side of my nose. Droves of famished wolves appeared from time to time and followed us howling, but as they kept at a safe distance we were not alarmed.

"The intense cold affected my lungs in such a manner that I found difficulty in breathing, and feared at one time that I could not continue my journey. Upon arriving in St. Louis I was put under the care of a physician—I, who fear American doctors as I do the pest. This one hastened to employ the entire resources of the apothecary: bleeding and leeches were the first prescription, then followed baths, powders, pills, plasters, and every known *tisane*,* sweet, bitter, hot, cold, and tepid; added to which a strict régime was ordered. Complete rest quickly restored my health and I immediately set about getting out of the hands of the doctor, who would soon have had all the flesh off my bones."[35]

If cheerfulness be a distinct mark of the missionary temperament, Father De Smet had reason to be thankful for this gift. Notwithstanding the trials and hardships of the mission and the silence of his friends which pained him, he brought a cheerful countenance to every fatigue and danger. The modest assurance of a heroism which ignored self was not the least attractive aspect of his personality.

No sooner was his health reestablished than he began to make arrangements to rejoin his post. He collected provisions, clothing, church ornaments, vestments, and agricultural implements, and was about to start, when he heard he was to be sent to another mission, and that

---

[34] On the first trips Father De Smet could only roughly calculate distances; hence there may be some inaccuracies.

* *Translator's Note.* A mild aqueous infusion possessing nourishing rather than medicinal properties.

[35] To the Carmelites of Termonde, Westport, April 27, 1840.

Father Christian Hoecken had been appointed to replace him with the Potawatomies.[36] The two years spent at Council Bluffs were but years of preparation; the great work of the missionary was about to begin. In another theater of action, and into the heart of the American wilderness, he was to carry the light of the Gospel, and be known henceforth as the "apostle of the Rocky Mountains."

[36] In September, 1841, Fathers Verreydt and Hoecken left Council Bluffs for St. Mary's Mission, established two years before at Sugar Creek for the Potawatomies of Kansas. From there Father Hoecken continued to visit the tribes on the Upper Missouri.

CHAPTER VI

THE FLATHEADS. FIRST JOURNEY TO THE ROCKY MOUNTAINS (1840)

The Growing Prosperity of the United States—The Indian Situation—
Admirable Dispositions of the Flatheads—Old Ignatius—The Indians
Who Four Times Made a Three-thousand-mile Journey to Obtain the
Black Robes—Father De Smet is Sent to the Rocky Mountains to
Prepare the Foundation of a New Mission—How One Traveled in
1840 Across the Prairies—A Meeting between Father De Smet and the
Flatheads—One of Napoleon's Grenadiers—A Sojourn in the Camp
of Big Face—The Missionary's Joys—On the Summit of the Rockies—
Sanctus Ignatius Patronus Montium—Father De Smet Leaves the
Flatheads—Dangers He Encountered in the Yellowstone—Triumphant
Reception by the Sioux—He Returns to St. Louis.

SINCE the separation of the Colonies from England
the United States had marched steadily on in the
path of progress and prosperity. In fifty years, "this
infant in swaddling-clothes," as spoken of by Joseph De
Maistre, had attained a development only equaled by
that of some of the great European countries. In 1780
the population of the United States numbered 3,000,000;
in 1840 it exceeded 17,000,000, and every year new States
and cities have sprung into existence.

The pioneer marched ever westward, hewing, with fire
and axe, a path through the virgin forests, and weaving a
trail in the tall grass of the prairies, pitching his tent
wherever he found agricultural land. Before this steady
conquest the wilderness receded, and colonization advanced at the rate of from twenty-four to thirty miles a
year.

But what became of the Indians, the original possessors
of the American soil? They beheld their domains diminishing continually, and numerous tribes driven from the
Eastern country sought refuge on the other side of the
Missouri. The Indian Territory had just been ceded to

the Indians, and there the Cherokees, the Creeks, the Chickasaws, the Seminoles, and the Kickapoos, etc., endeavored, under the supervision of the Government, to lead the life and acquire the habits of the white man. Other Indians had, like the Potawatomies of Council Bluffs, abandoned the greater part of their land to the Americans. They kept for themselves only an independent settlement called a "reservation," where the Government undertook to provide for their subsistence, at least for a limited number of years.

But the greater number of the redskins continued their roaming life in the desert, where the white man had not yet penetrated. Upon the banks of the Upper Missouri, in the territories of Nebraska, Wyoming, Dakota, and Montana, lived the great Sioux Nation, divided into several tribes.[1]

Further north, on the frontier of the British possessions, roamed the Blackfeet, the Crows, the Assiniboins, and the Grosventres. Lastly, in the heart of the Rocky Mountains, and in the fertile valleys watered by the tributaries of the Columbia River, gathered a large number of smaller tribes, strangers to the Missouri Indians, and often victims of their incursions. These were the Flatheads, the Pend d'Oreilles or Kalispels, the Cœur d'Alènes, the Chaudières, the Spokanes, the Kootenais, and the Nez Percés.

To these last tribes Father De Smet was henceforth to consecrate his ardent zeal and the resources of his great ability.

Of all the mountain tribes, the most interesting were the Flatheads.[2] Lewis and Clarke, the explorers, sent in 1804 on an expedition to discover the source of the Missouri River, were the first white men to penetrate the region of the Flatheads.[3] This tribe numbered scarcely

[1] See complete table of the Sioux tribes compiled by Father De Smet. Selected Letters, 1st series, p. 146.

[2] The origin of this name is unknown, as well as that of the Nez Percés, which is justified neither by their physical formation, nor the practices in use in their tribe.

Translator's Note: The Flatheads are said to belong to the Sá-lish-an stock found in Washington, British Columbia, and Montana.

[3] Cf. "Travels to the Source of the Missouri River," by Captains Lewis and Clarke, London, 1814.

two thousand souls; but if inferior in numbers to many of the neighboring tribes, they were unsurpassed in bravery and daring.

A member of that celebrated expedition, in speaking of the moral degradation in which many of the tribes were sunk, adds: "To the honor of the Flatheads who live on the eastern slopes of the Rocky Mountains, they must be cited as an exception. This is the only tribe that has any idea of chastity."[4]   Mr. Cox, who in 1812-1814 traded furs with them, tells us that the Flatheads possessed nobler qualities than any of the other Western tribes. They are, he says, honest, obedient to their chiefs, cleanly in their huts and personal habits, and hold lying in abhorrence.   Polygamy is almost unknown among them.   The women are excellent wives and mothers, and so celebrated for their fidelity that the contrary failing is a rare exception.[5]

Such a race was ready to receive the Gospel.   The French Jesuits who fell under the tomahawk of the Iroquois in the seventeenth century, little dreamed that the faith they had preached and sealed with their blood would one day be carried beyond the Mississippi to the Rocky Mountains and as far West as the Pacific Coast by the descendants of these same Indians who had treated them with such barbarity.

Let us here recall this extraordinary evangelization. Between the years 1812 and 1820 a band of Catholic Iroquois left the Caughnawaga Mission near Montreal, and, crossing the Mississippi valley, directed their steps to the unknown regions of the West.   What could have been their object in migrating to the far West?   Possibly, they were unconsciously serving the designs of Providence in behalf of those who were to become their brothers by adoption.   The chief of the band, Ignatius La Mousse, had been baptized and married by the Jesuits and remained for some time in their service.[6]

[4] Journal of Sergeant Patrick Gass, quoted by Father Palladino, "Indian and White in the Northwest," p. 4.

[5] Cf. Palladino, op. cit., pp. 4-8.   See Helen Hunt Jackson, "A Century of Dishonor," pp. 377, etc.

[6] These details have been taken from a letter of Father Hélias d'Huddeghem (July 4, 1836).   We see from it that he conversed for some time at St. Louis with Ignatius and his children.

The Indians called him Old Ignatius, to distinguish him from another Iroquois, the Young Ignatius of whom we will speak later on.

The travelers were so cordially received by the Flatheads that they decided to remain with them. Ties of marriage soon strengthened the bonds of friendship, and the new-comers became members of their people. Beneath his native ruggedness and rare intelligence, the soul of an apostle lay hidden in Old Ignatius. His courage and loyalty acquired for him an influence which he used for the good of the tribe. He often spoke to the Flatheads of the Catholic faith, of its beliefs, its prayers, and its ceremonies. The conclusion of his discourse was always the same appeal: to send for a Black Robe to instruct them and show them the way to heaven.

The Flatheads listened most attentively, and learned from him the principal mysteries of the Faith, the great precepts of Christianity, the Lord's Prayer, the Sign of the Cross, and other religious practices. Their lives were regulated by this teaching; they said morning and night prayers, sanctified Sunday, baptized the dying, and placed a cross over the graves of their dead.

The Pend d'Oreilles and Nez Percés, tribes friendly to the Flatheads, were eager to be instructed, and all ardently longed for the Black Robes. But how to obtain them? To reach the Montreal and Quebec Missions meant a journey of over four thousand miles.

Catholic priests, however, finally arrived in Missouri, and the news reached the mountains, doubtless brought by merchants who made yearly trips up the river. Old Ignatius at once assembled the tribe in council, and pro-posed sending a deputation to St. Louis in search of a missionary. The proposition was enthusiastically re-ceived, and four Indians offered to start at once. It was a bold undertaking. How were they to accomplish a journey of three thousand miles over high mountains, broad rivers, and across arid plains and the sands of the desert? How avoid meeting the Crows and Blackfeet, mortal enemies of the Flatheads?

The four travelers left their country in the spring of 1831, ready to brave every danger in order to obtain a priest.[7] It is very probable, however, that they joined a caravan of merchants who were going East. In the beginning of October the deputation arrived at St. Louis, repairing at once to a Catholic church to prostrate themselves before Him whom Ignatius had taught them to adore, praying fervently that their long journey would not be in vain, and that they might realize their hearts' desire. The dignified bearing and piety of the Indians greatly impressed all who met them, but unfortunately no one could understand their language.

Yet another trial awaited them. Worn out by the fatigues of a journey that had lasted several months, two members of the deputation fell ill and died within a few days.[8] The two surviving Indians set out for the mountains, but never reached their tribes, nor is it known whether they, too, succumbed to fatigue, or were massacred.

This expedition, however, was not in vain, for it made known the existence of the Flatheads, and gained the interest of the public. Catholic priests were so scarce at that time that a new mission could not be started. The Protestants, wishing to profit by this condition, endeavored on two occasions to get in touch with the Indians. In 1834 the Flatheads learned that a band of missionaries was en route to their tribe, and they concluded it was the Black Robes with the messengers who had been sent to fetch them. Great was their disappointment when the caravan arrived and they beheld not one of their tribe in the party. The missionaries, moreover, in no way resembled those the Iroquois had told them about. They were married and they did not wear either the black robe or the crucifix, neither did they recite the "big prayer" (the

---

[7] According to Father Hélias d'Huddeghem, the chief of the expedition was called Martin, and was Ignatius' uncle. He died shortly after arriving at St. Louis. His companions belonged to the Flatheads and the Nez Percés.

[8] "I was at that time absent from St. Louis," wrote Bishop Rosati. "Two of our priests went to see the poor Indians, who seemed delighted with their visit. They made the Sign of the Cross and other signs connected with baptism, which Sacrament was administered to them, to their great satisfaction. A crucifix was given to them which they seized eagerly, kissing it several times and clinging to it until they died. The bodies were taken to the church and buried with full Catholic ceremonies." (Annals of the Propagation of the Faith, Dec. 31, 1831.)

Mass). These were not the masters they expected. Realizing that it was useless to remain, the Methodists left to establish themselves in Oregon. Another attempt was made a year later by the American Board of Foreign Missions, with no greater measure of success.

The Flatheads, despairing of seeing again their brothers that had left the camp four years previously, decided to send a second deputation to St. Louis. This time Ignatius offered to go himself. Taking with him his two sons, whom he wished to have baptized, he left the mountains in the summer of 1835. After unspeakable fatigues and hardships the deputation reached St. Louis the beginning of December. Having been taught French when a child, Ignatius could explain the object of his journey. A Belgian Jesuit, Father Hélias d'Huddeghem, heard his confession and prepared his sons for baptism.

For some time the Fathers in St. Louis had wished to establish a mission on the other side of the Rocky Mountains, but as the number of priests hardly sufficed for the work of the college, the Father General could not then undertake another foundation. Ignatius, nevertheless, continued to plead for a priest, in the name of the tribes whose delegate he was. "I consoled him as best I could," wrote Father Hélias, "assuring him that our 'Black Chief' at Rome would shortly provide for the needs of his people, and that if permission was given to me, I would start at once for the mountains." [9] Bishop Rosati also promised to send missionaries, and cheered with this hope Ignatius returned to his country.

Eighteen months passed, and yet no Black Robe arrived. In the summer of 1837 a third deputation started for St. Louis. It was composed of three Flatheads, one Nez Percé, and their chief, Old Ignatius. In traversing the Sioux country they encountered a band of three hundred warriors. Ignatius, who was dressed as a white man, might have been spared, as the Sioux thought he belonged to a caravan of white men returning to St. Louis; but the valiant old man refused to be separated from his companions. Knowing they were lost, the Flatheads determined to at least uphold the honor of their tribe. Fifteen

[9] To Madam Hélias d'Huddeghem, July 4, 1836.

Sioux entered into combat with them. At last, defeated and outnumbered, they fell, offering their lives to God for the salvation of their brothers.

Upon learning this crushing news the poor Indians asked themselves if they would ever obtain a Catholic priest, and undaunted, decided to send a fourth deputation to St. Louis. Two Iroquois who had some knowledge of French offered to go. One was called Peter Gaucher, the other, the Young Ignatius. They left in 1839, joining a party of trappers traveling in the same direction. About the middle of September the deputation passed the St. Joseph Mission, at Council Bluffs. They visited the mission which had been established the year before for the Potawatomies, and there Father De Smet beheld for the first time those to whom he would soon begin his apostolate. "With tears in their eyes they begged me to return with them. If only my health would permit it, I might have the luck this time to get further up the Missouri. Should God deem me worthy of the honor, I would willingly give my life to help these Indians."[10]

A few weeks later our two travelers arrived at St. Louis. They made their confessions to one of the Fathers at the college, then went to the cathedral to hear Mass and receive holy communion, and there Bishop Rosati confirmed them.

After a long conversation with the Indians the good Bishop wrote to the General of the Society of Jesus, telling him of the sterling qualities of these Indians, and recounting their efforts of the past eight years to obtain a Catholic priest. The letter concluded in the following words: "For the love of God, Most Reverend Father, do not abandon these souls."[11] Touched by this earnest appeal, the Father General agreed to send a priest. At last the Flatheads were to realize their long-deferred desire. Peter Gaucher started at once to carry the good news to his tribe, Young Ignatius remaining in St. Louis to act as guide to the missionary, who would start in the spring.

When Father De Smet heard of the promise made to the Flatheads he offered at once to go to the Rocky Mountains.

[10] Letter to Francis De Smet, Council Bluffs, Oct. 29, 1839.
[11] St. Louis, Oct. 20, 1839.

Knowing his health was not yet entirely restored after the hardships of his recent journey, his Superiors for some time withheld their consent, but finally yielded to his importunities.[12]

At that time there was no question of definitely establishing a mission for the tribe, but simply of studying the country with this end in view. The missionary, moreover, entertained no illusions as to the difficulties of the enterprise: "It is a journey fraught with many dangers," he wrote to his brother, "but God, in whom I put my trust, will, I hope, guide me, for it is for His greater glory that I undertake it. The salvation of a whole nation is at stake. Pray for me; and have little Charles pray especially for me every day: *talium est regnum cœlorum*, their innocence makes them friends of God."[13]

His Superior had intended giving him an assistant, but the necessary money was not forthcoming, so he started alone, with only Young Ignatius as guide. They left St. Louis March 27, 1840, arriving a few days later at Westport,[14] the frontier city of Missouri, and the meeting-place of the merchants en route to the Rocky Mountains. He here procured horses for his journey, buying seven in all, one for himself, one for his guide, and five for transporting baggage and provisions. They were to join a caravan of about thirty men belonging to the American Fur Company. Before starting for the great desert, he placed himself under the protection of the Queen of heaven, and wrote for the last time to his brothers and sisters. In the firm belief that he was answering the call of God, he departed cheerfully and confidently: "God has surely great designs upon these poor tribes, and I thank Him with my whole heart for having chosen me for this mission. I fear nothing, and never in my life have I experienced greater happiness and tranquillity."[15]

---

[12] "He manifested," writes Father Verhaegen, "such eagerness and ardent zeal for the work; he possessed, moreover, such remarkable qualities, that it was hardly possible for us to make another choice. His prudence and ability assured the successful termination of his journey." (To Francis De Smet, St. Louis, April 24, 1840.)

[13] To Francis De Smet, St. Louis, March 16, 1840.

[14] To-day this is Kansas City.

[15] To Francis De Smet, Westport, April 24, 1840.

The caravan started April 30th, going west across arid plains that were intersected by deep gorges. Soon the intense heat began to affect them. "When only ten days out," writes Father De Smet, "I was seized with an attack of intermittent fever, with the chills which usually precede such an attack. My friends urged me to return, but my longing to see the mountain tribes was stronger than any argument they could offer to deter me from going.

"I followed the caravan as best as I could, holding myself on my horse until my strength was exhausted. They then laid me upon a cart, where I was jolted about like a bale of goods. Often in crossing deep and steep ravines I was thrown into extraordinary positions; sometimes my feet shot up in the air, and again I fell between packing-cases. I would shiver with cold one minute and the next be dripping with perspiration, and crimson from the raging fever. For three days—when my fever was at its height—I had only stale, salt water to quench my thirst."[16] On May 18th they reached the Platte or Nebraska River, "the most marvelous and useless of rivers," two miles wide, and in places only from three to six feet deep, which renders it unnavigable. Hence the caravan was obliged to continue the journey by land.

Father De Smet appreciated keenly the grandeur and beauty of the country, and gazed with delight upon the islands that lay in groups in the river, which from a distance resembled a flotilla of boats, their sails entwined with garlands of green and festoons of flowers.[17] Thousands of buffalo ranged the vast prairies, recalling to mind the flocks of the patriarchs that once covered the mountains in the East.

Then came the desert, with its arid, desolate plains, where the grass was parched and the rivers and streams dry; the deer, buffalo, and roebuck sought refuge in the few oases where life still existed. Piles of stone, steep peaks, and deep ravines were encountered; and walls of rock, seemingly unsurmountable, barred their progress. Father De Smet was greatly interested in meeting bands

[16] Narrative addressed to Francis De Smet, St. Louis, Jan. 25, 1841.
[17] *Ibid.*

of Indians of different tribes. Formerly these tribes were in peaceful possession of the prairies, and now they were being driven back into the forests and gorges. "Some day this country may be the cradle of a new people, composed of the original savage races, and of adventurers, fugitives, and the outcasts of society: a heterogeneous and dangerous population, that the American Union gathers like a sinister cloud upon its frontiers. The Indian tribes that are being transported from the country east of the Mississippi to the solitudes of the West, carry with them an implacable hatred of the white man, who has unjustly driven them from the tombs of their fathers and robbed them of their heritage. Hence their numbers are augmented, and resentment is rife. In time, will not these tribes assemble in bands to pillage and massacre—mounted upon the fleet-footed horses of the prairie—the desert for the theater of their brigandage, their lives and spoils sheltered behind inaccessible rocks?"[18]

The future alas! but too well justified his prevision.

After following the right bank of the Nebraska for a month the missionary reached the Rocky Mountains about the middle of June. "They are rocks piled upon rocks and seem the ruins of an entire world, covered with the shroud of eternal snows."[19] The caravan camped at Green River, one of the branches of the Colorado. The Indian and Canadian beaver-hunters assembled there every year to sell their furs, or exchange them for articles furnished by the white men.

Arriving at Green River June 30th, what must have been Father De Smet's joy when he beheld a group of Flatheads approaching. Peter Gaucher had brought back from St. Louis the news that a Black Robe would soon come with Young Ignatius. The great chief immediately dispatched ten warriors to meet the missionary and escort him to the camp. He himself followed with all his tribe.

"Our meeting," says Father De Smet, "was not that of strangers, but of friends. They were like children who, after a long absence, run to meet their father. I wept for joy in embracing them, and with tears in their eyes they

---

[18] Narrative cited. Cf. W. Irving, "Astoria," Chap. xxii.
[19] *Ibid.*

welcomed me with tender words, with childlike simplicity. The Flatheads gave me the news of the tribe, recounting their almost miraculous preservation in a battle that lasted five days, in which they killed about fifty of the enemy without losing a single man. 'We fought like braves,' they told me, 'sustained by our desire to see you. The Great Spirit had pity upon us, and helped us to clear of all danger the road you must follow. The Blackfeet retired weeping. It will be some time now before they molest us again.' Together we thanked God for His protection and begged for His assistance to the end."[20]

But the party had yet to traverse the most difficult and dangerous part of the way. While the horses were resting Father De Smet spent several days conversing with the Indians assembled upon the banks of the Green River. He saw for the first time the Snakes, who were reduced to feeding on roots they dug out of the ground, and the Ampajoots [Yampah Utes?], who were still more impoverished. "The country they inhabit is a veritable moor. They live in crevices in the rocks and in holes dug in the earth. These Indians wear no clothing, and their weapons consist of bow and arrow, and a sharp stick. They wander over the barren plains searching for ants and grasshoppers, which they eat; insipid roots and nauseous berries are regarded as a feast. Men, whose word I cannot doubt, have told me that they feed on the dead bodies of their relatives, and even eat their children."[21] Such misery appealed to the heart of our missionary, and he would gladly have stayed to consecrate his life to those degraded people. He had, however, the consolation of baptizing several of the tribe and giving them a glimpse of eternal joys.

The Nez Percés, the Spokanes, and the Cœur d'Alènes were more human in their habits and customs. They inhabited a fertile country and their wealth consisted principally of horses, some of the tribes possessing five or six hundred. All manifested a great desire to have a Black Robe among them. The Kalispels, or Pend d'Oreilles, resembled the Flatheads in character, language, and habits, and formed with them one people. Like the latter, they had led a wandering life, and merely awaited the arrival of the missionary to begin the cultivation of the soil, and to live according to the precepts of the Gospel.

While conversing with the Indians, Father De Smet took occasion to give some salutary advice to the Canadian hunters who seemed to him "to have great need of it." Great was his astonishment to find a compatriot among them, a Fleming of Ghent. John Baptiste De Velder had been an old grenadier in Napoleon's army. Taken prisoner in Spain, he escaped from the English colonies in an American ship, and for the past years had hunted beaver in the Rocky Mountains. Enchanted to have found a Belgian nine thousand miles from his country, he generously offered to accompany the missionary and serve him during his journey. He was resolved, he said, to spend the remainder of his life serving God. John Baptiste had almost entirely forgotten Flemish, remembering only his prayers, and a hymn in honor of the Blessed Virgin he had learned at his mother's knee, and which he recited daily.

July 3d was a Sunday. Father De Smet offered the Holy Sacrifice of the Mass at an altar erected upon elevated ground and decorated with wild flowers. This was the first time Mass had been said in the Rocky Mountains. "I preached in French and English (writes the missionary) to the American and Canadian hunters, and then through an interpreter addressed the Flatheads and the Snakes.[22] It was a consoling sight to see this cosmopolitan gathering following devoutly the Sacred Mysteries. The Canadians sang some hymns in French and Latin, while the Indians chanted in their own tongue. The service was truly *Catholic.* The place where the Holy Sacrifice was offered has since been called by the trappers, 'The plain of the Holy Sacrifice.'"[23]

The next day the gathering dispersed. Accompanied by his faithful Fleming and the delegates from the Flatheads, Father De Smet continued his journey. After crossing mountains and rivers, and scaling precipices for eight days, they arrived at the Indian camp.

The Flatheads, Pend d'Oreilles, and Nez Percés, came

[22] Also Shoshones or Rootdiggers. See Chittenden-Richardson, p. 219.
[23] Narrative addressed to the Carmelites at Termonde, March 1, 1841

from a distance of eight hundred miles to meet them,[24] and in their midst Father De Smet tasted the purest joys of his apostolic life. He himself shall tell us of it.

"The poles were already set up for my tent, and upon my arrival, men, women, and children, sixteen hundred souls in all, came to shake hands with me and bid me welcome. The old men cried for joy, and the children expressed gladness by gambols and screams of delight. These kind Indians conducted me to the tent of the great chief, a patriarchal person called Big Face, who, surrounded by his council, received me with great cordiality. 'Black Robe,' he said, 'welcome to my nation. Our hearts rejoice, for to-day the Great Spirit has granted our petition. You have come to a people poor, plain, and submerged in the darkness of ignorance. I have always exhorted my children to love the Great Spirit. We know that all that exists belongs to Him and everything we have comes from His generous hands. From time to time kind white men have given us good advice, which we have striven to follow. Our ardent desire to be instructed in what concerns our salvation has led us on several occasions to send a deputation of our people to the great Black Robe [the Bishop] of St. Louis to ask him to send a priest. Black Robe, speak! We are all your children. Show us the path we must follow to reach the place where abides the Great Spirit. Our ears are open, our hearts will heed your words! Speak, Black Robe! we will follow the words of your mouth!'

"I then spoke at length to these good people upon the subject of religion. I told them the object of my mission, and asked them to give up their wandering life and settle in a fertile district. All declared themselves ready and willing to exchange the bow and arrow for the spade and the plow. I drew up a set of rules for the religious exercises. One of the chiefs immediately brought me a bell, and that first evening it called the Indians to assemble around

[24] Father De Smet passed then quite near to "the land of wonders," since called the National Park of America. But he knew the country only later from the accounts of another traveler. (See Selected Letters, 1st Series, p. 97.)

my tent. After a short instruction, night prayers were said. Before retiring they sang in admirable harmony three hymns in praise of the Great Spirit of their own composition. No words can express how deeply I was touched.

"The great chief was up every morning at daybreak. He would mount his horse and make the tour of the camp, haranguing his people: 'Come,' said he, 'courage, my children! Tell Him you love Him, and ask Him to make you charitable! Courage, the sun is rising. Come, bathe in the river. Be punctual and at our Father's tent on the tap of the bell. Be still, open your ears to hear, and your hearts to retain the words he will speak.'

"When all were ready I rang the bell for prayers and instruction. From the day I arrived until I left the Flatheads, their avidity to hear the word of God increased daily. I preached regularly four times a day, and each time they ran eagerly to secure good places. Those who were sick were carried to the sermons.

"The morning after our arrival I began at once to translate the prayers through an interpreter. Fifteen days later I promised a medal of the Blessed Virgin to the one who would be the first to recite the *Pater*, *Ave*, and *Credo*, the Ten Commandments, and the four Acts without a fault. A chief arose. 'Father,' he said, 'your medal belongs to me'; and to my great surprise he recited all the prayers without missing a word. I embraced him, and made him my catechist. He performed this function so zealously that in ten days the whole tribe knew their prayers.

"I had the happiness of regenerating nearly three hundred Indians in the waters of baptism. They all begged for the Sacrament, and manifested the best possible dispositions. But as the absence of the missionary would be only temporary, I deemed it wiser to put off the others until the following year, not only with the intention of giving them an exalted idea of the Sacrament, but also to try them in regard to the indissolubility of marriage, something quite unknown among the Indian nations of America.

"Among the adults baptized were two great chiefs, one

belonging to the Flatheads, the other to the Pend d'Oreilles, both over eighty years of age. When I exhorted them to renew their sentiments of contrition for their sins, Walking Bear (the name of the second) replied: 'In my youth and even later in life I lived in complete ignorance of good and evil, and during that time I must often have displeased God. I sincerely ask for pardon. But when I fully realized that a thing was sinful I immediately banished it from my heart. I do not remember ever having deliberately offended the Great Spirit.'

"I have never discovered the least vice in these Indians, save gambling, in which they often risk all they possess. These games have been abolished by general consent, since they have learned that they are contrary to the commandment which says 'Thou shalt not covet thy neighbor's goods.' They are scrupulously honest in selling and buying, and none of them has ever been accused of stealing. Every article that is found is carried to the tent of the chief, who proclaims the object and returns it to the owner.

"Slander is unknown among the women; a lie is considered especially odious. 'We fear,' they say, 'to offend the Great Spirit, hence we hold liars in abhorrence.'

"All quarrels and fits of passion are severely punished. They share one another's sufferings, give help in time of need, and care for the orphans. They are well-mannered, gay, and very hospitable; their tent is open house; keys and locks are unknown. Often I said to myself 'These are the people that civilized men dare to call barbarians!'

"It is a great error to judge the Indians of the interior by those of the frontier. These last have learned the vices of the white men, whose insatiable greed of gain is served by corrupting the Indian, and whose bad example leads him into vicious habits."[25]

Father De Smet returned to the Flatheads in Pierre's Hole at the foot of the three Tetons.[26] A few days later they broke camp and started north by slow stages. On

[25] Narrative addressed to Francis De Smet.

[26] The Teton Mountains are the most interesting, historically and otherwise, in the United States. The principal summit, the Grand Teton, is 13,691 feet high. Cf. Chittenden-Richardson, p. 228.

July 22d, the caravan attained the ridge which separates the watersheds of the Missouri from those of the Columbia River. "I climbed a high mountain," writes the missionary, "in order to more accurately measure the distance of the source of these two rivers. I saw the stream descending from dizzy heights, leaping from rock to rock with a deafening noise. The two large streams are formed at their source, with scarcely a hundred feet between them. I wished very much to get to the summit, but a five-hour climb had exhausted my strength. I reached, I think, a height of 5,000 feet, and after crossing masses of snow twenty feet deep I yet was far from the top.

"Constrained to abandon my project, I seated myself and fell to thinking about the Jesuit Fathers who were serving the missions on the Mississippi from Council Bluffs to the Gulf of Mexico. The happy memories these thoughts awakened moved me to tears of joy. I thanked God for having deigned to bless the work of His servitors dispersed in this vast vineyard, and implored this grace for all the nations of Oregon, the Flatheads and Pend d'Oreilles in particular, these last who had just enrolled themselves under the banner of Jesus Christ. Then I wrote in large letters upon the soft surface of the rock the following inscription: *SANCTUS IGNATIUS PATRONUS MONTIUM. DIE JULII* 23, 1840. I said a Mass of thanksgiving at the foot of this mountain, surrounded by my Indians, who chanted canticles of praise to God, and took possession of the country in the name of our holy founder."[27]

The following day the travelers marched on the other side of the mountain, where they came upon a succession of smiling valleys, arid plateaux, steep hills, and narrow passes. The end of July found Father De Smet camped near the junction of the three sources of the Missouri. Immense herds of buffalo roamed over the plain, and the Flatheads, profiting by this occasion, replenished their food-supply.

Father De Smet shared in every way the wandering life of his Indians, living on roots and what game could be found. His bed was a buffalo hide, and, wrapped in a

[27] Narrative addressed to Francis De Smet.

blanket, he slept under the stars; storms and tempests he braved in a small tent. For four months he suffered from a fever which, he says: "Seemed loath to leave me; but the hard life I lead finally enabled me to throw it off, and since September I am in perfect health."[28]

The season was then far advanced, and the missionary was obliged to start at once in order to reach St. Louis before the winter set in.

"I decided to leave," he tells us, "on August 27th [1840]. Early in the morning of that day seventeen warriors, the pick of the two tribes, came with three chiefs to my tent. The old men in council had selected these braves to act as my escort through the country of the Blackfeet and the Crows, the two tribes most at enmity with the white man. Long before sunrise all the Flatheads had assembled to say good-by. No word was spoken, but sadness was written on every countenance. The only thing that consoled them was a formal promise to return the following spring, with a reinforcement of missionaries. Morning prayers were said amid the tears and sobs of the Indians, which drew tears from my own eyes, although I endeavored to control my emotions, trying to make them understand that my departure was imperative. I exhorted the tribe to serve the Great Spirit with fervor, and to avoid anything that might give scandal, dwelling once more upon the principal truths of our holy religion, and giving them, as spiritual chief, an intelligent Indian I had myself carefully instructed. He was to replace me during my absence. Night and morning and every Sunday they were to recite prayers in common, and he was to exhort them to the practice of virtue. I authorized my deputy, furthermore, to privately baptize the dying and infants in case of need. With one voice they promised to obey all my injunctions.

"With tears in their eyes the Indians wished me a good and safe journey. Old Big Face arose and said:

"Black Robe! may the Great Spirit accompany you on your long and dangerous journey. Morning and night we will pray that you may safely reach your brothers in St. Louis, and we will continue to pray thus until you return to your children of the mountains. When the

[28] To Francis De Smet.

snows of winter will have disappeared from the valleys, and when the first green of spring begins to appear, our hearts, which now are so sad, will once more rejoice. As the meadow grass grows higher and higher, we will go forth to meet you. Farewell, Black Robe, farewell.'"[29]

While the Flatheads were returning to their country upon the banks of the Clarke, Father De Smet, escorted by the band of Indian warriors and his devoted compatriot, traveled in the direction of the Yellowstone. His purpose was to follow this river to its junction with the Missouri, and on his way back to St. Louis to visit the forts established along the river, where he might possibly find a goodly number of half-breed children needing to be baptized.

For days they traveled through endless plains and arid wastes intersected with deep ravines, where at every step the enemy might be in hiding. Scouts were sent out in every direction to reconnoiter, and at night what seemed to be the least dangerous spot was chosen for encampment. A small fort hastily constructed with trunks of trees safeguarded them from a night attack.

The caravan soon came to a camp of the Crows, a tribe allied at that time with the Flatheads, and was received with great cordiality. The tribe's larder being well provisioned, the time was spent in feasting and rejoicing. Father De Smet tells us that in one afternoon he assisted at twenty successive banquets. "Scarcely was I seated in one tent before I was invited into another one. My digestion not being as accommodating as that of the Indians, I contented myself with only tasting their stews, and for a bit of tobacco, the eaters I had taken the precaution to include in my followers emptied the plates for me."[30]

When about to enter the country of the Blackfeet, Father De Smet, fearing to expose the faithful Flatheads, sent back his escort. Alone now, with only his honest

[29] To Francis De Smet.
[30] "The law of the feast was that each one must eat all that was given to him; however, one could get rid of his plate by giving it to another guest with a present of tobacco." (Narrative cited.)

Fleming, he traveled for several hundred miles through the most dangerous country any explorer has ever visited, a trackless land in which his compass was his sole guide. At every step they saw recent traces of the grizzly bear, that terror of the wilderness. In many places the travelers came upon forts that had been constructed by warring tribes, and behind which the enemy might be hiding.

"Upon awakening one morning," writes the missionary, "I saw, about a quarter of a mile distant, the smoke of a big fire, which turned out to be the camp of a party of savages. Being separated from them by only a point of rock, we hurriedly saddled our horses and galloped off. That day we made about fifty miles without stopping, arriving at camp two hours after sunset. Fearing the savages had seen our trail and might pursue us, we dared not light a fire, and went to bed supperless. I rolled myself in my blanket, lay down on the grass, and recommended my soul to God. My brave grenadier soon began to snore like a steam-engine under way, sounding all the notes of the gamut and ending in a deep sigh which harmonized with the prelude, while I tossed from one side to the other and spent a sleepless night.

"The next morning at daybreak we were off. Toward noon, another alarm. A buffalo had been killed scarcely two hours before at the place we were then passing; his tongue, marrow bones, and several other tidbits had been taken out. Providence provided us with a supper of what was left. We traveled in an opposite direction from the Indian tracks, and the following night camped in the midst of some rocks, once the lair of panthers and wolves. There, I slept well, undisturbed by my companion's music."[31]

Every day, in fact every hour, the travelers beheld signs of the near presence of the dreaded Blackfeet. "Such solitude, with its horrors and dangers, has one great advantage; man is face to face with death and realizes how completely he is in the hands of God. Hence, it is no great thing to make to God the sacrifice of a life that belongs less to one's self than to the first savage who wishes to take it. In the face of danger one prays more

[31] To Francis De Smet.

fervently, and when saved makes better resolutions. In the desert I made the best retreat of my whole life."[32]

At last they reached the Missouri, at a place where one hour before the enemy had passed. Father De Smet recounted to one of the chiefs the dangers he had run in the Yellowstone. "The Great Spirit has His manitous," said the Indian, "which He sent to accompany you and put to flight the enemy that would do you harm." Could any Christian have translated better the verse of the Psalm: *Angelus suis mandavit de te, ut custodiant te in omnibus viis tuis?*[33]

The travelers remained several days at Fort Union at the mouth of the Yellowstone, the most important post the Fur Company possessed upon the Missouri. Father De Smet baptized several half-breed children there, and on September 23d set out again, accompanied by the traders who were en route to the Aricaras. Three days later the travelers reached the camps of the Mandans. At the approach of strangers, the Mandans and the Grosventres rushed out prepared to make trouble, but when they caught sight of the minister of the Great Spirit, demonstrations of friendship quickly followed their threats of death. In every tent or lodge the pots were filled with good things. Like their neighbors, the Crows, they wished to feast the new arrivals. A series of invitations to dine followed, and the feasting was kept up until midnight.

The three merchants remained at Fort Clarke. Fort Pierre was a ten days' journey farther on. Father De Smet, failing a guide, started off with only John Baptiste De Velder and a Canadian traveling in the same direction. "But," says he, "one gradually accustoms one's self to brave every danger. Confident in God's protection, we continued our way across the sands of the plains, guided by our compass, like mariners upon a vast ocean.

"The fifth day found us in the neighborhood of the Sioux Blackfeet, an offshoot of the Blackfeet of the mountains. Their very name struck terror into our hearts. We crept through ravines to be out of range of the piercing eye of the Indian that ever searches the plain.

[32] To Francis De Smet.   [33] Ps. xc. 11.

"Toward noon a near-by spring invited us to rest and make our midday repast. We were congratulating ourselves upon having escaped the dreaded enemy, when suddenly a war-cry, accompanied by deafening noises, sounded from the direction overlooking our hiding-place. A band of Blackfeet that had been following our tracks for several hours, armed with guns, bows and arrows, half-naked, weirdly daubed with color, descended upon us at full gallop.

"I immediately rose and extended my hand to the one who appeared to be chief of the band. 'Why are you hiding in a ravine?' he said, 'Are you afraid of us?' 'We were hungry,' I replied, 'and the spring tempted us to take a few moments' rest.' The chief eyed me from head to foot. My cassock and the crucifix I wore on my breast excited his curiosity. Then addressing the Canadian, who spoke a little Sioux, he said: 'Never before in my life have I seen this kind of a man. Who is he, and where does he come from?' Given such an opportunity, the Canadian was not backward in according titles. 'This man,' he replied, 'converses with the Great Spirit. He is the *French Black Robe* [34] and is come here to visit the different Indian tribes.'

"At these words the savage softened, commanded his warriors to lay down their arms, and each one gave me his hand. I made them a present of a large package of tobacco, and immediately the warriors seated themselves in a circle to smoke the pipe of peace and friendship.

"The chief then invited me to come and spend the night in his village. Twelve warriors laid an immense buffalo hide on the ground before me. The chief took me by the arm and, conducting me to the hide, bade me sit down. Understanding nothing of the ceremony, I seated myself, and imagine my surprise when I saw the twelve Indians seize this would-be carpet by its extremities, lift me from the ground, and, preceded by the chief, carry me in triumph to the village.

"In an instant every one was out to see the Black Robe.

[34] The missionaries who until the end of the eighteenth century evangelized North America were all French; hence the title French Black Robe, given to them by the Indians.

I was given the place of honor in the chief's tent, who, surrounded by forty of his braves, addressed me in the following words: 'Black Robe, this is the happiest day of our lives, for to-day, for the first time, we see in our midst a man who is near to the Great Spirit. These are the principal warriors of my tribe. I have invited them to the feast I have prepared for you, that they may never forget the great day.'"[35]

It seems strange that with the savages the fact of being a Catholic priest merited a triumphal reception for the lowly missionary, while in other times, and to men proud of their civilization, he would have been the object of suspicion. During the repast the great chief showered attentions on his guest, even to giving him a mouthful of his own food to chew, a refined usage among his tribe.

At night, after the missionary had retired and was about to fall asleep, he saw the chief who had received him with so much honor, enter his tent. Brandishing a knife that gleamed in the light of the torch, he said: "Black Robe, are you afraid?" The missionary, taking the chief's hand, placed it on his breast and replied: "See if my heart beats more rapidly than usual! Why should I be afraid? You have fed me with your own hands, and I am as safe in your tent as I would be in my father's house." Flattered by this reply, the Blackfoot renewed his professions of friendship; he had wished only to test the confidence of his guest.

The next day Father De Smet continued his journey. The great chief gave him three Indians to accompany him to Fort Pierre; among them was his own son, whom he begged the priest to instruct. "I want to know," he said, "the words the Great Spirit has communicated to us through you."

From Fort Pierre the missionary went down to Fort Vermillion, where a bitter sorrow awaited him. The Sioux had violated the peace concluded the year before with the Potawatomies. A band of warriors had returned to camp bearing a scalp. Father De Smet at once called a council of the tribe, reproached the chiefs for breaking their word, menacing them with terrible reprisals if they did not at

[35] To Francis De Smet.

once repair the injury done. Thoroughly frightened, the Sioux entreated him to be once more their interpreter, and to assure the Potawatomies that they were resolved to forever bury the hatchet.

Happy to be the bearer of a message of peace to his neophytes, Father De Smet wished to start at once. His horse was exhausted, so with a half-breed Iroquois he started in a canoe. It was then the middle of November. The Missouri was filled with floating ice, which continually jammed the frail skiff against snags. Five times the travelers nearly perished. The nights were spent on sandbars with no nourishment save frozen sweet-potatoes and a little fresh meat. At last, after traveling ten days, they reached Council Bluffs. The following night the river froze over.

Fathers Verreydt and Hoecken were the first priests Father De Smet had seen since he left St. Louis. "You can readily imagine my joy in finding myself safe and sound in the midst of my fellow-priests after a journey of two thousand leagues, through every conceivable danger, and among barbarous tribes." In the name of the Sioux he renewed peace with his beloved Potawatomies. But he could not tear himself away from his dear Indians and only at the end of three weeks did he set out to finish his journey to St. Louis, arriving there New Year's Eve. His journey had lasted nine months.[36]

[36] It is very probable that John Baptiste De Velder accompanied Father De Smet to St. Louis, but from that time on his name no longer appears in the missionary's narratives.

CHAPTER VII

FATHER DE SMET had promised the Flatheads to
return to the Rocky Mountains and bring with him
new missionaries, but lack of funds again stood in the
way of realizing this project, the Fathers not having sufficient means to defray even one-half the expense of the
expedition. And how did our resourceful missionary meet
this situation? "The thought," he writes, "that the undertaking was doomed to failure, and that I could not
keep the promise I had made to the poor Indians, occasioned me keen sorrow and regret. But I had been the
recipient of direct help from on high too often to allow
myself in this instance to yield to discouragement. My
confidence in God remained unshaken."[1]

Shortly after his arrival in St. Louis, Father De Smet
circulated thousands of pamphlets recounting his life and
experiences among the Indians. Being thus informed of
the admirable dispositions of the Indian tribes, the Catholics east of the Mississippi generously contributed to establish a mission promising such abundant fruits.

Father De Smet started off on his begging expedition in
midwinter, going first to Louisiana. "I marvel at the
ways of Providence in choosing me as the means of ac-

[1] Letter to the editor of the *Catholic Herald*, May 1, 1841.

complishing His designs. My fondest hopes have been more than realized, for notwithstanding the critical financial condition actually existing in the United States, I collected $1,100 in New Orleans. Women brought me their jewels; even the slaves contributed their mite."[2]

Fathers Point and Mengarini and three lay Brothers were appointed to the mission, and returned with Father De Smet to the Rocky Mountains.

The Superior's choice of men proved a very happy one. Nicholas Point, born of humble parents at Rocroi, in the French Ardennes in 1799, early in life manifested great piety and love of work. Marshal Ney offered to adopt the lad and give him a career in life; but the youth had other aims in view. The lives of the Saints, particularly the life of St. Francis Xavier, revealed to him a higher and greater glory than that of arms, and he determined to become a missionary. Entering the novitiate of Montrouge, it was not long before he was appointed prefect of studies, filling that office first at St. Acheul, and afterward at Fribourg. In 1835 Father Point came to America and founded a college at Grand Coteau, which he left three years later in a flourishing condition.

In 1838 the Louisiana Mission in charge of the French Jesuits was attached to the Missouri Mission, Father Verhaegen remaining Superior with the title of Vice-Provincial. Profiting by this circumstance (the union of the two missions), Father Point begged to be allowed to go with Father De Smet to the Rocky Mountains.[3]

Father Gregory Mengarini was born in Rome on the feast of St. Ignatius Loyola, July 31, 1811. In 1828 he entered the Society of Jesus and made his course in theology at the Roman College. One day in the refectory he heard read a letter from Bishop Rosati, pleading the cause of the Indians. That letter was, for Mengarini, the call of God. Immediately after his ordination he started for the missions. A man of tried virtue and gentle nature; a skilful physician, a musician of no mean order, and a remarkable linguist, such was the new missionary to the Rocky Mountains.[4]

[2] Letter to Francis De Smet, April 27, 1841.
[3] See notice of Father Nicholas Point in The Woodstock Letters, 1882, p. 299.   [4] Cf. The Woodstock Letters, 1887, p. 93.

The lay Brothers, not less than the Fathers, rendered valuable services to the mission, Brother William Claessens filling the office of carpenter, Brother Specht that of blacksmith, and Charles Huet, general-utility man and "Jack-of-all-trades."[5] Besides the Fathers and lay Brothers, Father De Smet engaged three laborers, who under the direction of the Brothers were to undertake the hard work of the mission.

The missionaries set out on their journey April 24, 1841, and at Westport joined a party of sixty travelers, many of them bound for California in search of gold. "The caravan," writes Father De Smet, "was composed of a curious collection of individuals, every country in Europe being represented: in my little band of eleven were men of eight different nationalities."[6]

Several days were spent in loading the wagons and mules before the caravan could start. "I hope," writes the missionary, "that the journey will end well; it has begun badly. One of our wagons was burned on the steamboat; a horse ran away and was never found; a second fell ill, which I was obliged to exchange for another at a loss. Some of the mules took fright and ran off, leaving their wagons; others, with the wagons, have been stalled in the mud. We have faced perilous situations in crossing steep declivities, deep ravines, marshes, and rivers."[7]

The missionaries, as in the preceding year, followed the Nebraska River until reaching the first spurs of the Rocky Mountains. The immensity of that river and its verdant, graceful banks, in cheerful contrast to the lugubrious desert, compelled Father De Smet's admiration. "One feels himself transported to the dawn of creation, when the world came forth from the hands of its Maker."

But every now and then a destructive cyclone would devastate these enchanted shores.

"One day when the wind was spending its fury, we witnessed at a short distance from us a marvelous spectacle. A huge, whirling, funnel-shaped cloud appeared in the

[5] Brother Claessens of Beerendrecht in the province of Antwerp, Brother Specht of Alsace, and Brother Huet of Courtrai.
[6] Letter to Father Verhaegen, from the banks of the Platte, June 2, 1841.
[7] Letter to Father Elet, from Soldier River, May 16, 1841.

heavens, tearing through the air with a deafening noise, carrying with it every object in its path; while clouds lying beyond the influence of the wind massed and whirled in an opposite direction. Had we been in the track of the cyclone the whole caravan would have been swept into nothingness. But the Almighty said to the winds, as to the waves, so far and no further.

"Above us, we saw the storm retreating majestically to the north, finally spending its force in the bed of the Platte. Then occurred another upheaval of nature: in an instant the river was lashed into a foaming torrent, from which the water rose in the form of a vast horn of plenty, its sinuous movements resembling a serpent rising on its tail; trees were uprooted and the land laid waste. Such violence, however, soon spends itself. Shortly all was over; the waterspout fell of its own weight as rapidly as it had risen; the sun came out, nature's forces calmed, and we continued our journey."[8]

Upon nearing the source of the great river, the travelers found more somber vegetation, rugged hills, and mountains towering into the clouds. Behind those summits dwelt the tribes destined soon to hear the word of God. Our missionary, uplifted by this thought, became a poet, expressing his rapture in the following hymn:

> "Oh, no! It is no shadow vain
> That greets my sight—yon lofty chain
> That pierces the eternal blue,
> The Rocky Mounts appear in view.
>
> "I've seen the spotless virgin snow,
> Glistening like gems upon their brow,
> And o'er yon giant peak now streams
> The golden light of day's first beams.
>
> "All hail, majestic Rock! the home
> Where many a wanderer yet shall come;
> Where God Himself from His own heart,
> Shall health and peace and joy impart.
>
> "Father and God! How far above
> All human thought Thy wondrous love;
> How strange the paths by which Thy hand
> Would lead the tribes of this bleak land,
> From darkness, crime, and misery,
> To live and reign in bliss with Thee!"

[8] Letter to Father Verhaegen, Sweetwater River, July 14, 1841.

After resting two days on the shores of the Green River, the caravan started again in the direction of Fort Hall, situated on Snake River and north of Salt Lake.

"The crossing of a river, with a retinue such as ours, was no small affair. Commending ourselves to God, we ordered the drivers to whip up the mules; the animals tugged and strained valiantly and gained the other bank. Our train of wagons then worked its way through a labyrinth of valleys and mountains, opening, as we went, a trail in the depth of a ravine, or through dense brush on the slope of a steep rock. At this juncture the mules were taken out and hitched abreast, then every man's shoulder went to the wheels, and every inch of rope was requisitioned to steady the convoy on the edge of the chasm, or keep it from a too rapid descent! Yet all these precautions did not save us from many tumbles. Our Brothers, forced by circumstances to take the reins, would often find themselves, one on a mule's neck, another on his hind quarters, and a third under the fore feet of the animal, not knowing how they got there, and each time thanking God for a miraculous escape.

"Those on horseback were accorded the same divine protection. During the journey Father Mengarini was six times thrown from his horse, Father Point almost as often, and once in full gallop I was pitched over my horse's head; yet none of us had so much as a scratch."[9]

At Fort Hall on the feast of the Assumption they met the advance-guard of the Flatheads, who had traveled over three hundred miles to come and meet the Black Robes. Among them was Young Ignatius, Father De Smet's guide of the previous year. Ignatius had been running for four days without food or drink in order to be the first to salute the missionaries.

Simon, the oldest member of the tribe, was also in the advance-guard. Although so worn with age that even when seated he leaned upon a cane for support, the ardor of his youth revived upon hearing of the approach of the Black Robes. "My children," said he, as he mounted his horse, "I am one of you; if I succumb on the way our

[9] Letter to Father Verhaegen, Fort Hall, Aug. 16, 1841.

Fathers will know in what cause I die." During the journey he was often heard to say: "Courage, my children, remember we go to meet the Black Robes!" Then lashing their steeds and following their intrepid leader, the cavalcade covered fifty miles a day.

Father De Smet's heart rejoiced when he found that the year's interval had in no way diminished the fervor of the Flatheads. The greater number, even old men and little children, knew by heart the prayers he had taught them. Twice on week-days, and three times on Sundays, during his absence had the tribe assembled to say prayers in common. The box containing vestments, and the altar service left in their charge the preceding year, were carried on high like the Ark of the Covenant each time the camp moved.

Many of those baptized died saintly deaths. A girl twelve years of age exclaimed at the moment of death: "How beautiful! How beautiful! I see the heavens opening and the Mother of God is calling me to come!" Then turning to those about her she said: "Heed what the Black Robes tell you, for they speak the truth; they will come and in this place erect a house of prayer."

see p. 128

Enemies of Catholicism vainly endeavored to sow dissension and distrust, by insinuating that the missionaries had no intention of returning. "You are mistaken," replied Big Face. "I know our Father; his tongue does not lie. He said, 'I will return,' and return he will."

The missionaries left the caravan three days after their arrival at Fort Hall, going north to the Flathead encampment. One of the braves sent Father De Smet his finest horse, with strict orders that no one should mount the steed before it was presented to the Black Robe.

On August 30th, four months after their departure from St. Louis, the missionaries arrived at their destination. "As we approached the camp we saw one courier after another advancing. A gigantic Indian then appeared, coming toward us at full gallop. Cries of 'Paul! Paul!' were heard, and it was in fact Paul [Big Face], so named in baptism the year before. They thought him absent from the camp, but he had just returned, wishing himself to present us to his people. Toward nightfall an affecting scene took place. The neophytes—men, women, young men, and children in arms—struggled with one another to be the first to shake hands with us; our hearts were too full for utterance. It was a great day."[10]

Upon his first visit to the Flatheads, Father De Smet had urged them to look about for a fertile tract of land where the tribe could settle. They lived, principally, upon the fruits of the chase; hence, it was neither feasible nor possible to suppress this means of subsistence until agricultural development could replace it. Nor did Father De Smet expect to transform instantly a wandering tribe into a sedentary people. Hunting, for some time to come, would have to remain their principal means of subsistence, but, instead of encampments continually following in the wake of the roaming buffalo, their movable lodges would be transformed into fixed abodes, where, after the day's hunt, the men could join their families and experience the softening influence of home life. The Indian thus would be drawn from idleness; he would learn economy, and unconsciously acquire the habits of civilization.

The proposition was enthusiastically received. The Flatheads chose a suitable site which the missionaries went to inspect, at the source of the Clarke River, and beyond a barren territory. In traversing these arid wastes, the Indians and missionaries lived on fish for eight days; but the horses suffered for want of food, not a blade of grass being found on that desolate soil. After twice crossing the ridge of the Rocky Mountains, the caravan at last entered the valley destined to be the home of this wandering tribe, and pitched their tents a few miles south of what is now the town of Missoula,* between Stevensville and Fort Owen. The Bitter Root River, which further on becomes the Clarke, watered this extraordinarily fertile region. The richness of the soil, the beauty of the situation, and the proximity of other tribes decided the missionaries to make this place the seat of the mission.

It was September 24th, the feast of Our Lady of Mercy,

[10] Letter to the Father General, Madison Fort, Aug. 15, 1842.

* *Translator's Note:* On the main line of the Northern Pacific Railroad, not far from the town of Missoula, Montana, one may catch a passing glimpse of a small way-station painted red and bearing the sign "De Smet," a sorry monument to the memory of so intrepid a pioneer.

and that same day Father De Smet erected a cross in the center of the camp. "I should have liked all who are zealous Christians to be present at this ceremony: it was a moving spectacle to see the Flatheads, from the chief to the youngest child, come to press their lips reverently upon the emblem of our salvation, and swear upon their knees to die a thousand deaths rather than abandon their religion."[11]

The solemn inauguration of the mission took place the first Sunday in October, the feast of Our Lady of the Rosary. The mission was placed under the patronage of the Blessed Virgin and called St. Mary's Mission. It was a solemn moment! The marvels of the primitive Church were about to be renewed in those mountains. The missionaries sank on their knees, imploring the help of heaven. "What can we do," they asked themselves, "to fulfil our vocation?" being fully convinced that God had especially chosen them for the conversion of an entire people.

The plan of evangelization adopted by these intrepid apostles merits more than a passing mention. We find it outlined in a letter which Father De Smet wrote to his Superior, Father Verhaegen.[12]

"The little nation of the Flatheads appear to us to be a chosen people, out of which a model tribe can be made; they will be the kernel of a Christianity that even Paraguay could not surpass in fervor.[13]

"We have greater resources for obtaining such results than had the Spanish Fathers. Remoteness from corrupt influences; the Indian's aversion to the other sects; his horror of idolatry; his liking for the white man, and for

[11] To the Father General, Madison Fork, Aug. 15, 1842.

[12] St. Mary of the Rocky Mountains, Oct. 26, 1841.

[13] The celebrated *Reductions* of Paraguay were founded upon the right bank of the Parana River at the beginning of the seventeenth century. Spanish Jesuits converted the natives, and taught them to till the soil. It was a sort of theocratic state comprising thirty-two cities inhabited by relatively 40,000 families. In 1767 the Jesuits were driven out of the Spanish possession and the destruction of the reductions followed. (Cf. "Histoire du Paraguay," by Father De Charlevoix, 3 Vols. in 4, Paris, 1756.)

Translator's Note: The employment of the word "reduction" in conveying the idea of systematized settlement has sprung from the use of the word as constantly applied to the groups or colonies above referred to in the historical records of the Jesuit Missions.

the Black Robe in particular, whose name for him is synonymous with goodness, learning, and piety; the central position of the mission; sufficient land for several settlements; fertile soil; the protection of high mountains; no meddlesome and petty authority conflicting with that of God and those who represent Him upon earth; no tribute to pay but our prayers; such are the advantages our mission enjoys. Furthermore, the Indians are convinced that without religion there is no happiness either in this life or in the world to come."

Father De Smet was of the opinion that they could not do better than model their mission upon the celebrated *reductions* of Paraguay. "The end those Fathers had in view, and the means employed to attain that end, were approved by the highest authority. Furthermore, the results obtained called forth the admiration even of our enemies."

After a careful study of the Muratori [14] Relation, Father De Smet believed he could develop in the neophytes the following virtues:

"First, *with regard to God:* A simple, firm, lively faith in the practices and precepts of religion. A profound respect for the only true religion and all that relates to it. Tender devotion and respect for the Virgin Mary and the saints. Desire of conversion of others. Fortitude in trials and suffering.

"*With regard to one's neighbor:* Respect for authority, for the aged, and respect for parents. Justice, charity, and generosity to all men.

"*With regard to one's self:* Humility, modesty, discretion, gentleness, pure living, and love of work."

But to attain this ideal, the Indians would have to be kept away from all bad influences. "Here in this place we are far removed from the corruption of the times, and from all that the Gospel implies in the term 'the world.' A great advantage we must safeguard, by a strict surveillance over all intercourse between the Indians and white men, extending our watchfulness even to the workmen we employ."

[14] An account of the Missions of Paraguay, translated from the Italian, Paris, 1754.

In order to preserve the language of the neophytes, the missionaries taught them in their mother tongue. The curriculum of the mission comprised reading, writing, arithmetic, and singing. "A more advanced course of teaching, it seems to me, would be prejudicial to the simplicity of these excellent Indians." Exceptions were made only in favor of those who promised to labor for the propagation of the faith.

"Father Point, our architect, has already drawn plans for the village, in the center of which will stand a church one hundred feet long and fifty feet front, with the priests' house and school adjoining. Around this central point will be grouped the dwelling-houses, workshops, stores, and other buildings of common utility, the farming land beginning on the outskirts of the village."

Religious exercises, singing, music, instructions, catechism, administration of the Sacraments, in fact the division of labor and the general organization of the congregation, conformed as closely as possible to the regulations of the Paraguay Mission. "Such," says Father De Smet, "are the rules we have drawn up for our community. We now await their approval or amendment by those who have God's interests at heart, and who by virtue of their position of authority receive graces that enable them to keep alive in us the true spirit of the Society of Jesus."

Hardly had the missionaries arrived at their destination, when they began the work of construction. Every man became a laborer. The Flatheads cut thousands of stakes in the forest and fenced in their property. The priests' house and farm-house rose as by enchantment. In less than five weeks a temporary church with "pediment, colonnade, balustrade, choir, seats, etc.," was erected in the exact spot designated by the young Indian girl of whose happy death we have spoken: "The Black Robes will come to this spot and will build a house of prayer."

On the feast of St. Martin the catechumens assembled and instructions preparatory to the reception of baptism were begun. A number of neophytes were to receive the Sacrament on December 3d, the feast of St. Francis Xavier, but a series of unfortunate happenings seemed to conspire to interfere with the ceremony. The interpreter and the sacristan fell ill; the organ, through some unforeseen accident, got out of order; a hurricane swept over the valley, uprooting trees, carrying away three tents, and breaking the church windows. Happily, however, on the evening of December 2d the storm ceased.

The Indians were lost in wonder and admiration when they beheld the decorations and arrangements of the sanctuary. "Festoons of green covered the walls. Above the altar, artistically draped, the holy name of Jesus stood out in relief upon a background of blue sky. A statue of the Blessed Virgin stood at the end of the choir; an image of the Sacred Heart adorned the door of the tabernacle. The flaming torches, the silence of the night, and the approach of dawn—all this moved the hearts and minds of the Indians already touched by grace, and nowhere, I think, could be found a similar gathering of elect souls."[15]

What a joy indeed for the missionaries, this offering to St. Francis Xavier, on his feast, the spectacle of two hundred men and women just emerging from barbarism, replying intelligently to their catechism questions, and praying with great fervor while receiving the Sacrament of Baptism; then retiring to their places, each carrying a lighted candle. Being obliged at times to speak through an interpreter, the missionaries were in the church from eight o'clock in the morning until ten o'clock at night, taking only one hour for dinner.

The following day was devoted to legalizing marriages. This occasion proved the neophytes to be profoundly imbued with the spirit of Christianity. Up to the present time many of the Indians had lived in complete ignorance of the unity and indissolubility of the marriage-bond; but now having learned to love God above all things, they generously made Him the sacrifice of their affections—the women rivaling the men in heroism. "I love you dearly," said one woman to her husband, a prey to hesitation and indecision, "and I know you love me; but you also love another. I am old, she is young. Leave the children with me and remain with her. In so doing we will please God, and all will receive baptism."

[15] Letter to Father Verhaegen, Dec. 30, 1841.

Father De Smet, at that time, was absent from the mission.[16] He returned December 8th and began at once the preparation of those who had not yet received baptism. Besides lessons in catechism taught by the other Fathers, Father De Smet gave three instructions daily to the catechumens, who learned so quickly, and showed such admirable dispositions, that on Christmas day he administered baptism to one hundred and fifty souls, and performed thirty-two marriages.

"I began the day by saying Mass at seven o'clock, and at five in the afternoon I was still in the chapel. The emotions my heart then experienced are but poorly expressed in words.

"The next day I sang a solemn High Mass in thanksgiving for the favors God had showered upon His people. Between six and seven hundred converts, counting the children baptized the previous year, assembled in the heart of the wilds, where until now the name of God was unknown, offering the Creator their regenerated hearts and promising fidelity to Him until death. Such devotion must be very pleasing in God's sight and will assuredly call down blessings upon the Flatheads and the neighboring tribes."[17]

The Blessed Virgin now deigned to manifest in a striking manner how pleasing to her was the simple faith and innocence of her new children. Shortly after midnight Mass on Christmas eve, the Mother of God appeared in the tent of a poor woman to a little orphan named Paul. "His exemplary childhood," writes Father De Smet, "his piety and candor, and the account he gave of the apparition, preclude all doubt of the truth of his statement. The following is what he told me in his own words: 'Upon entering John's tent, where I went to ask help with the prayers I do not yet know, I saw a wonderfully beautiful person raised above the ground, clad in raiment white as snow, a star upon her brow and a serpent at her feet; in her hand she held a fruit I have never seen before,[18]

[16] See following chapter, his journey to Fort Colville.
[17] To Father Verhaegen, Dec. 30, 1841.
[18] Would it be temerity to see in this apparition an anticipated declaration of the dogma of the Immaculate Conception?

and from her heart rays of light radiated toward me. I was frightened at first; then fear vanished, my heart was warm, my mind clear, and although I cannot say how it happened, suddenly I knew my prayers.' The child then told me the same beautiful person had appeared to him many times in his sleep, and that she told him that it would please her if the first Flathead village would be called St. Mary.

"The boy had never seen nor heard tell of visions, nor did he even know whether the apparition was a man or woman, as the clothes were unfamiliar to him. Questioned by several others, he gave the identical description of all that had happened. The child grew in virtue and was the angel of the tribe."[19]

One can imagine Father De Smet's joy and thankfulness when he could write his Provincial on December 30th: "The whole Flathead nation has been converted, and baptism administered to many Kalispels, Nez Percés, Cœur d'Alènes, Snakes, and Kootenais: other tribes are asking for us, and a vast country only awaits the arrival of the missionary to range itself under the banner of Jesus Christ. This, Reverend Father, is the gift we offer you at the close of the year 1841."

The newly-born mission became in three months a flourishing Christian colony, and as it was essential to keep up, through regular religious practices, the good dispositions of the Indians, a rule of life was outlined and strictly adhered to. The Angelus gave the signal for rising in the morning; half an hour later morning prayers were said in common, then followed Mass and instruction.

Everything was done to render these exercises attractive to the Indians. Father Point, gifted with remarkable talent for drawing, made highly-colored pictures of the mysteries of our religion, the history of God's people, and the life of Jesus Christ; the full, melodious voice of Father Mengarini intoning hymns which told of the happiness of a Christian life and the joys of eternity, moved the Indians'

[19] Letter to the Father General, Aug. 15, 1842. Father Point relates the same facts in almost the same words. (*Recollections of the Rocky Mountains* in The Woodstock Letters, 1883, p. 140.)

hearts to thankfulness for the graces God had poured forth upon their tribe.

The sick were visited in the morning, the Fathers administering remedies and comforting the sufferers with words of encouragement and counsel. Catechism was taught at two o'clock in the afternoon, the children being divided into two categories, according to age and the amount of instruction already received. The missionaries adopted the method of teaching and awarding of prizes in use in the Christian Brothers' schools. Night-prayers were said at sundown, followed by an hour's instruction.

The time spent in church seemed all too short to the Indians: "After prayers said in common," writes Father De Smet, "the Indians prayed and sang hymns in their homes; these pious exercises were prolonged often far into the night, and if awakening during the night they began again to pray."[20] On Sunday the religious exercises were protracted and more numerous, but the Fathers knew that these humble souls found happiness in speaking to their celestial Father, and that no place was so attractive to them as the house of God. "Sunday, the day of rest, was religiously observed, and even before the coming of the missionaries a timid deer could have stayed among the people in perfect safety, even when the Indians were starving for food. To shoot an arrow from his bow on Sunday was as great an enormity in the eyes of the Indian as gathering wood was to the Jews. But, as the former has a better understanding of the law of grace, he is less slave to the letter which kills, although no less faithful to the spirit."[21]

In dealing with such Christians, one could ask more of them than the ordinary practices of religion, hence a few months after the founding of the mission, pious associations were formed. The inhabitants of the village were divided into four groups, each group having its separate rules, its officers, and its meeting-days.

The congregation of men was called the Society of the Sacred Heart. The Prefect, an Indian called Victor, was,

[20] To the Carmelites of Termonde, Oct. 28, 1841.
[21] See in the accounts of St. Mary's Mission the interesting *Memoires* of Father Mengarini, published in The Woodstock Letters, November, 1888, February and June, 1889.

after the death of Big Face, raised to the dignity of chief. In the opinion of all, "he had the best head and the kindest heart in the village." His wife, Agnes, was elected President of the Society of the Blessed Virgin. His son became President of the Young Men's Society, and his daughter acted in the same capacity for the young girls.

Grace working in the souls of the new converts moved them to perform acts of heroic virtue. Peter, chief of the Pend d'Oreilles,[22] having on one occasion to defend his family from the attacks of a Blackfoot outlaw, afterward threw himself on his knees and prayed for his enemy. "Great Spirit," he prayed, "You know why I killed the Blackfoot. It was not revenge; it was necessary to make an example of this man, that others of his tribe may take warning. I entreat You to be merciful to him in the other life. We willingly pardon him the evil he wished to do us, and to prove that I speak the truth, I will cover him with my cloak."

What a victory over self, in a man whose supreme joy, before his conversion, had been to revenge himself upon his enemy with all the refinements of cruelty!

Twice a year some of the Flatheads left the village to hunt buffalo. Not wishing to leave before receiving baptism, the Indians remained at St. Mary's as long as a morsel of food was left to eat, and even the dogs, driven by famine, devoured the leather straps which tethered the horses at night. The departure for the winter's hunt took place December 29th, and the expedition prepared for an absence of several months. Father Point accompanied the wandering camp, not wishing to leave a part of the tribe so long without spiritual help, and because his presence would prevent the disorders the hunt usually occasioned.

The winter was a severe one. It snowed without interruption for three months. Many of the Indians were attacked by snow-blindness, and during a terrific storm Father Point nearly succumbed. Had not some hunters quickly lighted a fire when they saw him turn a ghastly pallor, he would have died of cold. The crowning trial was that they saw no buffalo.

[22] This chief was the celebrated Walking Bear, baptized the year before.

But neither cold, nor wind, nor snow, nor famine, prevented the Flatheads from accomplishing their spiritual devotions. Night and morning the camp assembled in and around the missionary's tent, the greater number having no shelter but the sky above them. Nevertheless, they were most attentive to the sermon, and sang the hymns which preceded and followed the prayers. At daybreak and at sunset a bell summoned the hunters to recite the Angelus. Sunday was strictly kept.

Such fidelity touched the heart of God, as we shall see from notes taken from Father Point's diary.

"*February 6th:* To-day is Sunday. Strong wind, gray sky, bitter cold; no hay for the horses; the buffalo driven off by the Nez Percés.

"*February 7th:* The cold more piercing, the aridity of the plain increases, the snow a great hindrance. Notwithstanding yesterday, the day of rest was sanctified, to-day perfect resignation. Courage! confidence!

"Toward midday we reached the summit of a high mountain. What a transformation! The sun was shining and the cold less penetrating. We saw an immense plain before us, good pasturage, and herds of buffalo. The expedition halted, the hunters assembled and set off for the chase. Before sunset one hundred and fifty-three buffaloes fell to their bag. If this find of buffaloes was not a miracle, it resembled greatly the miraculous draft of fish. In God's name Peter cast his net and brought to shore one hundred and fifty-three fish. Confident in the power of God and in His name the Flatheads brought down one hundred and fifty-three buffaloes."

Several Pend d'Oreilles joined the Flatheads. Despite the difficulties of a nomad's life and the rigors of the season, Father Point found means to instruct and baptize a number of Indians. At the approach of Easter the hunters returned to St. Mary's, and on Holy Saturday the whole tribe assembled in the mission church to sing the *Regina cœli*.

The time was now come to prepare the neophytes for their first communion. The faith and piety that characterized their reception of the Sacrament of Baptism was evident in the same degree in their preparation for the other two Sacraments. When told about confession, some wished it to be public. The impenetrable mystery of the Holy Eucharist they accepted without question: "Yes, Father, we believe truly and sincerely."

The feast of Pentecost was chosen for the great celebration. In order to give greater solemnity to the occasion a procession was formed; the missionaries, wearing surplices and preceded by a crucifix-bearer, marched ahead of the neophytes. Silently, in a spirit of recollection, they entered the church. The sanctity of the spot, the clouds of incense, and the singing of the hymns, moved the hearts of the neophytes, awakening within them emotions they had never felt before. As the moment of the consecration and communion approached, the poor savages, kneeling, with bowed heads, adored and thanked their God. He whom they had learned to love and whom their fathers had so long desired, had become the Guest of their transfigured souls!

In the spring of 1842 a succession of touching feasts took place. The Rocky Mountains witnessed for the first time the month of May devotions, the celebration of the feast of the Sacred Heart, and the procession of the Blessed Sacrament. The fervor of the Indians was such that numbers were permitted to receive holy communion frequently. "There are entire families," writes Father De Smet, "who approach the holy table every Sunday. Often we hear twenty consecutive confessions without finding matter for absolution."[23]

The old chief Big Face was no longer witness of these wonders. He died during that same winter, after having, at ninety years of age, made his first communion.

"Have you no sins to repent of since your baptism?" asked the missionary.

"Sins?" he replied, astounded. "How could I commit sins when it is my duty to teach others to live well?"

He was buried wrapped in the flag he waved every Sunday to announce the Lord's Day. He also could chant his *Nunc Dimittis*, for he had lived to see his tribe a Christian people, practicing, in the heart of the desert, the highest Christian virtues.

[23] Letter to the Father General, Aug. 15, 1842.

CHAPTER VIII

ONE month after his arrival at St. Mary's, Father De
Smet was obliged to leave his fellow-missionaries to
go to Fort Colville on the Columbia River, about three
hundred miles northwest of the mission. The journey
was undertaken with two objects in view:

First, the needs of the colony, which was in dire poverty.
Brother Specht was clothed in a garment made of animal
skins, and one of the Fathers had been obliged to transform
an Indian blanket into a cassock. Moreover, provisions
for the winter, seeds for the spring crops, tools, agricultural
implements, beeves, cows, in a word all that was needed for
the establishment of a "reduction," had to be purchased.

The second object of his journey was to visit the Kalispels
(a tribe allied to the Pend d'Oreilles) who camped in the
autumn on the borders of the Clarke River.[1]

Father De Smet had left St. Mary's October 28th, escorted by ten Flathead warriors. On the feast of All
Saints he reached the principal camp of the Kalispels,

---

[1] The Kalispels were also called the Pend d'Oreilles of the Bay to distinguish them from the Pend d'Oreilles of the Mountains, who had been
visited by Father De Smet when he visited the Flatheads.

where he was enthusiastically received; and what was his surprise that evening to hear them recite night prayers, and to learn that this tribe was in a way converted before ever having seen a missionary!

The mystery was soon solved. Having heard the previous year of the arrival of a Black Robe in the mountains, the Kalispels sent an intelligent young Indian, possessing an excellent memory, to visit the Flatheads. In their camp he learned the prayers, the hymns, and the great truths of our religion, and upon his return was made the apostle of the tribe. His instructions were handed on from one lodge to the other, and before the winter was over, more than half the tribe was Christian.

Overjoyed at the admirable attitude of these people, Father De Smet at once baptized the children and the sick of the tribe, and when taking leave of the Kalispels he promised to send a priest who would remain with them.

His journey along the banks of the Clarke brought him to a gigantic chain of rocks. "I have been in many bad places," he writes, "but never before have I encountered such difficulties as this pass presented. Impossible to cross it on horseback, on foot it was equally out of the question, as I should have been exhausted before getting over." He then had recourse to an expedient that recalled the adventures of his youth. "Remembering I had in my caravan a gentle and staid old mule, I proceeded to take hold of its tail, and held on tight. Urged on by cries and the generous use of the whip, it patiently dragged me to the summit. For the descent I changed my position and hung on to the reins. The animal, descending step by step, landed me safely on the other side."[2]

The next day he entered a vast forest of pines and cedars, through which he traveled for three days. "This forest," writes the missionary, " is a marvel of its kind. The Indians tell me it is the finest forest in Oregon. It would, in fact, be difficult to find elsewhere such gigantic trees. The cedar towers majestically in a wilderness of birch, alder, and beech. I measured one forty-two feet in circumference; another fallen cedar lay two hundred feet

[2] Letter to one of the Fathers of the Society of Jesus, St. Mary's, Dec. 8, 1841.

along the ground. The branches of these colossi, inter-laced above the birch and beech trees, form a canopy so dense that the sun's rays never reach the moss and lichen-covered earth. A thousand trunks rising like so many columns to a green dome form a temple erected by nature to the glory of its Creator."[3]

Upon emerging from the forest one catches sight of Kalispel Lake with its islands and pine-trees, its sloping shores, its horizon of hills, one above the other, reaching up to summits of eternal snow.

For the missionary, however, the most entrancingly beautiful view is as nothing compared to the joy of gaining a soul for God. "One day, from the declivity of a hill upon which I was standing, I saw upon the river-bank a little log hut. I called several times—no reply. Feeling drawn to visit the hut, I descended, accompanied by an interpreter. We found there a poor old woman, very ill, and blind. I spoke to her about the Great Spirit, of what one must do to obtain salvation, of baptism, etc. The apostle St. Philip tells us that there are cases in which all the necessary dispositions are found in an act of faith and a sincere desire to know truth. The poor woman's replies breathed respect and love of God. 'Yes,' said she, 'I love God with all my heart. During my whole life He has cared for me. I wish to be His child and belong to Him forever.' The poor creature then fell on her knees and begged for baptism. I administered the Sacrament, giving her the name of Mary, and hung a medal of the Blessed Virgin around her neck. When leaving her hut and even at some distance away, I still heard her thanking God for this inestimable favor.

"Hardly had I regained the small mountain path when I met the woman's husband. Bent under the weight of years and infirmity, the wretched man could scarcely drag himself along. He was in the forest setting a deer-trap when my men told him of my coming. The poor Indian hurried as best he could, and catching sight of me, cried out from afar in a trembling voice: 'What happiness to see our Father before I die! The Great Spirit is good.

[3] Letter to one of the Fathers of the Society of Jesus, St. Mary's, Dec. 8, 1841.

I am now at peace!' The good man shook my hand effusively, repeating again and again the same words. I told him I had visited his hut and baptized his wife.

"'I heard of your arrival last year in the mountains,' he said, 'and that you had baptized many people there. I am old and poor; I never hoped to have the joy of seeing you. Black Robe, give me the happiness you have just given my wife. I also wish to belong to God, and will love Him forever.'

"I baptized the Indian in a torrent near-by, giving him the name of Simon. Continuing on my way, I heard him repeating, 'Oh! how good God is! I thank you, Black Robe, for the happiness you have procured me. My heart is at peace! Yes, I will love God always. How good God is! How good God is!' In that moment not for a kingdom would I have changed places with any one on earth. Such a meeting is, of itself, worth a journey to the mountains."

A little farther on another consolation awaited Father De Smet. He discovered in a miserably poor hut five old Kalispel Indians over eighty years of age. Three of them were blind, the other two had only one eye. They were pictures of human misery. "I spoke to them," he tells us, "of the necessity of salvation and the happiness of the future life. Their replies moved me to tears. All five of them, from different corners of the hut, cried out: 'O God! What happiness has come to us in our old age! We love You, Lord! and will continue to love You until death!' When I explained the necessity of baptism, they fell upon their knees to receive the Sacrament."

In order to awaken apostolic zeal in the souls of his fellow-priests Father De Smet addressed them in burning words that recall St. Francis Xavier's impassioned outpourings:

"Oh! good and beloved Fathers in Europe, in God's name I conjure you to come without delay to labor in this vineyard! The harvest is ripe and plentiful. The eagerness of these tribes to hear the Word of God is almost beyond belief. From every direction, and I mean by that, from great distances, they come, asking me to baptize their children. Many have followed me for a whole day, with the sole object of listening to the instructions. Everywhere I go, the old people beg for baptism. My heart aches at the thought of so many souls left to perish for lack of priests to instruct them. Of this place one can truly say: *Messis quidem multa, operarii autem pauci.*[4] Does there exist in the Society of Jesus a priest whose heart would not kindle with zeal at these words? Does a Christian exist who would refuse to contribute to such work as that of the Propagation of the Faith?

"Certainly the life of a missionary has its trials and dangers; yet, however great these may be, he guards the serenity of his soul by centering his mind upon God. The desert is immense and the journey across it monotonous. The howling of the wolves, the grunting of the bear, and the screams of the wildcat and panther are heard, but only in the distance, for these wild beasts flee at the sight of man. Providence has provided admirably for the needs of those who inhabit the wilderness; buffalo, deer, gazelle, roebuck, bighorn, and elk roam here in thousands. Yet a fast of a day or two—I speak from experience—gives zest to appetite. Should a storm keep one awake, one sleeps better the following night. The sight of the enemy lying in wait to take one's life teaches more confidence in God; teaches one to pray well, and to keep his account with God in order; but an abiding and grateful joy succeeds these disquieting moments, and I hope yet to learn what it is to suffer for the sweet name of Jesus. Here, in all its force, one experiences the truth of those divine words: *Jugum meum suave est, et onus meum leve.*"[5]

On November 14th, Father De Smet arrived at Fort Colville, the property of the Hudson Bay Fur Company. The commander, a Scotchman, welcomed the missionary, and furnished him with all the cattle he wanted, also foodstuffs and seeds. Furthermore, he added to the supplies (unknown to Father De Smet) a number of delicacies, such as sugar, coffee, tea, chocolate, butter, crackers, flour, poultry, etc. Four days later Father De Smet set out upon his return journey to the Bitter Root.[6] He arrived

---

[4] "The harvest indeed is great, but the laborers are few."—(Matt. ix, 37.)

[5] "My yoke is sweet and My burden light." (Matt. xi, 30.) Letter cited.

[6] An amusing incident happened which convinced our missionary that daughters of Eve exist in every latitude. "We had left five bales of dried meat with the Pend d'Oreilles. Finding but two upon my return, I enquired

at St. Mary's on the feast of the Immaculate Conception, December 8th, and was received with cheers and acclamations of joy by his dear Flatheads. He had been absent forty-two days, and during his journey had baptized one hundred and ninety souls and preached the Gospel to over two thousand Indians.

The missionary brought back from Fort Colville several bushels of oats, wheat, and potatoes for planting. Brother Claessens had already plowed an enclosed piece of land adjoining the mission, and in the spring he sowed the seeds and planted the potatoes.

The Indians, filled with wonder at this proceeding, thought it folly to plow and destroy grass that fed their horses and to bury seeds that were good to eat. In vain Brother Claessens assured them the seeds would rot in the ground and produce a hundredfold. No one believed him. When things began to sprout in the spring the Flatheads remained whole days at a time perched upon the fence to see if what was told them would come true. Shouts of joy greeted the first blades that appeared above the ground. Before long the ears formed upon the tender stalks, and when summer came the enclosure resembled a huge basket overflowing with golden harvest. The crops were divided among the Indians, who now could appreciate the advantage derived from tilling the soil. The missionaries seized this occasion to explain to them the mystery of the resurrection of the body.

In the spring of 1842 provisions again ran short. Unable, this time, to obtain them from Fort Colville, Father

---

of the chief what had become of the rest. 'Black Robe,' he said, 'I am ashamed and afraid to tell you. I was absent when you put your bales in my tent. My wife opened one to see if the meat was moldy. The fat looked so good and tempting! She tasted it, and when I returned offered it to me and the children. Soon the news spread through the village; the neighbors flocked in and we ate it all up.'

"Had the worthy man wished to repeat anew the story of our first parents, he did full justice to his rôle. This incident furnished me the occasion to instruct the Indians on original sin and its disastrous consequences. The chief then arose, and after severely reprimanding his wife, protested in the name of the tribe that a similar occurrence would never again happen." (Letter cited.)

De Smet journeyed to Fort Vancouver near the mouth of the Columbia, and about a thousand miles west of St. Mary's. This journey was destined to play a part in the religious future of Oregon that Father De Smet then little dreamed of.

Leaving St. Mary's Mission April 13th, he visited the Kalispels in passing, and while there preached to the tribe and strengthened them in their good resolutions. Further on, he came upon the camp of the Kootenais. This tribe had never seen a priest; but from an Iroquois who had been thirty years in their camp, they learned the principal articles of faith. Father De Smet baptized the infants, and the adults who had received some instruction.

After crossing the Bitter Root Mountains he came to the country of the Cœur d'Alènes, a fertile, lovely valley stretching westward hundreds of miles. Clusters of dark pines and cedars emerged from the green plain, in the center of which lay a lake well stocked with fish. A river ran through the valley, and to the north, east, and south snow-capped mountains pierced the clouds. Formerly the Cœur d'Alènes were considered the most barbarous and degraded of the mountain tribes; they adored animals, and lived in complete ignorance of God, the soul, and a future life. Even the precepts of natural law were but vaguely understood and pretty generally offended against in practice. About 1830, an Iroquois Catholic, it is supposed, taught them the first elements of Christianity. Shortly after this date, the tribe suffered the ravages of a violent epidemic. When the plague was at its height, a dying man heard a voice saying: "Leave your idols, adore Jesus Christ, and you will be cured." He obeyed, and was restored to health. Then, making a tour of the camp, the restored man related what had taken place and entreated his stricken brethren to follow his example. They did so and all likewise were cured.[7] This event produced a profound impression on the Cœur d'Alènes, but without a priest to further instruct them, a few of the tribe returned to the worship of idols;

[7] Father Point, who relates this fact, adds: "I heard the above from the lips of the Indian to whom it happened, who wept tears of gratitude in relating it. Furthermore, eye-witnesses confirmed his statement." (Cf. De Smet, "Missions de l'Oregon," p. 243; Father Point, *Recollections of the Rocky Mountains* in "The Woodstock Letters," 1883, p. 153.)

the conduct of many, however, since the revelation of the true God, had remained irreproachable.

Such was the condition of the Cœur d'Alènes when Father De Smet visited the tribe in 1842. "I was conducted in triumph to the lodge of the chief," he tells us, "and there, as in every other Indian camp, the calumet was brought forth. After it had been handed around several times and smoked in solemn silence the chief addressed me in the following words:

"'Black Robe, welcome to our country. Long have we desired to see you and be enlightened by your words. Our fathers worshiped the earth and the sun. I remember distinctly the day we first heard of the one and only true God. Since then it is to Him we have addressed our prayers and supplications, and yet we are much to be pitied. We do not know the teachings of the Great Spirit, and we sit in darkness. But now I hope you have come to bring us light. I have finished. Speak, Black Robe! Every ear is open and eager to hear your words.'

"During the two hours in which I spoke to them of salvation and the end of man, absolute silence and stillness reigned. The sun was just setting, and I recited the prayer I had some days before translated into their tongue. Refreshments were then offered, consisting of scraps of dried meat, a black moss cake that tasted like soap, and a glass of river-water, all of which were as nectar and ambrosia to a man who had not tasted food since sunrise. The chiefs expressing a desire to hear me again, I continued to instruct the tribe until far into the night, pausing every half-hour to hand around the calumet and give time for reflection. During these pauses the chiefs conversed about what they had just heard, explaining it to their subordinates.

"Upon awakening in the morning I found my tent invaded by Indians who had slipped in before dawn. Getting up at once, I knelt down, the Indians following my example, and together we offered our day and our hearts to God. 'Black Robe,' said the chief, 'we came here early this morning to watch you and imitate you. Your prayer is good, and we wish to adopt it. But you will stay here only two nights, and we have no one to teach it to us.' I rang the bell for morning prayers, and promised the chief they all would know the prayer before my departure."[8]

Then it was that Father De Smet laid down the method that would henceforth be used for teaching the tribes their prayers. He assembled the Indians, ranging the children in a circle, with instructions to keep the same place at every reunion. Then each one was made to learn a phrase of the prayer by heart. Two children repeated the Hail Mary, seven the Our Father, ten the Commandments, and twelve the Apostles' Creed. After repeating to each child his particular phrase until he knew it by heart, the missionary then made them recite the phrases each in turn. This made a continued prayer, which the tribe listened to night and morning. After a few days one of the chiefs knew all the prayers by heart, and from that time he recited them for the tribe.

Two days after his arrival at the Cœur d'Alène camp, Father De Smet baptized the children, the sick, and the old men and women of the tribe. It seemed as though God had only kept these last on earth to accord them this supreme favor. In listening to their expressions of joy and gratitude one seemed to hear again Simeon's praises to the Lord.

Torn with regret, the missionary took leave of his new Christians, promising to send them a priest to complete their instruction. "Never has a visit to the Indians given me so much consolation, and nowhere have I seen such unmistakable proof of true conversion, not even excepting the Flatheads in 1840." The future but confirmed his judgment, for the Cœur d'Alènes remained the most industrious and Christian of the mountain tribes.

Father De Smet then visited the Spokanes, who were eager for religious knowledge, and from there he went to Fort Colville. The melting of the snow having occasioned great floods, he was unable to travel overland to Vancouver. While his guides and followers were constructing a boat in which to make the journey on the Columbia, Father De Smet visited the Chaudières or Kettle Indians, and the Okinagans camped on the other side of the river.

[8] Letter to the Father General, Madison Fork, Aug. 15, 1842.

Young and old came running to him, all eager to receive instruction, and quickly applied themselves to learning the prayers. Here again the missionary could do no more than baptize the children and the sick. "Had we but a few more priests," he writes, "and the means of getting farming implements for the Indians, all the mountain tribes would soon be Catholic."[9]

On May 30th he set out on his journey to Vancouver. Numerous rapids and submerged rocks render navigation on the Columbia extremely dangerous, and once more Father De Smet was to experience that marvelous protection which accompanied him throughout all his travels.

"I had gone ashore," he tells us, "and was walking on the river-bank, little dreaming of the catastrophe that threatened. The men pushed out into the stream, and seeing them leisurely pulling along and singing as they bent to their oars, I began to regret having preferred a stony path on the edge of a rock to the smoothness of the river. Suddenly the prow struck, throwing the men almost out of their seats. Righting themselves quickly, they attempted to move off, when the boat was caught in a whirlpool. The river was white with foam, and above the roar of the waters I heard the pilot urging the men to row. Alas! it was all in vain. The boat whirled around in the maelstrom, its prow rose in the air, and then it plunged into the abyss.

"A cold sweat broke out all over me, and for the moment all was a blur. A cry, 'We are lost!' told me the fate of my men. Unable to render aid, I stood there helpless, a petrified spectator of the awful scene. No trace of the accident was visible in the spot where the boat had disappeared, but, as the waters calmed, I beheld the men in a life-and-death struggle. The oars, the mast, the upturned boat, with its contents, floated about upon the water. The men battled with the whirlpool that, forming again, engulfed five of the crew—forever. My interpreter twice touched bottom and thought himself lost, when, with a prayer on his lips, he landed safely on the bank. An Iroquois was saved by clinging to my bed; a third man

9 Letter to Francis De Smet, Fort Colville, May 25, 1842.

had the luck to grasp the handle of an empty trunk which kept him afloat until he could reach shore."[10]

The rest of the journey passed without incident. Father De Smet had the happiness of baptizing several children of the various tribes he visited, and on June 8th he arrived at Fort Vancouver.

The territory of Oregon at that time comprised the whole region lying between the Rocky Mountains and the Pacific Ocean.[11] The situation of that vast country and the grandeur of its scenery were unsurpassed. To the west lay the Pacific, with its deep bays and steep cliffs. A horizon of pine-clad hills marked the eastern boundary, behind which towered the great Rocky Mountain chain, its peaks shrouded in eternal snows. The country abounded with green valleys, sapphire lakes, and boundless prairies. Great rivers became cataracts, dashing down into deep and dark ravines.

Until the beginning of the last century, Oregon, to the white man, was an unexplored land. The Hudson Bay Company was the first to discover and exploit its richness.[12] The fertility of the soil, its rich vegetation, and the harvest of priceless furs to be obtained from every variety of animal, attracted bold and venturesome merchants, among whom were several Catholic Canadians.

In 1824, John McLoughlin, a man of undisputed ability, was appointed Governor of the Hudson Bay Company posts in Oregon.[13] Agents who had finished their years of service were permitted to locate in the country, and were given land, principally upon Willamette River. This colony, not wishing to be deprived of the helps and consolations of their religion, asked for a Catholic priest.

[10] Letter to the Father General, Madison Fork, Aug. 15, 1842.

[11] For a long time this country was disputed territory. The Oregon question was settled by the Powers in 1846. All land south of the 49th degree of latitude was given to the United States, and the rest became British possessions.

[12] The Hudson Bay Fur Company, founded in 1670, with its principal headquarters in Montreal, had the monopoly of all trade west of the British possessions and in Oregon. In the latter country the company had several trading-posts, the most important being Fort Vancouver.

[13] Born in Canada in 1784, Dr. McLoughlin was educated in Paris, and at an early age entered the service of the Hudson Bay Company. Brought up a Protestant, he later in life embraced the Catholic faith, and from that time his influence and services were always at the disposal of the missionaries.

In 1838 the Archbishop of Quebec obtained passage for two Canadian missionaries, Francis Norbert Blanchet, and Modeste Demers, on one of the Fur Company's boats. Francis Norbert Blanchet was appointed Vicar General, with jurisdiction over the whole country situated west of the mountains. The missionaries journeyed for several months over lakes and rivers before reaching the Rocky Mountains, from where they descended into the Columbia valley, where they found Protestant missionaries already installed.

As far back as 1834, Methodists, Presbyterians, and Anglicans swarmed into Oregon, each denomination establishing its own churches. The zeal of the Catholic missionaries accomplished prodigies in an effort to combat the work of these sects. Catholic churches were erected at Vancouver, Willamette, and at Cowlitz. Christian piety being revived, Canadian trappers were rescued from the disorders of a life of adventure; and the Indian was not forgotten.

In order to reach the tribes Father Demers retraced his steps and went up the Columbia to Walla Walla and Colville. But what were two priests in the vast work of converting a population of 200,000 souls, scattered over an area aggregating nine hundred miles in length and six hundred miles in width?

Hearing that Father De Smet, with five other missionaries, had arrived in the mountains, Father Blanchet hastened to acquaint him with the conditions existing in Oregon. "You can readily see," he says, in concluding his letter, "how timely the arrival of one of your Fathers and a lay Brother would be. In my opinion, this place is where the religious foundations in this part of the country should be laid: a college, a convent, and schools are an absolute necessity. This is the battle-ground, here we must conquer, and here the first large mission should be established. From central posts missionaries could visit the outlying posts, distributing the Bread of life to infidels still plunged in the darkness of death." [14]

---

[14] Fort Vancouver, Sept. 28, 1841. Dr. McLoughlin seconded Father Blanchet in this matter. "After many years' experience I am fully convinced that the most efficacious means of spreading Catholicity in this part

Going, some months later, to Fort Vancouver to revictual St. Mary's Mission, Father De Smet was able to investigate for himself the condition of the missions in Western Oregon. At St. Paul on the Willamette he met the Canadian missionaries.[15] Plans for Christianizing the country were discussed and decided upon. Father De Smet realized the necessity of establishing a large mission in Western Oregon, where civilization was rapidly advancing, and from where Catholicism would penetrate into the mountains. But alas! men and money were wanting. The Fathers from St. Louis hardly sufficed for the needs of the new converts, and, moreover, that immense territory required not one but many missionaries. Sisters were also needed to undertake the Christian education of the children.

Father De Smet decided to go himself to his Superior to plead the cause of the Oregon Mission, resolved that, failing to obtain help in St. Louis, he would seek it in Europe. A few days later the missionaries separated, as Father De Smet was eager to return to St. Mary's with the provisions, tools, and clothes he had purchased at Vancouver for the mission. He arrived there July 27th.

The Flatheads, accompanied by Father Point, were absent on the summer hunting expedition; Father Mengarini guarded the old people and the children left in camp during their absence. Without delay, Father De Smet departed to join the hunters, and on August 15th he celebrated Mass in a beautiful plain watered by the Madison: "I wanted to thank God for the many favors accorded me during the past year. I had the consolation of seeing fifty Flatheads approach the holy table. In their humility and devotion they resembled angels more than men."[16]

The missionary would have liked to linger and enjoy the

---

of the world would be the establishment of a large mission for the colonists at Willamette and Cowlitz. The Indian imitates the white man, and if one of your Fathers and a lay Brother could come here to labor with Fathers Blanchet and Demers until reinforcements arrive from Canada, it would be an immense gain for religion." (Vancouver, Sept. 27, 1841.)

[15] When Father De Smet found himself in the presence of the Vicar General, the humble religious fell upon his knees to ask his blessing. Father Blanchet, beholding Father De Smet, sank upon his knees to ask the same favor. Father Demers, a witness of this touching scene, liked to tell of it in after-life.

[16] Letter to the Father General, Madison Fork, Aug. 15, 1842.

fervor of his neophytes, but duty called him elsewhere. Father Mengarini was left in charge of the Flatheads and Pend d'Oreilles. Father Point, upon the return of the hunting expedition, was to go with Brother Huet to establish a mission for the Cœur d'Alènes. The missionary himself started out for the fourth time to cross the American desert, again in search of recruits for the mission.

Father De Smet's escort consisted of ten Indians. They crossed two mountain chains and made one hundred and fifty miles in three days across a country infested with Blackfeet, without, however, encountering one of the tribe. Then came a few days' rest with a friendly tribe before setting out for the Crows.

"The Crows spied us from afar, and when they recognized us cried out 'the Black Robe! the Black Robe!' Men, women, and children to the number of about three thousand poured out of their huts like bees out of a hive. My entry into the village occasioned a wild scene, of which I found myself, *ex abrupto*, the principal actor. The chiefs and highest braves, numbering about fifty in all, suddenly pressed around me, impeding my passage, one pulling me to the right. another to the left; a third held my cassock, and an athlete wished to carry me, all talking at once and appearing to be quarreling.

"Not understanding the language, I wondered if I should laugh or be serious. Happily, the interpreter relieved my embarrassment, telling me that this tumult was but an expression of politeness and high regard for my person. All solicited the honor of feeding and lodging the Black Robe. Acting upon the interpreter's advice, I chose my host. The others immediately fell back as I followed the chief into his lodge, the largest and most splendid one in the camp. Then the Crows began to pour into the lodge, offering me every conceivable attention. The social calumet, symbol of Indian unity and brotherhood, was kept lighted and passed around to the entire assembly."[17]

[17] "These Indians," wrote Father De Smet, "are without doubt the most enquiring, the most eager for instruction, the cleverest and most civilized of the Western tribes, and, furthermore, great friends and admirers of the

"Wild with joy, the Indians declared this to be the greatest day of their lives. They entreated me to take pity upon the tribe and remain to teach them and their children to know and serve the Great Spirit. I promised them a Black Robe, on condition that the chief would undertake to abolish thieving, so frequent among them, and reform the degrading corruption of morals that reigned in his tribe.

"These Indians have one thing in their favor upon which I base great hopes: So far they have resisted the efforts of American merchants to introduce intoxicating liquors into their tribe. 'What is your fire-water good for?' said the chief. 'It only does evil. It burns the throat and stomach and makes a bear of a man: he bites, growls, yells, and finally falls down like a dead body. Take this liquor to our enemies; they will kill each other, leaving their wives and children in a pitiable condition. We do not want whiskey. We are crazy enough without it.'

"Before departing I witnessed a touching scene. The chief asked to see my crucifix. Taking advantage of the occasion I told them about Our Lord's sufferings, why He gave His life for us, at the same time putting the crucifix into his hands. Reverently he kissed it, and pressing the image of Our Saviour to his breast, with eyes lifted toward heaven, cried out: 'Oh, Great Spirit, have pity upon Thy children, and show them mercy.'"[18]

After leaving the Crows' camp, Father De Smet, with

white man. They plied me with questions, and among others wished to know the population of the white man. 'Count,' said I, 'the blades of grass in your vast prairie and you will then have some idea of their number.' This occasioned general mirth. No such thing was possible, they said, but they nevertheless understood what I meant. I then told them of the white man's villages—London, Paris, etc.; of towers high as mountains, and churches vast enough to contain all the Crows and Blackfeet at one time; of the streets in these great villages filled with hurrying men and women in more compact masses than the buffaloes ranging their prairies. Such marvels left them speechless with wonder; and when I described moving tents drawn by a machine that vomited forth smoke and outdistanced the fleetest horse; boats that traversed the ocean, transporting in a few days the inhabitants of an entire village from one country to another; men rising in the air and soaring in the clouds like mountain eagles, their astonishment knew no bounds. Closing their hands over their mouths, they emitted screams indicating admiration. 'The Master of life is great,' said the chief, 'and the white men are His favorites.'"

[18] Letter to Francis De Smet, St. Louis, Nov. 3, 1842.

Young Ignatius, a half-breed named Gabriel, and two Protestant Americans, entered once more the valley of the Yellowstone, then infested with wild tribes. The perpetual warfare carried on between the Blackfeet, Sioux, Cheyennes, and Assiniboins made it the most dangerous spot in the wild Western country.

"After traveling six days we arrived at the scene of a recent massacre. About us lay the bloody remains of ten Assiniboins massacred three days before, their bodies already half devoured by wolves and birds of prey. The sight of these remains and the vultures circling over our heads filled me with secret terror; the little courage I possessed seemed to abandon me, although I tried to conquer this feeling and hide it from my companions. Each step but increased it, coming as we did upon fresh traces of men and horses, unmistakable signs of the proximity of the enemy. Our guide feared we were already discovered, but thought by proceeding cautiously we would escape pursuit.

"The next day the following line of march was adopted. At daybreak we were in the saddle. At ten o'clock a halt of an hour or two, a place being carefully chosen, offering some defence in case of attack. Then we started off again, going at a brisk trot until sundown. After the evening meal, in order to deceive the enemy, we built a big fire, hurriedly erected a cabin out of branches of trees, after which we got on our horses and rode until ten or eleven o'clock at night. We then dismounted and without fire or shelter rested as best we could."

The travelers at last reached the Missouri River and remained several days at Fort Union. The long trip across an arid desert had exhausted the horses, and yet eighteen hundred miles lay between the missionary and St. Louis. So Father De Smet, with Ignatius and Gabriel, procured a boat and in this frail bark abandoned themselves to the swift current of the Missouri.

"This time we were in luck. The third day out we heard a steamboat in the distance, and before long it hove in sight. Our first thought was to thank God for this present favor. The proprietors of the boat, as well as the captain, generously invited us to come aboard. I accepted thankfully, all the more when I learned that warring tribes were in hiding all along the river. The water was low, the snags and sand-bars frequent, and the boat was often in danger of being wrecked. Submerged rocks broke the paddle-wheels, a hurricane overturned the pilot's house, which would have been swept into the water had cables not been quickly attached, and after forty-six days of perilous navigation a skeleton of a boat landed us at St. Louis.

"The last Sunday in October found me kneeling before the Blessed Virgin's altar in the cathedral, thanking God for the protection He had accorded His unworthy servant. From the beginning of April I had covered five thousand miles; had been up and down the Columbia River, where five of my men perished before my eyes; I had been the length of the entire desert of the Yellowstone and descended the Missouri to St. Louis; and in this long voyage I had never received a scratch nor wanted for the necessities of life. *Dominus memor fuit nostri et benedixit nobis.*"[19]

[19] "The Lord hath been mindful of us and hath blessed us." (Ps. cxiii, 12.) Letter quoted.

CHAPTER IX

SECOND VOYAGE TO EUROPE (1843–1844)

Fathers De Vos and Adrian Hoecken are Sent to the Mountains—Father De Smet and Daniel O'Connell—A National Meeting—Journey to Rome—Father De Smet Received by the Pope—Gregory XVI Wishes to Make Him a Bishop—New Missionaries—Sisters of Notre Dame—From Antwerp to Vancouver around the Horn—A Seven Months' Journey—Storms, Shortage of Food, Reefs.

FATHER DE SMET remained in St. Louis only a few days, for he was eager to set about sending missionaries to the Rocky Mountains and to Oregon. Informed of the needs of the mission, Father Verhaegen, Vice-Provincial of Missouri, appointed two priests and a Brother to join Fathers Point and Mengarini. These were Father Peter De Vos, former Master of Novices at Florissant, Father Adrian Hoecken, the brother of Christian Hoecken, apostle to the Potawatomies, and Brother MacGean.[1]

Men were not sufficient: money was needed, and this the St. Louis Fathers were unable to furnish.[2] So Father De Smet again set about raising funds, and after publishing an account of his journeys,[3] started on a begging tour, visiting in turn New Orleans, Boston, Louisville, Cincinnati, Pittsburg, Cumberland, Baltimore, Washington, Philadelphia, and New York. By the end of the winter he had collected five thousand dollars, a sum sufficient to

---

[1] In Father De Smet's absence, Father De Vos was appointed Superior of the mission.

[2] "We are up to our eyes in debt," writes Father Van de Velde, "and God alone knows how we shall be able to extricate ourselves. The assistance formerly received from Belgium and Holland has decreased, and our expenses increase in the measure our resources diminish." (Letter to Mr. De Nef, St. Louis, Jan. 10, 1843.)

[3] "Letters and Sketches, with a Narrative of a Year's Residence among the Indian Tribes of the Rocky Mountains," Philadelphia, 1843.

defray the expense of the journey of the new missionaries, and to purchase necessities for the development of the colony.

In May, 1843, Father De Smet accompanied Father De Vos and his companions as far as Westport, and himself directed the departure of the caravan, happy to be able to send such a reinforcement to his beloved Indians.

But what were three missionaries in the work of evangelizing such a vast country? Since the American provinces were unable to furnish priests, Father De Smet decided to seek them in Europe, and on June 7th he sailed with Bishop Hughes, that valiant metropolitan, who was journeying to Rome. Dating from that voyage, an intimate and lasting friendship existed between the prelate and the missionary. On June 28th Father De Smet landed in Ireland, and there made the acquaintance of Daniel O'Connell, that great man that personified unshaken faith in the just claims of his unhappy country. The labors of Bishop Hughes in behalf of the Irish immigrants and the many organizations of which he was the very soul, assured him a cordial welcome from O'Connell. The Bishop himself introduced the "Apostle of the Indians" to the great agitator. The next day a national meeting was to be held in Dublin, and O'Connell invited his guests to accompany him.

"I have been present," writes Father De Smet, "at a gathering of two hundred thousand people, and had the honor of sitting in the same carriage with the great liberator, Daniel O'Connell. The people's enthusiasm knew no bounds: we were literally carried in triumph to the meeting-place near the city, amid the acclamations and blessings of the throng. Seated on the platform, not a word of the stirring discourse escaped me. That day Irish eloquence resounded in all its glory.

"What a spectacle it was for me, a missionary who, after being buried for five years in the heart of the American desert, and now thrown by chance upon Irish soil, found myself beside one of the greatest men of the day—the only agitator who has ever instigated a revolution without spilling one drop of blood.

"What a man! I cannot express my sensations and

feelings on that occasion. Never did I behold a brighter
eye, a more benevolent face, a more imposing and com-
manding person. His words flow like honey from his
lips; he enraptures and captivates and places you at your
ease in a moment, just like an old friend and acquaintance."[4]

Father De Smet and Bishop Hughes left Dublin together
and traveled to Liverpool. From there the missionary
journeyed to London and later on to Belgium.[5] Accounts
of Father De Smet's labors among the Indians had already
been circulated throughout Belgium, for during a period of
five years his letters had kept the benefactors of the missions informed of the progress religion had been making
among the Potawatomies and mountain tribes. The
people of Belgium vied with one another in doing honor to
the missionary, and all were eager to hear his picturesque
recitals.

July 30th found him in Brussels, where he gave a conference upon his missions to the pupils of St. Michael's
College. To amuse his young audience he introduced a
"redskin" by disguising his servant, who, thus attired,
struck the threatening and grotesque attitudes of the
Missouri Indians. Wild applause greeted this unexpected
performance, no one enjoying it more than Father De Smet
himself, who, while acquainting them with his Indian
mission, had at the same time amused the children.

The missionary permitted himself only a few days of
affectionate intercourse with his family and friends, for he
had come to Europe for other things than to secure sweet
repose and the easy success of a *raconteur* of adventures:
he was seeking laborers in the Lord's vineyard, who would
depart at once to undertake the Christianization of Oregon.
So, early in August he left Belgium for Rome to set forth
his needs to the Father General of the Society of Jesus.

Father Roothaan received Father De Smet with marks
of tender affection, and listened with interest and deep
emotion to the accounts of the labors and successes of his

[4] Letter to Francis De Smet, London, July 9, 1843.
[5] Bishop Hughes, while in Europe, collected money for his diocese.
He was introduced by Father De Smet to several charitably-disposed persons, among them the pious Queen of the Belgians, Marie Louise, who
presented the Bishop with a valuable pectoral cross.

heroic children. Convinced that no work was more worthy than the evangelization of the Indian, he promised to personally recommend Father De Smet to the different provinces of the Society. Then the Father General presented the first missionary of the Rocky Mountains to Gregory XVI. Imagine the emotions of the humble missionary when the Holy Father rose from his throne to embrace him! This touching reception more than repaid Father De Smet for all he had suffered in the service of the Church.

During the audience the Holy Father asked many questions about the Indians and their attitude toward religion. Father De Smet transmitted to His Holiness a message from Victor, the great chief of the Flatheads. When this zealous neophyte had learned that the Sovereign Pontiff was exposed to attacks from the impious, he had arisen and addressed the missionary in these words:

"Father, you speak upon paper [you write]: if the Great Chief of the Christians is in danger, send him a message from me. We will build him a lodge in the middle of our camp; we will hunt game that he may be fed; and we will be his guards to protect him from the enemy." Gregory XVI smiled benignly: the invitation touched His Holiness: then, seeming to read the future, he said, "In truth, the time is coming when we must leave Rome! And where shall we go? God alone knows! Give my apostolic blessing to those excellent Indians."

But Father De Smet's joy was not unalloyed, for soon it came to his ears that he was to be made a Bishop, with jurisdiction over the country lying between the Rocky Mountains and the Pacific Ocean. The distracted missionary implored his Superior to save him from an office he felt unworthy to receive and incapable of discharging. Thanks to the Father General's efforts in his behalf, Father De Smet was spared the burden, and Father Blanchet, Vicar General, was appointed Bishop of Oregon. Henceforth the Bishop found no more devoted and submissive collaborator than Father De Smet.[6]

Returning to Belgium, our missionary began the dis-

[6] Palladino, "Indian and White in the Northwest," p. 42.

agreeable task of begging.   The principal cities of Belgium
were visited as on the previous tour in behalf of the Indians,
and then he saw for the last time Mr. De Nef, for the following year the great benefactor of the missions died,
leaving to the Society of Jesus the direction of the college
which had been his life's work.   From Belgium Father
De Smet went to Holland.   In the dioceses of Bois-le-Duc
and Breda he aroused great zeal in behalf of the missions,
and The Hague, Amsterdam, and Rotterdam gave generously to the cause.[7]   The General of the Jesuits had been
faithful to his promises and had made appeals to Rome,
Naples, and Lyons, Spain and Germany, with the result
that three new missionaries started at once for the Rocky
Mountains.[8]   Five others were appointed to return with
Father De Smet: three were Italians, Fathers John Nobili,
Michael Accolti, and Anthony Ravalli; two were Belgians,
Father Louis Vercruysse, of Courtrai, and Brother Francis
Huybrechts, of Eeckeren, near Antwerp.   These additional
priests brought the number of Jesuits in the mission up to
seventeen, a number sufficient at that time for its most
urgent needs.

But for the education of the Indians, the help of teaching
Sisters was indispensable.   A Belgian community, the
Sisters of Notre Dame de Namur, had three years previously established a house at Cincinnati, and Father De
Smet, having visited their convent before leaving America,
was much impressed with the work accomplished by them.
The Sisters themselves were eager to share the missionaries' labors, so while in Belgium, November 10, 1843, he
visited their mother-house.   In the annals of the institution we read: "We were happy to see in person, if only
for a moment, this great missionary.   His letters, alive
with zeal and enthusiasm for apostolic work, had awakened
our interest.   We had imagined him an energetic, enterprising, enthusiastic man—but not at all!   Before us stood
a venerable priest, calm and humble, replying modestly
to our questions, and recounting most interestingly his
experiences.   Many times, it seems, he had miraculously

---

[7] Father De Smet and his companions left for America with nearly
$30,000.

[8] Fathers Joset and Zerbinati, with Brother Magri.

escaped death. 'When one is not worthy to die,' he said, 'one escapes easily.'"

Bishop Dehesselle of Namur demurred at the Sisters' request that they might join the Oregon Mission, but finally gave his consent. Six Sisters prepared for immediate departure. But how would it be possible to expose these frail women to the many dangers and hardships of crossing the American wilderness? Father De Smet did not contemplate such an undertaking, and decided, notwithstanding the long journey, to double Cape Horn and enter Oregon through the Columbia River. An Antwerp boat, the *Infatigable*, was about to set sail for Valparaiso, and on this vessel Father De Smet engaged passage for the Sisters and the missionaries.

The party set out from Antwerp December 12th. Fogs and contrary winds delayed the boat nearly a month in the Schelde, but the passengers knew how to employ their leisure profitably. "All's well aboard," writes Father De Smet. "We have a trustworthy skipper, and a good crew; the Sisters are calm and contented, the Fathers and Brothers courageous and hopeful. We live here a community life; every one is occupied; Father Vercruysse gives French lessons to the Italians, and I am teaching all my band English."[9]

At last, on January 9th, the vessel put out to sea. All "paid tribute to inexorable Neptune;" but a voyage lasting seven months brought trials other than seasickness to the missionaries, not the least of these being monotony. Father De Smet, indefatigable traveler that he was, found it interminably long. "Life on shipboard is dull and tedious. Nothing but water; now and then a sail on the horizon, or some sea-gulls and fish distract us for a moment from our dreams and musings on the far away. A more serious distraction is found in the storms, hurricanes, reefs, and steep rocks; and when the vessel is beaten about at the mercy of the winds, beyond the captain's control, we tremble for our lives."[10]

The missionary's thoughts traveled to the loved ones

[9] Letter to Charles De Smet, on board the *Infatigable*, Dec. 25, 1843.
[10] Letter to Francis De Smet, Valparaiso, May 1, 1844.

that he had left behind for the third time: "Often on a calm, clear night I sit on deck gazing for hours at the stars, and musing upon sweet memories. The Belt of Orion, commonly called 'the Three Kings,' recalls to my mind my two brothers and my sister. In looking at 'Berenice's Hair,' I imagine myself in the midst of the children of the family; I see and hear them; they climb upon my knees, their little arms around my neck; you know how dearly I love them."[11]

As they doubled Cape Horn, the boat, which until then had stood the sea extremely well, all but foundered. "From the 22d to the 30th of March," writes Father Vercruysse, "we experienced a furious hurricane which tore even the furled sails into ribbons, and drove the boat about at the whim of the wind. Mountains of water towered above us. The captain averred it was the severest storm he had ever encountered in his thirty years at sea. The hatches were battened down one entire week, and we hardly dared creep out on deck even for an instant to gaze upon the terrible spectacle. Death stared us in the face. On the 31st the waters calmed, and we breathed freely once more: but April 1st found the storm again in full blast, the wind driving us steadily upon the rock-bound coast of Patagonia, about a mile distant. All except the Sisters remained on deck, every eye fixed on the rocks threatening us with immediate destruction. Suddenly the captain's cry, 'We are lost! All is over!' broke the suspense. But God seemed to say: 'I am watching over you.'

"Father De Smet sought out the nuns, who like ourselves were imploring the help of our blessed Mother. He offered to hear their confessions, telling them that nothing short of a miracle could save the vessel: shipwreck was inevitable. These good women calmly and cheerfully replied that God would dispose of their lives as He chose; that they awaited with resignation the accomplishment of His divine will.

"It was eleven o'clock at night; the waves were heard breaking upon the reefs, when suddenly the wind veered to another quarter, driving us out to sea. Had the wind not

[11] Letter to Francis De Smet, St. Mary of Willamette, Oct. 9, 1844.

changed just at that moment we certainly should have perished."[12]

With the calming of the sea, the *Infatigable* resumed her northerly course, stopping at Valparaiso and Callao. While the vessel was in port, the missionaries visited Santiago and Lima, where they received a warm welcome from the religious orders. The captain hoped to make Vancouver in twenty-five days, but he reckoned without contrary winds. Forty days passed, and yet no land in sight. Provisions began to run low, and rations, that according to Father De Smet had never been good or abundant, were now cut down. The crew grumbled; the captain fell ill; still more, another hurricane threatened to wreck the ship. Father De Smet exhorted his band to storm heaven with their prayers. "We conceived the happy idea of making a vow, and sought refuge in Mary's immaculate heart, resolved to spend the following day in retirement and examination of conscience.

"The fury of the storm lashed the sea into mountainous waves that rose twenty-five feet above the vessel. Destruction seemed imminent. We all made good confessions and confidently placed our lives in God's hands. Toward evening I went on deck and saw a sight that rejoiced my heart. Floating on the water was a seaweed called *Adam's needle*, which indicated the proximity of land. Gradually the wind subsided, and once more we took heart and hoped to see land soon.

"On July 28th the shores of Oregon loomed before us. What joy! What transports of delight! What words of thanksgiving in our hearts and on our lips! What emotion at the sight of this vast country, where, for lack of missionaries, thousands of men are born, grow to manhood, and die in the darkness of infidelity! But now through our efforts, the greater number, if not all, shall know the truth."[13]

But the spirit of evil fought desperately to delay the landing of those whose conquest it dreaded. "The entry into the Columbia is a difficult and dangerous passage, even with charts, and our captain had none. As we advanced, breakers indicated the presence of a sand-bar

---

[12] Account of the voyage addressed to Father Broeckaert, Lima, May 20, 1844.
[13] Letter to Francis De Smet, St. Mary of Willamette, Oct. 9, 1844.

several miles in length: a reef of rocks running across the river seemed to impede our passage.[14] It was July 31st, the feast of St. Ignatius, and this coincidence heartened us and renewed our courage. Before long a launch taking soundings came alongside the *Infatigable*. The sailors' serious faces boded no good news: one hardly dared question them, but the lieutenant informed our captain that he had crossed the bar in five fathoms of water. Our sails were then set and we advanced slowly under a light breeze. The sky was blue and the sun shone in all its glory; not for a long time had we had such a day. It only wanted now our safe entry into the river to make it the happiest one of the whole journey. As the boat advanced our prayers redoubled.

"The captain began taking soundings. Two sailors lashed to the side of the vessel called out: 'Seven fathoms!' Every five minutes the same call was heard: then, 'Six fathoms! Five fathoms!' the number always decreasing. When 'Two and a half fathoms!' was heard, hope fled. But God was trying our faith: He had not willed our destruction. The cry, 'Four fathoms!' bade us hope again: we had still two miles of breakers to pass, and again our hearts sank when we heard 'Three fathoms!' At this juncture the lieutenant informed our captain we were out of the channel. 'Nonsense!' replied our skipper. 'The *Infatigable* can pass anywhere! Go ahead!'

"Heaven was certainly with us, for without help from on high, neither the captain's skill, nor the soundness of the boat, nor the discipline of the sailors could have saved us from certain death. We were over three hundred feet out of our course in the as yet untraveled and uncharted southern channel.[15] God seemed to wish to teach us that although He exposes us to danger, His power can save us. Blessed be His name!"[16]

[14] Since then the Government has facilitated the entrance into the Columbia by parallel jetties, which concentrate the flow over the bar, and scour out a deep channel.

[15] "At a short distance from its mouth the Columbia divides into two branches, forming two channels. The northerly one in the vicinity of Cape Disappointment is the one we should have taken; the southern one is avoided because of the breakers that bar its entrance. We were certainly the first and probably the last to enter it." (Father De Smet, letter quoted.)

[16] Letter to Francis De Smet, Oct. 9, 1844.

CHAPTER X

THE OREGON MISSIONS (1844–1846)

The Jesuits and Sisters of Notre Dame at Willamete—St. Francis Xavier's
Mission—Father De Smet, Organizer of the Missions—How He En-
couraged and Aided His Fellow-Missionaries—St. Ignatius' Mission at
the Kalispels; Father Adrian Hoecken—The Sacred Heart Mission at
the Cœur-d'Alènes; Fathers Point and Joset—Louise Sighouin—
Visit to St. Mary's; Fathers Mengarini and Zerbinati—Jesuits' Success
at Willamette; Fathers Accolti, Ravalli, Vercruysse, and De Vos—
Father Nobili is Sent to New Caledonia—Father De Smet's Visit to the
Chaudières, Flatbows, and Kootenais—The Missions of St. Paul,
Colville, St. Peter of the Lakes, St. Francis Regis, the Assumption, and
the Immaculate Heart of Mary—Father Ravalli Goes to Join Father
Hoecken at St. Ignatius' Mission—How Account for Father De Smet's
Success?—A Would-be Murderer who Became a Model Neophyte.

BISHOP BLANCHET was impatiently awaiting Father
De Smet's return: when the news came that his boat
had arrived, he left St. Paul's Mission and hastened to
Vancouver. The Catholics, though busy with the harvest,
abandoned their fields, and embarking in boats, descended
the Willamette; each one wished to be the first to greet
the missionary and bring him back in triumph. Upon
their return, a *Te Deum* was intoned in the mission
church, and next day, the feast of the Assumption, hymns
of thanksgiving were sung in honor of the Queen of heaven,
who once more had proved herself to merit the title of
"Star of the sea."

The Sisters took immediate possession of the convent
that had been built for them on the right bank of the
Willamette, though it was not wholly completed. Doors
and windows were lacking, but the Sisters took a hand with
saw and plane, and even undertook the glazing and paint-
ing. After a few weeks, St. Mary's Convent opened its
doors.

The Indians and Canadians were so eager for instruction,

that while awaiting the completing of the building, the Sisters held classes for women and children in the open air, and prepared them for first communion. Their ages ranged from fifteen to sixty years. Many of these poor creatures came from great distances, carrying a few days' provisions with them and sleeping at night in the forest.[1]

St. Joseph's College for young men was simultaneously opened by Father Bolduc, a late arrival from Canada. Hearing of this, the Protestants quickly dispersed. "It is significant," writes Father De Smet, "that the same boat that brought us to Vancouver is taking the Protestant ministers and their wives to the Sandwich Islands, whence they will return to the United States. After years of fruitless efforts to draw Catholic children from their faith, they have closed their school and quit the country, leaving us a free field."[2]

The Jesuits were desirous of establishing a training-school for young men near the Willamette, which would serve also as a central depot for provisioning the Rocky Mountain Missions, and for this purpose Bishop Blanchet offered them land. A salubrious climate, fertile soil, forests, and a diversified and imposing landscape made the situation a particularly advantageous one for the Jesuit foundation. Father De Smet beheld in it a second Florissant. "I hope," writes he, "that after the example of St. Stanislaus' Mission, whose influence now radiates over a large portion of Missouri, in Ohio and Louisiana, to the Rocky Mountains, and the extreme western boundaries of America, there will be established here one day a novitiate for missionaries who—and may the day be not far distant!—will labor among the different tribes of this vast territory, carrying the torch of faith."[3]

Work was begun at once, the missionaries and Canadians rivaling each other in untiring labors, with the result that

---

[1] Cf. Notice sur le Territoire et sur la mission de l'Orégon, suivie de quelques lettres des Sœurs de Notre-Dame, établies à S.-Paul du Willamette, Bruxelles, 1847.

[2] To the Mother General of the Sisters of Notre Dame, Aug. 28, 1844.

[3] To Francis De Smet, Oct. 9, 1844. The missionary's dream was only partly realized; the great distance of the missions from one another, and the hardships and difficulties of the journeys, rendered the new foundation impracticable; after a few years it was abandoned by the Fathers.

at the end of a few months the house was opened under the title of St. Francis Xavier.

Father De Smet set out once more to cross the wilderness. An extraordinary initiative characterized his apostolic labors. Having once conceived and developed his plans, he would then choose a site for a new station, lay it out, and start the work. When all difficulties had been surmounted, he sought other fields of activity, leaving to his colleagues the joy and satisfaction of completing the mission. From the end of 1844 to the close of 1846 was doubtless the most fruitful period of his life. During these years he crossed and recrossed the Western United States many times, going from one tribe to another, instructing one and sustaining another, establishing new "reductions," and departing, once the foundation was laid and the direction of affairs could be left to others.

While the Fathers lately arrived from Europe were occupied in studying the Indian language and in ministering to the Christians on the Willamette, Father De Smet journeyed across the mountains to winter with the Flatheads. On November 6th he entered the Kalispel valley, where he found Father Adrian Hoecken carrying on the work he had begun in 1841.

"I was received in camp with the ringing of bells and discharge of musketry. The accounts the young missionary gave me of the tribe show the work of grace in a people sincerely seeking truth.

"'We have no brilliant qualities of mind,' the Indians told him, 'but in default of intelligence we possess docility. Now that a Black Robe has come among us, we listen to him and obey him; his orders are executed without delay.'"[4]

The missionary was energetically seconded in his apostolic labors by the old chief, Loyola. "So long as a breath of life remains in me," he said, "every man here must live uprightly." The spirit of fraternity and mutual respect existing among the members of this tribe recall those happy days spoken of in Holy Writ, when Christians had but one heart and one soul.

[4] Letter to Madam Parmentier of Brooklyn, St. Ignatius' Mission, July 25, 1846.

But winter was coming on, and our missionary must get to St. Mary's before the cold set in. Father De Smet had hardly taken leave of the Kalispels when he encountered a deputation from the Cœur d'Alènes, who had come to beg him to visit their tribe. He accepted, not having the heart to refuse them, and hoped he would still be able to cross the Bitter Root Mountains before the trail had become impassable.

Father Point had been two years with the Cœur d'Alènes. He had arrived there the first Friday of the month and, on that day, had placed the mission under the protection of the Sacred Heart. "From that moment," he writes, "a Christian spirit animated the inhabitants of this happy valley. The nightly gatherings, sacrilegious ceremonies, and diabolical apparitions formerly so frequent, have now been done away with. Gambling, hitherto the absorbing occupation of the Indians, has also been abandoned. Marriage, which for centuries knew neither unity nor indissolubility, has been restored to its pristine purity. From Christmas until the feast of the Purification, the missionary's fire was made with the remains of their sorcery."[5]

When Father Point arrived at the mission, he had drawn the plan of the village, and the Indians had set to work to fell trees, dig ponds, make roads, and till the soil. A church was erected in the center of the settlement, and the religious celebrations acquainted the new converts with the solemnity and appeal of the new faith.

Father Joset, who came shortly to share Father Point's labors, was destined to pass many years of fruitful apostolic work in the mountains.[6] The neophytes' fervor daily increased, and Father Point tells us that "For several months not one grave offence has been committed in the Sacred Heart village, at least not among those who have received baptism."[7]

[5] Letter to one of the Jesuit Fathers, quoted by Father De Smet: "Mission de l'Orégon," p. 240, et seq."

[6] An account of Father Joset is found in The Woodstock Letters, Nov., 1901, p. 207.

[7] "It requires exceptional virtue on the part of the aged to become the pupils of their young children, and on the part of the children to be patient and serious preceptors of their aged fathers; on the part of mothers of families, who, not content with giving their children the food they deprive themselves of, pass long evenings in making known the divine word to relatives,

The faith and piety of this mission was due in large measure to Louise Sighouin, a zealous Christian baptized by Father De Smet in 1842. Although a daughter of the chief of the Cœur d'Alènes, she had left all to devote herself to the service of the missions. "I am ready," she said, "to follow the Black Robes to the end of the earth; my sole desire is to know the Great Spirit, to serve Him faithfully, and to adore Him with all my heart." Not only was she an example of piety and modesty to the tribe, but she spent hours every day teaching the children and old people and in visiting the poor and nursing the sick. Once she recoiled at the sight of a dreadful ulcer, then, filled with compunction for what she considered a grave fault, she returned to the invalid every day for two months and, like a veritable Sister of Charity, dressed the wound. Nor did she hesitate to make war on disorderly conduct. She faced the most redoubtable sorcerers, denouncing them as impostors, and through threatening them with God's judgments, finally brought the culprits, trembling and contrite, to the feet of the missionary.

When Father De Smet arrived at the mission, the Cœur d'Alènes were preparing for their first communion, friends, and even strangers, eager to hear them; for young men, who repeat a hundred times to their less intelligent companions, things the meaning of which they grasped at first hearing, and who spend whole nights in teaching the deaf and blind, who were the despair of the Black Robe. And chiefs, true fathers and pastors of their people, rise at dawn, and even in the night in cold, inclement weather, to arouse souls from their torpor. Hence is it astonishing that the faith and piety of these humble souls should have more than once obtained extraordinary favors?

"One morning," says Father Point, "upon leaving the church I met an Indian woman, who said, 'So-and-so is not well.' She was not yet a catechumen and I said I would go to see her. An hour later the same person, her sister, came to me saying she was dead. I ran to the tent, hoping she might be mistaken, and found a crowd of relatives around the bed, repeating, 'She is dead—she has not breathed for some time.' To assure myself, I leaned over the body; there was no sign of life. I reproved these excellent people for not telling me at once of the gravity of the situation, adding, 'May God forgive me!' Then, rather impatiently, I said, 'Pray!' and all fell on their knees and prayed devoutly.

"I again leaned over the supposed corpse and said, 'The Black Robe is here: do you wish him to baptize you?' At the word baptism I saw a slight tremor of the lower lip; then both lips moved, making me certain that she understood. She had already been instructed, so I at once baptized her, and she rose from her bier, making the sign of the cross. . . . To-day she is out hunting and is fully persuaded that she died at the time I have recounted." (Letter quoted.)

which they were to make in a few weeks. Night and
day the camp resounded with prayers and hymns. Such
piety and edifying conduct were a great consolation to
Father De Smet, and his joy would have been great could
he have led to the holy table those upon whom he had
lately poured the waters of baptism: but it had been
snowing several days and he could not delay, as he had
to cross the mountains that lay between him and the
country of the Flatheads.

He set out from the Sacred Heart Mission with an
escort of four Indian guides, who were to accompany
him as far as St. Mary's. The season was already far
advanced. It snowed and rained incessantly, and torrents,
ever increasing in volume rushed down the mountainsides.
After marching for eight days he was forced to return.

"In a night," writes Father De Smet, "tiny rivulets became raging torrents, arresting my progress at every step.
At the price of great suffering, many falls and duckings,
we finally reached the St. Ignatius River. It had risen
more than ten feet, carrying along with it huge trees,
which rendered my passage extremely dangerous. Once
I sank with my mule, but I clung to the beast and he
dragged me to the opposite bank.

"At night we camped in the shadow of a huge cross
erected by an Indian chief. As the river had not yet
overflowed its banks, we retired for the night with a
certain feeling of security, but before morning one of
the men awoke to find his legs in water; putting his head
out of the tent he gave the alarm. It was none too soon,
for we found ourselves in the midst of a huge lake, the
land being inundated for miles.

"Here again, as on former occasions, Providence came to
our aid. Two canoes had been left at the place of our
encampment, and thus we were able to take refuge, with
our arms and baggage, upon a hill two miles distant. I
sent one of my guides to the mission to inform them of my
mishap. Two days later five canoes commanded by two
chiefs came to my assistance and brought us back to the
village."[8]

The Indians blessed the accident that had given them

[8] Journal of the autumn of 1844.

back the missionary, but the intrepid Father De Smet did not abandon his project.   Now that the mountains were impassable, he determined to reach St. Mary's through the Kalispel valley, and it looked for a time as though he might succeed.   But as it was then the middle of December, the Clarke River began to freeze over, and the Indians in charge of the canoes declared that to continue was to advance to certain death.   Father Mengarini had written that he had nearly perished in the flood and had lost twelve horses in the forest.   Then only did Father De Smet decide to return to the Kalispels and to wait until spring before attempting to reach the Flatheads.

"The Indians put their best tent at my disposal and endeavored in every way to render my stay in their midst as agreeable as circumstances would permit.   On Christmas day one hundred and twenty-four adults received baptism: a few minutes before midnight a pistol-shot rang out in the night, followed by a discharge of musketry in honor of the Child Jesus, and three hundred voices in the forest intoned in the language of the tribe that beautiful hymn:

"The Almighty's glory all things proclaim!"

Immediately, the throng of worshipers crowded into the humble chapel constructed of trunks of trees, straw, and bark.   Pine branches, interspersed with wreaths and garlands of green, decorated the interior, and above the simple altar hung a paper star with a profusion of streamers that attracted the eyes of the Indians.

"I celebrated High Mass at midnight, at which the congregation chanted Christmas hymns, and never did the words of the *Gloria* seem more appropriate: 'Peace on earth to men of good will.'   Breakfast followed the Mass, and the joyousness of the reunion resembled the lovefeasts of the early Christians.   Later the catechumens presented themselves in the church to receive baptism. The old men and women I had baptized two years before, still preserving their baptismal innocence, acted as godfathers and godmothers.

"Not in vain did the priest pronounce those sublime words of the ritual: 'Receive the white garment which you will bring without blemish to God's tribunal, that you may enter into eternal life,' for he had the certainty that the larger part of the catechumens would preserve their innocence until death. When asked later on if they had offended God and if their consciences were free of all reproach, they replied, 'How can you ask, Father! In baptism I renounced evil. Is it not fitting that I should shun it? Even the thought of displeasing the Great Spirit makes me tremble.'

"In the evening solemn benediction of the Blessed Sacrament was given for the first time. After this ceremony, fifty couples, fathers and mothers of families, some of them over eighty years of age, came forward to renew their marriage vows. I could not restrain the tears, so deeply was I affected by the sincerity and affection with which they promised henceforth to have but one heart.

"After the last instruction, prayers of thanksgiving were said for the favors received during the day, and although it was getting late, prayers continued to be said and hymns sung in every lodge."[9]

At the first sign of spring Father De Smet set out again for St. Mary's, where this time he arrived without adventure and was received by Fathers Mengarini and Zerbinati. Great was their joy in welcoming the founder of the mission! A missionary's life in the mountains was an isolated one. Perhaps once a year he got news of the outside world, and then only at the price of a dangerous journey to Vancouver, whither he went under escort to provision the camp. It even happened that he did not receive letters that had been sent him; the letter from France transferring Father Point to Canada was three years in reaching him.

Father De Smet regaled the missionaries with accounts of his visit to Europe and to Rome; he recounted his reception by the Father General and by Gregory XVI, who had deigned to bless the mission in Oregon. He recalled the incidents of his recent voyage from Antwerp to Willamette, the founding of St. Francis Xavier's, and lastly the religious celebration at which he had assisted among the Cœur d'Alènes and Kalispels.

[9] Letter to Madam Parmentier, St. Ignatius, July 25, 1846.

The Flatheads also had remained faithful to their baptismal vows. The whole tribe approached the holy table at the Mass said on Easter by Father De Smet, and a choir of young men under Father Mengarini's direction sang several songs by the best German and Italian composers.

St. Francis Borgia's mission of the Pend d'Oreilles [10] had been annexed to St. Mary's Mission, and three hundred of the tribe, mostly adults, had presented themselves for baptism. Upon their lined and scarred foreheads was poured the water that confers eternal life, and these souls were gained for God.

Father Hoecken was awaiting Father De Smet's return before beginning the foundation of a "reduction" that was to be placed under the patronage of St. Ignatius; so with many regrets the indefatigable apostle took leave of St. Mary's Mission to return to the Kalispels. With the consent of the chiefs, he chose a vast plain bordered with cedars and pines. The fertile soil, abundant pasturage, rich quarries, and a waterfall, from which power could be obtained both for a flour and a saw mill, made it a most favorable situation for the new foundation.

Father De Smet drew the plans of the village, superintended the beginning of the work, and then went by water to Vancouver to provision the new colony. Swollen by the melting snow, the river had become a raging torrent in which four Americans had recently been engulfed. The missionary ran the risk of being caught in a whirlpool similar to the one in which his crew had been lost three years before; but trusting in Providence he embarked, and five days later arrived safely at Vancouver, where he was received by Father Nobili. That zealous missionary had learned the language of the country and was exercising a fruitful ministry among the employees of the fort and the neighboring Indians.

[10] The Pend d'Oreilles or Kalispels comprised, as we have seen, two principal groups: the Kalispels of the Mountains, belonging to St. Francis Borgia's Mission, north of St. Mary's, and the Kalispels of the Bay, belonging to St. Ignatius' Mission, near the mouth of the Clarke. The two missions were united in 1854 near the Flathead Lake under the name of St. Ignatius.

In order to avoid confusion we will continue to call the Pend d'Oreilles the Indians of the Mountains; those of the Bay, the Kalispels.

The two missionaries traveled up the Willamette to St. Francis Xavier's Mission, where they were warmly welcomed by the Fathers, who expressed their joy at meeting once again their intrepid chief, Father De Smet. He had crossed the whole of Oregon during the past eight months, preparing for each priest his field of apostolic work.

Father Accolti was the Superior of an active band of missionaries, while Father Ravalli's knowledge of medicine rendered great service to the sick of that region. Father Vercruysse had founded a new parish and built a church for the Canadians of the Grand Prairie, south of St. Francis Xavier's Mission, and Father De Vos had made many converts among the Protestants.

Adding these results to those obtained by the Fathers of the mountain missions and the Canadian missionaries, Father De Smet calculated that over six thousand souls in Oregon had received baptism in six years. "The grain of mustard seed," he writes, "grows apace, and extends its branches over this heretofore sterile and neglected land."[11]

In 1842 Father Demers, assistant to Bishop Blanchet, made a journey to New Caledonia, six hundred miles north of Vancouver,[12] during which he baptized seven hundred children. Since that time the inhabitants had ardently desired religious instruction, and although without a priest, they built three churches in the hope that one day a missionary would come to settle among them. To this mission Father Nobili was appointed, and proved himself worthy of the confidence of his Superior.

Born in Rome, young Nobili entered the Society of Jesus at the age of sixteen. Through his literary talent he soon achieved distinction, and after his ordination obtained permission to consecrate his life to the conversion of the Indians. We shall soon see the wonderful fruit of his apostolic labors. When June was drawing to a close, Father De Smet started for the mountains with a train of eleven horses, laden with plows, spades, hoes, saws, and every sort of implement for St. Ignatius' Mission. In crossing

[11] Letter to Bishop Hughes, St. Francis Xavier's Mission, June 20, 1845.
[12] New Caledonia, here spoken of, is to-day British Columbia.

the Cascade Range, he came upon heaps of bones of dead animals, the melancholy remains of a caravan that had been lost in the snow or buried in an avalanche.

The following month found him among the Kalispels. During his absence the neophytes had increased to more than four hundred. Several wooden houses had been built, the material prepared for constructing a church, and a large tract of farming land was already enclosed. The men were adepts in the use of the plow and axe, and it was evident the Indians had abandoned the nomad life for the regular pursuits of the colony.

The future of this "reduction" was assured, and the time had now come to seek out and carry the Gospel to new tribes.

Three years before, Father De Smet had met, near Fort Colville, Indians athirst for the knowledge of the Great Spirit. Hence he repaired first to this tribe, taking with him several Kalispels to act as choristers and catechists.

"Near the Falls of the Columbia," he writes, "from eight to nine hundred Indians, Chaudières, Okinagans, Sinpoils, and Zingomènes, had gathered for the salmon-fishing. Upon a rock overlooking the river I erected my little bark chapel, around which were grouped the Indians' huts, like a covey seeking shelter under the mother's wing.

"Never were people so hungry for the divine word, and to nourish and sustain such happy dispositions I gave several instructions, which were listened to with eager attention. I chose the feast of St. Ignatius for the closing of the religious exercises, when over a hundred children and eleven old people were baptized. Many of the latter, who were carried on buffalo hides, seemed only to await this grace before going to rest in the bosom of God.

"The oldest neophyte, nearly a hundred years old and blind, said to me: 'My life has been a long one, and for many years I have wept without ceasing for the loss of my children and friends. I am now alone, and live as a stranger among my tribe, with only sad and bitter memories for companions. Yet I have one consolation—I have always avoided bad company, my hands are clean of thieving, quarrels, and murder. To-day the Great Spirit has taken pity on me; I am happy and I offer Him my heart and life.'"[13]

Here Father De Smet founded a mission which he called St. Paul's. Another one, St. Peter's, was established a little farther north for the Indians inhabiting the lake regions.

On August 4th our missionary left the Falls of the Columbia, accompanied by several half-breeds who wished him to inspect a place they had chosen for a Christian foundation between the St. Ignatius and the Sacred Heart Missions. Many hunters wished to settle there with their families. Finding the site a favorable one, Father De Smet drew up the plans for a new "reduction," which he named St. Francis Regis.

There remained the Flatbows and the Kootenais, whom no priest had ever visited, so he decided to go to them and prepare the way for missionaries. After hewing his path through dense forests, frightful marshes, and swollen rivers, he finally arrived at the first of these camps.[14] The Flatbows numbered about ninety families. Thanks to a worthy Canadian who had lived among them for many years, they were already acquainted with the great truths of religion, they knew several hymns in French and in their native tongue, and all were desirous of becoming Christians.

"This year," writes the missionary, "as in preceding ones I have passed among the Indians, the feast of the Assumption of the Blessed Virgin was for me a day of happiness and consolation. I celebrated the first Mass ever said in this part of the world, and afterward baptized ninety-two children and ten adults advanced in years. In the evening the cross was erected, the standard of the Saviour being planted on the shore of the lake to the salvo of eighty guns. At its foot, the entire tribe offered

[13] Letter to Father Joset, Sept. 9, 1845.
[14] " The Flatbows are ignorant of industry, the arts, and science, and share in common the fruits of the earth. Like all Indians, they are improvident, and are either reveling in abundance or on the verge of famine. One day they feast until gorged, then for several succeeding days abstain entirely from food. These two extremes are equally pernicious, judging from the cadaverous, blank faces I see among them." (Letter to Bishop Hughes, Station of the Assumption, Aug. 17, 1845.)

their hearts to the Great Spirit, promising inviolable attachment to our holy religion, and they destroyed what remained of their ancient superstitions."[15]

This station was called the Assumption, and here, as everywhere that Father De Smet penetrated, civilization marched hand in hand with faith, for he made these Indians understand the advantages of tilling the soil, and promised to furnish them seeds and farming implements. Thanking God for the wonders of grace worked in their souls, he directed his steps to the country of the Kootenais.

"This," says our traveler, "is the *ne plus ultra* of the wilderness! The forest is so dense, that if the guide gets a few steps ahead, he is completely hidden. In order not to lose one's way one must abandon himself to the instinct of the horse, who follows the tracks of the wild beasts through the wood. Had I not resorted to this shift, I would have lost my road completely. These somber places engender gloomy thoughts; one seems condemned to never emerge from these labyrinthine haunts of bears and panthers.

"The path winds in the neighborhood of a stream, which follows in one place a mountain gorge, or rather a precipice of appalling height. Amid such obstacles one must travel for a distance of eight miles, scaling, by the aid of a pickaxe, steep declivities, awe-inspiring heights, and long and narrow sloping banks. At each step the danger is so evident that the blood freezes in one's veins and a cold sweat breaks out. After each crossing I thanked God as though I had just escaped death and its agonies."[16]

Father De Smet had met, in the spring of 1842, several Kootenais families living on the borders of the Clarke River, hence his present arrival was greeted by a discharge of musketry and lively manifestations of joy. "They showed me their diaries, which were long, narrow, oblong boards or sticks, upon which they had marked the days and weeks since they had first met me. Forty-one months and some days had already been counted."

From the Canadian who had lived for years with the Flatbows, the Kootenais had learned the first elements of

[15] Letter quoted.
[16] Letter to Bishop Hughes, Flatbow [Kootenai] River, Sept. 3, 1845.

religion.[17] They sang hymns, said morning and evening prayers in common, and observed strictly the Lord's Day.

"On the feast of the Immaculate Heart of Mary," writes our missionary, "I sang High Mass, and in God's name took possession of the new land visited for the first time by a Catholic priest. Afterward I baptized one hundred and five souls, of whom twenty were adults. Following the order of ceremonies I had observed with the Flatbows, the day ended with the planting of the cross. It was raised on high, and saluted by a discharge of all the guns in the camp. Then came the tribe in procession, headed by their chiefs, who prostrated themselves at the foot of the tree of salvation, and in a loud voice offered their hearts to Him whom they called their Master, the divine Pastor of souls. This station was called the Immaculate Heart of Mary."[18]

It is difficult to estimate at their full value the prodigious labors of our missionary. During six weeks' travel in an unknown country, through dense forests wherein he made his way with the utmost difficulty, he had baptized over three hundred souls and had founded five new stations. In order to assure the future of these Christians, Father Ravalli was sent to share Father Hoecken's labors. The new posts were grouped in a relatively small area around St. Ignatius' Mission, thus enabling the Fathers to go from one to the other to complete the instruction of the neophytes.

Nearly all the Oregon tribes now had missionaries, and those who were deprived of a resident priest were visited by the neighboring Fathers. The valleys were dotted with charming villages, and from the center of each rose "the lodge of prayer." The evening breezes wafted melodious Christian hymns that delighted and astonished the approaching traveler. Before the end of another year, the increasing number of the faithful necessitated the foundation of two new dioceses.[19]

[17] The Flatbows and Kootenais were two tribes belonging to the Skalzi family. [18] Letter quoted.

[19] In July, 1846, Bishop Blanchet was appointed Archbishop of Oregon City. His suffragans were Bishop Demers of Vancouver Island, and Bishop A. M. A. Blanchet (his brother), first Bishop of Walla Walla. The last-named See was transferred in 1850 to Nesqually.

With his soul inundated with joy, Father De Smet thanked God for having chosen him to be the instrument of His designs. "I believe firmly in the hundredfold promised by Our Saviour. What we have given up in this world is as nothing compared to what we have found and experienced in the wilderness."[20]

How is the phenomenal success of these missions to be explained? Many of the Indians possessed admirable natural virtues; they but needed to know Christianity to embrace it.[21] Even the most degraded had preserved a high ideal of the greatness of the power of God. Blasphemy was unknown among them: not presuming to address the "Great Spirit," they entreated their manitous to intercede for them. Superstition if you will, but beneath it was a religious sentiment which the missionary had only to enlighten and direct. None held back through false pride or prejudice. Even the Sioux, the proudest of the Western tribes, compared themselves to children bereft of a father's guiding hand, and to the ignorant animals of the prairie, and with touching humility begged the missionary to "take pity on them."

Such elevated, upright souls could, moreover, appreciate the chastity of the Catholic priesthood. With rare discernment, the Indian understood that, belonging as he does to all men, a priest cannot give himself to one person, and not for an instant did they hesitate to choose the Black Robe, who had consecrated his life to them, rather than the minister in lay dress, installed in a comfortable home with wife and children, devoted to the interests of his family, giving only the time that remained to distributing Bibles.[22]

Father De Smet was a man specially chosen by God to be an apostle to these tribes. An intrepid traveler, loving adventure, he could, thanks to his robust constitution,

[20] Letter to Madam Parmentier, St. Ignatius, July 25, 1846.
[21] "The North American Indian is the noblest type of pagan that exists. He acknowledges a Great Spirit; he believes in immortality; he has a lively intelligence and clear mind; is brave and intrepid, and so long as he is not deceived, is faithful to his word. He loves his children passionately, and dies gladly for his tribe." (Rev. H. B. Whipple, Protestant Bishop of Minnesota, quoted by Helen Hunt Jackson, in "A Century of Dishonor," p. 7.)
[22] Cf. Marshall, "The Christian Missions," Vol. ii, p. 300, et seq.

travel months at a time, eat all kinds of food, sleep in the open, and share in every way the rude life of the mountain Indian. Yet, more than his physical strength, did his moral qualities assure his success. Although as a rule he spoke only through an interpreter, he soon acquired an influence over the Indians that amounted to fascination. The dignity and sweetness of his manner, his calm assurance, the loyalty of his nature and compassionate goodness, merited for him the significant names that obtain even to-day among the tribes: "The Great Black Robe," "The white man of gentle speech," "The Indian's best friend." Though gentle in nature, he had energy and strength of character, and with these qualities he conquered the most stubborn natures.

While residing at one of the mountain missions, an overbearing, sullen Indian, who was feared on account of his gigantic strength, swore to kill the missionary, and do away with the religion he preached. One day Father De Smet started off on horseback to visit a neighboring post, armed only with his breviary and his riding-whip. Suddenly, he saw the enraged Indian descending upon him, brandishing his tomahawk and emitting war-whoops. Nothing would have been easier than to flee, but that would have meant a triumph for the fanatic. In a flash the Father sprang to the ground, and before his adversary could strike, gave him a blow with his fist that knocked the tomahawk out of his hand. The Indian stooped to get it, and as he did so Father De Smet seized him, threw him, and, holding him on the ground, administered a good cowhiding.

Blind with shame and fury, the would-be assassin struggled to free himself, but in vain. Then he begged for mercy, swearing to treat the Black Robe henceforth with the greatest respect. Father De Smet promised him his liberty upon condition that he would himself tell the whole tribe that he had been beaten by the Black Robe. Willy-nilly, the proud warrior was obliged to submit. He rose, but the missionary kept his hatchet, saying that if he wished to get it back he must come himself in a few days to the mission to fetch it.

The Indian was not yet converted, but the way was prepared. A week later he approached the mission and asked to speak to Father De Smet. The latter received him most kindly, ordered refreshments to be served, and encouraged him to talk about his victories and the number of scalps he had taken from the enemy. Gradually the Indian's face brightened. Then the conversation was changed to the subject of religion. The missionary exposed the absurdity of superstitious practices, and revealed the great truths of the Catholic faith. The Indian acknowledged he had been vanquished a second time, and asked to become a neophyte.

For several weeks the new catechumen faithfully attended the missionary's instructions, finally receiving baptism, and becoming one of the best Christians of the tribe.[23]

[23] This incident is related in the *Précis Historiques*, Brussels, 1873, p. 446, by a Father who heard it from Father De Smet's own lips.

CHAPTER XI

St. Mary's Mission Threatened—Father De Smet Goes in Search of the Blackfeet to Induce Them to Make Peace—Autumn in the Rocky Mountains—*Mirabilia opera Domini*—Coming upon the Camp of the Assiniboins—A Feast with the Indians—"Like a Fish on a Hook"—Father De Smet Arrives at Rocky Mountain House—A Band of Blackfeet Come to Join Him—The Dangerous Interpreter—The Inaccessible Tribe — The Missionary Decides to Pass the Winter at Fort Edmonton—He Visits St. Anne's Mission—On a Sledge from Saskatchewan to Athabasca—A Christian Who Had Not Seen a Priest for Forty Years—Crossing the Mountains when the Snow Was Melting —To Reduce His Weight Father De Smet Fasts for Thirty Days—Descent of the Columbia—A Meeting with Father Nobili—Journey to Vancouver and Willamette—The Grotesque Indian—Progress of the Missions—Victory of the Flatheads over the Crows—The Impression Produced on the Blackfeet—Father De Smet's Complete Success—"Exaltation of the Holy Cross"—Father Point is Charged to Open a Mission for the Blackfeet—Father De Smet's Return to St. Louis—The Aricaras—The Sioux—The Missionary's Prodigious Labors—Consoling Results.

NEITHER the zeal of the missionaries nor the fervor of the neophytes could assure the future of the new Christendom, so long as it was exposed to the incursions of the Blackfeet. The Flatheads were especially menaced, the yearly buffalo-hunt giving rise to new grievances. The Blackfeet claimed the exclusive right to hunt upon the eastern slope of the mountains. The Flatheads maintained that their ancestors had always enjoyed this privilege, and furthermore, that so long as a brave of their tribe could bear arms they would defend their rights. Hence sanguinary encounters ensued, in which the Flatheads, inferior in numbers, were defeated.

St. Mary's Mission was frequently attacked. In a country covered with thick underbrush, it was possible for the Blackfeet to remain hidden for days, waiting to attack at night any Flatheads returning alone to the village.

The unfortunate victims were killed and scalped, and the assassin escaped unseen. While the warriors were at the hunt, the missionaries dared not venture unarmed beyond the stockades, and night and day a sentinel stood guard, firing from time to time to intimidate the enemy.

For some time Father De Smet had been thinking of visiting these formidable neighbors, hoping thereby to induce them to bury the war-hatchet and conclude a lasting peace with the Western tribes. The undertaking was perilous in the extreme, for the missionary was without arms, and, so to speak, without escort. The Blackfeet were bitter enemies of the whites, whom they murdered without scruple to satisfy their hate and superstitions.

"What will befall me?" writes Father De Smet when about to penetrate into the enemy's country. "I confess to being assailed by a multitude of fears. Poor human nature! this frail, timid *meus homo* is affrighted, and would have me look back and listen to my dreams. But duty calls, Forward, march! I trust in God: He can, if it please Him, soften the wildest natures. I take courage in the prayers that are being said for my safety. The salvation of souls and the preservation of St. Mary's are at stake, and no consideration shall turn me from a project I have cherished since my first visit to the mountains."[1]

The Blackfeet lived on the other side of the Rockies upon the Upper Missouri. Going in an easterly direction, Father De Smet would doubtless have been able to encounter them after a few days' travel. But he preferred to journey north and across the mountains near the source of the Saskatchewan, in the hope of discovering new tribes to whom he might preach the Gospel. His object was to take possession in the name of Christ of the entire region, as yet untrodden by a Catholic priest.

After founding the mission of the Immaculate Heart of Mary he started off at the end of August, accompanied by the Kootenais guides, and a third Indian who was to serve as hunter and interpreter. But a year was destined to pass before he should encounter the Blackfeet. The events of this journey throw into relief the missionary's daring initiative and untiring perseverance.

---

[1] Letter to Bishop Hughes, Sept. 26, 1845.

On September 4th Father De Smet arrived at the source of the Columbia. He was spellbound with admiration at the grandeur of the spectacle that lay before him, and gazed at the stream dashing and foaming down the mountainside, which becomes, in its capricious turns and windings, the most dangerous of the Western rivers. "The famous Cheops and Cephren dwindle into insignificance before these gigantic peaks. The natural pyramids of the Rocky Mountains seem to hurl defiance at all human construction. The hand of God laid the foundations, permitting the elements to fashion them, and through the centuries they proclaim His glory and power."[2]

From there he traveled east through a narrow gorge into which daylight hardly penetrated. Trees of various species clung to the mountain's rugged flank, and pines and cedars cast their dark shadows upon the jagged rocks. The poplar rustled in the autumn breeze, the slender birch waved its golden plumes, and the blue turpentine and the juniper-tree, heavy with its crimson berries, filled the valley with their perfume.

When he came across plants not indigenous to Belgian soil, he got off his horse and filled his pockets with seeds for the friends and benefactors of the missions. "In four or five years one could fancy one's self in America when in John's garden,[3] or in Charles' country-place." The route lay through dense forests, raging torrents, and beside appalling precipices. A slight noise at times indicated that all life was not banished from these solitudes. It was the deer calling to its mate, or the elk giving the alarm at the hunter's approach, or a herd of caribou lying couched on the snow; disturbed by the sound of the horses' hoofs, they started up and instantly disappeared behind inaccessible peaks. Now and then a buck crossed the traveler's path, his ears cocked and straight as the point of a lance; he stopped a moment, regarded the caravan, and then bounded into a thicket. High above, near the ice-bound summits, white forms moved as though suspended upon the flanks of the rock. They were mountain-goats, quietly

---

[2] Letter quoted.
[3] He speaks here most likely of Dr. Frederick John Lutens, his brother-in-law.

browsing upon the edge of precipices, beyond the reach of the most daring hunter.

Always interested in the habits of animals, Father De Smet studied with pleasure and interest these inhabitants of the forest, from the redoubtable grizzly bear "which in Oregon corresponds to the lion in Africa" to the little mountain rabbit, "only six inches long, and not of sufficient importance to find mention in natural history." Emerging from the forest, he beheld the aurora borealis. "Huge shafts of light play across the heavens, straight as columns, or in undulating waves appear and disappear in infinitely varied aspects. Then suddenly the whole horizon is brilliantly illuminated, the rays uniting at the zenith to separate in divers forms."[4]

Up to this point the journey had gone smoothly. The missionary thanked God, whose sublime works he had just admired. "All that one sees and hears in the wilderness is delightful and instructive; one is impressed, captivated, and elevated toward the Author of all nature. '*Mirabilia opera Domini.*'"[5]

On September 15th, Father De Smet crossed the range that separates the waters of the Columbia from the Saskatchewan. On the summit he planted a large cross, "The Cross of Peace," and then began the descent of the eastern side of the mountain. After three days, he came upon traces of a band of Indians. Could these be the Blackfeet? Fear seized his escort, and in the hope of turning the missionary from his project, they related their dreams of evil omen. One saw himself devoured by a bear; the other beheld crows and vultures circling over the missionary's tent; a third saw blood. To reassure them the jovial missionary recited a fable.

"Midst the dark horrors of the sable night,
  (No idle dream I tell nor fancy's strain)
Thrice rose the red man's shade upon my sight,
  Thrice vanished into dusky air again.

"With courage high my panting bosom swells,
  Onward I rushed upon the threatening foe,
When, hark! horrific rise the specter's yells,
  He points the steel and aims the fatal blow.

[4] Letter to Bishop Hughes, from the Cross of Peace, Sept. 15, 1845.
[5] *Ibid.*

"Guard, sentinel! to arms! to arms! to arms!
Indians! Indians! my voice swelled loud and deep.
The camp is roused at dread of my alarms,
They wake and find—*that I am sound asleep!*" [6]

Laughter dispelled fear, and the guides saw how little importance Father De Smet attached to such dreams. "Come what may," they cried, "we will never forsake you until we see you in safety."

"And yet," writes Father De Smet, "I had no illusions as to the danger, for I found myself in a land, the scene of bloody encounters, in close proximity to a barbarous people, the enemies of the white man, whom I may never see again." [7]

For two days they followed the tracks of the unknown travelers, whose traces became ever more distinct. "I sent my guides to reconnoiter," says the missionary; "one of them returned at nightfall, saying he had come upon a small camp of the Assiniboins of the Forest, where he had been well received and all had manifested a great desire to see me." The next day he joined the tribe and journeyed several days with them. "This tribe, numbering not more than fifty families, live in the woods and the mountains. Agriculture is unknown to them, and they feed on animal flesh, especially porcupines, which abound in this region. When short of food they eat roots, seeds, and the inner bark of the cypress. The chief of the tribe told me that last winter a man in the extremity of hunger had eaten his wife and four children."

In default of horses, the Assiniboins possessed a large number of dogs, and more voracious animals could scarcely be imagined. "One night I neglected to put stakes around my tent, and in consequence found myself in the morning shoeless, my cassock minus a collar, and my breeches short a leg.

"The Assiniboins are filthy beyond description, and devoured by vermin which they themselves eat. 'Are you not ashamed,' I asked an Indian, 'to eat these insects?' 'They eat me first,' he replied, 'and I have the right to retaliate.' Wishing to be particularly amiable, one day I

[6] Cf. Chittenden-Richardson, pp. 506, 507.
[7] Letter to Bishop Hughes, Camp Assiniboin, Sept. 26, 1845.

assisted at a porcupine feast, a scene that would have turned the strongest stomach. Failing a table-cloth and dishes, several of the company took off their leather shirts shining with grease and laid them on the ground. Upon this covering the meat was cut and served; to dry their hands they wiped them on their hair. An old woman whose face was smeared with blood—a sign of mourning—presented me with a wooden bowl of soup. The horn spoon reeked with grease, which she kindly licked before putting it in my soup.

"The Indians have a bizarre method of cooking certain dishes which they, however, consider delicious. The cooking is done solely by the women, who first work up a mixture of grease and blood in their hands and then boil this in a little water. Then they fill a kettle with grease and meat which they have chewed into a pulp. Often half a dozen women are occupied for hours preparing this rare stew. They chew and chew again mouthful after mouthful, then put the whole in the kettle. This is the far-famed Rocky Mountain hash! Add to this delectable dish cakes made of crushed ants and grasshoppers dried in the sun, and you will have some idea of the delicacies of the Assiniboin table."[8]

These people were not wholly disposed to be taught the Gospel. Jealousy divided families, and quarrels, disputes, and murders were not infrequent. Protestant ministers of doubtful morals had traversed the country defaming the Black Robes; but, undaunted, the missionary gave instruction every evening, and baptized some children and an old man who, dying a few days later, was interred with Catholic rites.

After a few weeks' sojourn at the Assiniboin camp, Father De Smet started off with his three guides. The interlaced branches of the cypress forest which they traversed tore and scraped their hands, faces, and clothes, as the travelers pushed their way through. Nor did our missionary escape without an adventure. He says:

"I had to pass under a tree that hung over the path; one of its branches, broken off at the end, presented a dangerous hook. I bent down on my horse's neck, but this was a

[8] Letter to Bishop Hughes, Camp Assiniboin, Sept. 26, 1845.

useless maneuver, for it seized me by the collar of my coat and lifted me up, my horse passing on from under me. There I hung like a fish on a hook. My battered hat, black eye, and torn cheek in a civilized land would have laid me open to suspicion as being a highwayman from the Black Forest, rather than a missionary in search of souls."[9]

After pushing their way for several weeks through the mountains, the caravan descended into the vast plain that lies between the Saskatchewan and Upper Missouri. Here, besides the Blackfeet, lived the Crows, Aricaras, Crees, Assiniboins of the Forest, the Cheyennes, the Sioux, and others. Canadian missionaries had just begun to evangelize these barbarous tribes. "The difference in physiognomy between these Indians and those who inhabit the shores of the Columbia is as great as the mountains which separate them. These latter are renowned for their frankness, gentleness, and amiability, while cruelty, craft, and thirst for blood give their impress to the lineaments of the Blackfeet. Hands unstained by blood are a rarity in this nation."[10]

On October 4th they arrived at the Rocky Mountain House, belonging to the Hudson Bay Company. Although a Protestant, the commander was disposed to aid the missionary. A detachment of Blackfeet was due at the fort and he promised to bring about a friendly meeting. Father De Smet then discharged his escort, and while awaiting the Blackfeet prepared for baptism twenty Crees who had learned of Christianity from a Canadian priest.

On October 25th a band of thirteen Blackfeet arrived at the Fort. "They greeted me," writes Father De Smet, "after the fashion of Indians, with politeness at once uncouth and cordial. Upon learning the object of my journey, the old chief embraced me. His accoutrements distinguished him from his companions, for he was covered from head to foot with eagle feathers and wore upon his chest a medallion consisting of a large plate decorated with blue flowers. Every mark of friendship was shown me, and each time I visited him he seated me beside him,

---

[9] Letter to Bishop Hughes, Rocky Mountain House, Oct. 5, 1845.
[10] *Ibid.*, Oct. 30, 1845.

13

shook my hand affectionately, and rubbed his vermilion-painted nose first on one of my cheeks and then on the other. He invited me at once to visit his country and offered to personally act as my guide and introduce me to his people."[11]

That year had been a disastrous one for the Blackfeet. Twenty-one warriors had been killed in two skirmishes with the Flatheads and Kalispels; six hundred horses had been stolen, and twenty-seven men scalped by the Crees; fifty families massacred by the Crows, and one hundred and sixty women and children led into captivity. Such misfortunes had rendered tractable the chiefs of this ferocious tribe.

The main difficulty was to find a competent interpreter. The only one at the Fort was not considered trustworthy, and could not be recommended by the travelers who had employed him; but his professions of fidelity finally decided Father De Smet to engage him, as he wished to reach the Blackfeet before winter set in. Before long he had reason to regret his decision.

On October 31st he left the Post, accompanied by the interpreter and a young half-breed Cree to care for the horses. The Blackfeet had gone before to prepare the tribe for the missionary's visit, and dispose them to accord him a friendly reception. "Despite his promises," writes Father De Smet, "the interpreter soon showed his hand. He became sullen and bad-tempered, and behaved as though the weight of the universe had been placed on his shoulders. He pitched camp in places where the poor horses could not find a blade of grass after a long day's journey. The further we advanced into the wilds, the more surly he became. Not a pleasant word escaped his lips, and his incoherent mutterings finally alarmed me.

"I had marched unintermittently ten days, and the last two nights were nights of anguish and watching. Just then I had the luck to meet a Canadian, whom I prevailed on to remain with me for a few days. The next morning the interpreter disappeared. Although my situation was critical in the extreme, with neither guide nor interpreter, the departure of my disagreeable companion lifted a weight

[11] Letter quoted.

off my heart, for had I not met the Canadian, in all likelihood I would have fallen a victim to his fell designs to do away with me."[12]

Father De Smet then set about to find another interpreter, as he was determined not to turn back. He was told that further on he would find one who was also en route for the Blackfeet. For eight days he searched for him through a labyrinth of narrow valleys, but all in vain. Nor did he come upon any Indians. The Crees, who were on the war-path, overran the country in every direction, the Blackfeet fleeing before them. For four days it snowed heavily; the horses were exhausted. Father De Smet's rations were at low ebb. The passage of the mountains was blocked, and nothing now remained but to try to reach one of the Fur Company's posts and winter there, putting off until spring his visit to the Blackfeet. So Father De Smet hastily retraced his steps, going to Fort Edmonton on the Saskatchewan. The warm reception given him compensated in a measure for the disappointments and mishaps of the past two months. The population of the Fort was in large part Catholic. The missionary explained the catechism every morning to the children, and in the evening before night-prayers gave an instruction, at which the commander and his household were present.

St. Anne's Mission lay fifty miles west of the Fort. This was the headquarters of the Canadian priests, Fathers Thibault and Bourassa, who from this center extended their apostolic labors to Athabasca, Peace River, Slave Lake, and the Mackenzie. Father De Smet visited them, and was rejoiced to find that the Indians in this part of Canada were not less fervent than the most religious of the Western tribes. In the course of one journey Father Thibault had baptized nearly five hundred souls.

Winter was drawing to a close, and yet grave difficulties stood in the way of reaching the Blackfeet. An interpreter was not to be had. Armed bands terrorized the country; thieving and carnage were rife. While determined not to give up his project, Father De Smet deemed it wiser for the present to retire again to St. Ignatius' Mission. He

[12] Letter to Bishop Hughes, Fort Edmonton, Dec. 31, 1845.

still hoped to reach, by another route, this inaccessible tribe.

On March 12th he left Fort Edmonton with an escort of three trustworthy half-breeds given him by Father Thibault. His plan was to approach the mountains through the Athabasca valley and from there to descend the Columbia to Fort Colville. As the ground was covered with snow, they traveled in a sleigh drawn by four dogs, and after six days reached Fort Assiniboin on the Athabasca. Then following the river for three hundred miles, they arrived at Fort Jasper.

There he met an Iroquois who had not seen a priest since he left his country forty years before. The old Indian's joy knew no bounds, for now his children could be baptized. Father De Smet remained several days to instruct this interesting family, thirty-six in number. He celebrated Mass on Easter, and afterward administered baptism and married seven couples.

The moment of separation was impressive. "The new Christians," writes Father De Smet, "wished to honor me in a way that would leave a lasting impression on their children and keep before them ever the name of him who had placed them in 'the way of life.' The assembled family gave three rousing hurrahs, at the same time firing their guns in the direction of the mountain to which they gave my name. The men escorted me ten miles on my journey, each one shaking my hand effusively at parting. We exchanged good wishes and mingled our tears, and when they departed we found ourselves alone in one of those wild ravines enclosed by mountains rising like insurmountable barriers."[13]

Father De Smet reached the top of the highest peaks in the Rocky Mountains, and beheld Mount Brown lifting its snow-clad summit over ten thousand feet in the empyrean. Crossing these mountains is difficult at all seasons, but it was especially difficult now, at the beginning of May, for the melting snow caused frequent avalanches, carrying with them enormous rocks that

[13] Letter to Bishop Hughes, from the foot of the Great Glacier, May 6, 1846.

bounded down the mountainside with deafening noise, felling trees, crushing herds and flocks, and filling up the valleys. Before this undertaking, the most perilous perhaps that he had ever encountered, the intrepid missionary, already exhausted by a useless journey of several months, seems to have lost courage temporarily. To his family he writes:

"My health is no longer what it was. Every time I climb a mountain now, my strength seems to leave me. The rigors of the climate, fasts, sleepless nights, with ever-increasing anxieties, and the dangers and agonizing moments I pass through, are sapping my constitution. Only lately did I miraculously escape the hands of a vile assassin."

In writing to his Belgian friends he says, "You are always in my heart, and I sigh and long for you. If God permits me to again behold my country I shall never leave it."[14] It would, however, have been difficult for Father De Smet to keep this resolution, for he was to see his native Belgium seven times more, and each time, despite his love for his family, the thought of the salvation of souls was to bring him back to his adopted country.[15] Nor does it displease us to see the great missionary momentarily bend under his burden; his personality is the more winning for being so human, since there is often more pride than virtue in bearing up under trial.

Before long Father De Smet recovered his wonted spirits, and again his letters tell us of the difficulties and accidents of this appalling journey. "We had sixty miles to make on snow-shoes before reaching the boat encampment on the Columbia, and we determined to make the trip in two and a half days. The commanders at Rocky Mountain House and at Fort Edmonton endeavored to dissuade me from undertaking this journey, thinking me too heavy for the exertion it required. But a strict fast for thirty days reduced my flesh, and, finding myself considerably lighter, I bravely set out to journey through snow from

[14] Letter to Francis De Smet, from the foot of the Great Glacier in the Upper Athabasca, May 6, 1846.
[15] In 1833 Father De Smet became a naturalized citizen of the United States.

sixteen to twenty feet deep. We went single file across a plain covered with the débris of an avalanche; now over lakes or torrents hidden under the snow; and now through a cypress forest buried in snow to its top branches. I do not know how many times I tumbled, for every minute I was having trouble with my snow-shoes, or was caught by the branch of a tree. When one falls the arms are instinctively stretched out to save one's self. In deep snow the danger is not great; the arms sink in up to the shoulder, and one lies struggling and laughing. My guides were most obliging, and after each tumble hastened to my assistance and got me on my feet again.

"After tramping thirty miles the first day, we made our camp. We cut pine branches, which we laid on the snow for our beds. Sleeping on the snow and in the open may sound uncomfortable to those accustomed to soft mattresses and warm rooms, but never was there a greater mistake. Come and breathe the pure air of the mountains, where coughs and colds are unknown, and where condiments are not needed to excite the appetite! Come and try a nomad's life and see how the fatigues of a long day's journey are forgotten; come and experience the joy of health and sound sleep, wrapped in a buffalo hide, lying upon pine branches beside a crackling fire!

"The next day we began the steep descent of what is known as the Great Western Slope. It took five hours. The whole side of the mountain is covered with a dense forest of huge pines, larches, and cedars. Woe to the man with a heavy body or who makes a false step! I speak from experience—for many times I gathered myself together twenty or thirty feet from where I fell, happy indeed if I did not strike my head against the trunk of some great tree.

"At the foot of the mountain the scene changed. The barriers of snow and the many banks which until now had held the mountain torrents, lakes, and streams in check were broken up during the night, putting the Great Portage River in freshet. Through a valley scarcely a mile wide this river winds with so many turns, that in one day we crossed it forty times in water up to our shoulders; and so swift is its current that we were obliged to hold tightly to one another to prevent being swept away. The rest of the journey was made in dripping garments. The cold, together with extreme fatigue, caused my legs to swell; my toe nails came off and the blood coagulated in my boots. Four times I felt my strength failing, and I should have perished in this grim wilderness if the courage and strength of my companions had not sustained me.

"We left the Portage valley and entered a thick and mountainous forest, where the ground was encumbered with thousands of trees felled by the tempests. Then followed marshes through which we crossed in mud and water up to our knees; but these troubles were trifling compared to those which we had encountered in the beginning of our journey. Finally we came to the boat encampment on the Columbia, at the mouth of the Portage River. Those who have crossed the Rocky Mountains at 53° of north latitude when the snow is melting know what it means to be a good traveler. It had required all my strength to accomplish this crossing, and I confess I would not dare to undertake it again."[16]

After a few hours' rest, Father De Smet and his guides embarked upon the Columbia. After the horrors of the dark mountain passes, they were cheered by the smiling aspect of spring. The river islands were a mass of blossom and the mantle of snow was thinning on the mountainsides; a thousand little rivulets leaped singing from rock to rock. In the hands of his skilful guides the canoe shot the rapids, made its way safely through the rocks, and descended swift as an arrow.

At one time Father De Smet feared a repetition of the accident that had befallen his men four years before. He had just stepped ashore to avoid a difficult passage; the Canadians, confident in their ability to manage the canoe, refused to leave it, when suddenly it was caught in a whirlpool. Despite their desperate efforts, it was sucked in and the boat filled with water. The missionary on the bank fell on his knees and implored heaven to save his men, who seemed doomed to destruction. In a flash the gulf closed again, throwing the canoe into safe water.

At St. Peter of the Lakes, on the right bank of the

[16] Letter to Father Van de Velde, Boat Encampment, May 10, 1846.

river, there lived twenty families of the Chaudière tribe, who had not received baptism the previous year. Father De Smet stopped to instruct them, and a few days later they all became Christians. Toward the end of May he arrived at Fort Colville, where the Indians of the St. Paul Mission were waiting to receive him and conduct him to their mission. Great was the missionary's joy to find that the whole tribe had been instructed and baptized by Father Hoecken, and still greater was his happiness in celebrating Mass in the humble chapel built by the Indians.

It was an added pleasure to meet Father Nobili, the apostle to New Caledonia. He likewise had passed through many trials. Obliged to follow these wandering tribes from camp to camp, he had traversed hundreds of miles through ice and snow, with often no food other than dog or wolf meat, and for months he had lived on a sort of moss mixed with insipid roots. But such privations endured for God were not in vain. Everywhere the Indians received the missionary enthusiastically, asking him to baptize their children. Many were converted and remained faithful to their marriage vows. A cross had been erected in every village that did not possess a church. Father Nobili felt the need of a rest and was now about to leave to spend a few weeks at St. Ignatius' Mission.

As we have seen, it was Father De Smet's intention to repair to the same mission, and from there to work his way to the Blackfeet. The commander at Fort Colville had kindly offered him passage in a boat going to Vancouver, which would permit him to revictual the different mountain posts. Father De Smet accepted his invitation.

During the year, Catholicism had made rapid progress in the Willamette valley. Fathers Accolti and De Vos of St. Francis Xavier's Mission expected many conversions in the contiguous territory. Father Vercruysse had accomplished marvels with the Grand Prairie Indians, and the Sisters of Notre Dame rejoiced in an ever-increasing number of pupils. But the number of missionaries was not sufficient for the work. Archbishop Blanchet, however, was soon to return from Europe with both missionaries and Sisters.[17]

Laden with supplies for the missions, Father De Smet started again to cross the mountains. He had hardly left Vancouver when a powder-horn exploded, burning one side of his face, though not seriously enough to impede his travels. As he journeyed, he studied the habits of the Indians, and found endless pleasure in the beauties of the river.

At a place called the Great Dalles, Father De Smet came upon a band of grotesque Indians. When the German, Canadian, and Spanish emigrants descended the Columbia valley they were frequently in need of provisions, canoes, and guides. In payment for these they gave the Indians their old clothing, hence a rare collection of coats, trousers, hats, and shoes were worn indiscriminately by men and women, regardless of age or stature.

"Two big, stalwart Indians paraded before us in the apparent belief that their new acquisitions embellished their persons. One wore a pair of trousers turned inside out, another a coat much too short, with a torn pair of skintight trousers which betrayed the absence of a shirt; a lace head-dress was the crowning touch to this bizarre costume. I met Indians wearing one shoe, others both shoes. Some go through the camp in the habiliments of a wagoner, others in a mixture composed of the clothes of a sailor, a workman, and a lawyer, arranged according to fancy; some again with only one article of dress. I have seen an old Indian showing off a pair of boots, the only article of his wardrobe. Indian squaws are attired in long calico gowns which they have besmeared with fish oil through choice or negligence. If they can afford it, they superadd a vest of flannel, or the *ne plus ultra* of elegance, a man's overcoat."[18]

The spectacle amused our missionary, but he could not forget the moral degradation of these unfortunate people. "With the greater number idolatry extends even to the worship of the lowest animals, and some even sacrifice

---

[17] Of this number six were Jesuits: Father Anthony Goetz, Joseph Ménétrey, and Gregory Gazzoli, with three lay Brothers.

[18] Letter to Father Van de Velde, Fort Walla Walla, June 18, 1846.

human beings to appease their gods. Add to this, licentiousness, a passion for gambling, and an idleness that famine alone stimulates into action, hypocrisy, and gluttony, and all that is base, and you will then have an idea of the vileness in which the Indians of the Columbia stagnate."[19]

Father De Smet hoped to be able to send missionaries to these tribes, but for the moment the future of the existing missions must be assured. At Walla Walla he left the Columbia, struck out overland, and with a caravan of mules and horses crossed for the second time the immense country of the Spokanes and Nez Percés. He visited, in passing, St. Francis Regis' Mission, where seventy half-breeds were leading Christian lives, and on July 17th arrived at St. Ignatius' Mission.

Under Father Hoecken's wise direction the new "reduction" had prospered. The Kalispel converts numbered about four hundred and were distinguished not only for their fervent piety, but for industry and love of work. The men had three hundred acres of land under cultivation and the women had learned to milk cows and make butter. Besides cattle, they had large poultry-yards. To sustain the growing colony Father De Smet gave Father Hoecken part of his supplies. He then departed for the Cœur d'Alènes.

Above all others, the Sacred Heart Mission manifested in a striking manner the wonderful effects of grace in the soul of the savage. "God," they said, "took pity on us; He has opened our eyes: He is infinitely merciful." The neophytes applied themselves to agriculture, and under Father Joset's direction sowed enough grain to nourish many families. Thus gradually these nomadic children of the desert began to appreciate the joy of domestic life. Father Point had been recalled, and was to be replaced by Father Gazzoli. In union with Father Joset he carried on for many years a fruitful apostolate.

After a few days spent with the Cœur d'Alènes, Father De Smet, accompanied by Father Point, left for St. Mary's, thus, at the same time revictualing the missions, and also approaching the land of the Blackfeet. St. Mary's, the

[19] Letter quoted.

first foundation, always remained the principal mountain settlement, and like a glowing and luminous hearth, radiated civilization through the desert.

Father Zerbinati died in the autumn of 1845 after a short apostolate of only two years, and was succeeded by Father Ravalli from St. Ignatius' Mission.[20]   The rapid development of this mission was due to Father Mengarini's powers of organization.   A large church now replaced the little chapel; a priest's house and other wooden houses in the same style had been built, and cattle and poultry gave the touch of a civilized community to the prosperous village.   The wheat crop amounted to thousands of bushels, and a quantity of potatoes, more than sufficient for the tribe, had been grown.   Even after the Easter celebrations the granaries and cellars were still so well filled that the missionaries invited the Snakes, the Bannocks, the Nez Percés, and the Pend d'Oreilles to a feast composed of dishes unknown to many of them.   Father Mengarini had also succeeded in extracting the sugar from potatoes, and with barley and some native roots made a sort of non-intoxicating drink that was both agreeable to the taste and nourishing.   But they still lacked flour, for the result obtained from crushing wheat between stones or grinding it in a coffee-mill was anything but flour.   Father Ravalli immediately set about supplying this need.   With the assistance of Brother Claessens and Brother Specht he constructed a water-mill capable of turning out daily several sacks of flour, and, at the same time, a saw-mill for cutting boards and beams needed in building.   The saw he made from the tire of a wheel, beaten out thin, and from four other tires, welded together, he made a fly-wheel.   The whole was run by the same waterfall that worked the flour-mill.

The spiritual and moral condition of this mission was as satisfactory as its material prosperity.   Since the abolition of polygamy the population had sensibly increased.   The abandonment of children, divorce, and the shedding of

[20] Born at Ferrara in 1812, Anthony Ravalli evinced in early youth a strong desire for foreign missionary work.   With this end in view, besides philosophy and theology, he had studied medicine, drawing, and mechanics. His devotion, simplicity, and happy nature won for him, during his labor of forty years, the esteem and confidence of both the white man and the Indian.

blood were now unknown among the Flatheads. Young girls were permitted to marry for choice. The sick were cared for, and no longer allowed to die in misery. The education of the children was regarded as a religious duty, and gave promise to the missionaries of a Christian generation.

Bands of unfriendly tribes, it is true, continued to trouble the tranquillity of the village. But the courage of the braves, sustained by extraordinary faith in divine protection, finally made allies of the most hostile. Shortly before Father De Smet's arrival, an encounter had taken place with the Crows, who had stolen thirty of the Flatheads' horses. Two who were innocent of the theft had been punished. When the mistake was discovered, every effort was made to make amends, but all in vain. The Crows gladly seized a pretext for warfare.

One morning, the Flatheads saw a cloud of dust on the horizon; it was the enemy. The chief then assembled his tribe and addressed them thus: "My friends, if God wills that we be conquered, we shall be; but His will be done, and above all trust in Him!" When the Crows came within range of their rifles, a volley was poured upon them. Disconcerted by this resistance, they changed their plan of attack and began a series of fantastic evolutions, which only resulted in wearing out their horses.

"To horse!" cried the Flathead chief. In a flash every man vaulted into the saddle and started in pursuit of the Crows, whom they forced to retreat two miles from the camp. Their number was large enough, however, to permit them to continue the struggle until sundown, when they fled in disorder, leaving fourteen dead and nine wounded. The Flatheads did not lose a single man. Even their women distinguished themselves in action. After having pursued a band of Crows, hatchet in hand, one squaw returned, saying, "I thought these braggarts were men: they are not even worthy of being pursued by women."

This encounter brought matters to a point that facilitated the reconciliation that Father De Smet had sought for more than a year. Father Mengarini's kindness and

charity conquered the savage natures of the Blackfeet
living in the neighborhood of St. Mary's, and the daring
courage of the Flatheads, to which they owed their preservation from the common enemy, finally won them over.
Burning to avenge the disaster experienced the year before,
the Blackfeet united with the Flatheads in an effort to beat
back the Crows. Returning victorious, they at once
sought out the missionary.

"Such a victory," they said, "could only have been
obtained by prayer. All during the battle we saw the
old men, the women, and the children on their knees,
imploring help from on high. We have often taken part
in their night and morning prayers and listened to the
chiefs' instructions. Black Robe, deign to take pity on us;
we have decided henceforth to follow the teachings of the
white man's great manitou."

And now Father De Smet was nearing the realization
of the plan for which he had so long labored and suffered.
Conducted by a band of Blackfeet, he was going to penetrate
into the very heart of the redoubtable tribe in order to bring
about a lasting peace between them and the Flatheads,
and to prepare the way for Christian teaching.

The day after the feast of the Assumption, he left
St. Mary's valley, accompanied by Father Point and a
group of Flatheads charged with the expression of the
peaceful intentions of their nation toward the Blackfeet.
After crossing the Rocky Mountains, he entered for the
third time the dangerous Yellowstone valley. Near the
mouth of the Big Horn he turned northwest, crossing an
arid and mountainous country, and for days had only
brackish, stagnant water to drink. At last, on September
14th, the feast of the Exaltation of the Cross, on the
shores of the Judith River, a tributary of the Missouri,
he came upon the principal camp of the Blackfeet. The
news of the Flatheads' victory had already reached them.

"The religion of the Black Robes," they said, "is more
powerful than ours." Hence they received Father De
Smet with the honors due a man who spoke to the Great
Spirit. Profiting by such favorable dispositions, the missionary explained to the Indians the elements of Christianity, dwelling at length upon the protection God accords

those who trust in Him. Then the Blackfeet who had fought in the last battle against the Crows related what they had witnessed in the Flathead camp. They extolled above all the power of the Sign of the Cross, which appeared to them a sure indication of victory. "To-day is truly the feast of the Exaltation of the Cross," writes Father De Smet in his journal.

For their own interest, as well as out of consideration for the Black Robe, these fierce warriors made a truce, and received as allies their former enemies. That night the Flatheads and Blackfeet recited evening prayers together. The missionary's soul was filled with joy at seeing prostrate before the cross men who had once wounded each other in bloody battles and whom deadly hatred had divided. In chorus they invoked "the Master of life," calling Him for the first time their common Father. All seemed to be of one heart and soul.

The next day was the octave of the Nativity of the Blessed Virgin. "I sang Mass in the open air under a canopy of green boughs, the work of the Indians, and implored the blessing of heaven upon these wandering tribes of the desert, begging God to unite them by the ties of peace. Flatheads, Nez Percés, Piegans, Bloods, Grosventres, and Blackfeet of different tribes, to the number of more than two thousand, surrounded the humble altar on which the Victim without blemish was offered for them. The perfect harmony which seems to animate the Flatheads and the representatives of the other tribes is unexampled. One would think that their old quarrels had long since been forgotten, and this is the more remarkable, for it is a part of the Indian's creed to cherish vengeance against his enemy until death."[21]

Father De Smet remained several weeks among the Blackfeet, in order to strengthen their peaceful intentions, and continued to prepare them to receive the Gospel. But the conversion of the Blackfeet presented difficulties he had not encountered among the Oregon tribes. "These are savages in the full sense of the word, accustomed to satiate their vengeance and to revel in blood and carnage. They are plunged in the grossest superstitions; they wor-

[21] Letter to Father Van de Velde, Fort Lewis, Sept. 26, 1846.

ship the sun and moon, offering them sacrifices of pro-
pitiation and thanksgiving. They cut deep into their
own flesh and even cut off the joints of the fingers. 'I
offer you my blood,' they say to their divinity; 'now give
me success in arms, and on my return I will offer you the
homage of the scalps of my enemies.'"[22]

But despite their degraded condition, Father De Smet
still hoped to accomplish some good among them. He had
baptized several children and every evening the Indians
crowded to his instructions; all seemed to understand that
the missionaries were devoted heart and soul to their
welfare. Father Point, who had been so successful with
the Cœur d'Alènes remained with the Blackfeet to complete their instruction and establish a mission for them
like those on the other side of the mountains.

Fathers were too few in number, however, to evangelize all the Western tribes, so Father De Smet set out once
more for St. Louis to procure men and money. He was
eager, moreover, to acquaint his Superiors with the progress the missions were making, and to gain for his work the
sanction of obedience.

On September 28th, our missionary embarked upon the
Missouri in a light canoe with only two guides, and began a journey that lasted two months before he reached
Westport. He stopped frequently en route to visit the
employees of the forts, and to instruct and baptize their
children. Along the river, bands of Indians would signal
to him from the shore. "To refuse to land would anger
them and expose us to their thirst for vengeance, so through
prudence we landed, and rarely had cause to regret it.
We accepted the calumet and filled it for them, and
exchanged news. If they saw our provisions were low,
they insisted upon giving us the best spoils of the chase;
then we embraced and parted friends."[23]

One night, however, they encountered a real danger.
Their bivouac fire betrayed their location to a band of
Aricaras, the sworn enemies of the white man. They
descended upon them, armed to the teeth, but happily

[22] Letter to Father Van de Velde, Sept. 27, 1846.
[23] Letter to the Father General, St. Louis, Jan. 1, 1847.

the chief knew Father De Smet, and at sight of the copper cross on his breast he flung away his tomahawk and, running to the missionary, embraced him, saying: "I see you are about to leave for the country of souls. We did not know you were near, and took you for an enemy." Then they exchanged all the marks of politeness and friendship, and the evening was passed in rejoicing. Before his departure the Indians promised the missionary that henceforth they would greet the white man with calumet in hand.

Soon they came to the country of the Sioux, and found the principal chiefs assembled at Fort Lookout. He told them of the conversion of the mountain tribes and of his recent visit to the Blackfeet. "And you," he said to the Sioux in conclusion, "will you receive the Black Robe who wishes to live in your plains and dwell in the midst of you? Will you listen to his words and follow the path that Jesus Christ, Son of the Master of life, came on earth to show us, for in this path all nations must tread? Speak, Sioux! I am listening and will carry your words to the great chiefs of the Black Robes; speak from your hearts." The Sioux deliberated a few moments, then the great orator arose:

"Black Robe," he said, "I speak in the name of the chiefs and braves. You have spoken beautiful words about the Master of life. We like them. To-day is the first time that we have heard them. Black Robe, you are only passing through our country: to-morrow we will no longer hear your voice; we shall be as we have always been, children without a father to guide them, like ignorant beasts of the prairie. Black Robe, come and build your lodge in our midst; my heart tells me that you will be listened to. We are wicked, we have bad hearts, but those who carry the good word have never come to us. Come, Black Robe, the Sioux will listen to you and our children shall be instructed by you." [24]

Unfortunately the winter was approaching; the river was already filling with ice, and Father De Smet could not delay an instant if he wished to reach St. Louis, so it was with regret that he had to put off the present evangelization

[24] Letter quoted.

of this tribe, and start to meet his colleagues. At Westport he discharged his boatmen and traveled overland, and on December 10th arrived at the University. Many, many times in the course of his journey his life was in danger.

Seven years had elapsed since his first journey to the Rocky Mountains. "His prodigious labors, travels, hardships, and perils must be placed," say Chittenden and Richardson, "in the very first rank of similar exploits. In these seven years he had traveled, by methods of the time, a distance equal to more than twice the circumference of the earth. He had traveled in almost every clime and by every sort of conveyance. From the burning summer of the equator, he had passed to the frozen winters of $54°$ $30'$ north. He had traveled by sailing-vessel, by river barge, and by canoe; by dog-sled and snow-shoes; on horseback and in wagon, and many a long mile on foot. He had endured hardships that seem to us almost impossible, and which undoubtedly were the foundation of the ills he later suffered." [25]

But if the work was arduous, the results were most consoling. Oregon possessed more than twenty Christian centers. Upon the banks of the Columbia numerous tribes begged for baptism. In New Caledonia and Western Canada more than a hundred thousand Indians were disposed to receive the word of God. "Three zealous priests," writes Father Accolti, "would suffice to carry the name of Jesus Christ to the Behring Straits." [26] Subjugated by the softening influence of the Gospel, the Missouri Indians gradually conquered their bloodthirsty instincts. The Blackfeet made peace with the mountain tribes, and the Sioux were impatiently awaiting the arrival of the missionary.

In the course of his travels, Father De Smet came in contact with the greater part of the Western tribes. He knew their habits and customs because he had lived their life. His frankness, kindness, and self-confidence had gained for him enormous influence and authority among the Indians.

---

[25] Chittenden-Richardson, pp. 56, 57.
[26] Letter to Father Van de Velde, St. Francis Xavier on the Willamette, June 1, 1847.

CHAPTER XII

Father De Smet Goes to Europe with Father Elet—The "Journeys to the
Rocky Mountains" and "The Missions of Oregon"—Interest Manifested
in the Works of Father De Smet—"Such a Book Revives Our Faith
in the Gospel of St. John"—The Revolution of 1848—Arrival in
America of the Jesuits Driven Out of Europe—Across the "Bad Lands"
—The Poncas—Father De Smet with the Sioux—The "Scalp Dance"
—The Daughter of Red Fish—Plans for a New Mission.

FATHER VAN DE VELDE, who three years before
had succeeded Father Verhaegen as Vice-Provincial,
listened with lively interest to Father De Smet's account
of the progress the missions were making. At all costs,
these thousands of Indians asking for baptism must be
saved. But where to find the missionaries? The Vice-
Province had just lost, through Father De Theux' death,
one of its most energetic workers,[1] and the priests that
remained scarcely sufficed for the needs of Missouri.
An appeal must be made again to Belgium. Father Elet
was about to leave for Rome as Procurator,[2] and it was
decided that Father De Smet should accompany him.

Father Elet had not seen his native land for twenty-six
years, and since Father De Smet's last visit to Belgium
he had received no word from his family. The two
priests arrived in Belgium in the spring of 1847, and after
spending some days with his people, Father De Smet accompanied Father Elet to Paris. While there he visited the
church of Notre Dame des Victoires, where he returned
thanks to his powerful Protectress for the success of the
missions. Before leaving he conversed with the eminent

[1] Father De Theux died at St. Charles, Feb. 28, 1846.
[2] Every three years each province sent one of its members under the title
of "Procurator" to confer in its behalf with the Father General.

curé of the parish, Father Desgenettes, and enrolled a large number of the newly-converted Indians in the celebrated arch confraternity. Returning to Belgium, he went to Tronchiennes to make a retreat, and there undertook a new publication of his "Letters."

A French edition of his *Voyages aux Montagnes Rocheuses* —"Journeys to the Rocky Mountains"[3]—had appeared in 1844. The work, originally published in English, was soon translated into Dutch, German, and Italian.[4] As Father De Smet left America, a second volume from his pen was about to appear. This was an account of his travels during 1845–1846. "I hope," he writes to his brothers, "that you have received my letters from the Upper Athabasca. Fifteen others have just been published in all the Catholic magazines in the United States. The entire collection is now being printed in New York, and will appear in a volume of four hundred pages with illustrations. One hundred copies will be sent to Belgium, where I propose to publish them in French and Flemish. Moreover, I am bringing a map of all the lakes and rivers in the mountains through which I have traveled."[5] The work appeared under the title of "The Oregon Missions"[6] and was not less of a success than its predecessor.

The accounts of the Far West published hitherto by others had betrayed only a superficial observation, the authors' main object being the discovery of the source of the Missouri or a route to the Pacific across the Rocky Mountains.[7] The regions that Father De Smet describes he knew thoroughly. He, of all men of his time, had the most profound knowledge of the Indians, having studied their savage and primitive habits during a long sojourn among the different tribes, and he had many times found himself in situations more alarming than the imagination

[3] Published by P. J. Hanicq, Mechlin.

[4] For the different editions of Father De Smet's Letters, see Sommervogel, *Bibliothèque de la Compagnie de Jésus*, Vol. vii, Cols. 1307–1310.

[5] Liverpool, May 7, 1847.

[6] Published by Van der Schelden, Ghent.

[7] Lewis and Clarke, "Travels to the Source of the Missouri River" (1810); Washington Irving, "Tour on the Prairies" (1835); "Astoria" (1838); "Adventures of Captain Bonneville."—To these may be added G. Catlin's picturesque publication, "Illustration of the Manners, Customs, and Conditions of the North American Indians" (1840).

of the writers of adventure had conceived of. He had shared with the Indians the perils and excitements of the hunt; rather than hurt their feelings, he had partaken of feasts that turned his stomach, and had been the instrument of those marvels of grace, conversions *en masse*.[8] He possessed, moreover, rare powers of observation, solid common sense, and a decided talent for narrative. His expressions are original and his words picturesque. From dramatic scenes he passes to amusing anecdotes and reflections. His style at times is prolix and long drawn out, but a certain misuse of terms is pardonable when one considers that these letters were written offhand and under circumstances little favorable to style or composition. Often it is on a boat, in the confusion of the coming and going of passengers, or during a halt after a long day's march, that the missionary takes his pen to describe a scene or record events. Moreover, is it not to be wondered at that this Fleming who left Belgium before completing his studies, and who spoke for twenty years practically only English and the Indian dialects, should have retained his knowledge of French and been able to write it fluently?

But Father De Smet was devoid of all the vanity of an author and quite frankly excuses his "*Français un peu sauvage.*"[9] On several occasions he begged his confrères in Belgium to revise his letters before giving them to the public, "to polish the style and to correct the faults of orthography."[10] This revision was made, perhaps with more zeal than success, for it seems to us that the original, even with its faults, was more virile and possessed of a certain charm of its own.

His letters cover an infinite variety of subjects. A profound lover of nature, he describes its grandeur with eloquence. The majestic solitudes of Oregon perhaps inspired him more than all else and at times he reads like an echo of the Psalmist, *Mirabilia opera Domini*. He describes delightful nooks and verdant oases. He con-

---

[8] What Father De Smet did not see with his own eyes he was informed of from absolutely reliable sources. Among his friends were trappers, traders, interpreters, and pilots who had lived for years in the West and shared the life of the Indians. Cf. Chittenden-Richardson, p. 141.

[9] Letter to the Vicar General of Canada, Sept. 23, 1852.

[10] Letter to Father Terwecoren, April 5, 1856.

templates with equal pleasure the tiny rivulets and the starry heavens. As a naturalist, he studied the habits of animals; he was engrossed with botany, and often the recital of his labors is interrupted by the enumeration of plants he has discovered and to which he gives charming names.[11] He was probably the first to realize the wealth that industry was afterward to find hidden in the soil of the Far West.[12]

But the Indians were his absorbing interest. He studied their origin,[13] their tribes, and mode of life, but above all their religious ideas. Before Longfellow had embodied in his "Hiawatha" the ancient traditions of a race doomed to extinction, Father De Smet had collected their simple legends, in which one discerns their belief in a Creator, the fall of our first parents, the deluge, the dispersion of mankind, and in a divine Mediator who intercedes for us with the "Master of life."[14]

One often wonders why Father De Smet did not profit by the knowledge he had acquired to make a name for himself as a geographer or a natural scientist. The answer is that he had other desires than for human glory. Following the example of the Master, who sacrificed Himself for the salvation of sinners, his sole ambition was to gain souls to God, his preference ever being work among the poor, the ignorant, and the despised. He passionately loved the Indians. He could not think of them without emotion, nor speak of them without tenderness; "my dear Potawatomies," "my dear Flatheads," "the children

[11] See particularly, "Journeys to the Rocky Mountains," letter to his uncle Rollier.

[12] "The Oregon Missions," edition of 1848, pp. 82, 107, 122.

[13] The origin of the redskins is still a disputed point in ethnology. With many learned authorities, Father De Smet maintains that "the Tartars, Mongolians, and certain other races of Asia have successively peopled the American Continent. However, it appears equally certain that the peoples of the ancient continent (the Scandinavians) also founded colonies here." He bases his opinion on the physiological characteristics, tombs, customs, traditions, languages, religions, and astronomical systems of these divers peoples, and further adds: "A certain amount of obscurity will ever stand in the way of knowing the particular origin of any one people in the New World; but does not the same obscurity obtain with regard to many peoples of the Old World?" (See "The Oregon Missions," edition of 1848, No. XXXII. Origin of the American Races.)

[14] See especially "The Oregon Missions," No. XXVII. Chittenden-Richardson, pp. 1052–1107.

of my heart," he called them.   And it was this that made his letters eloquent sermons.   "Such a book," says a Protestant newspaper, "revives our faith in the Gospel of St. John.   Here we find a religion inspired by love, and capable of ruling the world, a religion that kneels humbly under the dome of St. Peter's in Rome and at the same time regards the heavens from the rocky summits of Oregon."[15]

After publishing his "Letters," Father De Smet began another begging tour in the principal towns of Belgium and Holland, to obtain not only money, but men.   Meeting those attracted by a taste for adventure, he candidly told them of the dangers of a missionary's life.   "In our wilds," he said, "a man takes his life in his hands, not because the climate is unhealthy—far from it; if men died only of sickness, they would live to an advanced age; but because of rivers, forest, and prairie, of fires, and the guns and shafts of savages.   Of every hundred men who journey through our country, not ten escape them."[16]

Despite his warnings, however, many young men were won over by the apostle to the Indians, and said farewell to their families.   Among them was Father Charles Elet, brother of Father John Elet, a young priest destined to die a saintly death a few months after his arrival in the United States.

On April 3, 1848, Father De Smet and Father Elet sailed for America.   The crossing was a bad one.   "For several days," he tells us, "I suffered from that illness which does not kill, but tries the most patient of men.   A mountainous sea tumbled us about, and we staggered around on deck in grotesque positions.   After a wearing day, I sought repose, only to be thrown out of my berth by the violence of the sea."[17]

On arriving in New York, the travelers learned that the Revolution that had dethroned Louis Philippe threatened to sweep Europe.   In Paris, Rome, Naples, Berlin, Vienna, and Prague the people were in revolt.   "The latest news

<hr />

[15] *Evening Mirror* of New York, after the publication of "The Oregon Missions."

[16] "Journeys to the Rocky Mountains," 13th letter.

[17] To Francis De Smet, New York, May 5, 1848.

from Rome," writes the missionary, "has greatly perturbed me. Our poor Pontiff! Our poor religious orders! what is to become of them? Yet God's will be done! The persecutors will soon be in a more pitiful condition than their victims."[18]

The Jesuits, as usual, were the first attacked, and many sought refuge in America. Hearing that some priests were about to arrive, Father De Smet remained several weeks in New York to receive them. After supplying them with money and starting them safely to their destinations, he left for St. Louis. This time he went west by the Lake route, the least expensive and most agreeable way, stopping one day to see the sublime Falls of Niagara, that marvel of American scenery. On July 4th he arrived in St. Louis.

The Jesuits recently arrived from Switzerland and Italy were, before long, appointed to their different posts. "Cast off by the Old World," writes Father De Smet, "they have come to offer themselves for the evangelization of the New, and are received with open arms. The Bishops all over the country have asked for these priests, and already a hundred of them are exercising a peaceful ministry."[19] Many, wishing to labor among the Indians, joined the Oregon Missions.

After a few weeks spent in St. Louis, Father De Smet left for another mission. It will be recalled that on his return journey from the Rocky Mountains in the autumn of 1846 Father De Smet remained some time with the Sioux tribes on the Upper Missouri. From that time on he was consumed with a desire to return to these Indians, in order to study their habits and to see if they were not ready to receive a missionary. Joining some agents of the Fur Company, he ascended the Missouri to the mouth of the Nebraska. From there he went overland on horseback in the direction of the Niobrara and White rivers, choosing this mode of travel as best suited for studying the country.

The difficulties of this journey in summer through the most arid part of the American plains were indescribable. Clouds of mosquitoes swarmed about the caravan; their cooking was done over fires made of buffalo dung; after a march of twelve hours they found that there was no water

[18] To Father Parrin, New York, May 5, 1848.
[19] To Charles De Smet, St. Louis, July 30, 1848.

at their place of encampment, and mirage, that phenomenon of the desert, aggravated the torments of thirst. They beheld shimmering lakes and flowing rivers upon the horizon, and dreaming of shade and verdure, pressed on. As the hours sped by, their illusions increased. Exhausted and panting, they fought their way, unconscious that the illusive vision was ever-receding, and would finally disappear.

The caravan marched for six days without seeing an Indian or any habitation until they came to the mouth of the Niobrara, the home of the Poncas. Father De Smet seems to have kept an agreeable remembrance of this courageous tribe, which he calls "the Flatheads of the Plains." The Black Robe was most cordially received by the Indians, and the calumet was passed from mouth to mouth. The assembly, numbering nearly a thousand, heard for the first time the name of Jesus Christ from the mouth of a Catholic priest. Unable to remain with them, Father De Smet baptized the young children and left, as catechist, a well-instructed half-breed Catholic.

The route to the Sioux lay through the Bad Lands. "This region is the most unique of any I have met in my journeys," says Father De Smet. "The action of the rain, snow, and wind upon the argillaceous soil is scarcely credible; and the combined influence of these elements renders it the theater of most singular scenery. Viewed at a distance, these lands exhibit the appearance of great villages and ancient castles, but of such a capricious style of architecture that they seem to belong to some new world, or to ages far remote. Here a majestic Gothic tower, surrounded with turrets, rises in noble grandeur, and there enormous columns seem reared to support the vault of heaven. Further on you may descry a fort with mantellated walls, beaten by the tempest; its hoary parapets seem to have sustained, during many successive ages, the assaults of tempests, earthquakes, and thunder. Cupolas of colossal proportions, and pyramids which recall the gigantic labors of ancient Egypt, rise in air. The atmospheric agents act upon them with such effect that probably in the course of a year or two these strange constructions are transformed or destroyed.

"The settler will try in vain to cultivate this fluctuating and sterile soil. But though it offers no interest to the farmer or botanist, the geologist may find abundant material for study and illustration; here are found petrified remains of the largest of known quadrupeds, the mastodon, mingled with those of the mountain hare. I have seen well-preserved skulls, horns, and tortoises so large that two men could scarcely lift them." [20]

After crossing this arid region, the missionary at last reached the Sioux camp. The Sioux or Dakotas, divided into several groups, numbered thirty or forty thousand, and formed the most powerful and warlike of the North American Indian tribes. The different Sioux tribes spoke much the same language and were scattered over both sides of the Missouri River north of the Niobrara.

Some of these tribes, such as the Santees, the Yanktons, the Brûlés, and the Ogallalas, were at that time camped in the neighborhood of Fort Peter, between the White and Cheyenne rivers. When Father De Smet came upon the Sioux, he found them reveling in all the horrors of their primitive savagery. Several warriors had just returned from an expedition against the Omahas, carrying thirty-two scalps dangling from their lances and horses' bits. At the sight of these hideous trophies the whole tribe jumped and shouted with joy. The "scalp dance and feast" was celebrated with the most discordant yells and horrible contortions. They planted a post daubed with vermilion in the middle of the camp; the warriors danced around it, the scalps swaying with each movement. To the deafening accompaniment of drums, each man howled his war-song, then, striking the pole with his tomahawk, proclaimed the victims it had immolated, exhibiting ostentatiously the scars of the wounds he had received. These depraved customs were the natural consequence of their barbarous instincts. Contact with the white man had developed vices unknown among the Oregon tribes, but despite all this, the Sioux received the ambassador of the Great Spirit enthusiastically. An event that took place

[20] Letter to Victorine Van Kerckhove, St. Louis, May 2, 1848. The American geologist, Hayden, visited this desert in 1855 and brought back numerous specimens which he gave to the National Museum at Washington.

two days after his arrival won for Father De Smet the confidence of the Indians.

The Ogallalas had invaded the country of the Crows, and had met them in battle. The latter fought bravely, killing ten or twelve of their aggressors and driving the others off with clubs. The daughter of Red Fish, the great chief of the Ogallalas, was taken captive by the Crows. Crushed and humiliated, he left his tribe to go to Fort Peter, to ask the officers' assistance in obtaining his daughter's release, offering eighty beautiful buffalo robes for her ransom as well as his best horses. He then sought out Father De Smet.

"Black Robe," he sobbed, "you see before you an unhappy father who has lost his beloved daughter. Have pity on me! I have been told that the Black Robe's prayers are powerful with the Great Spirit. Speak to the Master of life for me, and I shall not then despair of again seeing my child."

These words, and the old man's deep sorrow, moved the missionary. He promised to pray for his daughter's return, but admonished the chief that it rested with himself to dispose heaven in his favor, through his own good conduct. He then made him forswear all unjust aggressions against the neighboring tribes, and summoned him, with his tribe, to listen to the commands of the Great Spirit.

The next day Father De Smet offered the Holy Sacrifice, at which the Indian chief assisted, imploring, in a loud voice, the help of God. When Red Fish returned to his camp, he assembled his warriors and informed them of his interview with the Black Robe. Suddenly, joyful cries came from the extremity of the camp. They rushed forth to inquire the cause, and saw the captive daughter returning. The old chief could scarcely believe his senses. He ran from his tent to receive his child, who threw herself into his arms. But how did it happen? The young girl told her story:

"From the time of my capture I was tied by my hands and feet to stakes driven into the ground. One night an unknown woman came and loosened my cords. She then gave me food and several pairs of moccasins, and said to me

in low tones, 'Rise and return to your father.' I started
off at once and walked all night. At daybreak I hid in
the hollow of a tree. Some hours later, a band of warriors
who were looking for me passed by without seeing me.
Not finding my tracks on the other side of the river, they
returned to camp. At nightfall I again set out, and in
this manner I walked six days and nights until I had the
joy of finding my father."

Who was this woman who liberated her? Father De
Smet does not tell us, but he asserts the event happened
during the night of the day he celebrated Mass at Fort
Peter.[21] During the daughter's recital the Indians raised
their hands toward heaven in thanksgiving to the Great
Spirit. Soon the news spread from tribe to tribe. The
Sioux, after this proof of the efficacy of Christian prayer,
showed themselves disposed to listen to the missionary.
Father De Smet spent several weeks visiting the Indians.
All sought the honor of receiving him in their lodges, where
he sat at the feasts spread for him, and, taking advantage
of these reunions, instructed his hosts, showing them the
folly of their superstitious practices, exhorting them to live
in peace with their neighbors, preaching temperance and
justice, and dwelling upon the Last Judgment, which will
bring joy to the elect and despair to the wicked.

The Sioux listened to him with respectful attention;
many asked for baptism and promised to live Christian
lives. Judging that they were not yet sufficiently instructed, and wishing to put their perseverance to the test,
Father De Smet baptized only the children and some old
men, two of whom were nonagenarians.

"We have always loved the Great Spirit," they said.
"Knowing no other prayer, we have offered Him daily the
first smoke of the calumet."

Winter was now coming on, and the missionary was
obliged to quit his neophytes. He embarked on the
Missouri and duly covered the fifteen hundred miles to
St. Louis. Ordinarily so confident of the future of the
Indian missions, Father De Smet this time showed a certain reserve in speaking about his plans. "What I have seen
is far from encouraging for a missionary. There is a great

[21] Cf. Selected Letters, 3d Series, pp. 151-153.

difference between the Flatheads and the other tribes west of the mountains and the Sioux. Would a mission be feasible? My own experience and my sojourn among the Sioux compel me to place confidence in Him alone who holds in His hands the most hardened of hearts and most recalcitrant of wills. I hope that in the course of this year something may be done for these unfortunate Indians." [22]

This hope, alas! was not to be realized. Although he labored unremittingly in their behalf, Father De Smet never lived to see a mission established among the Sioux. For years he continued to visit them and instruct and baptize their children and old people, and he prolonged the existence of the tribe by fighting against and defeating the efforts of the white man to exterminate them.

[22] Letter to Emilie Van Kerckhove, St. Louis, May 4, 1849.

CHAPTER XIII

FATHER DE SMET, ASSISTANT TO THE VICE-PROVINCIAL AND PROCURATOR GENERAL OF MISSOURI (1849)

Father Van de Velde, Appointed Bishop of Chicago, is Replaced by
Father De Smet—The Missouri Vice-Province in 1849—Father De
Smet *Socius*—His Firmness—His Goodness—History of Watomika—
Father De Smet's Attachment to the Kansas Missions—St. Mary's
Mission to the Potawatomies—Fathers C. Hoecken, Duerinck, etc.—
St. Francis Hieronymo's Mission to the Osages—Fathers Schoenmakers
and Bax—A New Apostolic Vicariate—Bishop Miège—Father De
Smet as Procurator—His Capable Administration—His Efforts to
Obtain Money—Providence Comes to His Aid—Gratitude to Bene-
factors—"A Year of Accidents"—Father De Smet during the Cholera
and the Great Fire—St. Louis University Saved through the Inter-
cession of the Blessed Virgin.

FATHER DE SMET was wholly wrapped up in his
plans for new mission foundations, when his Superiors'
orders suspended the work. On Father Elet had devolved,
for several months, the duties of Vice-Provincial. Father
Van de Velde was named Assistant Vice-Provincial and
Procurator of Missouri, but hardly had he entered upon his
duties when he was appointed by the Sovereign Pontiff
to the See of Chicago.

A zealous worker, possessed of rare intellectual culture,
coupled with a gentle, lovable nature, Father Van de Velde
was recognized as one of the most distinguished priests in
the United States. In looking about for a successor, the
Fathers remembered that Father De Smet had, on a
former occasion, when Procurator of the college, evinced
undoubted administrative ability. So to him was confided
(at least provisionally) the duties and responsibilities of the
office which Father Van de Velde had vacated.[1]

[1] "The duties of the office I now occupy absorb my whole time, and there
is no one to relieve me. We have many churches, colleges, and schools in
the United States and are, alas! too few in number for this heavy charge.

This appointment demanded a painful sacrifice from the missionary engaged upon work rich in promise. Nevertheless, Father De Smet obeyed cheerfully. "Father Van de Velde's duties have for the moment been laid upon my poor shoulders," he writes, "and I shall endeavor to discharge them to the best of my ability, and render every service within my power to the different houses in the Vice-Province." [2]

We will now follow him in the discharge of his new functions.

The Vice-Province of Missouri at that time numbered about two hundred Jesuits. Besides the St. Louis University and the Florissant novitiate, it possessed colleges at Bardstown, Louisville, and Cincinnati, and ten small houses.

The Louisiana Mission had been restored in 1847 to the French Jesuits of the Lyons Province.[3] The Oregon and Rocky Mountain Missions passed, in 1851, under the immediate control of the General of the Jesuits, and three years later were attached to the Turin Province. The Osage and Potawatomi Missions in Kansas were each served by ten Jesuits, who ministered to flourishing Christian communities.

In his quality of *socius* or assistant, Father De Smet aided Father Elet in the administration of the Province, attended to a large part of the correspondence, and accompanied him on his visits to the colleges and missions.

While the office of Assistant Vice-Provincial was not one of responsibility, it entailed routine work and left little initiative to the incumbent. God alone knows what it cost that energetic, enterprising missionary to submit to the limitations and drudgery of secretarial work. "I am like a soldier," he writes one of his friends. "Upon receiving an order I obey instantly and go where I am sent,

I trust other Fathers will soon arrive from Europe. When I can be relieved of this position, I hope to receive the longed-for permission to return once more to the Indians." (Letter of Father De Smet to Mr. Monroe, the Blackfeet's interpreter, St. Louis, June 12, 1850.)

[2] Letter to Father Smedts, St. Louis, March 5, 1849.

[3] This mission, it will be remembered, was annexed to the Missouri Vice-Province in 1840.

but, like the soldier, I too have my preferences, and need I say they are for the land of the Indians?" And again, "I long for the plains, the deserts, the wild life of the Indians, with its dangers, privation, and fatigues, which were, in truth, treats compared to the monotony of my present existence."[4]

But if the work weighed heavily upon him, Father De Smet's Superiors had no reason to regret his choice as Assistant Vice-Provincial. During the absence or illness of the Vice-Provincial he was forced to decide grave matters and solve difficulties; to say the word of encouragement or administer reproof. Every line of his correspondence reveals sound judgment, breadth of view, and fair and kindly dealings with his fellow-workers. Obliged to treat with men of different nationalities, he applied himself to inspire them with the sole object of laboring for God's glory. "In the world in which we live, few people are content, and the greater number murmur and find much to complain of. Happy are those, especially in our Society, who keep in view only *ad majorem Dei gloriam*, regardless of national prejudices, the pest of religious communities. I pity with all my heart the man subject to this frailty."[5]

His upright nature scorned the subterfuges of self-love, and practiced rigid obedience. "He who is not content unless exercising authority or left to do his own will— such a man is not religious.[6] If our motive in entering the Society was to occupy positions of authority, and to seek only work that pleased us, we had done better to remain in the world. The spirit of domination and attachment to one's own will are stumbling-blocks and obstacles in the path of virtue. From these follow, not infrequently, lukewarmness in meditation and prayer, distaste for our holy vocation, and the habit of complaining against the attitude and orders of our Superiors. This path leads not to heaven, and in it we find only ennui, restlessness, and dejection. . . . Ever present must be the object for which we have left all, father, mother, brothers,

[4] Quoted by Chittenden-Richardson, p. 58.
[5] To Father Hélias d'Huddeghem, St. Louis, July 19, 1850.
[6] To Father Druyts, July 4, 1854.

sisters, and country. Nor must trifles or inordinate affections distract us from it. Heaven is truly a great reward." [7]

Although frank and outspoken, Father De Smet was ever considerate of the feelings of others. If he had reason to suspect that a fellow-priest nourished any resentment toward him, he at once assured him of his unalterable friendship: "Tell Father X—— that all is long since pardoned and forgotten, and that I have never entertained any feelings of bitterness. There have been in his regard, alas, misunderstandings and differences, which have had sad results, but I attribute them to the devil, jealous of the good intentions of the Indians and the great good that is being accomplished by the missions." [8]

Being of a sensitive nature, the slightest suspicion or sign of distrust caused him acute suffering. "It would give me great pleasure to see you in St. Louis," he writes to his Superior, "and I am confident that ten minutes' conversation would put things right, and dispel the prejudices and unfriendliness your letters so often betray. What has occasioned these feelings, I am at a loss to explain, but I can assure you I have never experienced other sentiments than respect and love for your Reverence." [9]

Father De Smet's genial nature was devoid of harshness; he was always approachable and kindly considerate in his dealing with his fellows. He understood the value of kind words, of timely encouragement, and was not sparing in merited praise, a necessity in many circumstances. All, even the youngest, were treated with the utmost consideration. On one occasion, a scholastic wrote to ask his prayers. In reply, he received the following charming letter: "You ask me to say a Mass for your intentions. I will say not one Mass, but six, as soon as possible. Whenever you wish prayers for some particular intention, let me know and I will say Masses for you." [10]

That Father De Smet's subordinates remained his friends

[7] To Father Maes, Feb. 13, 1851.
[8] To Father Joset, Jan. 21, 1851.
[9] St. Louis, July 31, 1849.
[10] To Brother L. Heylen, April 19, 1856.

is due to his simplicity of manner and his cordial kindness: among these he counted none more devoted than a young Jesuit, Jacques Bouchard, better known by his Indian name, Watomika, "The Swift-footed Man." The story of this convert written by himself is singularly touching. Through his mother, Marie Bouchard, Watomika was descended from an Auvergne family that had emigrated during the Revolution. His father, Kistalwa, belonged to the Delaware tribe, formerly one of the most powerful tribes in America. Kistalwa's integrity and courage won for him the greatest distinction his tribe could bestow: he was made chief. He cherished a burning resentment against the United States for having usurped the lands of his fathers, and he instilled in his son a hatred of the white man. Watomika was brought up in paganism, and in his early childhood was, of course, taught to ride and use the bow and tomahawk. At nine years of age he accompanied the chief, his father, to the hunt, astonishing by his daring the most intrepid hunters. One day the news came that a Delaware had just been killed by a band of Sioux. Kistalwa at once assembled his braves and started in pursuit of the enemy. Watomika begged to join the expedition.

"Are you not afraid of being scalped by the Sioux?" asked his father.

"If my father is a coward, then I, too, am a coward," replied the child.

Delighted with this reply, Kistalwa consented. But Monotawan, "the white gazelle"—it was thus the Indians called Marie Bouchard—was in despair. Placing her hands upon her son's head, she implored the protection of the Great Spirit, and as the warriors disappeared in the distance the poor mother repeated, sobbing: "Watomika, my dear Watomika! I shall never see you again!"

Soon the Delawares overtook the Sioux, and, though inferior in numbers, descended upon them and a frightful encounter ensued. Kistalwa's thunderous voice urged on the combat. Watomika, though wounded in the leg, fought valiantly at his father's side. Suddenly Kistalwa fell mortally wounded, and then the Delawares, goaded to madness by the loss of their chief, succeeded in putting the Sioux to flight.

Following the custom of his tribe, Watomika daily placed on his father's tomb his favorite dishes, until he dreamed that the deceased had entered "the land of the living." But God was already preparing to enlighten his soul with the light of true faith.

Soon afterward a Protestant mission was established in his country. The Presbyterian minister in charge was greatly impressed by this Indian boy's intelligence, and offered to send him to Marietta College in Ohio, in order that he might study the religion of the white man. The idea filled the child of the wilderness with revulsion at first. Abandon the land of his ancestors and the mother he loved, to live among strangers whom he had been taught to hate? But as time passed, an irresistible impulse decided him to accept the minister's offer.

This neophyte of twelve years, just emerged from savagery, applied himself diligently to the study of what he was told was truth. Gifted with rare intelligence and marked religious propensities, Watomika possessed, moreover, a delicately sensitive nature. He spent hours every day in prayer and meditation upon divine things. He fasted strictly once a week, eating his first meal at sundown. His studies once completed, the ardent neophyte longed to devote his life to preaching the new Gospel and prepared himself for his work by prayer and fasting. But in probing the doctrine of Calvin, he was assailed by doubts and unrest of mind, which his austerities could not calm. In his great distress, Watomika sought light from on high, ready to follow it at any sacrifice. Just at this time an order came for him to proceed to St. Louis to replace an absent colleague. There God awaited him.

A chance stroll brought him one day before the Jesuit church at the hour when the children attended catechism class. He entered. The altar, the crucifix, the image of the Blessed Virgin made an impression upon him which he could not explain. With respectful attention he followed the priest's instructions.[11] The lesson that day dealt with the very questions upon which this distracted soul had longed for enlightenment. He returned home in a more

---

[11] This priest was, most probably, Father Damen.

tranquil frame of mind; but now only the full light of truth could satisfy him.

Watomika's knowledge of Catholicism was based upon calumnious reports, but notwithstanding this he did not hesitate to seek relief from a priest, nay, even a Jesuit. To him he told all his doubts and troubles. Grace did the rest. Watomika abjured his errors and a few months later asked to be admitted to the Society of Jesus.

Entering the Florissant novitiate at twenty-four years of age, he was in due time ordained priest. This proud descendant of the Delaware chiefs, and erstwhile disciple of Calvin, wrote to Father De Smet: "My one desire, and the object for which I pray daily, is to live and die a true son of the Society of Jesus, in whatever function or place God assigns me through the voice of my Superiors."

One can easily imagine the tender friendship that sprang up between these two Jesuits. The apostle to the Indians felt that in this new convert, uplifted to an exalted state, he beheld the first fruits of a race that had been unjustly despised. Watomika, now called Father Bouchard, in turn recognized in the missionary the most devoted defender of his oppressed people. When he beheld the Delawares despoiled of their lands in defiance of treaties, it was to Father De Smet that he confided his grief.[12]

Father Bouchard was appointed to the San Francisco Mission, and during a residence there of thirty years he enjoyed the reputation of being a distinguished orator and was venerated for his virtues. During this time he never forgot the missionary who had received him so paternally when he was entering upon his new life. "Pray for me and write to me often," he said. "Would that I could always be near you."[13]

But the missions ever remained Father De Smet's chief

---

[12] "Had the insolent American put his foot upon my throat, I could not have suffered greater pain and bitterness." (Letter to Father De Smet, Chicago, Nov. 11, 1857.) "I can but weep and sigh over the ruin of my beloved tribe. They deserve a better fate. But what can one expect from a Government devoid of loyalty, and an avaricious nation whose only God is the almighty dollar and which covets the land of a defenceless people? My heart bleeds at the thought of the future of my tribe, ruined, corrupted, destroyed by the blood-stained hands of a so-called liberal Government." (To Father De Smet, Leavenworth, July 1, 1857.)

[13] It was doubtless at the time of his departure for California that Father

preoccupation. Further on we shall tell what he did for the Oregon Missions. At present let us review his efforts in behalf of the missions in Kansas. We have already spoken about the Potawatomies of Council Bluffs.[14] Shortly after Father De Smet's departure, Fathers Verreydt and Hoecken, despairing of reforming incorrigible drunkards, departed for Sugar Creek, south of Westport, where another band of Potawatomies in the charge of a Breton priest, Father Petit,[15] had lately arrived. This tribe, comprising two thousand Indians, was already half Christian,[16] and hence it was imperative that they should have schools. Father De Smet immediately thought of the Ladies of the Sacred Heart.

"Believe me," he said to Mother Gallitzin, who at that time was upon a tour of inspection of the American houses, "you will never succeed in this country unless you call down the blessing of heaven by founding schools for the Indians."

"Such is my earnest wish, Father. But we have neither money nor teachers."

"Nevertheless, Reverend Mother, it must be done."

Then he addressed Madam Duchesne, and represented the advantages of a foundation at Sugar Creek, for the place had to be secured at once in order to forestall the Presbyterians and Methodists. Although she was in her seventy-first year, that heroic woman asked to be allowed to go herself to the Indians. "How good it is to serve

Bouchard sent Father De Smet the following acrostic, *Remember Watomika:*

> **W**hen friends once linked by ties so dea*r*
> *A* long and sad farewell must giv*e,*
> *T*heir former woes and pleasures see*m*
> *O*ft does the heart when all alon*e*
> *M*indful regard the parted for*m*
> *I*n all that can the soul absor*b.*
> *K*ind friend, 'tis thus I'll muse on the*e*
> *A*nd think that thou art always nea*r.*
> Farewell!

In regard to the apostolate of Father Bouchard at San Francisco, see The Woodstock Letters, Vol. XIX, p. 302.

[14] See Chapter V.

[15] In regard to the life and virtues of this admirable missionary, see The Annals of the Propagation of the Faith, July, 1839, p. 379, *et seq.*

[16] Father Badin of New Orleans and Father Desseille of Bruges preceded Father Petit at this mission.

God gratuitously and at His expense! If we can obtain four hundred dollars to begin with we will leave in the spring."

Father De Smet soon carried to Mother Gallitzin five hundred dollars he had himself collected and thus assured the foundation.[17]

In 1848 the Potawatomies, again driven back by the Americans, were forced to leave Sugar Creek and emigrate further west to a reserve fifty miles square on the borders of Kansas. The Jesuits and the Ladies of the Sacred Heart followed them there and founded the prosperous St. Mary's Mission. Here again Father De Smet was able to render signal services to his confrères. In leaving Sugar Creek, the missionaries forfeited the subsidy heretofore paid by the United States for the education of the children of the Indians. After a lengthy correspondence with the Superintendent of Indian Affairs, Father De Smet finally won the cause of his protégés. Nor was this all: he gave valuable information to the missionaries in regard to their dealings with the Government agents; put them on guard against the proceedings of the Protestants, and in addition sent them large sums of money.

The Ladies of the Sacred Heart were not forgotten. "I have bought you all you have asked for, and your things will arrive with the merchandise we are sending the Fathers. Whenever I can be of service to you, you have only to ask. The Provincial has received $750 for the Potawatomi Mission, half of which he will give you to dispose of as you think best." [18]

The devotion of such men as Fathers Hoecken, Duerinck, Gaillard, and Dumortier, sustained and upheld by Father De Smet's aid and encouragement, soon bore fruit in St. Mary's Mission. The Superintendent of Indian Affairs declared that the Jesuits had accomplished more with the Indians than all the Methodists together. At the Sacred Heart School young Indian girls passed from the wilderness to the novitiate.[19]

[17] Cf. Baunard, *Histoire de Madam Duchesne*, p. 433, *et seq.*

[18] To Madam Lucile Mathevon, St. Louis, Aug. 18, 1849.

[19] From President Pierce's message to Congress in 1854 we quote the following: "The schools in charge of the Jesuit Fathers are in a flourishing condition. I have had the good fortune to be present at the examination

Southeast on the Neosho, the St. Francis Hieronymo Mission was established. Father Schoenmakers, a Hollander, and Father Bax, a Fleming, went in 1847 to minister to the Osages, who had been converted twenty years before by Father Van Quickenborne. The Osages were among the most degraded tribes of the desert. Idle, filthy, drunkards, corrupted by contact with the whites, they became hostile to the Black Robes, against whom they had been warned by Protestants. "The spectacle of so much misery and degradation brought tears to the eyes of those sent to labor for the salvation of this unfortunate tribe." To this was added bitter privations. "We suffer hunger and thirst and cold, and sleep in the open during the wettest season of the year, with only a buffalo skin and one cover by way of bedding."[20]

Father De Smet hastened to relieve their distress, and obtained a subsidy for the schools. To encourage the missionaries in their arduous task he recalled to them his own labors, and the sufferings he had endured in Oregon. "I, too, have tasted the bitter privations to which one is exposed in the Indian countries. Let me tell you some of them, but I hope you may be spared similar sufferings. For several years I was a wanderer in the wilderness and during three years I never received a single letter. I lived for two years in the mountains without ever tasting bread, salt, coffee, tea, or sugar. During four years I knew neither shelter nor bed; six months I was without underlinen, and often days and nights I have gone without food or drink. Pardon me if I speak thus, and believe me, I do so neither to reproach you nor to glorify myself. I only recall what I have endured. Nor do I regret it. On

of their pupils, and I can heartily approve of their methods of teaching. I doubt if there exist in the Indian Territory any other schools that can be compared to these. The pupils make rapid progress in their studies; they are, moreover, well fed and clothed, and appear happy and contented."

In 1856, Major Clarke, directed by the Government to inspect the Catholic schools among the Potawatomies, made the following report: "I cannot speak too highly of these schools. Besides the ordinary course of instruction, the girls are taught to sew, to knit, to embroider, and to do housework. The boys have an industrial school, where they learn useful arts, such as agriculture, horticulture, etc. Father Duerinck is a most energetic man and excellent manager, and is devoted heart and soul to the well-being of the Potawatomies, to whom he is both father and friend."

[20] To Father De Smet, June 1, 1850.

the contrary, I thank God for it and would gladly exchange my present situation for the hardships of mission work."[21]

The missionaries to the Osages were men capable of appreciating these words, and despite unspeakable fatigues and difficulties without number, Father Schoenmakers endured for forty years this rude apostolate. Small-pox broke out in the tribe: Father Bax went from village to village, from cabin to cabin, carrying help and religious consolation until he, at thirty-three years of age, fell a victim to his heroic charity.

Occasionally the Fathers at St. Mary's and at St. Francis Hieronymo Missions found means of visiting the neighboring tribes, namely the Peorias, the Miamis, the Senecas, and the Creeks. Father Hoecken has left us an account of a journey he made to the Sioux,[22] in the depth of winter, through snow from fifteen to twenty feet deep. He was mounted on a lame horse; his feet, nose, and ears were frostbitten, his legs were stiffened with rheumatism, and he was starving. At night the storms raged and the wolves howled around the camp. Yet his soul overflowed with joy: "My one desire is, with the help of God's grace, to bear suffering and fatigue as long as it is within my power to endure them. I place my hopes in the bosom of my Saviour and await my reward from His bounty, not in this life, but in the life to come." Such heroism and devotion yielded abundant fruit. The Christians increased rapidly in numbers among both the Indians and the American settlers.

In 1851 the Osage and Potawatomi Missions were raised by Pius IX to a vicariate apostolic, and Father Miège, a Jesuit, was appointed titular Bishop, with jurisdiction over the territory east of the Rocky Mountains. The new Bishop asked Father De Smet to accompany him and introduce him to his new and immense diocese, and in so doing recognized the eminent services the apostle to the Indians had rendered the missionaries.[23]

---

[21] To Father Schoenmakers, St. Louis, June 5, 1849.

[22] Quoted from Selected Letters, 2d Series, p. 65, *et seq.*

[23] Father De Smet being unable to comply with the Bishop's request, Father Ponziglione, lately appointed to the Osage Mission, was his companion.

Father De Smet discharged not only the duties of Assistant to the Vice-Provincial, but those of Procurator General as well, in which latter capacity he provided for the material needs of the different Jesuit houses and the missions in particular.

The financial condition of the Jesuits rendered this task a difficult one. Mr. De Nef's death had sensibly reduced the financial assistance formerly given by the Belgian Province, and following the troubles of 1848, the Propagation of the Faith had discontinued its assistance. An increasing number of applicants for admission to the Florissant novitiate necessitated larger accommodations, and the maintenance of the Jesuits expelled from Europe was a fresh charge upon the Province. From all sides came demands for help. "We have pressing debts to pay," writes Father De Smet, "and only empty coffers."[24] In appealing to a friend, he says, "We may perhaps never meet again on earth, but I trust we will meet in heaven, where there will be neither question of figures, nor demands for money, nor account-books."[25]

The new Procurator labored valiantly to keep the expenses within the limits of his budget. With minute exactitude he kept track of receipts and expenses. In his accounts with the subsidy furnished by the Government to the schools in Kansas, he entered seriously in his books:

The United States, Dr. to Father De Smet, $0.35.

His correspondence betrays his unflagging efforts to avoid debt. Five times in one month he writes to one of the Fathers to urge him to reduce his expenses. His warning producing no effect, he threatened to stop payment: "If you exceed your allowance your note will be protested."[26] The ablest administrator, however, is powerless before a total absence of capital—but Father De Smet was not ashamed to ask assistance. He wrote to Belgium, France, Holland, and to several dioceses in Canada, and in the hope of interesting his benefactors in the missions, gave them detailed accounts of his travels. When the

[24] Letter to Father Erensberger, St. Louis, March 13, 1849.
[25] Quoted by Chittenden-Richardson, p. 59.
[26] Letter of Dec. 27, 1849.

seventh Council of Baltimore was about to take place he presented a petition to the Archbishop asking for the establishment of a league similar to the one in Lyons, for the propagation of the faith among the Indian tribes of the West.[27]

Generous contributions flowed in. One Belgian benefactor alone sent twenty thousand dollars: the money was distributed as fast as it arrived, and yet many needs remained unprovided for. "I was obliged to send supplies to the mountain missions, and had not a cent *ad hoc*, hence I proceeded to beg money. From morning until night I went my rounds. I wrote letters, journeyed from place to place to secure contributions, and now when all is done I still lack one hundred dollars. I trust to Providence for the rest."[28]

And Providence responded generously. Many times commercial houses furnished several hundred dollars' worth of merchandise gratis. Rich ship-owners, old pupils of Father De Smet, and personal friends paid transportation fees. The American Fur Company offered the missionaries free carriage for their goods on their boats going up the Missouri. Money often came in in most unexpected ways.

"A few months ago," writes the Procurator, "the Superior of a mission informed me that he was in urgent need of money, and without it he would be obliged to abandon the work. In the same post came another letter from the Vicar General of Quebec in which he said, 'I have a sum of money to dispose of and your name has come to my mind. Let me know if you are in need of money.' In reply I gave him some details regarding our missions, leaving it to him to decide if they were deserving of assistance. I allowed the distressed missionary to draw on me for six hundred dollars. Some months later I received from him a letter of thanks with a bill of exchange payable on sight within three days, and two days later I received from the Vicar General a bank-note that more than covered my charity."[29]

Encouraged by such experiences, Father De Smet never

[27] See Chittenden-Richardson, p. 1306.
[28] Letter to Charles De Smet, May 15, 1860.
[29] Letter to Charles Van Mossevelde, Sept. 27, 1854.

despaired. "I have so often been rescued by a kind Providence that it would be ungrateful of me not to trust Him implicitly. He who feeds the birds of the air and clothes the lilies of the field will not abandon His children who have left all for the glory of His name." [30]

Father De Smet never forgot a favor, nor did he ever presume upon the generosity of his benefactors. The duties of Vice-Provincial brought him frequently in contact with church dignitaries, and among the laity who interested themselves in the missions are found the best names of Belgium: Count de Meeus, Countess d'Aspremont, Countess de Mérode, and the Duke de Brabant, who later ascended the throne under the title of Leopold II. In this distinguished society our missionary moved with ease and dignity, and even after twenty years spent among the savage tribes of North America he remained ever a gentleman of polished manners and address.

As in former years, he collected plants, insects, minerals, and Indian curiosities to send to Europe. He named the lakes and rivers he discovered after his benefactors, but above all he prayed constantly for them: "I have ordered the Flatheads, the Cœur d'Alènes, and the Pend d'Oreilles to recite the rosary once a week for one of their greatest benefactors—it is of you I speak. As the rosary is said at nightfall by every Indian family, already several thousand rosaries have been offered for you. These children of the wilds will continue thus to show their gratitude until otherwise instructed, which will not be soon." [31]

When a benefactor died, Father De Smet said several Masses for the repose of his soul. Many times members of his family sent the missionary large sums of money. In return he offered Mass for them twice a week. "It is," he says, "a debt of gratitude, and one that it gives me pleasure to discharge, for despite the distance that separates us, I still feel in touch with you. Every Thursday and Sunday you make your intentions, and I take them to the altar; thus we remain strongly united until death, by the sublime and consoling tie of religion." [32]

---

[30] Letter quoted.
[31] Letter to Madam Parmentier of Brooklyn, July 25, 1846.
[32] Letter to Charles Van Mossevelde, Bardstown, Aug. 20, 1855.

Father De Smet's assumption of the office of Procurator in 1849 coincided with a series of disasters in the United States, which gave to that year the name of "the year of accidents." St. Louis was not spared, for on the eve of the feast of the Ascension a disastrous fire destroyed twenty-seven boats anchored at the levee, and, spreading to the town, laid waste five hundred houses. The Orphanage, the cathedral, and the Archbishop's residence were threatened.

Being one of the first on the scene, Father De Smet rescued the archives and papers of the Missouri See, had the library carried to a place of safety, and then offered the orphans a shelter in the college. When the danger was over he returned thanks to the Sacred Heart. "Shall we ever be able to make a worthy return for such signal protection?" he asks.[33]

About the same time a scourge more terrible than fire devastated the city—cholera—and it claimed as many as two hundred victims a day during a period of several months. "There is general mourning," wrote Father De Smet. "All who have the means leave the city; business is dead. Often, friends whom I have seen in the morning are lying in their coffins in the evening."[34] Night and day the Fathers at the University were found at the bedsides of the dying. Father De Smet did not take time to undress, he was so constantly on duty. We have before us a letter written by him in which he states he was twice interrupted in its writing by visits to the sick and dying.

One of his nieces invited him to return to Belgium, but he replied: "America lacks priests to minister to the suffering and dying, and yet you have the temerity to propose that I should seek safety and die elsewhere but in the breach! When old veterans desert the battle-field for the repose of family life, what will the young recruits say and do?"

But even the cholera had its consoling aspect. "It strikes an impartial blow, respecting neither name, station, nor religion: it helps the good to become better, the wicked to repent, and rouses the lukewarm from their torpor. Why should we dread the cause of so much good?"[35]

[33] To a nun, May 22, 1849.
[34] To Madam Meersman, July 4, 1849.
[35] To Sylvia De Smet, July 8, 1849.

The self-sacrificing devotion of the Jesuit Fathers called down the blessing of heaven. At that time the University, besides its entire staff, numbered two hundred boarders. The Fathers implored the help of the Blessed Virgin: "We placed ourselves and all our pupils under her powerful protection, promising to adorn her statue with a silver crown should all escape the scourge. Mary loves her children too well to allow them to perish."[36] Nor was Father De Smet's confidence misplaced. Although the college was situated in a part of the city where the infection raged, it was not attacked, nor were the classes interrupted for a single day. The Fathers continued their ministrations to the sick without catching the contagion.

When the scourge had ceased, all hastened to keep the promises made to our most blessed Lady. One evening during the month of October, professors and students met in the chapel. The statue was solemnly crowned, and then carried in procession amid the grateful prayers and tears of all who were present. His heart filled with intensest joy, Father De Smet took part in the triumph of his Mother in heaven. Once more she had proven her claim to his confidence and gratitude.

[36] To Charles Van Kerckhove, July 9, 1849.

CHAPTER XIV

Discovery of Gold in California—The White Invasion—The American
Government Invites the Tribes to a Conference in which Fathers De
Smet and C. Hoecken are to Take Part—Cholera on Board the *St. Ange*
—Father De Smet's Serious Illness—Father Hoecken's Death—His
Health Hardly Reestablished, Father De Smet Visits the Indians
during an Epidemic of Smallpox—A Journey across the Wilderness—
The Highway to the Pacific—The Great Council—Points Submitted
for Deliberation—Father De Smet's Successful Efforts—An Era of
Peace for the Redskins—Return to St. Louis—Visit to St. Mary's
Mission.

FATHER DE SMET had filled the office of Procurator
and Assistant to the Vice-Provincial for six months,
when he was offered an opportunity of visiting the Indians.
Gold had just been discovered in California, and thousands
of immigrants crossed the desert, lured by the promise of
the new Eldorado. In a few months these traveling hordes
had cut a large route from Missouri to the Pacific. San
Francisco, which in 1848 had but five hundred inhabitants,
in two years increased to a population of 25,000. The
Indians, notably the Cheyennes, viewed with irritation the
"Pale Face" invasion of this territory, which had been
guaranteed to them by the United States Government,
and sanguinary conflicts were feared.

Colonel Mitchell, the Superintendent of Indian Affairs
stationed in St. Louis, conceived the idea of a Council,
in which all the Eastern tribes would be represented, and
in which, furthermore, they would be offered an indemnity
for land taken by the whites for a highway and the forts
that would be constructed along the route. It was decided
that the Council should take place at Fort Laramie in the
summer of 1851.

The Superintendent, charged with negotiating the affair,
sought advice and assistance from Father De Smet, who

had not only crossed the plains many times, but understood the nature of the different tribes. He knew his influence over the Indians to be more powerful than the promises and threats of any Government. "Should your present duties permit," writes the Superintendent, "I would like very much for you to take part in the Fort Laramie Council. Your maps and drawings of the prairies and mountains, as well as any information you can furnish with regard to their habits, the history of the country, in fact, all that concerns the Indians, will be of valuable assistance to us, and will be greatly appreciated by the Government."[1]

Here was an occasion for revisiting the Sioux and other tribes on the Upper Missouri. Father De Smet at once accepted, and Father Christian Hoecken, the apostle of the Potawatomies, obtained permission to accompany him. The latter, in joining this expedition, was to crown a life of self-sacrificing devotion with a heroic death.[2]

On June 7th, the Fathers embarked on the *St. Ange*, a steamboat going up the river to Fort Union, about 2,000 miles northwest of St. Louis. Their intention was to visit the Indians camped along the river, and then cross the Yellowstone valley to Fort Laramie upon the upper course of the Nebraska. The *St. Ange* was commanded by Captain La Barge, an intimate friend of Father De Smet. Several members of the fur companies, bound for different trading-posts in the Indian Territory, were also on board. "These men," says our missionary, "were in search of the goods of the world; Father Hoecken and I were seeking the treasures of heaven in the conversion of souls."[3]

The spring that year was late and wet. Melting snows and continued rain had swollen the rivers until the muddy waters of the Missouri inundated the land for miles. The boat pushed its way through floating débris; houses, barns, stables, and fences were carried along pell-mell, with thousands of uprooted trees. It required skilful steering

[1] St. Louis, April 19, 1851. An account of these maps is found in Chittenden-Richardson, p. 137.

[2] Father Christian Hoecken of Tilbourg in Holland was, as we know, the brother of Father Adrian Hoecken of the Oregon Mission.

[3] St. Louis, Jan. 16, 1852.

to avoid striking these floating masses, and at the same time breast the mighty current. Several times the boat became unmanageable. But all this was as nothing in comparison to the trials that yet awaited the missionaries.

Three days after leaving St. Louis cholera broke out on board the *St. Ange*, and the merry songs of the passengers were turned into mournful silence. Thirteen persons, one after the other, fell victims to the scourge. Father De Smet was confined to bed by an attack of bilious fever. Father Hoecken, eager to aid others, watched day and night by the bedsides of the dying, administering the consolations of religion and offering his untiring personal service. "I suffered," writes Father De Smet, "at seeing him labor alone at his heroic task, but I was too weak to assist him in any way. On the 18th what we thought were symptoms of cholera appeared, and I begged Father Hoecken to hear my confession and give me Extreme Unction. Just at that moment he was called to a death-bed. 'There is no immediate danger for you,' he said; 'we can wait until to-morrow.' That day he assisted at three deaths. I shall never forget the scene that took place a few hours later.

"Father Hoecken's cabin adjoined mine, and in the early silence, between one and two o'clock in the morning, I heard him call me. I dragged myself to his bedside, to find him in his death-agony. He asked me to hear his confession, which I did, and while I administered Extreme Unction, he replied to all the prayers. His recollection and piety but added to the veneration in which he was held by the passengers. Finding myself in a condition in which I might die at any moment, I asked him to hear my confession. He was still conscious of what I was saying. With tears streaming down my face, I knelt by the bedside of my faithful friend and sole companion, and to him, in his death-agony, I confessed, being myself in an almost dying condition. He soon became speechless. Resigned to God's will, I read the prayers for the dying. Ripe for heaven, Father Hoecken rendered his soul to God June 19, 1851, twelve days after his departure from St. Louis." [4]

The deceased was only forty-three years of age, and in

[4] Letter quoted.

him was centered the richest qualities of an apostle: ardent zeal, robust health, invincible courage, extreme prudence, simplicity of manner, and a calm and cheerful nature. During the fifteen years of his life spent among the Indians he had built several churches, and established fervent Christian congregations. A martyr to charity, he, even in the throes of death, exercised his ministry of salvation.

Father De Smet was bent upon assisting personally at the burial of his friend. Enclosed in a heavy coffin, the body was lowered into a trench on the edge of the forest, to the accompaniment of the prayers of the Church. A month later Captain La Barge, on his return trip to St. Louis, exhumed the venerated remains and transported them to the cemetery at the Florissant novitiate. "In other circumstances," writes Father De Smet, "his death would have deterred me from continuing my perilous journey. But God gave the strength which nature refused."

Gradually the fever disappeared, Father De Smet's strength returned, and he, in turn, ministered to the sick and dying. Five passengers succumbed later, each receiving the Last Sacraments. Many who had not been to their duties for years came to Father De Smet's cabin, where they confessed their sins and were reconciled with God. Father Hoecken's death made a deep impression on all, and bore immediate fruit. Finally the steamboat reached the high lands of the Indian Territory. The fresh, bracing air dispelled the epidemic. But they soon learned that another scourge, smallpox, was devastating the homes of the Indians, who died by hundreds. Bodies remained unburied, exposed to the summer heat, and for miles the air was infected with the odor of decaying flesh.

Although hardly convalescent himself, Father De Smet went ashore, and visited the entire stricken region, where he baptized children, nursed the sick, and ministered to the dying. Astonished by his courage and touched by his goodness, the Yanktons, Mandans, Aricaras, and Grosventres listened to the words of the Great Spirit, and invited the missionary to remain among them. Although Father De Smet was obliged to rejoin the *St. Ange* and continue his journey, he did not forget these far-off tribes, and later we will see how he labored to establish a mission for them.

While going up the river the burden of his thoughts was the future of these great solitudes. "Nature has been lavish in her gifts to this country, and one need not be a prophet to predict a prosperous future for this land. Before long one could apply to this region the words of the Psalmist: 'The earth was created for the abode of man and to manifest the glory and perfection of the Lord.' These fertile, smiling fields invite the husbandman to till the soil. Ancient oaks await the woodsman, the rocks the stone-cutter. One day the sound of the axe and hammer will ring through the wilderness. Extensive farms, surrounded by orchards and vineyards, herds and flocks of domestic animals, will cover the uninhabited places, and will provision the towns that shall rise up as by enchantment." But what will then become of the Indian who from time immemorial has possessed the land? A grave and disquieting question to one who had followed the encroaching policy of the States in regard to the red man's territory.

"I still keep a ray of hope for the future of these unfortunate tribes. The Indians willingly send their children to school; they make progress in agriculture and mechanical arts. It is not too much to hope that they may one day be incorporated into the Union with the rights of citizens. This is their sole chance of salvation. Humanity and justice demand it."

On July 14th Father De Smet arrived at Fort Union, a post situated above the mouth of the Yellowstone, and from there set out upon his journey overland. He parted with sincere regret from the traveling companions who had shared his trials during the months they had spent together on the *St. Ange*. During the fifteen days he remained at Fort Union he instructed the inhabitants, and made the necessary preparations for the eight-hundred-mile journey he was about to undertake. He then set forth with several Government agents and a number of Indian chiefs who were also en route for Fort Laramie. After ten days' travel the party arrived at Fort Alexander on the Yellowstone.

"The silence of death reigns in this vast wild," wrote the missionary. "Weeks pass without seeing a living creature, but one becomes accustomed to the solitude and ends by liking it. The mind becomes clearer, the faculties are more alive, and ideas spring forth spontaneously. The soul is drawn to prayer and meditation and confidence in God, and one's thoughts dwell upon Him who is our sole refuge and who can supply all our needs."

After crossing the Yellowstone the caravan entered the heart of the Great Desert, where the rocky soil furnished but meager sustenance for the horses, and lack of water caused intense suffering to both man and beast. A pest of mosquitoes forced the travelers to cover their faces and hands, while their heavy carts toiled up steep rocks and down deep ravines.

At last, on September 2d, the caravan reached the great highway to the Pacific. "This immense avenue," writes Father De Smet, "resembles a wind-swept surface, worn bare by the perpetual march of Europeans and Americans marching to California. The Indians, familiar with only the paths of the chase, thought, upon beholding this beaten track, that the entire nation of the white man had traversed it and that the country of the rising sun must be deserted."[5] Eight days later they arrived at their destination, where Father De Smet was received by the Superintendent of Indian Affairs and invited to be his guest during the Great Council.

The Great Council was held at some distance from Fort Laramie, in a vast plain watered by the Nebraska. Ten thousand Indians, belonging, for the most part, to the various Sioux tribes, assembled there to hear the proposition offered by the United States Government. The most complete unity now reigned among these peoples, only yesterday divided by hate and dissension. Remembering their common origin, the children of the wilderness stood in serried ranks to defend their common interests.

[5] Letter from Father De Smet to the editor of the *Brussels Journal*, June 30, 1853.

On September 12th the Council opened, and the following points were submitted for deliberation:

I. The Indians must recognize the right of the United States to construct roads and military posts in their territory.

II. The Indians, in the interests of peace, must undertake to repair the loss and damage suffered by the whites at their hands.

III. An indemnity of $50,000 in gold would be paid immediately to the Indians for all damage caused to their hunting-grounds, roads, and prairies by travelers crossing their country.

IV. The Indians would receive, moreover, annually during a period of fifty years, $50,000 in gold to be used according to their best judgment.

The treaty was read and explained point by point to the interpreters, who went from group to group of the different tribes, informing them of the nature of the Government's propositions. Confident in the good faith of the United States, Father De Smet sincerely desired the success of the Council.

Received by the chiefs and invited to their feasts, the missionary constantly used his influence to assure peace. His loyal, disinterested attitude greatly impressed the Indians, who harkened to his wise advice. He knew, moreover, that religion is the surest guarantee of union between people. "Promises, threats, firearms, and swords," said he, "are less effective than the Black Robe's words of peace and the civilizing banner of the cross." [6]

Finding this the one occasion to preach the Gospel to all the tribes, Father De Smet gave daily several instructions upon the Commandments, and the recompense or punishment in the life to come. He explained, moreover, the necessity of baptism, and administered the Sacrament to about twelve hundred children. One, perhaps, doubts the efficacy of these detached instructions, given to a passing audience, who to-morrow would return to their superstitious practices. But this is an error. In the field of paganism the missionary could be compared to a fruitful tree, which in autumn gives forth its seeds, abandoning

[6] Letter quoted.

them to the winds of heaven. What matters it that thousands fall on sterile ground and come to naught, if only one seed grows and bears fruit? Father De Smet in his travels often met Indians so permeated with the spirit of Christianity that they were quite ready for the regenerating waters of baptism. Upon questioning them he found to his surprise that they had once listened to his instructions, and his words, falling upon their sincere, well-disposed souls, had borne the fruit he now witnessed. On this occasion also he could rely upon the lasting effects of his apostolate, for the Indians had listened to him with pious attention and expressed a desire to become Christians.

"Father," said they, "we are faulty and sinful because we are ignorant of the word of the Great Spirit. If you will remain here to instruct us, we will try henceforth to lead better lives." Powerless to accede to their request, Father De Smet was heard repeatedly to exclaim, "If European priests knew the good a missionary could accomplish here, they would hasten to America to bring joy to our Mother the Church in giving her thousands of new children."

And now the Great Council was about to conclude. The different articles so long under discussion were finally, one after the other, adopted by the tribes. The treaty was signed by the representatives of the United States and the principal Indian chiefs. The next day the United States flag flying from the Superintendent's tent, and the firing of a cannon, announced the arrival of the presents sent by the Government—a division of which would now take place. The Indians assembled without delay, ranging themselves in a circle around the exposed gifts. The great chiefs were first presented with an outfit of clothing, which they immediately donned. Proud of their new habiliments and courting admiration, they naïvely showed themselves to the missionary, decked out in generals' uniforms and magnificent gold-plated swords, which contrasted singularly with their long hair and vermilion-painted faces. Thus accoutered, the chiefs divided among the members of their tribes the bounty of the Government. Perfect order reigned, and strict justice presided at the distribution of the gifts. When the Indians retired, charmed with the Superintendent's amiability and kindness, they were satisfied, and confident in his promises of peace. Father De Smet likewise shared in the general feeling of confidence and good will. "This Council," he says, "will be the beginning of a new era for the redskins; an era of peace when travelers will be able to cross the desert unmolested, and the Indians in turn will have nothing to fear from the white man."

The Great Council lasted twelve days. On September 24th the Indians began the preparations for their departure. Father De Smet requested them to pray daily to the Master of life, and promised to use his influence to obtain a missionary for them. He then shook hands for the last time with the chiefs, and set out for St. Louis with the American delegates and a deputation of Indians en route for Washington.

After journeying for some time along the Nebraska, the caravan turned south in order to visit the Potawatomi Mission. This was an opportune occasion of impressing the Indians with the advantages of industrious and persevering work. The St. Mary's missionaries gave a banquet in honor of the travelers, consisting of quantities of vegetables and fruits. Sweet potatoes, carrots, turnips, pumpkins, melons, apples, and peaches were served to the Indian deputation, to which all did justice. At the conclusion of the repast, Eagle Head arose and addressed Father De Smet in the following words: "To-day we understand your words. You told us in the camp that the buffalo would disappear from our territory in a few years, but that we could draw from the earth sustenance for ourselves and our children. When you spoke thus our ears were closed; to-day they are open, now that we have eaten the fruits of the earth. We see before us a people happy, well fed, and well clothed. We will welcome the Black Robes and will listen to their words."

The next day being Sunday, all assisted at High Mass. The prayers, hymns, and piety of the faithful made a profound impression upon the visiting Indians, who incessantly interrogated the missionary upon the doctrines that gave happiness here below and would conduct them to heaven in the world to come.

Upon leaving St. Mary's the travelers directed their steps to Westport, where they embarked on a steamboat descending the Missouri. One can easily imagine the wonder and amazement of the redskins in passing suddenly from the wilderness into a rich and civilized country. Every town and scattered village resounded with their cries of joy and admiration. At last, on October 22d, the party arrived at St. Louis, where the Indian deputation was cordially received at the St. Louis University, the Provincial even promising to send them a Black Robe.

In reviewing the events of the past five months, Father De Smet was filled with gratitude to God. He writes: "During my journey across the plains and mountains God watched over me. I escaped from a dangerous malady; from the attacks of the enemy and wild beasts; from smallpox and cholera. I came safely through a camp where men were dying and rotting before me, and remained over a month among the dying and dead, handling and nursing the cholera-stricken victims without contracting the disease. To me was given the happiness of pouring the waters of baptism upon the foreheads of 1,586 children and adults, many of whom have since succumbed to the scourge, and whose eternal happiness is now assured."[7]

The missionary's modesty did not permit him to recall the part he had taken in the success of the Conference, but the United States recognized it, and before long it was admitted in Washington that his mediation had been more effective than that of an army.[8] As will be seen, in new conflicts later to occur between the white man and the Indian, he was destined to again fill the rôle of pacificator.

[7] Letter to Father Hélias d'Huddeghem, St. Louis, Nov. 13, 1851.
[8] Chittenden-Richardson, p. 1566.

CHAPTER XV

THE YEARS OF TRIAL (1848–1855)

Father De Smet Ardently Desires to Again Take Up His Mission Work—The
Indians Petition Him to Come to Them—The Father General Dis-
approves of His Project—What Could Have Happened?—Complaints
Made Against Father De Smet by Some of His Assistants—His Reply—
New Complaints—Again Father De Smet is Justified—The Flathead
Mission Must Be Abandoned—The Father General Renders Justice to
Father De Smet's Zeal and Sincerity, but Does Not Deem It Prudent
to Open New Missions—The Missionary's Work Must Stand the
Test of Time—How it is Judged Fifty Years Later—Death of Father
Elet, Madam Duchesne, and Father Roothaan—"Why, My Soul,
Would You Escape the Cross?"—Father De Smet's Superiors Think
of Sending Him to Reside Permanently in One of the European Prov-
inces—His Letter to the Holland Provincial—He is Left in St. Louis—
He Pronounces His Solemn Vows—His Courageous Obedience Wins
for Him New and Greater Successes.

DURING Father De Smet's trip to Fort Laramie
Father Verhaegen took his place as Assistant Procurator of the Province. Doubtless the former hoped
that he would not be obliged to again take up his functions, as it will be remembered he had assumed the post
only temporarily and on several occasions had expressed
a desire to return to the missions.

On February 2, 1850, he writes to the Father General
of the Jesuits: "Your Paternity, in your letter of August
29th, deigns to enquire after my health. Thank God I
am very well, and, save for slight attacks of rheumatism,[1]
I feel quite capable of again facing and enduring the privations inseparable from long journeys. At a word from
your Paternity, I will immediately start for the Western
plains, where thousands of souls languish under the rule
of Satan. The hope of baptizing those little children and

[1] The malady in question, rheumatism, had been contracted by the
missionary during his journey to the Sioux.

preparing the aged, whose dispositions are admirable, for death, gives me courage to return to a post I left with much regret."

The Indians awaited impatiently the return of the Black Robe. Since 1847 the Blackfeet had been without a missionary. Father Point had been called to Canada by his Superiors, and was obliged to abandon his neophytes—eleven hundred in all—who thus were in danger of falling back into barbarism.[2] The Crows reminded Father De Smet of his promises, and entreated him to do something for them. "Remember," said the Sioux, "that the waters of baptism have been poured on the foreheads of our children." The chief of the Assiniboins sent a long letter begging for the Black Robes, promising to contribute a portion of the Government money to their support. "I am getting old," he says in conclusion. "Could I see my wish realized I would then die willingly."

Father De Smet deemed it imperative to respond to these appeals, inasmuch as he wished to forestall the arrival of the Protestant ministers, and prevent error from being sown in this well-prepared soil. He had hoped to be able to accomplish this in the spring of 1851. Bishop Miège asked Father De Smet to introduce him to the Indian tribes recently placed under his jurisdiction. "I hope," he writes, "to soon see new missions established east of the Rocky Mountains, which will labor for the conversion and civilization of these Indian tribes."[3]

Father De Smet's letters, written at that time, betray the joy he experienced in seeing his long-cherished dream about to be realized. He spoke of his projects and recommended them to the prayers of his friends. "My journey will be long and beset with dangers. Beg heaven to give me strength and courage to fulfil my task."[4] The preparations were completed, and everything was in readiness for the journey, when a letter arrived from Rome, disapproving of his return to the missions. It is true he had assisted at the Indian Council, but his local Superiors, not

---

[2] Father Point died at the Jesuit house in Quebec, July 4, 1868.
[3] To his brother Charles, St. Louis, April 27, 1851.
[4] To his niece Rosalie, who had just made her first communion, April 28, 1851.

wishing to fail in a promise they had made to the Government, had taken upon themselves the responsibility of allowing him to go.

What had happened?

We now come to the period of trial in the life of our missionary. Aspersed by men who had been misinformed, he felt that his judgment and prudence, nay even his character, was doubted by his Superiors. His trials were many and varied. He lived through hours of bitter discouragement. Years passed before he regained peace and felt confidence in those he loved and venerated. But this period of trial and discouragement can be easily explained. Father De Smet's extremely sensitive nature suffered acutely from the exaggerations and false reports that had gained the ears of his Superiors, too far off themselves to judge of the merits of the case. The ardor with which the valiant apostle labored at his task exposed his measures to criticism and false interpretations.

The first friction and trouble began when Father De Smet established the Oregon Missions. Among his auxiliaries were fellow-missionaries who, chafing under his authority, complained to Rome. The missionary, conscious of his conservative measures and his labors to keep peace, was consequently able to enlighten the Father General as to the cause of the trouble, and of his innocence of the unmerited charges.

In the spring of 1848 Father Roothaan charged Father Elet to assure the former Superior of Oregon "that he enjoyed his full confidence." However, this was but a short respite. In a letter dated February 17, 1849, Father Roothaan informs Father De Smet that he is accused of offending against holy poverty, and of dispensing funds as though the management of money were his own affair. These accusations determined Father De Smet to resign his post of Procurator General. With tears in his eyes he begged Father Elet to relieve him of a charge he was judged unworthy of holding, for he felt that henceforth the burden would be more than he could bear. Nevertheless, he felt it incumbent upon him to reply to these imputations, which attacked his honor as a priest and a Jesuit. Hence, he forwarded to the General of the

Jesuits an exact account of his administration since 1840, when the mission funds were given into his hands. This account had been several times submitted to the inspection and control of Fathers Van de Velde and Elet. Had useless expenditures been made, as the amount of debt proved, it was because "neither his advice nor his orders had been complied with."

"In what concerns my personal expenditures, apart from the modest sum paid my guide, I made three journeys from the Rocky Mountains to St. Louis without spending a dollar. Last year when I visited the Indians, I traversed three thousand miles of territory, was absent four months, and the entire expense of my journey amounted to $50." Even during his travels in Europe he lived most modestly. "When in Paris, finding myself at a distance from the Jesuit house, I more than once dined on two or three pennies' worth of chestnuts. I journeyed once from Marseilles to Rome and back again upon the main deck of the boat, my food consisting of a piece of bread and some meat I bought before embarking, to save expense. I regret to be obliged to enter into these details, but I am forced to do so to clear myself of the false charge made against me. If I have erred, I crave pardon."[5]

In Father De Smet's statement of his case, he gives not only convincing reasons for his line of conduct, but running through it is a note of sincerity that cannot be doubted. Father Roothaan was too clear-sighted and loyal not to accept his explanation, and retain the missionary in his office of Procurator and Assistant to the Provincial. His relations with his Superior were becoming most cordial, and he hoped before long to be allowed to go West to open new missions. Affairs had reached this point, when new complications arose which profoundly impressed the Father General and led him to doubt the ultimate success of the Oregon Missions.

On May 1, 1852, Father De Smet wrote to Bishop Van de Velde, "When you were my Superior, you often reproached me for being too easily affected and discouraged by things said in my disfavor, and I knew you were right.

[5] Letter of April 3, 1849.

Again I am being criticised, and am completely crushed by the disapproval that comes from the highest authorities, for not only are the accusations false, but the consequence of this will be the abandonment of a large number of the Indians, for whom I would gladly sacrifice the remainder of my life."

What then was the nature of these accusations? They are formulated in the letter from the General of the Jesuits, which had all but prevented Father De Smet's departure for Fort Laramie.

The following are the specific charges: First, the reports published by the missionary contained fantastic statements, which misled and caused bitter disappointment to missionaries arriving in these places. Second, that Father De Smet had compromised the future of the missions in giving too generously to the Indians, and in making promises he was unable to keep.[6]

In reply to the first charge, Father De Smet dispatched immediately to Rome the testimony of the principal Oregon missionaries, notably, Fathers Accolti, Ravalli, Mengarini, Joset, and De Vos. We will cite but two passages in this letter. On June 1, 1847, a year after Father De Smet's departure from the mountains, Father Accolti, Superior of the Willamette Mission, wrote to the Provincial, "You may possibly meet critical men, who will find our reports of the missions exaggerated. Do not heed them, for I can assure you that when conditions are viewed without prejudice, the reality surpasses all the reports that have been hitherto recorded. I state facts, and exaggerate nothing. Nay, more, I voice the general opinion of strangers, even Protestants, who are forced to believe the evidence of facts."[7]

Father Ravalli says, in a letter written the same year to Father Van de Velde: "I can say in all sincerity that in the

[6] Letter of April 14, 1851.

[7] Washington Irving, in speaking of the Flatheads, declares: "To say these people are religious gives but a faint idea of the piety and devotion they manifest in their conduct in life. They are honest to a fault, upright in their intentions, and their religious fidelity is truly remarkable. It is a nation of saints rather than a horde of barbarians." ("Adventures of Captain Bonneville," quoted by Helen Hunt Jackson, in "A Century of Dishonor," p. 377.)

midst of the Flatheads I find myself in a terrestrial paradise. In Father De Smet's letters which I read in Rome, and in the different reports he wrote while I was in Willamette, I feared his statements were exaggerated, and that his rhetorical flights were intended to charm the reader; but since Providence has granted my desire in sending me to the mountains, I know now that if any criticism could be made of those letters it would be that Father De Smet had minimized the good dispositions of these Indians." Along with this testimony, Father De Smet sent the General a letter from Bishop Blanchet, in which he expresses his gratitude to the missionary for the marvelous results he had obtained in Oregon. How was it possible, after such testimony, to see invention and inexactitude in Father De Smet's reports?

We will cite from the reply of Father Cataldo, who was best qualified to judge the facts and men of that far-off period.[8]

"Some," says he, "seeing only a small number of the stations, and not finding there conditions Father De Smet had experienced, concluded that his accounts were exaggerated or the work of imagination. I learned to appreciate Father De Smet when I came in contact with the Indians, and, when occasion presented, I spoke my mind to those who undervalued the author of the 'Letters.' I have always denounced their accusations."[9]

As to the second charge, that he had by undue liberality and rash promises compromised the future of the missions, Father De Smet again quotes the testimony of his fellow-priests. "I could fill many pages with extracts from letters written by the Oregon Fathers who praise my work among the Indians, and these letters were written years after I had left them."[10]

He quotes in particular a letter from Father Joset, written November 1, 1851. "You will be delighted to hear that the Pend d'Oreilles, Cœur d'Alènes, Chaudières, and the tribes of the Columbia Lakes give entire satisfac-

[8] Father Cataldo arrived in Oregon in 1864, and was for many years Superior of the Rocky Mountain Mission.
[9] Pendleton, March 5, 1909.
[10] Letter to Bishop Van de Velde, May 1, 1852.

tion to the missionaries, and, I may add, have never been better behaved."

The future of the missions was far from being compromised, though one event which took place at the close of 1850 was calculated to cause the Father General legitimate apprehension. St. Mary's Mission, the first established in the mountains, was abandoned. Situated in a smiling, fertile valley, and well provisioned, the "reduction" offered great facilities to the traveler. Every year trappers and American hunters returned to winter there, wishing, they said, to fulfil their religious duties. As a matter of fact, many only sought comfortable winter quarters in the mission, and abandoned themselves, under the eyes of the Indians, to shameful disorders. The Fathers reproved these men for their licentious living, and they, to revenge themselves, incited the Indians against the missionaries, saying they were ambitious men, whose sole object in coming from the other side of the ocean was to seize their land and oppress them. These calumnies, in conjunction with the intrigues of an Indian who wished to become chief, did not lack success, for however sincere may have been the conversion of the Flatheads, their unstable nature still remained. From being docile and devoted to the Black Robes they gradually drew away from their benefactors, and forswore the promises made in baptism. Their passion for play was awakened, and whiskey brought by the white man began its ravages.

The summer hunt of 1849 was the occasion of dire excesses. Ashamed of their conduct, the neophytes scarcely dared return to St. Mary's. Father Mengarini received them cordially, but all in vain. They felt that every eye reproached them for their disorderly life. All those who had taken part in the hunt mounted their steeds one morning and went away to pitch their tents nine miles distant. Only a few old people, deploring the misconduct of the tribe, remained with the missionary. Victor, the chief, had, unfortunately, neither the energy nor the influence of Big Face. When asked to intervene, his only reply was, "What can I do?"

Wishing at all costs to win back his wayward children, Father Mengarini went in pursuit of them. Alas! his advances produced no effect. At a loss to know how to reclaim them, he consulted his Superior, Father Accolti, who deemed it wise to close the "reduction" for a time. The departure of the Fathers would perhaps bring the Flatheads to their senses, and realizing the services rendered by the Black Robes, they might become docile once more and beg the missionaries to return.[11] With death in their souls, the missionaries departed from St. Mary's, where, formerly, the neophytes' fervor had given them sweetest joy. Father Mengarini retired to Willamette, and Father Ravalli to the Cœur d'Alènes.[12]

The Superiors saw in this abandonment of St. Mary's the fruit of Father De Smet's liberality and rash promises, but the missionaries protested vigorously that the accusations were "false in every respect."[13]

The missionary's grief and anxiety were augmented by the fear that the Father General might not this time exonerate him from all blame, for he had now waited a year for a reply to his letters. At last the long-looked-for letter arrived from Rome, in which Father Roothaan rendered justice to Father De Smet's zeal and sincerity, although he could not understand what had taken place. "The reverses of these last years," he said, "are still inexplicable, especially the change that has taken place in the Flatheads."[14]

The future of the "reductions" was a never-ceasing cause of anxiety to the Father General.[15] While con-

---

[11] Such measures had been taken with the Cœur d'Alènes, for a time refractory, with great success.

[12] Cf. Father Mengarini's *Mémoires* in The Woodstock Letters, June, 1889, pp. 149–152. Palladino, "Indian and White in the Northwest," p. 50. In consequence of circumstances that will be related further on, the mission was not opened until sixteen years later. Father Mengarini never again saw St. Mary's. After a short stay at Willamette he, with Fathers Nobili and De Vos, was put in charge of the new California Mission. He never forgot his dear Flatheads, and consecrated his meager leisure to composing a grammar destined to be of great service to the missionaries. (*A Selish or Flathead Grammar*, New York, 1861.) He died at Santa Clara, Sept. 23, 1886.

[13] Letter to Father Murphy, Vice-Provincial of Missouri, March 1, 1852.

[14] Letter of April 15, 1852.

[15] "Now that St. Mary's Mission is closed," he said, "I fear greatly for the others." (The Woodstock Letters, 1887, p. 96.)

vinced that the reports were exaggerated, he feared, nevertheless, that Father De Smet had been too optimistic, and had entertained projects too vast. Moreover, the situation could not have completely changed since the former Superior's departure five years previous. Before permitting new missions to be opened, and even before justifying Father De Smet's conduct and management, the General decided to suspend judgment and await more definite news.

Such difficulties are not of rare occurrence in the history of apostolic work. The missionary who carries the Gospel into a new country is usually eager and impatient to assure his conquest, and at the risk of seeming importunate, seeks more abundant resources, and an increasing number of co-workers. His enterprise may appear too daring. The difficulties of the beginning, and the inevitable checks invite the condemnation of the faint-hearted, the criticism of the short-sighted. Even Superiors, before engaging themselves to support a venture, require certain guarantees. But when it is evident that the work has God's blessing and promises an abundant harvest, and the future seems assured, those who at first counseled moderation applaud success and give unstinted approval.

Father De Smet's work, like that of all who have initiative, must be tried by the test of time. To-day no one questions the valiant missionary's right to the glory of having opened a fruitful field to Catholic apostolic work.

"It is beyond all question," writes Father Cataldo, "that Father De Smet was a superior man, and one sent by Providence to the missions. Humanly speaking, without him, or some one of the same caliber, the mountain missions would never have existed, and failing these, the California Missions would not now be in existence.[16] He was not a resident missionary, it is true, but he was the great organizer of the missions. He knew how to approach and charm the Indians, and to lead them under the direction of a Father. He found not only the means, but the men, whom he accompanied to the scenes of their labors, taught them

[16] The California Missions and the Rocky Mountain Missions, which were united on July 31, 1909, form now the California Province.

how to manage the Indians, and only departed when he saw them with the work well in hand." [17]

In 1891 Bishop Brondel of Helena called upon the faithful in his diocese to celebrate, on the first Sunday of October, the fiftieth anniversary of the introduction of Catholicism into Montana. "If to-day," said he, in speaking of the founders of St. Mary's, "there is not an Indian tribe without schools and churches, not a hamlet without its Catholic chapel, not a city of importance without its churches and schools and hospitals, we owe it in a large part to the heroic pioneers of the faith." [18]

As with the apostles of our blessed Lord, what Father De Smet sowed in sorrow, others reaped in joy.

When the Master's cross was pressing heaviest upon the shoulders of the missionary, he was deprived, gradually, of all human support. We know already the details of Father Hoecken's death. A few months later Father Elet died at Florissant, and when Father De Smet returned from Fort Laramie, he whom he called "the truest brother and friend," [19] he, whose gentleness and charity had supported him in hours of trial, was no more. These two Jesuits had been intimately connected from the time they were young men. Sons of Flanders, both crossed to America together and together shared the labors of those heroic days in Whitemarsh and Florissant. They were ordained at the same time, they took part in the colonization of Missouri, aided materially in founding the St. Louis College, and for years shared the government of the Vice-Province. Faithful to the memory of his sainted friend, Father De Smet writes touchingly, not only in sorrow for his loss, but in admiration of his virtues.[20]

We remember Madam Duchesne, that remarkable religious of the Sacred Heart, who, in 1823, received Father Van Quickenborne's valiant band of missionaries upon

[17] Letter quoted. Father de la Motte, who succeeded Father Cataldo as Superior of the Rocky Mountain and California Missions, shared absolutely the opinion of his predecessors. "Father De Smet's hopes," said he, "have been more than realized." (Santa Clara, March 16, 1909.)
[18] Sept. 27, 1891.
[19] Letter to Francis De Smet, St. Louis, April 17, 1851.
[20] Selected Letters, 2d Series, p. 51.

their arrival in Missouri. The evangelization of the Indians absorbed her thoughts and energies. "My whole pleasure," she writes, "is to hear about the promising future of the Rocky Mountain Mission. In realizing the expense such a foundation entails, one is tempted to wish for money." [21]

Encouraged and seconded by this valiant woman since his novitiate, Father De Smet venerated her as a mother, and each time he returned from his missions his greatest pleasure was to repair at once to the convent to give her an account of the progress the Gospel was making. "Never did I leave her," he says, "without feeling that I had been conversing with a saint. I have always regarded this Mother as the greatest protector of our missions. For several years she offered two communions a week and daily prayers for the conversion of the Indians, whom she dearly loved." [22]

Madam Duchesne was now over eighty years of age. Feeling the end approaching, she wished to take leave of what she held most dear in life: The Sacred Heart Community, her family, and the Indian Missions. "My very dear Father," she writes to the apostle of the Rocky Mountains, "I cannot leave this life without expressing to you my gratitude. Do not forget, after her death, her to whom you were so good upon earth. Your prayers will plead for me with the Sovereign Judge whom I have so often offended." She then promises to pray for the Indians, and especially for their good Father.

On November 18, 1852, the eminent foundress expired at St. Charles, leaving her community well established in America and animated with her spirit. Father De Smet received, before long, assurance of her happiness. It had been agreed between them that the first to die would obtain, if possible, a special favor for the other. Immediately after Madam Duchesne's death, Father De Smet experienced the fulfilment of the saintly woman's promise.[23]

The following year Father Roothaan passed to his re-

---

[21] See Bishop Baunard. "Histoire de Madam Duchesne," p. 469.
[22] Letter of Oct. 9, 1872.
[23] Bishop Baunard, *op. cit.*, p. 489. We do not know the nature of the favor.

ward. Until the last, he felt concern for the future of the Oregon Missions. Father De Smet sorrowed for the loss of a man he esteemed, loved, and venerated, and from whom he had received much kindness.[24]

The surviving friends were dispersed. With Father Van de Velde, now Bishop of Chicago, and Bishop Miège, Vicar Apostolic to the Indian Territory, Father De Smet would henceforth have but remote connections. Moreover, he had arrived at an age where it is difficult to form new ties. His friends disappearing one by one, the missionary attached himself more and more to the one Friend who remains when all others have passed away, making Him the confidant of his most intimate sufferings. He courageously embraced the cross, and dwelt continually upon thoughts that for some time past had occupied his mind. "Why, my soul, wouldst thou avoid the cross? Whichever way thou mayst turn thou canst not escape it. To evade one cross is but to encounter two others. Perhaps it is the suffering thou dost fear? Be wise! Welcome the cross that is sent by heaven, and try to comprehend its value. In it thou wilt find thy happiness; it is soaked with the blood of Christ, so generously spilled to wash away sin and open heaven." [25]

Strengthened by these thoughts, Father De Smet met unflinchingly a new sacrifice. There was a question of taking him not only from the missions, but from America, his adopted country. On March 12, 1852, he wrote to the Provincial in Holland: "Perhaps you are already in receipt of the letter in which the Provincial of Missouri communicates his intention, and that of his consultors, to send me to Europe as Procurator of the Vice-Province and the Indian Missions, and seeks your advice upon the advisability of the step. Father Elet formed this project

[24] Letter to Bishop Van de Velde, May 1, 1852.

[25] The following words, translated from the Flemish, were inscribed upon a picture given by Father De Smet to a benefactress of the missions: "I hope you will accept this little remembrance. It is one of my faithful companions. In 1821 it crossed the Atlantic with me for the first time. May it be as fruitful for you as it has been for me! Whenever I have been in affliction, to look at it has encouraged me to bear patiently the contradictions and trials God has been pleased to send me." (St. Louis, May 22, 1849.)

during his Provincialship, and it appears that your Paternity has already given to it your approval.

"With regard to myself, I wish to at once assure you that I have no desire to influence the decision of my Superiors, and am ready and willing to execute their orders; furthermore, after mature reflection and prayer, I wish to see them carried out, because I would gladly spend the few remaining years of my life in the strict observance of our holy rules, and in perfect submission to orders. I feel this to be a need, after so many years spent in the far missions of America.

"Father Hoecken's enviable death upon the battle-field, and that of the venerated Father Elet, who for many years was not only my brother in Christ, but a guide by his advice and example, make me sincerely desire this change. I assure you, Most Reverend Father, that I will endeavor to give complete satisfaction, and that should you deign to accept the Provincial's proposition, I shall be most grateful to you. To be able to live the life of a religious in the practice of obedience, and, when occasion presents, to still be useful to America, if such be the will of my Superiors, is, before God, my earnest desire."

God was content with this generous offer, and the Superiors of the Society let the project drop. Father De Smet remained in St. Louis and continued under the new Provincial, Father Murphy, to fill the office he had occupied under Father Elet. The fact that he remained Procurator of Missouri until his death is the best proof of the wisdom of his administration. Peace again entered his soul, and on August 15, 1855, he bound himself by further solemn vows more closely to the Master whom he promised to serve to the end.[26]

These years of bitter trial had but strengthened his virtue, and by the enlightenment that came from on high he realized that trial is an inevitable condition of all fruitful work. After the example of a crucified Saviour, the apostle must be willing to suffer. Seeing himself so

---

[26] Jesuits are ordinarily not ordained until seventeen years after they enter the novitiate. Father De Smet, received for the second time into the Society at the close of 1837, was obliged to wait until 1855 for his final incorporation.

quickly downcast and crushed, he became more humble and more compassionate for human suffering about him, and he acquired, especially, the habit of looking to God for support. "Our strength consists in a knowledge of our own weakness, and in the possession of that great remedy, the grace of Jesus Christ our Mediator." [27] These words translate admirably St. Paul's *Cum infirmor, tunc potens sum.* [28]

In taking him away from his dear missions, God imposed a heavy sacrifice upon Father De Smet, but his courageous obedience, far from curtailing his work, brought him even more important achievements.

[27] Letter to Laura Blondel, wife of Charles De Smet, nephew of the missionary, June 1, 1860.

[28] "When I am weak, then am I powerful." (2 Cor. xii, 10.)

CHAPTER XVI

PROGRESS MADE BY CATHOLICISM IN THE UNITED STATES—
FATHER DE SMET'S APOSTOLATE IN ST. LOUIS—THE
"KNOW-NOTHINGS"—(1849–1858)

Extraordinary Growth of Colonization—Progress of Catholicism—The
First Plenary Council of Baltimore—The Oxford Movement and Its
Effect in America—Eccleston, Brownson, Hecker—Success of the
Jesuits in St. Louis—Fathers Smarius, Damen, Weninger—Father
De Smet's Apostolate—The Emigrants—His Former Traveling Com-
panions—St. Anne's Church—The Direction of Souls—Protestant
Conversions—The Conversion of Randolph Benton—Attacks from
Enemies of the Church—Boernstein, Kossuth, Lola Montez—The
"Know-Nothings"—Attack upon Archbishop Bedini—"There is No
Other Country in the World where Honest Men Enjoy so Little Liberty"
—The Jesuits are Not Spared—Fathers Bapst and Nachon—End of
the Agitation which Served but to Strengthen Catholicism—Father
De Smet is Again Spoken of for the Episcopate—"My Heart is Always
with the Indians."

SINCE the coming of the Jesuits to Missouri, colonization west of the Alleghanies had progressed at an
astonishing rate. To this country, as vast in extent as
the continent of Europe, there flocked, yearly, thousands
of emigrants attracted by the richness of the virgin soil.
Before long the wilderness began to develop. In thirty
years the population of the United States increased from
ten million to twenty-five million inhabitants.

"I remember," writes Father De Smet, "when St. Louis,
Cincinnati, and Pittsburg were simple villages; these towns
now number over 200,000 souls. Ten years ago, Chicago
and Milwaukee were small inland ports; to-day the former
counts 80,000, and the latter 40,000 inhabitants, and resemble huge beehives teeming with activity. Follow the
course of the rivers; penetrate into the interior of the
country, and from one day to the next you will see beautiful
parks replacing forests, and vast prairies transformed into
prosperous farms, possessing herds of cows and sheep,

254 THE LIFE OF FATHER DE SMET, S.J.

droves of horses, and barns filled with wheat, while railways and macadamized roads traverse the land in every direction." [1]

Catholicism marched hand in hand with colonization. At the beginning of his episcopate, Archbishop Carroll had difficulty in finding a synod of twenty-five priests, ministering to the 40,000 Catholics of the Union. The first Plenary Council held in Baltimore on May 9, 1852, was composed of six Archbishops and thirty-five Bishops. Not counting the missionaries, America then possessed about 1,500 priests, ministering to 1,600,000 Catholics. Churches, seminaries, colleges, convents, schools, and hospitals abounded. "When I first came to St. Louis," says Father De Smet, "the town boasted of about 4,000 inhabitants, one poor church, and two small schools. To-day the population exceeds 120,000 souls, of which at least 50,000 are Catholics. It possesses a beautiful cathedral, eleven churches, a seminary for secular priests, and a large and well-equipped hospital in charge of the Sisters of Charity, a Jesuit college with one hundred and fifty boarders, one hundred and twenty half-boarders and day scholars, not counting about four hundred free pupils. The Christian Brothers have a college where the sons of good families are educated. The Ladies of the Sacred Heart and the Visitation and Ursuline Sisters have opened large boarding-schools for girls. Besides these, St. Louis possesses ten or twelve schools in charge of nuns and priests of religious orders, five orphanages containing over five hundred infants, a foundling asylum, a refuge for fallen women and for young girls exposed to doubtful surroundings.

"All the Masses are so well-attended that the churches can hardly accommodate their congregations, and the fervor of the faithful responds to the zeal of the pastors. The harmony existing between the secular and regular clergy contributes largely to the progress religion is making." [2]

[1] Letter to Mr. Conway, gentleman-in-waiting to the Duke de Brabant, St. Louis, July 10, 1855.
[2] Letter to Mr. Blondel of Antwerp, Louisville, April 21, 1855. St. Louis became an Archiepiscopal See in 1847. The first Bishop of the diocese, Right Rev. Joseph Rosati, died in Rome, Sept. 25, 1843, and was succeeded by Bishop, later Archbishop, Peter Richard Kenrick.

To what can we attribute these consoling results? To the large numbers of Canadian, Irish, German, and Polish emigrants who had settled in the Mississippi valley, on the prairies, and in the regions of the Great Lakes. Poor, for the most part, but robust, patient, and enterprising, they pushed to the Far West, and to them we owe the material prosperity of the United States. Desirous of bringing up their children in the Faith of their fathers, these men enriched America with churches, schools, and convents. While the Puritan families in New England had but one or two children, the new-comers, with their numerous offspring, fast became the controlling element in the country. The progress of Catholicism outstripped the increase in population. Since the beginning of the century, the number of Catholics had increased from one to ten per cent. of the inhabitants.

Catholicism becoming better known, conversions from Protestantism were of frequent occurrence. The closing ceremonies of the eighth Provincial Council of Baltimore lent prestige to Catholicism. The Bishops, whose dioceses extended from Louisiana to Oregon, went in procession to the cathedral to the accompaniment of hymns and the ringing of joy-bells. The thousands of faithful who composed these various dioceses harkened to the voice of their Bishops, and an immense concourse of Catholics acknowledged the only religion which can claim the right of directing souls.

The Oxford Movement, which, in 1840, sundered from the Church of England the élite of its ministers, had its echo in America. Those sincerely seeking truth severed the closest ties to embrace the true religion. Men distinguished in the intellectual world—among whom can be cited Archbishop Eccleston, Brownson the writer, and Father Hecker the apostle—came over to Rome. Many entered the priesthood, and later on were elevated to the ranks of the princes of the Church.

The Jesuits in St. Louis contributed largely to the success of the religious movement.

"The following," writes Father De Smet, "is what we are accomplishing in one church only. In St. Francis

Xavier's, our college church, last year (1854) the number of communicants exceeded 50,000 and between sixty and eighty conversions were made. The two Sodalities of the Blessed Virgin count among their four hundred members, lawyers, doctors, bankers, merchants, clerks, etc. All are monthly communicants, and wear the miraculous medal. The Archconfraternity of Our Lady of Victory numbers between 5,000 and 6,000 members, the Association of the Sacred Heart, 2,000, and 1,000 children attend the parish school." [3]

The University possessed one eminent controversialist and renowned preacher. Father Smarius of Brabant, Holland, attracted crowds of Catholics and Protestants every Sunday, who studied religious questions in order to reply to his arguments. A Protestant newspaper, *The Republic*, published the conferences and the replies, and thus spread, through the States of the Union, the defence of Catholicism.

Another Hollander, Father Damen, preached without respite in town and country, often receiving as many as sixty-seven converts into the Church in one day. He, with his assistants, gave over two hundred missions and brought 12,000 souls into the Church. With equal success, Father Weninger taught the word of God for thirty years in both German and English, and his many controversial works and pious writings proved as potent for good as his spoken word, meriting for him words of praise from the Sovereign Pontiffs.

Occupied as he was with the administration of the Vice-Province, Father De Smet had little leisure to consecrate to the ministry. He found means, however, of influencing souls, and effected many conversions in St. Louis. His greatest care was for the emigrants on the levee. He recognized at once the fair hair, bright coloring, and direct glance of the Flemish, and when the rough idioms of his native tongue betrayed, unmistakably, his countryman, he approached, told him who he was, and asked for news of Belgium. From him they received money and encouragement, and were told where to settle in their new country. Above all, he recommended the emigrants.

[3] Letter to Mr. Blondel, April 22, 1855.

to be ever faithful to their religious duties, and informed them where they could find a priest to minister to their needs.

For the greater number, the exodus was attended with disastrous results. Emigrant-boats were then more like slave-ships. Packed together below the decks, the people perished by hundreds, the mortality being ten per cent. in American boats and thirty per cent. in English boats. Those who survived became the prey, upon debarking, of unscrupulous railway agents.

"Two or three thousand Europeans," writes Father De Smet, "often pass through St. Louis in one week on their way to the West. Every steamboat is crowded to the rails, and it is no exaggeration to state that from fifteen to twenty persons die on each boat between New Orleans and St. Louis." But, considering conditions, one marvels that the mortality was not greater. "Imagine several hundred men, women, and children, and infants of a few months old, packed behind the boilers in a space fifty feet square, the sick breathing the infected air. When I visited these death-traps it turned my stomach. It is a miracle that any one escapes alive from such horrible, unhealthy holes. The emigrant transports now in use on the Mississippi are a disgrace to civilization, and sordid speculation is responsible for these conditions. No matter how overcrowded the boat may be, there is always room for one more. Each passenger represents so much money, and the sacrifice of human life from overcrowding is of no moment. Whole families are wiped out through disease, and thousands of children are left orphans in a strange country." [4]

One day a Flemish family consisting of father, mother, and nine children landed in St. Louis. The parents and four of the children had fallen ill on the boat. The mayor [5] had them taken to the Protestant hospital, where the father succumbed at once, followed a few days later by the mother; shortly afterward a little girl of seven died. Informed of this distressing case, Father De Smet took the eight children, of which the eldest was seventeen

[4] Letter to his brother Charles, St. Louis, Dec., 1849.
[5] Bryan Mullanphy, Mayor of St. Louis.

and the youngest eight months, under his protection. He writes to his brother: "It will doubtless be a consolation to their friends in Belgium to know that I have placed the little girls with the Sisters of Charity, and the two small boys with the Sisters of St. Joseph. The eldest boy and a girl of thirteen are with good Catholic families, where they will be taught a trade or some means of gaining a livelihood." [6]

From 1850, the Government, aided by charitable organizations, undertook to ameliorate the condition of the emigrants. The great Archbishop Hughes of New York established an Emigrants' Savings Bank which was later to become one of the most prosperous banks in the world. Yet years passed before the emigrant problem was solved. [7]

Father De Smet wrote to Belgium again and again, warning young men, especially, against the fate that awaited them. He sent his destitute and discouraged compatriots in St. Louis with letters of recommendation to other places, where a livelihood could be gained under more favorable circumstances. Often he advised them to return to Europe, defraying out of the personal means at his disposal at least a part of the expenses of the return journey.

The missionary's long sojourn in the wilds had brought him in touch with the trappers of the West, fort commanders, and agents of the fur companies. Among these were highly educated Catholics, forced by circumstances to remain years without approaching the Sacraments. To serve as a counter influence against indifference and error, he sent them such books as "Symbolism," by Moehler, and Balmes' "Protestantism and Catholicism Compared." [8]

"You will not regret," he says, in speaking of the last work, "consecrating a few hours of your leisure to this book, which contains varied subjects and new and fruitful ideas.

[6] Letter quoted.

[7] Extract from will of Bryan Mullanphy, who died in 1851: "I, Bryan Mullanphy, do make and declare the following to be my last will and testament: one undivided third of all my property, real, personal, and otherwise, I leave to the City of St. Louis in the State of Missouri, in trust, to be and constitute a fund to furnish relief to all poor emigrants and travelers coming to St. Louis on their way bona fide to settle in the West."

[8] *Le Protestantisme comparé au Catholicisme, dans ses rapports avec la civilisation européenne.*

Balmes is at once a savant and philosopher, a profound thinker, the popular man of the nineteenth century and the valiant defender of Catholic tradition." [9]

Upon hearing that one of his former traveling companions had abandoned his religious practices, Father De Smet immediately wrote, remonstrating with the delinquent in a friendly manner. "You tell me you have visited several churches in Baltimore, where you have admired the architecture and been impressed with the services. Dear friend, you have but a step to take now that you are in the midst of pious, zealous priests; join in the ceremonies of the Church in mind and heart, approach the tribunal of confession, and receive the Bread of angels. You will find in it, be assured, an inestimable treasure, a source of joy, consolation, and peace of mind and soul which the world cannot give. You have not been to your duties for years. Profit by the present occasion, I beg you, and return to God." [10]

Few resisted his appeals. The agents and business men who knew Father De Smet in the Far West, would, upon their return to St. Louis after years spent in the Indian countries, come to confess their sins, and to have him bless their marriages and baptize their children.[11] Unable to return to the missions, Father De Smet endeavored to contribute to the spiritual welfare of the Catholics in St. Louis. The ever-increasing population was in need of churches. He undertook to supply this need, and begged sufficient money to build a church which was dedicated to St. Anne, and consecrated by Archbishop Kenrick, July 27, 1856. To his exterior activities, the zealous priest joined interior work of the soul. His correspondence reveals a director vigilant and solicitous for the soul's progress and perfection. Prudently and delicately he interpreted the maxims of the Gospel and the teachings of the saints, applying them to individual needs. Moreover, it is not without interest to see a man whose activities were far removed from the study of mysticism, quoting such authors as Father Surin.

[9] Letter to Edwin Denig, St. Louis, May, 1852.
[10] Letter to Charles Larpenteur, St. Louis, Dec. 17, 1849.
[11] Cf. Chittenden-Richardson, *op. cit.*, p. 1499, *et seq.*

The esteem Father De Smet's virtues called forth is expressed in the words of Madam Duchesne: "God must be infinitely good to give me such an intercessor." [12] The prestige of his priestly labors, the dignity of his life, and the charm of his manner gained for Father De Smet great influence with both Protestants and Catholics. On April 22, 1854, he writes to Belgium: "Since the new year I have baptized six Protestants, among them a lawyer, a cousin of former President Taylor, and the wife of an ex-superintendent of the Indians. I have also converted a Freemason and am now preparing twenty Protestants for baptism." These lines give some idea of his success, but no conversion was so remarkable as that of Randolph Benton, the only son of Senator Thomas Benton, one of the best-known men of the United States. A gifted youth, twenty-two years of age, he had been brought up a Protestant, but was, unknown to his family, thinking of becoming a Catholic when an attack of dysentery brought him to the point of death. His father, for years on friendly terms with the college, hastened to inform Father De Smet of the danger that threatened. "At his express wish I visited his son, and found his condition alarming. He expressed his joy at seeing me and thanked me for my visit. I seated myself at his bedside and exhorted him to have confidence in God. He listened attentively to every word. 'Yes,' replied the young man, 'Our Lord sends only what is good for us.' I explained the principal articles of religion, which he accepted piously and in firm belief. The Senator was present during the interview. Charmed and edified by the Christian disposition of his son, he pressed my hand affectionately—then drawing me aside, exclaimed: 'What a great consolation this is! Despite the sorrow which tears my heart, my son's words fill me with joy. God be praised! If he dies, he will die a Christian.' No longer able to restrain his tears, the old man retired to another room to hide his emotion.

"I returned to Randolph, who declared his intention of becoming a Catholic. 'With all my heart I desire to receive baptism. Heaven grants me this inestimable favor, and I feel sure my father will not object.' I im-

[12] Baunard, "Histoire de Madam Duchesne," p. 485.

mediately sought the Senator in the adjoining room to ask his consent, which he gave willingly. Filled with joy, the young man prepared himself for the Sacrament. During the ceremony of baptism his arms were devoutly crossed on his breast, and with uplifted eyes he prayed fervently, thanking God for the grace accorded him." [13]

Father De Smet then administered the Viaticum. After he had returned to the college he received the following lines from the Senator: "Dear Father De Smet: After your departure, I returned to my son, who immediately asked me if I was pleased with what he had done. 'Very pleased,' I replied, and then advised him to rest and be quiet. 'Peace and happiness,' he said, 'are more potent than sleep.' Shortly afterward, with his eyes raised to heaven, serenity of soul written on his face, he exclaimed, in a clear, firm voice: 'Through God's infinite goodness, I am perfectly happy!' Then addressing me, said, 'I have wished for some time to become a Catholic, but I did not know if you would approve.' I replied that far from being displeased, I was truly happy, and that this was the first happy moment I had known since his illness. To you, dear Father, we owe all. You have restored peace to my heart in giving it to my son."

Randolph Benton had but a few hours to live. With touching piety he received the Last Sacraments, and on March 17, 1852, at sunrise, his soul, which had never "sinned against the light" entered into the joys of the Lord. The Archbishop of St. Louis assisted at the funeral services, and spoke eloquently of the deceased. Although a Presbyterian, Senator Benton had a hundred Masses said for the repose of his son's soul. Father De Smet hoped to receive the father into the Church. He never became a Catholic,[14] but to the end of his life the eminent statesman honored Father De Smet with his friendship.[15]

[13] Letter to Father Murphy, St. Louis, April 1, 1852.

[14] Thomas Benton died in Washington, April 10, 1858. He was given a public funeral, at which 20,000 persons assisted. Nothing in the accounts of his last moments indicates that he embraced the Catholic faith.

[15] Among the souvenirs of the missionary, his family preserve a copy of "Une Histoire des Tribus Indiennes," by Schoolcraft, in which is found the following inscription: "Offert par l'ex-sénateur Benton au Révérend Père De Smet, en témoignage d'affectueuse considération et de vive gratitude

The progress Catholicism was making began to disgust the enemies of the Church, who soon began their attacks. Many Italians, Swiss, Germans, and Hungarians, revolutionaries fleeing from Europe after the events of 1848, sought in the United States a more favorable ground to make propaganda for their so-called liberal ideas, and nowhere was the propaganda so actively carried on as in St. Louis. "We have here," writes Father De Smet, "between 30,000 and 40,000 Germans, among whom are many radicals, socialists, and visionaries recently driven out of Europe. Their chief, a demagogue named Boernstein, has been expelled successively from Germany, France, and Italy. Upon arriving here he declared war on the Jesuits, secular priests, and Catholics, and has labored for two years to incite his followers against us. Yesterday, at his instigation, they attempted to invade the locality where the election of a new mayor was taking place in order to get votes for their candidate. A bloody encounter took place; one man was killed instantly, and five or six houses were burned.

"Kossuth, chief of the revolutionary Hungarians, has come to St. Louis to associate himself with Boernstein, and, like the latter, is attacking the Jesuits. His popularity is diminishing from day to day. Doubtless, he will shortly retire to some obscure corner of the world, there to live in luxury upon the fruits of his new speculation, namely, the issuance of Hungarian bonds payable when Hungary becomes a Republic with Kossuth its first President.

"After Kossuth, came Lola Montez—she also attacked the Jesuits bitterly, avowing they were responsible for her expulsion from Bavaria. The Jesuits, she says, govern Bavaria, their Provincial is Prime Minister, etc." [16]

The Carbonari, then numerous in America, received their orders direct from European lodges. They edited a paper, *L'Eco d'Italia*, and labored unceasingly to prejudice

pour les consolations dont, après Dieu, il a été l'instrument, en assistant un fils mourant, lui faisant trouver, à vingt-deux ans, sur son lit de mort, un lit de fleurs, lui découvrant au sortir de ce monde, le printemps de la vie, l'aurore d'un jour radieux: spectacle inoubliable de joie douce et sereine, de confiante espérance et de reconnaissance à Dieu." (St. Louis, May, 1852.)

[16] To Francis De Smet, April 7, 1852.

the people against the Church and trammel the authority of the Bishops. In the hope of recovering their waning influence, the Protestant ministers made common cause with the revolutionaries. This was the beginning of a vast conspiracy, which imperiled, for a time, Catholic liberty in the United States.

The *Know-Nothings*, a new society,[17] began to be organized about 1852. Theirs was a secret order, which bound its members by a solemn oath. It was formed, ostensibly, to defend the rights of the poor against European invasion. "America for the Americans" was its slogan. With this object in view, they endeavored to have severe naturalization laws enacted against the new arrivals from Europe, and exclude citizens born of foreign parents from holding public offices. In reality, these fanatics combated not so much the foreign immigration as the fidelity of the Europeans, especially the Irish, to the Church of Rome. To base calumnies they added murder, pillage, incendiarism, and, before long, found an occasion for opening the campaign. In the spring of 1853 the Papal Nuncio to Brazil, Archbishop Bedini, arrived in New York, bringing the Sovereign Pontiff's blessing to the faithful in the United States. He was charged, moreover, to investigate the conditions of Catholicism in the great Republic.

The *Know-Nothings* saw in this mission a grave attack upon American liberties. Their newspapers denounced the perfidious and ambitious intrigues of Rome. The apostate priest Gavazzi came from London and placed his eloquence at the service of his fellow-socialists and friends. For several months he followed the Envoy from one city to the other, vomiting forth lies, threatening him with dire reprisals, and through fiery denunciation endeavored to stir up the masses against "Papists."

From vituperation and abuse there was but one step to action. On Christmas day in Cincinnati a band of assassins attempted to do away with the Nuncio. Driven off by the police, they revenged themselves by burning him in effigy. This odious scene was enacted in several

---

[17] Know-Nothing means literally, "I know nothing." Whenever questioned about their society, the members feigned ignorance.

towns. Conditions pointing to renewed attacks, Archbishop Bedini was forced to depart after a short sojourn in the United States.[18] But hostilities did not cease with the departure of the Nuncio. The campaign lasted for three years, attended by violent outrages and attacks, and armed forces had presently to interfere to defend life and property. A witness of these disorders, Father De Smet draws a gloomy picture of existing conditions in his letters. "The times are becoming terrible for Catholics in these unhappy States. Nowhere in the world do honest men enjoy less liberty." [19]

"European demagogues, followers of Kossuth, Mazzini, etc., have sworn to exterminate us. Seven Catholic churches have been sacked and burned; those courageous enough to defend them have been assassinated." [20] "The future grows darker, and we are menaced from every side. If our enemies succeed in electing a President from their ranks—until now the chances have been in their favor—Catholics will be debarred from practicing their religion; our churches and schools will be burned and pillaged, and murder will result from these brawls. During this present year (1854) over twenty thousand Catholics have fled to other countries seeking refuge from persecution, and many more talk of following them. The right to defame and exile is the order of the day in this great Republic, now the rendezvous of the demagogues and outlaws of every country." [21]

No laws were enacted for the protection of Catholics, and in some States the authorities were openly hostile. "The legislators of New York and Pennsylvania are now busy with the temporal affairs of the Church, which they wish to take out of the hands of the Bishops. These States have taken the initiative, and others will soon follow. In Massachusetts, a mischief-making inquisition has just been instituted, with the object of investigating affairs in religious houses. In Boston, a committee of

[18] See De Courcy and Shea, "The Catholic Church in the United States," 2d edition, New York, 1857, Chapters xxvii and xxviii.
[19] To his brother Francis, St. Louis, Sept. 8, 1854.
[20] To his brother Charles, St. Louis, Sept. 25, 1854.
[21] To his brother Francis, St. Louis, Oct. 24, 1854.

twenty-four rascals, chosen from among the legislators, of which sixty are Protestant ministers, searched and inspected a convent of the Sisters of Notre Dame de Namur." [22]

While making a tour of the Jesuit houses with the Provincial, Father De Smet more than once braved the fury of the fanatics. In Cincinnati, a priest could not show himself in the street without being insulted by renegade Germans, Swiss, and Italians. In Louisville, thirty Catholics were killed in an open square and burned alive in their houses. Those who attempted to flee were driven back into the flames at the point of pistols and knives. Even in St. Louis, several attempts were made in one week upon the lives of citizens. The Jesuits were not spared. At Ellsworth, Maine, Father Bapst was taken by force from the house of a Catholic where he was hearing confessions, was covered with pitch, rolled in feathers, tied, swung by his hands and feet to a pole, and carried through the city to the accompaniment of gross insults.

Some months later, Father Nachon was arrested and brutally beaten in the environs of Mobile, when on his way to say Mass in a neighboring village. One of the assailants, pointing a knife at his heart, said, "If you attempt to enter that village again, you will feel the steel of this knife." Father De Smet, who witnessed other criminal attempts, confines himself to the following simple statement: "Our situation is far from pleasant. We live in constant apprehension, yet not in fear. In any case, it is well to be prepared and pray much." [23] Far from being intimidated by the situation, he opened a college in Milwaukee, never doubting the religious future of the United States. From the beginning of the troubles he wrote, "The Church, as in all former persecutions, will come forth victorious. Undoubtedly there will be martyrs, but when the law which promises liberty of conscience to every citizen shall be menaced, Catholics will rise up to a man to defend it." [24]

But Catholics were not the only ones to protest. The

[22] To M. Blondel of Antwerp, Bardstown, April 22, 1855.
[23] To his nephew Paul, St. Louis, Aug. 22, 1855.
[24] To a Jesuit in Brussels, Bardstown, June 17, 1854.

Know-Nothings' excesses brought protests from the honest men of all parties. The press denounced them before the tribunal of the nation. In 1856, when the party hoped to grasp power, Buchanan's election to the Presidency shattered the dreams of the agitators.

This persecution was the last effort of Puritan bigotry. The storm had served but to strengthen the roots of the tree of faith, which now bore more abundant fruit. Just and serious-minded men investigated this attack on religion, with the result that ignorance and prejudice disappeared, and an eloquent defence of Catholicism was made in Congress. New conversions added to its prestige. The Governors of Illinois and California publicly abjured heresy, and Dr. Ives laid at the feet of Pius IX his Protestant Bishop's ring. The zeal and enthusiasm of the new converts made it possible for Father Hecker to found a new congregation devoted to the conversion of Protestants.[25]

In 1860 America possessed forty-three Archbishops and Bishops, 2,500 priests, and 4,500,000 Catholics, one-seventh of the entire population. "Throughout the length and breadth of the land, religion is preached openly and without hindrance, and Mass is said in private chapels as well as in the churches. With God's help, we have every reason for believing that before the close of the century, the Church in America will occupy an honorable place in the Catholic hierarchy." [26]

The work accomplished by the Jesuits met with just appreciation from the Bishops, and in 1855 five members of the Society of Jesus were proposed for the Episcopate. Father De Smet, in announcing this news to the Father General, entreated him to oppose his nomination. His name had been sent to Rome,[27] but the humble religious felt himself unfitted for the discharge of such high functions. His sole ambition was to return to the mountains. "The

[25] The first Paulist foundation was laid in New York in 1858.

[26] Letter from Father De Smet to his nephew Paul, St. Louis, May 15, 1860.

[27] "The new Sees will soon be occupied by the priests whose names have been sent to Rome. Their nomination is expected at the new consistory. Father De Smet of Termonde was proposed by the Synod of St. Louis, also Father Arnold Damen of Brabant, Holland." (Letter of Father Hélias d'Huddeghem to his family, Taos, Jan. 30, 1856.)

best part of my life," says he, "has been given to the Indians. I have had the happiness of drying tears, dressing wounds, especially wounds of the soul, and directing those poor people in the way of man's true destiny. My robust health has been weakened, and my hair has turned gray in their service." [28]

And again, "My heart, I admit, is ever with the Indians. They frequently send me pressing invitations to return. I am happy to be of use to them here, at least in temporal affairs, and to be able to send our missionaries the means to continue the evangelization of the tribes. The scarcity of our Fathers in St. Louis makes it impossible for me to be relieved of my duties at present, but I have not given up hope, and I beg God unceasingly, if such be His will, to allow me to pass my remaining years in the Far West."[29]

At the moment of writing these lines Providence was preparing for him the great joy of seeing once again, and perhaps saving from ruin, the Christian missions in Oregon.

[28] Letter to his nieces, April 20, 1853.
[29] Letter to W. A. Smets, St. Louis, Jan. 12, 1855.

CHAPTER XVII

EXPEDITION AGAINST THE MORMONS—PACIFICATION OF OREGON—CONDITION OF THE MISSIONS (1858–1859)

Father De Smet is Authorized by the Father General to Return to the Missions—The Government Sends Troops Against the Mormons—Father De Smet is Appointed Chaplain of the Troops—The Oregon Missions Prosper—Testimony of Protestants—The Arrival of the Whites in the Far West—Their Treatment of the Indians—The Missions are in Danger—St. Paul's at Fort Colville Must Be Abandoned for a Time—The Uprising of the Tribes—Colonel Steptoe's Defeat—General Harney, Sent to Subdue Oregon, Asks Father De Smet to Mediate—Colonel Wright's Victory—Indians Conquered, but Not Reconciled—Father De Smet Visits the Cœur d'Alènes and afterward the Other Tribes—The Chiefs Accompany Him to Vancouver to Sign the Peace Treaty—He Sees Signs of New Uprisings—General Harney Informs the Secretary of War of the Plan of Father De Smet—Captain Pleaston's Letter—State of the "Reductions"—Father Hoecken Founds St. Peter's Mission for the Blackfeet—Father De Smet Returns to St. Louis—He Has Traveled Fifteen Thousand Miles in One Year.

OPPOSITION to Father De Smet's work had been withdrawn for some time. In the light of facts, truth triumphed over false imputations. The missionary's upright conduct and the wisdom of his plans were recognized at Rome, and henceforth his Superiors would not oppose his desire to labor for the missions.

In 1854 Bishop Lamy of Santa Fé asked Father Beckx, Father Roothaan's successor, to send Father De Smet to convert tribes in New Mexico; but the return to Europe of the exiled Jesuits in 1848 forced the missionary to remain some time longer in St. Louis. The appeal of the Indians became more and more pressing. Smallpox had claimed four thousand victims, many of whom died without receiving baptism. "If the wishes of my Superiors, which are for me the will of God, accorded with those of the Indians, I would set forth at once to contribute my feeble assistance."[1]   At last, in the spring of 1858, he was free to go.   He had waited ten years for permission to rejoin his neophytes and carry to them the light of faith and the blessing of peace.

Before going to Oregon, Father De Smet accompanied a Government expedition against the Mormons.   Driven first from Illinois, then from Missouri, because of their low morals, the Latter Day Saints retired in 1847 to Salt Lake, a town situated west of the Rocky Mountains.[2] The head of the sect, Brigham Young, exercising autocratic authority over his followers, aspired to establish Mormonism throughout the entire American Continent.   Occupying the post of Governor of Utah Territory, he declared his independence of the Federal Government. From his "New Jerusalem" the prophet defied the President in Washington.   Government officials were forced to leave the State, or forbidden to exercise their functions. Congress appointed a new Governor of Utah, who set out in the autumn of 1857 with an escort of three thousand soldiers to enforce his authority.   Brigham Young lay in wait for the enemy, and surprising a convoy of foodstuff, burned the wagons and made off with the beeves, horses, and mules, leaving the small army destitute in the heart of the desert.

This news decided the Government to send a second expedition in the spring, commanded by General Harney, a well-known Indian fighter, who had suppressed the Indian uprisings in Florida, Texas, and New Mexico. Prudent and energetic, he was the man eminently fitted to undertake the subjection of the Mormons.   Before en-

---

[1] Letter to Gustave Van Kerckhove, St. Louis, July 25, 1857.
[2] Father De Smet knew the Mormon country.   "In the autumn of 1846," he wrote, "on approaching the Missouri border, I found an advance-guard of about ten thousand Mormons camped upon the Omahas' lands, not far from old Council Bluffs.   The sect had, for the second time, been driven out of one of the States of the Union.   Their intention was to winter in the great desert, and penetrate further into the interior to escape their persecutors, but the place of residence was not yet decided upon.   They plied me with questions about the regions I had traversed.   My accounts of the villages in Utah pleased them greatly.   Did this determine them to select Salt Lake?   I cannot say."   (Letter to Charles De Smet, St. Louis, March 10, 1851.)

tering upon the campaign, the General, wishing to assure religious ministrations to his soldiers, of whom three-quarters were Catholics, asked to have Father De Smet appointed chaplain.

On May 13, 1858, our missionary received his official appointment from the Secretary of War, which read as follows:

"It is the President's intention to attach you to the army of Utah in the capacity of chaplain, in the belief that in this position you will render important services to the country. The President himself charges me to express to you his desire, in the hope that this charge will neither be incompatible with your ecclesiastical duties, nor against your own inclination." Father De Smet, hoping to combine a visit to the Oregon tribes with this journey, submitted the proposition to his Superior. The Provincial advised him to accept, and a few days later the new chaplain left St. Louis to join the army at Fort Leavenworth, Kansas.

General Harney received the missionary courteously, assuring him that every facility would be given him for exercising his ministry. "He kept his word loyally," writes Father De Smet, "and his officers imitated his example. The soldiers were allowed to come to my tent for instructions and confession. Often at daybreak I had the consolation of celebrating the Holy Sacrifice, and of seeing a goodly number of soldiers approach the holy table." [3]

Although forming a part of the army of Utah, the missionary had opportunity of ministering to the Indians through whose country he passed. He gave several instructions to the Pawnees, Sioux, and Cheyennes, and baptized many children. In going up the Nebraska they met bands of Mormons en route for Kansas and Missouri, who expressed their joy at escaping from the despotism of Brigham Young. General Harney was informed by them that many others had decided to renounce the sect. This news encouraged the General in expecting a speedy subjugation of the country. Some days later, in fact, came the news that the Mormons would offer no resistance.

[3] Letter to the Father General, St. Louis, Nov. 1, 1859.

The new Governor had been installed and his authority recognized by the people. General Harney then received orders to return East with his troops. Judging his mission at an end, Father De Smet, upon his return to St. Louis, offered his resignation as chaplain to the Secretary of War, but as new difficulties were then threatening west of the Rocky Mountains, his resignation was not accepted.

For fifteen years the Oregon tribes had lived peacefully and happily under the watchful eyes of the missionaries. Great numbers of Indians had received baptism. All were taught agriculture; the harvests were abundant; the mills worked regularly; and new ground for cultivation was being broken continually. When, in 1854, the Government agents penetrated to the mountain tribes, they marveled at the results obtained, and were loud in their praise of the bravery, piety, honesty, intelligence, and industry of the new Christians. "I could hardly believe my eyes," said one of them. "I asked myself 'Am I among the Indians—among people the world calls savages?'"[4] Knowing the former abject condition of the tribes, they voiced their admiration in the following words: "Thanks to the untiring labors of the missionaries, the Indians have made great progress in agriculture. They are being instructed in the Christian religion; they have abandoned polygamy, are pure in morals, and edifying in conduct. The work of these Fathers is truly marvelous."[5]

This testimony from Protestant pens permits us to realize, faintly, what the Indians might have become if the United States had left to the Catholics the task of civilizing them, instead of following a policy of extermination. But the missionaries were not destined to reap the fruits of their labors. The same combination of circumstances that brought about the closing of St. Mary's in 1850 would, several years later, imperil the other "reductions."

Since the discovery of gold, the white man had invaded the West. "Imagine," writes Father De Smet, "thousands

[4] See Selected Letters, 2d Series, pp. 206–217. Long extracts of reports sent by Governor Stevens to the President.
[5] Lieutenant Mullan, "Explorations from the Mississippi River to the Pacific Ocean." Vol. I, p. 308.

of adventurers from every country; deserters, thieves, murderers, the scum of the United States, Mexico, Peru, Chili, and the Sandwich Islands, living together, free of all law and restraint." [6] From California this gold-seeking army spread to the territories of Oregon and Washington. In defiance of all law they drove out the natives, forcing them to seek refuge in the mountains. There is no darker page in history than the story of the "White Conquest." [7] In exchange for their lands, horses, and furs, the whites gave whiskey to the Indians. Drink being the passion of the race, they eagerly seized upon the fatal liquor. We remember the drunken orgies of the Potawatomies; the same scenes were now enacted in Oregon and California. Men slaughtered each other by the hundreds, and the women and children dragged themselves like animals around their wigwams.

Yet fatal as was the effect of alcohol, its action was too slow to satisfy the invaders. They concluded that the revolver was more expeditious than whiskey, and offered twenty dollars for every Indian scalp. Men killed as a training in marksmanship, and to try their weapons. What value had an Indian's life, when that of the white man was held so lightly?

Yet still more revolting machinations were resorted to. Arsenic was mixed with the flour and sugar sold to the Indians; their springs, from which they obtained drinking-water, were poisoned with strychnine, and clothing reeking with infection was given to them. "The following," says a missionary, "was told me by an eye-witness. It happened on the Pacific coast. The whites had decided to destroy an Indian camp, and to accomplish their fell purpose they hung from a tree in front of the camp the clothing of a man who had just died from small-pox. The Indians, catching sight of the garments, were enchanted, and proceeded to don them at once. Before long this terrible malady appeared, and of several hundred Indians, only a dozen poor wretches remained to weep over

[6] Letter to his brother Charles, St. Louis, April 26, 1849.
[7] "It would require a volume to recount the injustice, brutality, and murders committed in the last thirty years upon the Pacific coast, the details of which are too horrible to be believed." Helen Hunt Jackson, "A Century of Dishonor," p. 337.

the ravages wrought by the disease."[8] If to these destructive causes are added the evils engendered by the immorality of the whites, one readily understands how the Indian population in California fell in ten years from 100,000 to 30,000 souls.

Reascending the valley of the Columbia, the gold-seekers occupied the lands of the Cayuses, Walla Wallas, Nez Percés, Yakimas, and Spokanes. The "reductions" were threatened. What then would become of Father De Smet's work? The St. Paul-Colville Mission, founded for the Chaudières in 1845, had rapidly developed under Father De Vos' direction. It counted at least a thousand baptized Indians, all faithful to religious practices. After 1855 the aspect of things changed. The whites seized the lands under cultivation, and the villages, given over to debauchery and drunkenness, became theaters of the worst excesses.

Father Vercruysse, who had labored six years in Colville, wrote in 1857, "Since these hordes of foreigners have arrived in search of gold the Indian is no longer the same man. Demoralized by bad language and bad example, they no longer heed us. Gambling, stealing, illicit dealings, divorce, and sorcery have again begun and reduced them to the condition they were in before the arrival of the Fathers. Their sole means of salvation lies in separating them from the whites."[9] "The Indians are not innately wicked," adds the missionary, "only frivolous and stupid. They are kind-hearted, and if left to our care and influence would be angels."[10]

For three years Fathers Vercruysse and Ravalli contended with the invaders for the souls of their neophytes. "For the love of God and the salvation of the Indians, I am happy to be here, otherwise a day seems a century."

Finally, at the close of the year 1858, the mission was abandoned, and the Fathers, with a few remaining Chris-

[8] Article by Father de Rouge in *Les Études*, 1890, Vol. I, p. 492. "It is certain that the whites sought to poison all the Indian tribes, and I have heard them discussing which method would be the best." Julius Froebel, quoted by Marshall, "Christian Missions," Vol. II, p. 438.

[9] Letter to Father Broeckaert, Colville, Nov. 13, 1857.

[10] *Ibid.*, June 13, 1859.

tians, retired to the Cœur d'Alènes. The Sacred Heart
Mission, in charge of Father Joset, also began to suffer
from the proximity of the emigrants. Many Christian
Indians fell into the vice of gambling, and ceased attendance at church. The last Easter the Fathers were there,
only half of the tribe approached the Sacraments. "You
told us the religion of the whites would make us better
men," they said to the missionaries, "yet the whites we
see are worse than we are."

The Indians, nevertheless, struggled against the invasion of their territory. First in California and then in
Lower Oregon they attempted terrible reprisals. In the
endeavor to establish peace, the Government offered, in
1855, to buy the lands lying between the Willamette and
the country of the Blackfeet. The tribes returning to the
north would then have nothing more to fear from the
incursions of the emigrants. But the Indians had been
too often deceived to believe now in the good faith of the
whites. Far from accepting the proposition, the Cayuses,
Yakimas, Nez Percés, and the Palooses excited the Oregon
tribes against the invaders. Christian Indians who demurred to take up arms were taunted and called "women"
and "Little dogs, that can only bark when danger threat-
ens." The missionaries were denounced as enemies.
"They are white, like the Americans," said the chief of the
Yakimas, "and all are alike."

In the spring of 1858 Colonel Steptoe, at the head of a
company of cavalry, arrived in Willamette to establish
peace around Fort Colville. He camped in the neighborhood of the Cœur d'Alènes, who, judging their tribe
threatened, despite Father Joset's protestations to the
contrary, deemed the moment propitious for measuring
their strength with the United States. Surprising the
small command, they killed two officers and several soldiers. Inferior in numbers, the Americans retired precipitately, abandoning their baggage and cannon. The
Indians, carried away with this easy victory, thought
themselves invincible, and the mountains rang with their
cries and threats of revenge.

Determined to put an end to this condition, the Federal
Government summoned General Harney, who, in accepting

command of the troops, asked once more to have Father
De Smet appointed chaplain. Knowing the missionary's
influence over the Indians, he believed his mediation would
put an end to hostilities. The mission was a delicate one.
What would the Indians think when they saw the missionary attached to the army that had come to make war
on them? But peace in Oregon meant the saving of the
"reductions." Trusting in God, Father De Smet, with
the consent of his Superiors, prepared for immediate departure.

In order to avoid crossing the wilderness, General
Harney decided to go across the Isthmus of Panama and
enter Oregon through the mouth of the Columbia. Leaving New York September 20th, he arrived a month later
at Vancouver. Upon his arrival, the General heard, to
his great surprise, that peace had been made. Wishing to
avenge Steptoe's defeat, Colonel Wright left for Walla
Walla the end of August and, through his clever tactics,
routed the united forces of the Cœur d'Alènes, Spokanes,
and Kalispels early in September. Disconcerted by this
prompt reprisal, the tribes were ready to make peace.
They gave hostages, and, moreover, surrendered several
Indians, guilty of having assassinated Americans, to be
hanged.

The Indians were vanquished, but not reconciled.
Neither had the promises of the victors dispelled mistrust
nor calmed resentment. Hence it was imperative to
make the tribes realize that they must submit, and effect
a friendly understanding with the Government which was
prepared to guarantee them against further inroads of
emigrants. Otherwise the war could at any moment
break out again. The season was too far advanced to
permit troops to set out for the mountains. Father De Smet
offered to go alone to spend the winter with the Indians
and consolidate the peace, and to return in the spring
to give his report to the General.

On October 29th Father De Smet left Vancouver.
Four hundred miles lay between him and the nearest mission, that of the Cœur d'Alènes. At Fort Walla Walla
he met the hostages taken two months previously by

Colonel Wright. "Fearing they were in danger of being corrupted," says Father Vercruysse, "Father De Smet asked that the Indians might be allowed to return with him to their country. 'Impossible,' replied the Colonel, 'without express authorization from General Harney.' 'Very good,' said Father De Smet. 'I will answer for it that you will not be reproved by him for acceding to my request. I know well the Spokanes, Cœur d'Alènes, and the Kalispels. They are my children, and I will answer for their loyalty with my head, which will be at the disposition of the General should these Indians be untrue to their word.' The Colonel no longer opposed the departure of the hostages, who set out with their Father, happy as souls escaping from limbo." [11]

This arrangement furnished Father De Smet with guides and traveling companions, and, above all, assured him a welcome from the tribes. Arriving at the Cœur d'Alènes November 21st, he was enthusiastically welcomed as the friend, father, and liberator of the Indians. After an absence of twelve years, the missionary again found himself in the midst of those to whom he had given the light of faith. The "reduction" had steadily prospered, possessing now a beautiful church, comfortable houses, a mill, workshops, rich pastures, and fields of prodigious fertility. But even their prosperity was a menace, for the whites began to covet the mission lands. The thought of being obliged to one day leave the tombs of their fathers plunged the Indians into black despair. Father De Smet vigorously denounced the conduct of the emigrants, and the Christian Indians promised to have no further dealings with them. Moreover, he assured the Government that while repressing the violent acts of the Indians, he must at the same time defend their rights.

To recommence hostilities would be folly. General Harney informed the tribes that the Government, always generous to a conquered foe, was prepared, nevertheless, to protect its citizens in every part of the territory, and that entire obedience to the Government would be their only safeguard. The troops they had attacked the previous autumn were still in Oregon, and at the slightest sign

[11] Letter to Father Broeckaert, June 13, 1859.

of rebellion they would leave for the mountains with orders to show no quarter.[12]

The Cœur d'Alènes, it will be remembered, had taken up arms only at the instigation of the pagan tribes, with the sole object of defending their lands. Hence they were easily brought to terms of peace. But Father De Smet looked to religion as the sole means of subduing the cruel instincts of the Indians. The three months he spent at the mission were consecrated, in a large part, to instructing the neophytes, and in bringing back to Christian practices those who were led away through contact with the whites.

"I sang midnight Mass on Christmas," he writes. "The Indians—men, women, and children—chanted the *Vivat Jesus*, the *Gloria*, and the *Credo*, and sang hymns in their native tongue in perfect accord. I cannot express the joy and consolation this solemnity occasioned me in the vasts of the desert. It reminded me of the reunions of the early Christians, who were of one mind and one soul. Eight days before Christmas the Indians began their preparation for confession, and all, with few exceptions, approached the holy table. Such occasions are not forgotten, and the memory of this feast will remain one of the most agreeable of my life." [13]

Impatient to visit the other tribes, Father De Smet departed the middle of February for St. Ignatius' Mission.[14] A severe winter rendered the journey a perilous one. Shooting the rapids in the Clarke River in a frail canoe was attended with grave dangers, but the joy of seeing his neophytes again, and the hope of effecting peace, rendered him indifferent to fatigue and danger. Finally the missionary arrived at the Kalispels, who received him with joyful demonstrations befitting the Black Robe who had been the first to give them the knowledge of the Master of life. This, the most prosperous of the Oregon Missions, counted two thousand Christian Indians. Less exposed to contact with the whites than the St. Paul or Sacred Heart missions, this tribe, under Father Hoecken's watchful

[12] Quoted from Chittenden-Richardson, p. 1572.
[13] Letter to the Father General, St. Louis, Nov. 1, 1859.
[14] This "reduction," founded fifteen years before, near the mouth of the Clarke River, was transferred in 1854 to a more favorable situation some miles north of St. Mary's, and became part of St. Francis Borgia's Mission.

care, still adhered to its first fervor. Shortly after Father
De Smet's arrival the Kootenais appeared, having traveled
for days through the deep snow to come and shake the
missionary's hand and assure him of their fidelity to his
teachings. Only the Flatheads now remained. Despite
the sorrow of finding everything in ruins, Father De Smet
wished to see once more the old and ever dear St. Mary's
Mission.

The passion for gambling had evidently brought about
grave disorders, but the evil was not irreparable. The old
Indians deplored the blindness of the tribe, and all ardently desired the return of the missionaries. The chief
had traversed Oregon in search of Father Mengarini.
The year before, upon the occasion of a visit of one of the
Fathers from St. Ignatius, the greater number had approached the Sacraments, and began again to say their
prayers.

Following the example of the Cœur d'Alènes, the other
Christian tribes promised not to begin war. The Flatheads and Kalispels boasted of never having spilled the
blood of the white man, and of having entered the coalition
solely for the defence of their rights.

The pacifier encountered greater opposition from the
pagan tribes, but Father De Smet's uprightness and
touching kindness so influenced the Indians, that he succeeded in modifying their defiant attitude. The Spokanes,
Yakimas, Palooses, Okinagans, and the Chaudières promised to accept the Government's conditions. On April 16,
1859, the missionary started for Vancouver accompanied
by nine Indian chiefs, delegated by their respective tribes
to sign a treaty of peace with the agents of the Republic.
Alone and unarmed, a Jesuit priest had been able to do
more to restore peace in the country than the American
troops.

Father De Smet's efforts in behalf of peace were crowned
with success, but the journey had been a most difficult one.
It required more than a month's travel to reach general
headquarters. "We ran many dangers by reason of deep
snows and high waters. For ten days we steadily hacked
our way through dense forests where the ground was encumbered with thousands of fallen trees blown down by

tempests and covered with a blanket of snow from six to eight feet deep. I fell with my horse many times a day, but apart from some bruises I came forth safe and sound in limb from this awful journey." [15]

The chiefs finally arrived at headquarters, where they were ushered into the presence of General Harney and the Superintendent of Indian Affairs. They renewed their assurances of submission, asked for the friendship of the Americans, and expressed regret for the blindness that had led them to taking up arms. They promised, moreover, that no further molestations would be made upon the whites crossing their lands, if the Government in turn would consent to give the Indians "reserves," and engage itself to protect them.

Such dispositions won for the Indians a cordial reception from the General. He gave them presents, and promised them the protection of the United States. Nor did he delay in informing the Government of the important services rendered by Father De Smet to the army. "I am convinced that with prudence we have nothing further to fear from a serious outbreak in this country." [16]

Not content with negotiating peace, Father De Smet labored to prevent future conflicts, and to accomplish this he saw no other means save to cut off the savage from all contact with the white. In an interesting report he exposes his plan to General Harney. "The United States was to cede to the Indians 'reserves' comprising the country lying between the Rocky Mountains, the Bitter Root Mountains, and the Kootenais River, where, under direction of the missionaries and Government protection, would be assembled all the tribes scattered over the territories of Oregon and Washington." [17]

Impressed by the advantage this project offered, the General communicated the proposition to the Secretary of War. "The region in question," he said, "will not be occupied by the white man for at least twenty years; it is difficult of access and does not offer the colonists the advantages they find everywhere on the coast. The system

---

[15] Letter to the Father General, Nov. 1, 1859.
[16] Quoted from Chittenden-Richardson, p. 1576.
[17] *Ibid.*, p. 970 *et seq.*

in use in California of gathering into one 'reserve' large numbers of Indians and of forcing them to adopt immediately the habits of the white man, has failed because of the too sudden transition imposed upon the primitive and rebellious tribes.   Father De Smet's plan avoids this disadvantage.   He would place the Indians in a country abounding with game and fish, and where there is sufficient agricultural land to encourage tilling the soil.   The missionaries in charge possess complete authority over the tribes, and, enjoying their full confidence, would lead them gradually to accept the exigencies of civilization, when the inevitable decree of time shall bring the onward march of progress to their door.

"The history of the Indian race on our continent shows that the missionaries succeeded when military and civil authorities failed.   In an affair that affects the white man not less than the Indian, it would be wisdom to profit by the lessons of experience, and adopt Father De Smet's plan."[18]   The Government, unfortunately, thought otherwise.   Nevertheless, General Harney must be given credit for having tried to turn to account wise and humanitarian counsels.

Father De Smet's mission was now finished.   Wishing to see once again the mountain stations, and to visit the Missouri tribes, he obtained permission from his Superior to return to St. Louis overland.   On June 15th he left Vancouver with an escort of Indian chiefs returning to their respective countries.   Some months later he received the following lines from Alfred Pleasonton, an officer in the army of Oregon:

"My dear Father: We all deplore your departure.   I have yet to meet an officer who does not express his regret. To you we owe the good understanding that now exists between the whites and the Indians.   The General asks me to express to you his sincere gratitude for the valuable services you rendered the country during your sojourn here.   He wishes to renew to you his assurances of high regard and lasting friendship.   As for myself, I am conscious of my loss in this separation.   Your goodness and kindness impressed me greatly, and helped me to conquer my own

[18] Chittenden-Richardson, p. 1579.

intractable nature. Be my friend, I beg of you, and help me to acquire the priceless blessings that religion and virtue offer." [19]

The author of this letter became one of the leading generals in the United States army, and this testimony proves that Father De Smet had filled worthily his office of chaplain.

The Rocky Mountain Mission, as we have seen in the preceding pages, had been attached since 1854 to the Turin Province. Notwithstanding this, the Fathers in Oregon continued to regard Father De Smet as the main support of the "reduction." He collected funds, and sent yearly from St. Louis ample provisions of foodstuff, clothing, grain, farm implements, and tools. He obtained authorizations and subsidies from the Government, and he never left Europe without bringing back with him several missionaries. Unceasingly he recommended his "poor children of the desert" to the solicitude of the Father General.

Profiting by his presence in the country, Father Congiato, Superior of the missions, sought his advice. Since the abandonment of the St. Mary's and the St. Paul-Colville Missions, the Jesuits had but two "reductions" in Oregon—the Cœur · d'Alènes and the Kalispels. It was deemed wise to reconstruct the ruined missions, profiting by the good dispositions of the Indians, if possible also to establish new posts. Like the Flatheads, the Chaudières regretted the departure of the missionaries. "Black Robe," they said, "we wish to be good, and do the will of the Great Spirit. But see how exposed we are! The whites are daily becoming more numerous in our country; they offer us whiskey, and say we are not forbidden to drink it. Before their arrival we found no difficulty in being good; to-day all is changed."

In answer to this appeal it was decided that Father Joset should leave to open a mission at Colville. The Fathers were unable to take immediate possession of St. Mary's. The recently founded California Mission [20] had

[19] Fort Vancouver, Nov. 9, 1859.
[20] In 1849, at the urgent wish of the Bishop of Monterey, Fathers Accolti and Nobili had been sent to California to look after the Catholic emigrants,

reduced to six the number of priests laboring in the mountains. Notwithstanding this the Flatheads were not abandoned. Several times a year the missionaries from St. Ignatius' went to instruct them and administer the Sacraments.

Of all the Indian tribes, the Kootenais were the most interesting. "In this tribe," writes Father De Smet, "evangelical fraternity, simplicity, innocence, and peace reign. Their honesty is so well known that a merchant can absent himself for a week at a time and leave his store open. During his absence the Indians enter, take what they want, and upon the proprietor's return he is faithfully paid. One of the storekeepers assured me that he had never missed the value of a pin." [21]

The Kootenais built a church with their own hands in which they assembled night and day for prayers. Two or three times a year they received a visit from the missionary. At Easter and the principal feasts the tribe repaired to St. Ignatius' to receive the Sacraments and devoted several days to religious exercises.

East of the mountains, Father Hoecken was preparing to found a mission for the Blackfeet, who, since the Gospel had been preached to them, had ceased molesting the Oregon tribes. Still, the missionaries feared that their savage instincts might reawaken. The Father General finally acceded to Father De Smet's insistent supplications, and allowed him to take up Father Point's work. In a few months St. Peter's Mission near the Sun River counted one hundred neophytes. Peace now seemed firmly established. The "reductions" were again prospering, and Father De Smet decided to return to St. Louis.

Father Congiato accompanied him to the Oregon border, and this journey enabled him to see for himself and admire Father De Smet's relations with the Indians. "Never shall I forget the happiness I experienced during the journey I made with Father De Smet to the different tribes. With my own eyes I saw the respect, love, and

---

and were soon joined by Fathers De Vos and Mengarini. They founded large missions at San Francisco, Santa Clara, and San José. The Mission definitely constituted in 1854 was later detached from the Oregon Mission.

[21] Letter to the Father General, Nov. 1, 1859.

esteem in which he is held by the Indians, and which he richly deserves. One cannot fail to be touched by his charity and his tenderness for a race universally despised and persecuted. The Indians call him their father, but his feelings for them are more those of a mother." [22]

It was no easy task in those days to cross the mountains that separated the Sacred Heart Mission from that of St. Ignatius. "Imagine a dense virgin forest, the ground strewn with thousands of uprooted trees. The paths are hidden and obstructed by these barricades that imperil the life of horse and rider at every step. Two large streams wind through the forest, whose beds are formed of boulders of fallen rock and glistening stones deposited by the rushing water. The path crosses the first of these streams thirty-nine times, the other thirty-two times. Often my horse stood in water to his breast and at times even over the saddle, but one is lucky to escape with only soaked legs. A mountain of 5,000 feet lies between the two rivers, with here and there vast plateaux covered with eight feet of snow. After eight hours of hard climbing we arrived in a flowering plain, where, sixteen years before, during my first journey, a cross had been erected. This beautiful spot tempted me to pitch our camp; but Father Congiato, convinced that a two hours' walk would bring us to the foot of the mountain, advised us to push on.

"The two hours passed, then four hours, and night overtook us in the midst of a thousand difficulties. Mounds of snow and barricades of fallen trees were again encountered; at times we were obliged to creep along the edge of pointed rocks and down almost perpendicular inclines. The least false step would have precipitated us God knows where. In pitch-black darkness, without a guide, and off the path, we fell time and again, groping our way on all-fours and then rolling down the declivity. At last the roar of the stream we were seeking was heard in the distance, and each of us directed his steps in that direction. About midnight we came straggling in in a state of exhaustion, after a sixteen hours' march, our clothes in ribbons. We were bruised and cut all over, but had no serious injuries.

[22] Letter of Jan. 20, 1860; published in the *San Francisco Monitor.*

"The evening meal was hastily prepared, and each one recited his troubles and experiences to the great amusement of the entire camp. The excellent Father Congiato admitted he had miscalculated the distance and was the first to laugh heartily over the adventure." [23]

Father De Smet undoubtedly possessed a cheerful nature and robust health. The unexpected in his travels never annoyed or disconcerted him, but nothing short of his love for the Indians could have induced him, at fifty-eight years of age, to face such hardships and adventures.

At Fort Benton he and Father Congiato separated. In the hope of meeting an even greater number of the tribes, he wished to make the long journey to St. Louis on horseback, but finding that his six horses were exhausted, and their unshod hoofs worn down by the stones and rocks of the mountain roads, he was forced to abandon the project. A skiff was hastily constructed, three rowers and a pilot were engaged, and on August 5th he embarked on the Missouri River for St. Louis.

"We slept in the open," he writes, "or under a little tent, at times on a sand-bar or again on the edge of the plains or in the forest. Wolves, bears, and wildcats howled in the distance, but we were undismayed, 'for God has implanted the fear of men in all animals.' [24]

"In the desert, we wondered at the paternal Providence of God and were filled with sentiments of gratitude over His wonderful provision for the needs of His children. Food was not lacking; we even lived in abundance. The river provided us with excellent fish, water-hens, ducks, bustards, and swans; the forest yielded fruits and nuts, and game was not lacking. Herds of buffalo roamed the plains, and roebuck, venison, young kids, big-horns, pheasants, partridges, and wild turkeys abounded." [25]

On the way Father De Smet met thousands of Indians: Assiniboins, Crows, Mandans, Grosventres, Sioux, etc. He remained two or three days with each tribe, baptizing the children, instructing adults, comforting the dying, and,

[23] Letter from Father De Smet to the Father General, Nov. 1, 1859.
[24] *Terror vester ac tremor sit super cuncta animalia terræ.* (Genesis, ix, 2.)
[25] Letter to Laura Blondel, wife of Charles De Smet, St. Louis, Oct. 13, 1859.

incidentally, looking about with the object of establishing missions. Everywhere he was cordially received. The Missouri River Indians had long wished for a Black Robe, and Father De Smet promised to support their petition with his Superiors and to come himself to visit them.

After traveling several hundred leagues in his skiff the missionary went aboard a steamboat, and six days later, on September 23d, arrived in St. Louis. "To God alone be all the glory," he writes, "and to the Blessed Virgin my humble and profound gratitude for the blessings and protection accorded me during this journey! My greatest consolation is to have been God's instrument of salvation to about nine hundred dying children on whom I conferred baptism; many of these seemed but to await this grace before winging their flight to heaven, there to praise God for all eternity." [26]

During the year that had passed the missionary, in his various journeys, had covered about fifteen thousand miles.

[26] Letter to the Father General, Nov. 1, 1859.

CHAPTER XVIII

"The Rule of St. Ignatius Does Not Forbid Us to Love Our Family"—
Father De Smet's Devotion to His Family—He Shared in All Their Joys
and Sorrows—Even His Letters Are an Apostolate—His Many Journeys
in Belgium—Death of His Brother Charles—Father De Smet's Conferences—His Timidity—His Tales—Impressions of a Belgian Seminarian—Scenes on Board the *Humboldt*—Shipwreck—A Sunrise at Sea—
The Missionary Receives an Ovation upon His Return to St. Louis.

NEITHER his long journeys nor his multiple labors
ever altered or affected Father De Smet's intercourse
with his family and friends in Belgium. "Separation," he
writes, "even when voluntary or, rather, when imposed
by conscience and religion, can never destroy in the heart
of man the tenderness engendered by memories of family
and country. My hair may turn white, my sight fail,
my strength diminish, but my affection for you suffers no
change. Every day at the altar I beg the help and protection of heaven for my family. All I ask in return is
that you will keep me ever in your affections, and that
you will sometimes pray for your Uncle Peter, and for
the conversion of his poor Indians."[1]

As neither age nor distance affected his family relations,
neither did his religious life render him indifferent to his
people. "Surely the rule of St. Ignatius does not forbid
us to love our own, and I must say that Charles has always
held a special place in my affections."[2] Should any of his
fellow-religious refuse to their families the consideration he
thought due them, they were reproached for excessive
severity. "It is wrong not to write to one's relatives.

[1] Letter to his nieces, Sylvia, Elmira, and Rosalie, daughters of his brother
Charles, St. Louis, April 22, 1853.
[2] Letter to Mr. Blondel of Antwerp, St. Louis, April 22, 1855. Charles,
the eldest son of Father De Smet's brother Francis, had just married
Mr. Blondel's daughter.

Every one is then dissatisfied; both family and acquaintances."[3]

Father De Smet's correspondence shows that he never neglected any of his family, and always longed to have news of them. "Write me often, I beg you. Tell me about your good wife, and your dear little children, about your parents, sisters, 'Monsieur le Curé,' and other friends and acquaintances. Have any new marriages and baptisms taken place? Believe that I take a lively interest in all that concerns the happiness of the family."[4]

To Charles his nephew: "I want to remind you of the solemn compact we made before my last departure from Belgium, that you would write me once a month, and I in turn would say Mass for your intention every Saturday. I can assure you I have never once failed in my promise. Write me then at once, to dispel the sadness your silence has caused, and tell your brother Paul to add a few lines to your letter."[5] In return he promised to be generous. "Why does Charles delay so long in writing to me? I am quite ready to write twenty lines for every line he sends me."[6]

In order to keep himself fresh in their memory he frequently sent his family souvenirs of the Far West, such as richly embroidered moccasins, soft buffalo robes, and suits made of deer-skin embroidered with porcupine quills. One day a magnificent map of the United States arrived in Termonde. "Hang this map in a conspicuous place in your house, and now and then glance at it. You will be able to trace the countries through which I have traveled in my journeys from New Orleans to Halifax, and from Nova Scotia to the Athabasca glaciers north of the Rocky Mountains. Quietly seated in your chair, you can follow me through the seas, prairies, and mountains I have traversed, beset with innumerable dangers; in steamboats, bark canoes, on horseback, and on foot. Thus you will often think of me, and the idea of writing to me will oftener occur to you."[7]

[3] Letter to Father Truyens, St. Louis, Jan. 16, 1854.
[4] Letter to Gustave Van Kerckhove of Antwerp, a nephew of Father De Smet by marriage, St. Louis, July 3, 1856.
[5] Cincinnati, Aug. 2, 1854.   [6] To his brother Francis.
[7] To Charles and Rosalie Van Mossevelde, Bardstown, April 20, 1855.

When the long-looked-for letter arrived, the happy uncle quickly forgot the months of waiting. But notwithstanding his impatience for news, he seems always to have found excuses for the delinquent. "A little negligence or idleness is not to be wondered at in poor human nature, when the mind is filled with important affairs. One is justified in putting off the person who will suffer the least from the delay." [8]

Those who accuse the religious life of destroying natural ties could read Father De Smet's letters with profit. Never was a missionary so devoted to his family. Even when six thousand miles separated him from his country he still seemed always to live in spirit with his own. He shared their sorrows and joys and the minutest detail was of interest. His predilection, like that of his divine Master, was always for children and the young. Upon receiving news of the birth of his nephews he writes, "In God's name I bless them from afar. Send me their names that I may add them to my list of *mementoes* at Mass." [9] He loved these innocent souls even before they were born. "The enclosed holy picture is for Elmira's first child. Please give it to her with my best wishes the day of its birth." [10] Paul made his first communion at twelve years of age. "Tell him he must offer a communion for his Uncle Peter, who will say ten Masses for him." [11]

To Charles, about to be married, he writes, "I share in the joy these events bring to the family. Although the wedding-day in the month of May is not mentioned in your letter, I will offer the holy sacrifice every day for your and Alice's happiness. The movement of the boat upon which an altar has been erected in no way prevents me from keeping my promise. I send you a wedding-present of a large and beautiful Indian calumet." [12]

The feast-days of his brothers and sisters were never forgotten. He always joined his good wishes to those of

[8] To his nephew Charles, St. Louis, April 22, 1854.
[9] To Gustave Van Kerckhove, St. Louis, Dec. 11, 1859.
[10] To Charles and Rosalie Van Mossevelde, Bardstown, April 20, 1855.
[11] To his nephew Charles, St. Louis, April 22, 1854.
[12] St. Louis, April 20, 1862. He referred in this letter to Alice De Witte, second wife of Charles De Smet.

the children of the family.   Sometimes his congratulations were expressed in verse, and with what joy these French or Flemish poems were read and sung in the family circle! In 1854, to distract himself from the *Know-Nothing* movement, he gave free vent to his poetic strain.   One of his compositions contains not less than a hundred Alexandrines: A dialogue between St. Teresa and St. Rosalie, the patron saints of his two sisters, and while the style can hardly be called classic, the verses breathe profound religious sentiment and delicate affection.

The rugged worker had his hours of naïve and charming pleasantry.   "Now that I love my nephew Mr. De Bare as much as I love my niece Sylvia,[13] you will kindly give him a faithful description of his uncle, so that, should I arrive in your absence, he will recognize me.   Uncle Peter, you must tell him, is a man of medium height, with gray hair rapidly turning white.   A nose, of which neither Greek nor Roman could complain, occupies the center of a large face.   A near neighbor to the nose is a mouth of ordinary size which only opens to laugh and make others merry.   A peculiarity of his is to inculcate in others the love of God.   The rest proclaims a man of fifty years of age, weighing 210 pounds.   Should you ever build a house, widen the doors by six inches, for I do not like to squeeze through a doorway in entering my room."[14]   Father De Smet's letters terminate with greetings from afar to a long list of friends and relatives whom he assures of his unfailing remembrances, or of whom he asks prayers.   The list sometimes contains thirty or forty names.   Neither the barber nor the humblest servant is forgotten.

The photographs of his dear absent ones were a source of great happiness.   "I have in St. Louis several photographs of my family arranged around a beautiful engraving of the Blessed Virgin, which is the principal ornament of my poor cell.   When I open my eyes in the morning, and every time I enter my room, my eyes rest upon the image of my good Mother; and in recommending myself

---

[13] Mr. De Bare had just married Sylvia De Smet.
[14] To Sylvia De Smet, October, 1850. Upon the ample proportions of Father De Smet see Chittenden-Richardson, p. 105.

to her protection I implore her protection for all those who encircle her." [15]

This constant thought of his family may seem inconsistent with religious detachment. We must remember, however, that perfection does not consist precisely in loving God alone, but in loving Him above all other creatures. Certain saints whose austerities are well known had an abiding affection for their families. St. Francis Borgia maintained his intercourse with his family, sought them out on all occasions, and complained of the rarity of their visits and letters. Upon his death-bed he named his sons, brothers, and relatives one by one, that he might recommend them to God, and even begged his brother to look after a donkey-driver who had accompanied him in his travels.[16]

Father De Smet's solicitude for his family never interfered with the discharge of his missionary duties. In his tenderest and most affectionate letters, one recognizes the priest and religious firmly fixed on God, interested in all things, yet judging all in the light from on high. These same letters were to him as a phase of his apostolate. Delicately, yet firmly, he addressed to each one a warning or a counsel. "I feel justified in speaking thus, being the only priest in the family."

Hearing that one of his nephews delighted in reading and meditating upon the *Imitation*, he writes, "This is excellent, but not enough. A little courage will make you add practice to meditation. It does not suffice to know Jesus Christ; we must love and imitate Him, or our sublimest conceptions are sterile and worthless." [17] To a relative suffering from a long illness he sent weekly letters of encouragement and consolation, and begged the prayers of the religious orders in St. Louis for her. In every letter he urged her to imitate the courage and patience of

[15] To Charles De Smet, St. Louis, May 5, 1865.

[16] Cf. Father Suau, S. J., "Histoire de St. François de Borgia," Paris, 1910, p. 530. As to St. Francis Xavier, that model of missionaries, we know how devotedly attached he was to his fellow religious in Europe. "In order to keep you ever with me, I have cut off your signatures from your letters, and these names are such a consolation to me that I carry them and the formula of my vows always with me." (To the Fathers and Brothers at Rome, Amboina, May 10, 1546.)

[17] St. Louis, Sept. 25, 1854.

the saints. "In the words of St. Augustine: 'Can you
not do what so many others have done?' If of yourself
you feel incapable of accomplishing the least good action,
say with the Apostle: 'I can do all things in Him who
strengthens me.'" [18]

A few weeks later the pious invalid was called to her
reward. Father De Smet wrote at once to her husband
to encourage and console him with words of faith and
hope. "The news of Laura's death grieves me beyond
words, and I realize fully the sorrow this loss, as irreparable
as it is premature, has caused you. You have lost a companion who made the happiness of your life, and whose
amiable qualities were only equaled by her solid virtues.

"Dear Charles, the angels have claimed her for whom
you weep. She has been admitted, I dare hope, to the
celestial banquet, and has entered upon her immediate
reward for the sufferings she endured with so much patience
and resignation. I have recommended her soul to the
prayers of our Fathers and the religious orders in St. Louis,
and since receiving the sad news, I have offered the Holy
Sacrifice daily for her soul.

"It is a great consolation to hear that you have accepted
this heavy trial in a truly Christian spirit. You weep,
but not like those who weep without hope. Your dear
Laura has only exchanged her fragile, terrestrial body for
a tabernacle not built by the hands of man. On earth
she was your faithful and beloved companion; in heaven
she will be your angel and will intercede for you." [19]

Father De Smet's intercourse with his family was not
confined solely to correspondence. Three times in seven
years, from 1853 to 1860, he returned to Belgium.[20] What
joy for him to find at each visit a more numerous family;
to perform marriage ceremonies, receive souvenirs, and to
see that the affection of his family and friends had stood
the test of time. Now and then a great sorrow would
darken their lives. In November, 1860, Charles De Smet,

---

[18] To Laura Blondel, Charles De Smet's first wife, St. Louis, June 1, 1860.
[19] To his nephew Charles, St. Louis, July 12, 1860.
[20] In 1853, 1856, 1860. In 1853 President Pierce sent letters by Father
De Smet to different European Governments.

the missionary's eldest brother, died at his country-place, Grembergen, in the neighborhood of Termonde. A just judge, a fervent Christian, his generosity merited the gratitude of the missions.[21] Father De Smet had the consolation of assisting at his last moments, and following him to the grave.

But it was not to visit his family that he crossed the ocean. In his capacity of Procurator of the Missions he had to provide for the needs of the Vice-Province, and, moreover, find men and money for his mountain missions. That Father De Smet, above all others, was best fitted for this delicate task is proven by the fact that he secured one hundred apostles for the New World, and collected, in all, over $200,000.

His manner of procedure was as follows: Arriving in Belgium, he heralded through the press the object of his visit.[22] Then he began his begging tour, in Belgium and Holland, followed by similar journeys to France, Italy, Germany, England, and Ireland. His first visits were made to the families of the missionaries, to the benefactors of the missions, and to the heads of the Propagation of the

[21] Monsieur Charles De Smet, former President, held for several years the post of Counselor of the Court of Appeals at Ghent. In a statement of accounts in Father De Smet's handwriting we read: "*Don de C (harles) à son fr(ère) P(ierre) 20,000 francs.*"

[22] "After long journeys in the American wilderness, I see again my own country and am happy to be able to personally express the missionaries' gratitude to our benefactors for their generosity to the poor Indians.

"Since my last visit to Belgium I have traversed districts devoid of missions, and where probably no European has ever set foot. Providence has upheld my feeble courage, guided my steps, and fructified the seed of the Gospel in lands where it was heretofore unknown. I have recognized the good that can be accomplished among these wandering tribes ever at war with each other, who, having no hope of eternity, are bereft of all consolation.

"The small number of priests in America are insufficient to minister to the Catholics and at the same time to the Indians who clamor for a Black Robe. Hence, I have come to Europe to appeal to your generous hearts. I come also to ask for material assistance. I know that Belgium is besieged by missionaries from America, India, and the Orient, and I realize that benefactors are taxed to the limit of their resources to satisfy these constant demands. But no one in Europe can form any idea of the need we have for priests to prevent defection from our ranks, to convert the heathen, and to train missionaries; for money to build churches, support schools, establish reductions, and thus illumine the desert with the light of faith and the dawn of civilization." (Letter to the editor of the *Brussels Journal*, July 2, 1853.)

Faith. Then came the turn of the colleges, boarding-schools, and seminaries. Everywhere he was feasted and made welcome. Those privileged ones who attended his conferences retained a vivid picture of the priest with flowing locks, who, with touching simplicity, begged bread for his children. His address, ordinarily calm, almost cold, and devoid of sentimental demonstration, rang with enthusiasm in speaking about the Flatheads or Cœur d'Alènes and their needs; and in proclaiming the white man's iniquitous proceedings, his voice warmed and the tears that trembled on his eyelids rained down his noble, handsome face. His eloquence gained for the missions the interest of the entire audience.

Although his appeals were always successful, Father De Smet disliked appearing in public, and on such occasions this man, daring to the point of temerity, betrayed a pitiful timidity. Once he had promised to speak in the little church of St. Catherine in Liège, but when the day arrived, filled with embarrassment, he was heard to say: "I cannot do it. I do not know what to say." "Show yourself," they said, "and simply say you have come to make an appeal for your Indians." But the humble missionary drew back. At the last moment one was obliged to drag him from his room and conduct him to the church. He mounted the pulpit, addressed the congregation, and in a few moments was so carried away by his subject that his audience, moved and enchanted, could have listened to him for hours.[23]

With the children he was at his best. He loved the simple, naïve reception he received from nuns [24] and innocent little girls and boys, and always asked for a list of their Christian names in order to give them to the Indian children he baptized. In many schools [25] he dressed up young men as redskins and paraded them before the students amid storms of applause, overjoyed at the pleasure

---

[23] The fact is recounted by Father Broeckaert, then Pastor of St. Catherine's. Cf. *Précis Historiques*, 1873, p. 328.

[24] In particular at the Ursuline convents of Saventhem and Thildonck, and at the Servants of Mary at Erps-Querbs. The Superior of the last community was Father De Smet's cousin.

[25] At Brussels, Ghent, Antwerp, and Namur, and even before the students of the Sorbonne. Cf. Chittenden-Richardson, p. 66.

he occasioned, and laughing heartily with the little ones.

But he excelled in recounting tales and adventures, and like all missionaries, had many at hand, such as the story of Louise Sighouin, the Cœur d'Alène saint,[26] and terrifying ones of Tchatka, the Assiniboin chief, worthy imitator of Nero and Caligula.[27] Some of his recitals had quite a savage flavor—for example, the tale of the mouthful of whiskey which the Indians passed from mouth to mouth, the last one being allowed to swallow it. Only on rare occasions did he speak about himself, but when pressed to recount his adventures, yielded with his customary simplicity and humor. Once in the Rocky Mountains, in turning a path, a gray bear pounced upon him, burying his claws in his chest. Believing himself lost, he repeated the act of contrition, then, with the gigantic strength born of danger, he seized the beast by the throat and strangled him.[28] Through a sulphur match, he acquired great prestige with the Crows. In wonder at the facility with which the missionary lighted his pipe, the Indians concluded he possessed magic power, and treated him with great respect. Before taking leave of them he distributed boxes of the "mysterious fire." Four years later, when again visiting the country, Father De Smet was surprised to see the entire tribe coming forth to receive him. Chiefs and warriors in gala attire conducted him from lodge to lodge, where feasts awaited him. The great chief professed undying friendship. "Black Robe," he said, "to you I owe my success at arms," and taking from his neck a little bag, he displayed the remainder of the matches which Father De Smet had given him. "I take them with me whenever I go to war, and if the match lights the first time I strike it, I fall upon my enemies, sure of victory." The missionary had the utmost difficulty in abolishing this ridiculous superstition. "You see," he said, in conclusion, "with what trifles man wins renown with the Indians. The possessor

[26] Cf. Selected Letters, 2d Series, p. 357.

[27] *Ibid.*, 1st Series, p. 223.

[28] Father Deynoodt, an intimate friend of Father De Smet, records this fact in his notes. Baron de Woelmont avers that he heard the missionary recount a similar story. Cf. "L'Habit d'Arlequin," Brussels, 1892, p. 343.

of a few matches passes for a great man and receives distinguished honors!"

The following anecdote greatly amused his audience: Surprised one night in the depth of the forest by a snowstorm, Father De Smet climbed a tree, and, in searching about for a safe spot in which to spend the night, discovered that the tree was hollow. "Aha!" said he, "here I will be safely sheltered," and proceeded to descend inside. Arriving at the bottom, he felt something move under his feet, which turned out to be a brood of harmless young cubs. Soon, however, the sound of heavy grunts reached him. The mother bear was returning; her claws were already on the bark. She climbed up, then down she came, backward. What was the next move? With great presence of mind the missionary seized her tail with both hands and pulled it violently. The frightened bear quickly climbed up again and disappeared into the forest. Master of the lodging, he remained there quietly until daylight permitted him to continue on his way.[29]

In listening to these tales the children saw before them only a kindly old man who entertained and amused them, little dreaming that this priest was one of the greatest explorers of his time and the protector of the Indian race. That he knew how to move and impress the seminarians is evident from the numbers he gained to the apostolate. Yet he never forced a vocation, nor did he endeavor to directly influence any one to accompany him. His method was to expose the condition of the missions. He spoke affectionately of his dear Indians, awakened interest in them, and the rest followed naturally.

Among the spiritual notes of a Belgian seminarian we find the following lines, dated October 28, 1860: "Father De Smet spoke to us to-day for half an hour. He is unquestionably the greatest missionary in the world. His face is noble and gentle, but worn from fatigue. He speaks French badly, but even this carelessness of speech is agreeable. He has done us much good. Here is a true apostle; a man dead to self, telling of his travels and labors as though he were speaking about a third person, and edifying

[29] This extraordinary adventure is vouched for by several people who heard it from the lips of the missionary.

us at every turn. How splendid it is to see this priest, celebrated throughout the world for his achievements, submissive as a child to his Superiors' orders. 'I will return to America in May,' he said. 'Such are my Superiors' orders.' Yes, go, grand old man, and our prayers and good wishes will follow you! Work, you who have accomplished so much, work for those who sank into a cowardly repose when the heat of the day began; work for me, who am weak and sinful, or, rather, may your merits obtain for me the grace to do my part in the Lord's vineyard! Would that I could follow you there, where the work is great and the laborers few! May Your divine will be accomplished in me, O Lord! I submit myself to You in all things; let not my cowardice stand in the way."

After a sojourn of several months in Europe, Father De Smet began to prepare for his return to America. This event, a painful parting to all he left behind, was none the less so for the missionary, who, having proven the loyalty of his family and friends, left them with deep regret. Wishing to keep them in touch with his journeys, he sent letters from Southampton and Halifax, in which assurances of affection were mingled with descriptions of picturesque and lugubrious scenes.

In April, 1857, Father De Smet embarked at Antwerp with seven new missionaries. "The weather was splendid, and the steamer alive with animation. We have a multitude of emigrants, Germans, Dutch, Swiss, Belgians, and French on board. A day's journey brought us to Southampton, where the vessel remained until the next day to take on the English and Irish passengers. We numbered in all six hundred souls. All day long the ship resounded with the songs of the Germans and Dutch gathered on deck, where they danced to the accompaniment of violin and guitar and accordion. The main deck resembled a village kermess. But joy does not always tarry long, as was soon proved.

"Hardly had we passed the Isle of Wight than the aspect of things changed. A heavy sea came on, the vessel began to pitch as it rose and fell with the waves, carried up on the crest one moment, then plunged into an abyss of foaming water. Song and dance ceased; the dining-saloon was deserted; hunger and gayety disappeared together. Here and there were dilapidated groups of haggard men and women and children; pale and livid specters leaned over the rails in apparent converse with the sea. Even well ones, who, however, had eaten and drunk too generously, were wan and the color of parchment." [30] Father De Smet suffered greatly from seasickness, and notwithstanding the many voyages he made, he was never free from this humiliating malady. But this was the least of the trials he experienced on his various journeys.

In December, 1853, he had taken thirteen young men to America. Bishop Miège, who had come to Europe to assist at the election of Father Beckx, also returned with him upon the same boat, the *Humboldt*. The coal running short, orders were given to make for Halifax. Some distance from port, a fisherman came and offered to take the vessel in. "Are you a pilot?" asked the captain. "Yes," replied the fisherman. "I can go and fetch my certificate." The captain, believing him, entrusted him with the management of the ship. Against the advice of the officers, the pretended pilot at once changed the direction and soon the *Humboldt* was heading for the reefs near Devil's Island. It was six o'clock in the morning and the greater number of passengers were still in bed. Awakening with a shock, they rushed up on deck to see pieces of the ship floating on the water, torn off by a collision with the rocks. Water rushed into the hold and fire broke out near the boiler. Lifeboats were lowered, which were immediately filled by the passengers. But it was impossible to steer a boat in such a sea through a dense fog.

Vain efforts were made to run the ship on shore, but it was already settling. Consternation seized all the passengers, save Bishop Miège and Father De Smet, who remained calm, says a witness. A third collision threw every one pell-mell on the deck, and all seemed lost. But God stayed His hand; the vessel touched ground and rested firmly upon a rock until help could be obtained. Almost at the same moment the fog lifted, revealing land not a hundred feet away. The waters grew calm, the wind

[30] To Charles De Smet, New York, May 14, 1857.

dropped, and radiant sunshine bathed land and sea. The next day Father De Smet celebrated a Mass of thanksgiving in the cathedral of Halifax; his traveling companions made communions of thanksgiving in the firm conviction that they owed their safety to a special interposition of heaven.

Intrepid in the face of danger, once it had passed, our missionary gave himself up to contemplating the works of God. One evening in May after witnessing a glorious sunset, he lingered to contemplate the stars reflected in the water. "Never," says he in his *Itinerary*, "have I seen such a divine night. I remained on deck to enjoy it, and only retired to my cabin at two o'clock in the morning." Rising before dawn, he went immediately on deck to greet the new-born day. "The heavens were pure, the sea calm; only a faint breeze ruffled the face of the waters. From the bosom of the deep the sun rose majestically; then burst forth in glory, its dazzling rays radiating to all points of the horizon. In the east the ocean was aflame, a vast mass of molten gold. A sunrise at sea is a great, a sublime spectacle. *Mirabilia opera tua, Domine, et anima mea cognoscit minis.*" [31]

At St. Louis many were impatiently awaiting the return of Father De Smet. Arriving unexpectedly, he appeared at the University during the distribution of prizes. The crowded entertainment hall resounded with applause when the missionary entered. Speeches were suspended, the victors forgot their crowns, and the humble religious was forced to submit to a long ovation. "I admit that at that moment I was far from being at my ease." Finally he was allowed to retire, and kneeling, he kissed the doorstep of his cell, and thanked God for having restored him to his dear Indians.

[31] "Wonderful are Thy works, and my soul knoweth right well." (Ps. cxxxviii, 14.)

CHAPTER XIX

THE WAR OF SECESSION (1861–1865)

Civil War in the United States—The Battle of Bull Run—Anarchy in Missouri—Father De Smet's Trials—Father De Smet Secures a Subsidy for the Indian Schools—Obtains Military Exemption for the Jesuits —His Intercourse with Lincoln—A Dinner at the Belgian Legation—Publication of the "Western Missions and Missionaries" and the "New Indian Sketches"—It is Said that Father De Smet Did Not Write the "Letters"—He Addresses a Protest to the German Provincial—The Sisters of St. Mary in America—The War Ends—Jesuit Chaplains— Missions Given in the Large Cities—"The Church of These Fathers Must Be the Church of Jesus Christ"—The Oath Required by the State of Missouri—Catholicism Makes Great Progress.

UPON landing in New York in the month of April, 1861, Father De Smet found his adopted country in the throes of civil war. For a long time there had been division between the South, anxious to maintain slavery, and the North, the partisan of emancipation. The election of President Lincoln, a strong abolitionist, had precipitated the conflict. The Confederates had seized Fort Sumter and several arsenals, and the North retaliated by arming two hundred thousand men and proclaiming a blockade of the coast States in revolt. It was a terrible war, in which men of the same blood and country fought with unexampled ardor and persistency. A million men killed, towns and cities bombarded, the entire South devastated, the work of half a century destroyed, two billion dollars expended, the entire population affected; such was the balance-sheet of this sanguinary conflict.

Distressed beyond measure by this news, Father De Smet hastened to St. Louis. A passionate advocate of peace and liberty, he deplored the military régime to which the country had been subjected. The press and telegraph were under Government control, newspapers suppressed, railway lines cut, canal and river transportation intercepted, and citizens suspected of treason imprisoned without trial. "It cannot be denied that the great Republic is as completely given over to despotism as though it were in the hands of the Czar of all the Russias." [1]

But more than the loss of liberty, Father De Smet deplored the lives sacrificed to implacable rivalry. He was in Washington at the time of the famous battle of Bull Run, and from the heights overlooking the city he heard the cannon's roar. After a bloody conflict the Federals began to give way, and were finally routed. "The entrance of the fleeing men into Washington is the saddest scene I have ever witnessed. For miles, a straggling line of haggard officers and soldiers of every branch of the service, in tattered uniforms, without arms and knapsacks, pushed their way pell-mell among carts, ambulances, and vehicles of every description." [2]

But defeat in no way diminished the courage of the North. A call was made for five hundred thousand men and for five hundred million dollars, and the war continued with varying success for both the combatants.

Two years after the outbreak of hostilities, Father De Smet writes: "God alone can in His mercy put an end to this disastrous struggle. Up to this time no one can predict the final result. Numerous battles have been fought without leading to any definite result. A horrible war in which brothers cut each other's throats, and in which battles are often butcheries." [3]

Missouri, being on the border between the free States and the slave States, was the scene of the worst excesses. [4] Both North and South were largely represented, every town and village was divided into two opposing camps,

[1] Letter to Francis De Smet, St. Louis, April 16, 1862.   [2] Ibid., July, 1861.
[3] To Mr. J. Van Jersel, St. Louis, Feb., 1863.
[4] "You have read of the horrors of the French Revolution and the civil wars of different centuries and countries; but all that gives only a faint idea of the condition to which Missouri is reduced. Her own children, divided between the North and the South, tear one another to pieces and burn and sack one another's houses, while enemies from without overrun the State to satisfy their hatred and thirst for pillage. The head of the rebels has just published a manifesto in which he promises two hundred million dollars' worth of spoils to fifty thousand brigands willing to fight under his flag. To this condition has Missouri been reduced by detestable Secession, and yet we are only at the first page of its history." (Letter of Father De Smet to his brother Francis, St. Louis, Dec. 4, 1861.)

and in the general conflict it was difficult to distinguish a murder from an act of war.

Murders were on the increase in St. Louis; in two months there were seventy. The rumor spread that Father De Smet had been rescued by an armed force from being burned to death, but the report was unfounded. "I do not think," he writes, "that I am disliked to such a point." [5] Yet he was none the less horrified at what was taking place under his eyes. The city he had seen built, and the University he and Father Van Quickenborne had founded, seemed destined to early ruin. "Only a few months ago business flourished and the population was increasing. Since then forty thousand people have left St. Louis and thousands of houses and stores are vacant. Landed property has fallen to one-fourth its value,[6] our great river is blockaded, and hundreds of steamboats are lying idle along the levee. Farm products rot in barns and sheds. The college has opened with only a third of its pupils. When and how will it all end? No man can predict." [7]

But Father De Smet was not idle during this time. When the war was at its height, he, provided with a passport, three times went through the belligerent lines to visit the tribes on the Upper Missouri and to revictual the Oregon Missions. Several times he journeyed to Washington to claim Government subsidies for the Indian schools, and to obtain exemption from military service for the members of religious orders. The war was a great drain on the national treasury. The sum of $13,800 was due to the Osage and Potawatomi Missions. Father De Smet argued to the officials that the subsidies were guaranteed by treaties, and a longer delay would antagonize the Indians, who up to the present had shown themselves faithful subjects of the Union. Should the missions, for want of funds, be forced to send the hundreds of children back to their families, the tribes might make common

---

[5] To Father Terwecoren, St. Louis, Feb. 17, 1862.

[6] "I am acquainted with families who enjoyed incomes of $20,000 up to 1860, who are now reduced to $2,000 a year." (Letter of Father De Smet to the Mother General of the Sisters of St. Mary, March 1, 1862.)

[7] To Charles and Rosalie Van Mossevelde, St. Louis, Sept. 10, 1861.

cause with the rebels. This argument appeared to have weight, for ten thousand dollars was paid at once, and a promise was given that the rest would soon follow.

In the spring of 1863, Congress passed a law calling to the colors all men old enough to bear arms. Neither secular nor regular clergy were exempt, and already some had been enrolled. The Jesuits, while willing to expose their lives in the interests of their country, did not feel at liberty to go against ecclesiastical orders. "We are ministers of peace," writes Father De Smet, "and from all times the sacred character of the priesthood has been judged incompatible with war and the shedding of blood. It is a law of the Church, and one binding on our consciences." [8]

An act of Congress permitted the conscripts to buy release from military duties by the payment of three hundred dollars, but the St. Louis Province was too poor, and such an expenditure spelled ruin. Father De Smet appealed to the Secretary of War, who, in recognition of the missionary's services during the Oregon campaign, allowed the Jesuits to follow their avocations "until further orders." It was a tacit exemption, which lasted as long as the war. In passing through Washington, Father De Smet had had several interviews with President Lincoln. Between the emancipator of the slaves and the defender of the Indians a friendly understanding was easily established. The President showed himself well disposed toward the Indians and promised his support.

Everywhere the missionary was well received. Statesmen invited him to their tables; one day he dined at the Belgian Legation with the French, Spanish, and Russian ambassadors. "All the ambassadors were resplendent with their orders. I was arrayed in a worn frock-coat lacking two buttons. Nevertheless, it passed off very pleasantly and I held my own in this distinguished gathering. But I would have been more at my ease seated on the ground in the midst of my Indians, listening to their badinage, while eating with relish a buffalo steak or a fat roast dog." [9]

[8] Letter to Thurlow Weed, April 11, 1863.
[9] Letter to Father Terwecoren, St. Louis, Feb. 17, 1862.

In order to make known the missions and to obtain funds for them, Father De Smet published in New York, in 1863, two new editions of his "Letters." The first, entitled "Western Missions and Missionaries," was a translation of *Cinquante Nouvelle Lettres*, which had appeared in 1858.[10] Besides accounts of his journeys and studies of the habits and customs of the people, it contained several sketches of the first Jesuits in Missouri. The second volume, "New Indian Sketches," contained the story of Louise Sighouin, an account of the pacification of the Cœur d'Alènes, and the missionary's correspondence with General Harney. These publications were similar to his "Journeys in the Rocky Mountains," and "The Oregon Missions," and were written in the same interesting vein, with the same note of sincerity, freshness of style, and breathing the same charity for the Indians and the same zeal to save them.

"The facts related in these letters," says an American journal, "form an important chapter in the history of the Church in our country, and bring out strongly the difference between the labors of the Catholic and Protestant missionary. Can the American Board of Foreign Missions give the public a volume like this one of Father De Smet? What have their agents done with the enormous sums of money placed in their hands? Their labors are counted by the number of Bibles distributed. The letter killeth, but the spirit quickeneth."[11]

Yet there were men who contested the value of these recitals. Formerly Father De Smet had been reproached with embellishing facts beyond all recognition; now they claimed that the "Letters" were not written by him, that he had only lent his name to the publication. Who started the calumny? It was never traced to its source, but it spread to Europe, and was even believed by the German Jesuits. It grieved and perturbed the missionary that his good faith should be doubted, and once more he felt obliged to clear himself of this false accusation. In the following humble terms he addressed the German Provincial:

"Personally, I deserve small consideration, but our Missouri Province feels its honor has been attacked in

[10] Published by Casterman, Paris.
[11] *The Pilot*, Dec. 29, 1863.

supposing it could authorize an imposture. I alone am responsible for letters written over my name and with the consent of my Superiors. The accounts of some of our Fathers have been taken from authentic documents, which I obtained from different sources, and which were revised and published by me. In my travels I have drawn my information from authentic sources, and given it to the public for what it was worth, citing always my authority. While working among the Indians, I have not only instructed them, but have questioned and studied them, and have faithfully recorded the facts, both adverse and favorable. Every word has been written *ad majorem Dei gloriam*, and in compliance with my Superiors' express desire. Hence, I declare that the letters published as mine were written by me, which fact gives me the right to protest to your Reverence against the accusations of those in your Province who deny their authenticity. If need be, the entire Missouri Province is ready to attest my declaration."

The missionary's words could not be doubted, nor could one remain untouched in reading these words: "I am weak and sensitive; I have suffered many wrongs through false reports about my publications. Chapter xxxvi of the third book of the *Imitation* [12] comforts me and I endeavor to put it in practice. Moreover, Thomas à Kempis tells us that even St. Paul justified himself on more than one occasion, for fear his silence might be an occasion of scandal to the weak." [13]

Father De Smet not only spent himself in the service of his fellow-missionaries and in the support of the missions, but his help and counsel were ever at the service of whoever asked his aid. The Sisters of Namur were anxious to establish themselves in America, and in 1861 the Superior approached Father De Smet upon the subject. Conversant with the success obtained by European religious orders in the United States, he encouraged the project and promised to further its realization.

---

[12] "Against the vain judgments of man."
[13] Letter to Father Roder, St. Louis, Aug. 30, 1867. See upon the same subject, *Précis Historiques*, 1868, p. 58.

Then came the Civil War. The Bishops dared not undertake new foundations. Well-known convents lost three-fourths of their pupils and found themselves in straitened circumstances. The Sisters must await a more favorable moment. Yet several dioceses, notably that of Buffalo, were less affected by existing circumstances. Bishop Timon was the personal friend of Father De Smet and he spoke to him about the Namur Sisters. The Bishop considered the proposition favorably and offered the Mother General a foundation at Lockport, a town of fifteen thousand inhabitants. The house in question was extremely modest, but pupils were assured, and even novices.

Although the Bishop offered the best he had, the Mother General was prudent, and, before accepting the offer, sought Father De Smet's advice. His reply bespeaks the wisdom and supernatural motives of a priest: "After much reflection before God, I am of the opinion that you should accept the offer of Bishop Timon. Generally speaking, Catholic establishments in America have begun in poverty. Our first foundation in Missouri began with two log huts covered with bark, eighteen feet square, with dirt floors. The first convent of the Ladies of the Sacred Heart was established in a village of six hundred inhabitants. Their house was so small it hardly met the needs of the community. To-day they possess flourishing schools in all our larger cities. . . . The Bishop tells me that Buffalo, with its hundred thousand souls, has all the convents it can support. In ten years the town will probably number three hundred thousand. But before that time, if you come to Lockport, you will have an establishment in Buffalo and I hope in other large cities in America and Canada." [14]

This letter decided the Mother General to accept the Bishop's offer, and five months later five of her community left for America. They succeeded from the outset, and Bishop Timon asked for a second foundation. To-day the Sisters of St. Mary number nearly two hundred nuns, and possess well-known educational institutions in the large cities of the United States. [15]

[14] St. Louis, March 19, 1863.
[15] See "La Vie de la Révérende Mère Marie Claire de Jésus," by the Sisters of St. Mary de Namur, 1895, Chap. xiii.

The war, which for four years had laid the country desolate, was drawing to a close. Several Confederate army corps had surrendered, as well as Richmond, the Confederate capital. The North was victorious, and the slaves were set free.

"We must thank God," wrote Montalembert, "that a great nation is risen up again, and is purified of a hideous leprosy which served as a pretext and reason to all friends of liberty to denounce and defame her. She now justifies all the hopes we built upon her, we have need of her and she is given back to us, repentant, triumphant, and saved."[16]

Father De Smet thanked God for the abolition of slavery, "that festering sore,"[17] and he also rejoiced over the progress Catholicism was making. From 1863 the Missouri Vice-Province took rank with the other Provinces of the Society.

Although neutral in the question that divided the North and South, the Jesuits, the Sisters of Charity, and the Christian Brothers labored indiscriminately in behalf of the victims of the war. They opened hospitals in several cities, where their devotion and zeal obtained consoling results. Sinners were reconciled with God and many converts were made. "The Church of these Fathers," they said, "must be the Church of Jesus Christ."

The Jesuit Fathers serving as chaplains in the army won, by their courageous charity, the hearts and esteem of both soldiers and officers. "What are our Protestant chaplains good for?" asked General Butler. "They do well enough in peace, but are useless in war. They administer no Sacraments, and the humblest soldier is invested with as much spiritual power as they. Catholic priests alone can be of spiritual help to soldiers on the battlefield." [18]

Between battles, the chaplains instructed, baptized, and prepared the soldiers for their first communion. The Archbishop of New York himself came on one occasion to confirm four hundred men. Still more extraordinary, the Jesuit Fathers managed to preach three-day retreats, which were attended by both officers and men. In some

---

[16] *La victoire du Nord aux États-Unis*, in the *Correspondent*, May, 1865, p. 7.
[17] Letter to Paul De Smet, St. Louis, July 7, 1861.
[18] See The Annals of the Propagation of the Faith, 1865, p. 469.

regiments fifty communions were distributed every morning.

Towns and cities were as much aflame with religious zeal as the military camps. The extraordinary prosperity enjoyed by the United States previous to the outbreak of the war had resulted in a falling off of religious practices. Money and pleasure were the sole objects of life with many. But the horrors of war, the dark future, and the sudden loss of fortunes, gave other preoccupations to the frivolous. The Jesuits seized this moment to hold missions throughout the country. In St. Louis, Boston, Cincinnati, Louisville, New York, and Washington, the spiritual results of these missions exceeded all hopes. Fathers Weninger, Smarius, Damen, Maguire, and O'Reilly preached to enormous and mixed congregations. Father Smarius alone distributed fifty thousand communions in less than three months, and received into the Church two hundred and fifty Protestants. Many who, formerly, would not hear the word Catholic, now evinced great eagerness to be instructed.[19]

In Missouri, however, a sectarian movement hampered the action of the clergy. The legislature required priests to swear, before they were given the right to teach or preach, that during the war they had evinced no sympathy with the South. The refusal to take the oath meant a fine of five hundred dollars or six months in prison.

"Should this law be enforced," writes Father De Smet, "our churches will be closed and our schools ruined. Furthermore, since the State does not confer on us the right to preach and teach, to take such an oath would be to compromise the independence of the Church."[20]

But Catholicism had sunk deep roots in American soil, which her enemies could neither destroy nor weaken. The very day the ruling was to become a law the University opened its doors with six hundred pupils. The friends of liberty carried the acts of the legislature to the Supreme Court of the United States and in January, 1867, the oath was declared unconstitutional.

[19] In regard to the Catholic apostolate in the United States during the war, see *Les Études*, Dec., 1862, and Oct., 1863.
[20] Letter to Gustave Van Kerckhove, St. Louis, Sept. 23, 1865.

Some months later Father De Smet wrote jubilantly: "The Church, it is true, has many battles to fight; sectarians of every shade make war on her, but notwithstanding the propaganda, the speeches and writings of her enemies, our cause steadily gains a foothold. Churches, seminaries, colleges, academies, schools, religious houses, orphanages, and hospitals rise as by enchantment on American soil. Thousands of Protestant parents confide the education of their children to Jesuits, priests, Christian Brothers, and the Sisters, and the greater number of these children become Catholics, and later on apostles in their families. The Catholic population of St. Louis numbers one hundred thousand souls. It is the Rome of America." [21]

One sees that even if his mission work frequently withdrew him to remote scenes, Father De Smet was conversant with the strides Catholicism was making. His correspondence shows he was equally attentive to what was taking place in Belgium, Italy, and Mexico. With passionate interest he followed in every country the eternal struggle between good and evil. To him the issue never was doubtful. He would willingly have assented to these words of Montalembert: "It is always difficult to do good, but good prevails, and since the coming of Our Lord Jesus Christ into the world, virtue has slowly but incontestably progressed. History and reason prove this truth more and more every day to those who sincerely study the question. The present is better than the past, and the future will be better than the present." [22]

[21] Letter to Emile de Meren, Oct., 1867.
[22] Letter to Swiss students, Aug. 25, 1869.

CHAPTER XX

A TOUR OF THE MISSIONS (1862–1863)

The Needs of the Missions—Father De Smet Sends Yearly Assistance to the Oregon Missions—The Journey in 1862—St. Peter's Mission—The Journey in 1863—"This Is the Black Robe Who Saved My Sister"—Triumphal Journey through Oregon—The Fervor of the Cœur d'Alènes—Sad Forebodings—Return Journey by California, Panama, and New York—The Lost Returns—Father De Smet's Illness—His Friends are Dying One by One—"I Have an Inner Conviction that My End is Approaching. *Fiat voluntas Dei!*"—Restoration to Health.

SINCE 1849 Father De Smet had occupied in Missouri the posts of Procurator and of assistant to the Provincial. The first-mentioned office he exercised until his death, but as his many and long journeys were incompatible with the duties of Provincial, he was relieved of that position in 1862. From that time, every spring, he traveled up the Missouri to visit the missions or to pacify the Sioux tribes.

For many years the Oregon establishments had received no Government subsidies. Father Hoecken wrote from Oregon to acquaint Father De Smet with his financial embarrassment, and added: "Not for human gain have we given our lives to work and to suffer as we do here. Although all the gold in the world could not pay for our devotion, neither could any privation induce us to abandon our undertaking." [1]

Yet, however disinterested were the missionaries, a less precarious situation would have facilitated their labors and assured their success. Father De Smet relieved their poverty with yearly consignments of foodstuffs, clothing, seeds, and farm implements; and with what joy was this largess received! "Upon the arrival of such a shipment,"

[1] St. Ignatius' Mission, April 15, 1857.

writes Father Hoecken, "we wept tears of joy and thanks-giving. I did not close my eyes that night, and was unable to calm my emotions. The next day I reproached myself for my weakness, but you know what a missionary's life is among the Indians, with its anguish and privations, and you will excuse my sensibility." [2]

With his shipments, Father De Smet included books and a budget of news of all that was taking place in St. Louis. On one occasion his photograph accompanied the provi-sions. The Indians learned of this, and rushed at once to salute their benefactor. But his likeness was not enough; they clamored that he should come in person. He in turn was no less anxious to see once more his children of the wilderness, and in 1861 the visit was arranged. The death, however, of Father Druyts, the Provincial, delayed his departure until the following spring. Instead of going to them, he sent by steamboat fifty plows, a mill, tools, and household utensils and took pleasure in the thought of the joy these articles would give the missionaries. Then the news came that both boats and all the cargo had been destroyed by fire. Another consignment was immediately packed, and this time he took it himself. He planned to visit also the numerous tribes on the Upper Missouri who were asking for Black Robes.

In May, 1862, the missionary left St. Louis on a steam-boat bound for Fort Benton. The captain, Charles Chou-teau, one of the first pupils of the University, offered his former professor yearly free transportation for himself and the supplies destined for the missions. As they ascended the Missouri, they came upon numerous bands of Indians camping on its banks. When the boat landed for the distribution of the yearly pensions and presents of the Government, the Indians gathered around the Black Robe, offering him the calumet, and listening attentively to his words. Mothers brought their children to be blessed and offered to the Great Spirit, and he had the joy of baptizing over seven hundred souls—a great triumph, if one remem-bers that three-fourths of the children of these tribes died before attaining the age of reason.

An old squaw, crippled in arms and legs, dragged herself

[2] Letter quoted.

to the missionary's lodge, and, stretching out her withered arms, cried: "Father, have pity on me! I also wish to be a child of the Great Spirit. Pour water on my brow and pronounce the sacred words. The whites call me Marie, the name of the good and great Mother in heaven to whom I wish to go after death." Touched by such faith, Father De Smet instructed and baptized her and left her in transports of joy.

When he left St. Louis it was Father De Smet's intention to spend several months evangelizing the Sioux, but war had just broken out between this tribe and the Americans.[3] A chief suspected of being friendly to the whites had been killed by his braves. As neither guide nor interpreter could be found, he was obliged to renounce the project for the present. He reached Fort Benton, three thousand miles above St. Louis, where he was received by two Italian Jesuits, Fathers Giorda and Imoda, who had replaced Father Hoecken, lately recalled to the States after spending seventeen years in Oregon.[4] The flourishing St. Peter's Mission, founded a year before on the left bank of the Missouri in the neighborhood of the Sun River, counted over seven hundred Christians.

What joy for the missionary to see a tribe, formerly numbered among the most cruel of the mountain Indians, worshiping Christ! The fatigue endured and dangers encountered during the terrible winter of 1846 to succor the Blackfeet rendered this tribe dear to the missionary's heart. He celebrated in their midst a Mass of thanksgiving; many Christian Indians approached the holy table, and hundreds of voices chanted the *Magnificat*.

But if the future was full of promise, the missionaries were at the time in need of the bare necessities of life. Father De Smet came to their aid, and with the funds collected in Europe purchased for them large supplies of

---

[3] See the following chapter.

[4] Father Adrian Hoecken, seventeen years younger than his brother Christian, was born at Tilbourg in Brabant, Holland, March 18, 1815. In 1839 he entered the novitiate at Florissant; left for the mountains in 1844, and until 1861 labored with great success among the Flatheads. Returning east, he occupied different posts, being first appointed to the Osages, then to Cincinnati, and finally to St. Charles. He died in Milwaukee, April 19, 1897. (Cf. The Woodstock Letters, Nov., 1897, p. 364.)

food, clothing, and coverings. To encourage the Indians in their efforts at agriculture and trade, he left them two carts, several plows, and every sort of utensil.

On his return to St. Louis, Father De Smet made new purchases, and in the spring of 1863 went up the river, taking with him two lay Brothers and a cargo valued at three thousand dollars, destined for the missions. For several days they traveled through country infested with bands of secessionists, and in several places they passed dead bodies lying on the river-bank. Safety required that all travelers should be armed, and a heavy cannon was stationed in the prow of the boat. "As for myself," says the missionary, "I make use only of spiritual arms. I offer the Holy Sacrifice daily in my cabin, and the Brothers as well as myself are filled with confidence in protection from on high. When God is with us who can be against us?"[5] Even in such moments he quietly composed verses upon the sorrows of the times.

When he reached the Indian country he visited several bands of Crows, Assiniboins, Grosventres, Mandans, and Aricaras, administered more than five hundred baptisms, and arranged for the founding of a new mission near the mouth of the Yellowstone.

The heat of summer had already dried up the streams, and the river was too low to permit a steamboat to navigate further. The captain unloaded his cargo near the Milk River, three hundred miles from Fort Benton. The ninety passengers were forced to camp in a forest until wagons from the Fort came to fetch them and their baggage. War was still being waged between the Sioux and the whites; several steamboats had been attacked, and the loss of life was considerable. One day a band of six hundred warriors surprised the camp. Every man seized a gun and prepared to resist. Father De Smet wished to avoid bloodshed, so he went out to meet the enemy and was recognized at once by the Sioux. The son of Red Fish, the great chief of the Ogallalas, grasped his hand and exclaimed: "Here is the Black Robe who saved my sister!"

[5] To G. Van Kerckhove, on board the *Nellie Rogers*, May 15, 1863.

These words recalled one of the most touching episodes in the life of the missionary.[6]   The warriors surrounded the Black Robe, and showed him every mark of respect.   After he had talked some time with the Sioux, he distributed coffee, sugar, and sweet crackers.   They then departed to return no more.

After a month's weary waiting a long line of carts was seen approaching, also a carriage in which the three missionaries were to make the journey of three hundred miles through country laid waste by drought.   At last, on the feast of the Assumption, Father De Smet and his companions reached Fort Benton, and from there journeyed to St. Peter's Mission.

In a year's time the number of Christians had doubled. Fathers Giorda and Imoda worked for the evangelization of the Blackfeet, and at the same time ministered also to the Catholic emigrants living in the neighborhood.   These priests heartily welcomed the two Brothers who had come to share their labors.   As in the preceding year, Father De Smet's intention was to push on to the Sioux tribes, but the revolt of the Indians rendered this more and more impossible.   From every direction came news of massacres, and even the steamboats on the river were in danger. Mr. Chouteau had lost a number of his crew in going down the river, so Father De Smet decided to visit the Western missions, one after the other, and to return by way of California, Panama, and New York.

The Black Robe's arrival in Oregon was signaled from one tribe to another by lighting great bonfires on the mountains.   His journey was a two months' triumphal march, accompanied by every conceivable demonstration of gratitude: for was it not to him that the Indians owed the grace of baptism and the pacification of the country?

He had just left the mountains when he witnessed an affecting scene.   A camp of Kalispels and Flatheads were returning from a buffalo-hunt.   Suddenly a silvery bell was heard.   The chief was ringing the *Angelus*.   The whole band knelt down and devoutly recited the *Ave Maria*. Moved to tears, Father De Smet fell on his knees and

[6] See Chap. xii, p. 210.

21

united his prayers with those of his children. The next day he celebrated Mass upon a humble altar decorated with willow branches. The Indians chanted the litany of the Blessed Virgin and many made their first communion. The day passed in pious conversation. He baptized the children, and after distributing rosaries, medals, and scapulars, he departed for St. Ignatius' Mission.

Here Father Grassi, an Italian, had replaced Father Hoecken. He had collected the material for a hospital and a boarding-school, but Sisters were needed to carry these on. Father De Smet appealed to the Sisters of Providence of Montreal, and they responded promptly and eagerly. Before the year was out they were installed and ready to receive pupils and care for the sick.

St. Mary's Mission, the first mountain foundation, had been closed in 1850. The Flatheads had made several appeals for a Black Robe, but the Fathers could not then be spared. Three years later the cherished "reduction" was opened by Fathers Giorda and Ravalli, and again the fervor of former days revived in that fertile valley.

At Colville, Father Joset had succeeded in establishing the St. Paul Mission. From there the missionary visited the neighboring Columbian tribes. "Although the abuse of whiskey has demoralized the Indians, through God's mercy a large number of the faithful have escaped corruption, and show the same desire to hear the word of life and approach the Sacraments." [7]

But of all the tribes, the Cœur d'Alènes was the most satisfactory. Nothing had interrupted the peace concluded in 1859 with the Americans, and Fathers Gazzoli and Caruana, successors to Father Joset, marveled to see a people, formerly the most ferocious of the Western tribes, become the models of the new center of Christianity. Absolute confidence in the missionaries, great purity of morals, a spirit of penitence worthy of the cloister, and tender devotion to the Mother of God, such were the virtues of the new converts. [8]

[7] Cited by Father De Smet, Selected Letters, 3d Series, p. 173.

[8] "The Cœur d'Alènes fast nearly every Saturday in honor of the Blessed Virgin, a fast more rigorous than ours, for it is not broken till sunset. To prepare themselves to celebrate worthily the feast, some wear belts of thorns, others flay themselves with briers, and others again retire to the forest in

Both the Sacred Heart and St. Ignatius' Missions possessed churches that were the admiration of all newcomers. In the neighborhood of the principal stations many chapels were built, the greater number, however, being devoid of everything required by the rubrics of the Church. Father De Smet arrived one day from St. Louis with vestments and sacred vessels. As he opened his treasures the missionaries compared him to good St. Nicholas. He even gave Father Grassi his little traveling chapel. "His joy," he says, "made me forget the privation this gift imposed upon me."

This was Father De Smet's last visit to the Oregon Missions. Although the condition of the missions was most satisfactory, he could not put away a presentiment of coming disaster. Every day the invasion of the white man penetrated further; cargoes of whiskey arrived in many places, and the Indians fell victims to the fury and immorality of the pioneer Americans.[9] It seemed certain that the lands cultivated by the missionaries would be seized by the invaders and the Christians exterminated or driven into the arid mountain defiles. The most tolerant of the Government agents says in his report, "The red man must disappear before the approach of the white man. The question is, how can this be accomplished with the least suffering to the Indians and the minimum of expense to ourselves."[10] The missionary was destined to suffer untold sorrow in this sad perspective. The work of his life seemed doomed to destruction; whatever became of the Indians, they remained ever "the children of his heart." His heroic devotion to them to the very end proved what price he attached to their souls.

order to observe complete silence. There they pray and work, only returning to camp for the prayers said in common. Everything is referred to the missionaries, who are obliged to restrain, rather than excite their zeal. A chief of a neighboring tribe witnessed the charity that animates these Christians and wished to remain, saying, 'This mission is a paradise.'" (Letter from Father Grassi, *Catholic Missions*, 1870, p. 251.)

[9] "One must see this to believe it," writes Father De Smet.—"Were it not for the desire to save souls, we would flee the camp." (Letter from Father Vercruysse to Father Broeckaert, St. Ignatius' Mission, June 12, 1862.)

[10] Captain Mullan's report. Cf. Father De Smet, Selected Letters, 3d Series, p. 169.

With the approach of autumn, Father De Smet turned his steps homeward. After visiting Bishop Blanchet, the first apostle in that country, and the Sisters of Notre Dame, established in several cities in Oregon and California, he embarked at San Francisco on November 3d.

For many long months the Jesuits in St. Louis had been without news of the missionary. They had heard only of his enforced landing at Milk River, but not of his arrival at Fort Benton. Could he with his companions have fallen under the hatchets of the Sioux? "What increases our anxiety," writes Father Arnould from Belgium, "is that the provisions he had with him might have excited the cupidity of the Indians. Moreover, the crucifix by which the Indians recognized him, which he always wore on his breast, had by mistake been left in St. Louis." [11]

When winter came and he did not return, all hope was abandoned and the *suffrages* were said for the repose of his soul.[12] One can imagine the astonishment of the community when, on December 17th, he suddenly appeared at the University. In eight months he had traveled 11,400 miles without suffering injury from the bands of secessionists or from the Indians in revolt against the whites.

Such a journey had entailed excessive fatigue, and the traveler returned to St. Louis broken in health, tortured with neuralgia, and crippled with rheumatism. Three months later he writes: "It is only on rare occasions that I am able to leave my room or the house. My greatest privation is my inability to say Mass. Since my ordination in 1827 this is the first time that illness has deprived me of this happiness." [13]

In the solitude of his cell he looked back upon the past, and thought of the friends who were gone. How many new-made graves! After only seven years of the episcopate Bishop Van de Velde of Natchez was gone to his reward;

[11] Letter to Father Van der Hofstadt, Sept. 1, 1863. Father De Smet's crucifix is to-day the property of his nephew, Paul De Smet.

[12] Suffrages in the Society of Jesus are the prayers and Masses offered by each member for the deceased members.

[13] To Gustave Van Kerckhove, March 15, 1864.

Father Smedts, a fellow-companion of 1821 and for years Master of Novices at Florissant; Father Bax, the apostle of the Osages, fallen a victim of his charity at thirty-three years of age; Father Duerinck, engulfed in the waters of the Missouri, while en route to St. Louis to make his last vows;[14] Father De Vos, a Belgian friend, and the heroic Father Nobili, both dying just after founding the California Mission. One after the other these valiant souls seemed to pass before the missionary, calling him to eternal repose. "Insensibly," he writes, "life seems to ebb away. I am now in my sixty-fourth year, and I have an inward conviction that my end is near. *Fiat voluntas Dei.*"[15]

To his ardent nature, death was preferable to inactivity: "After enjoying robust health for so many years, and after so many years of travel, I find the change hard to bear. But we are in God's hands. With patience, which I pray for, and aided by His grace, I hope to be able to resign myself to His will."[16]

After prayer, family letters were his greatest consolation. "I hope," he writes his brother, "that your letters and those of your children will come regularly to cheer me. I have need of consolation, and this you will not refuse me after the many marks of kindness that you have shown me for forty-four years. Our correspondence must continue to the very end."[17]

However, his health seemed to slowly return, and the old missionary took up active life again. "Though my legs are unsteady, my heart is still strong."[18] To while away the weary hours, he wrote long accounts of his journeys to the Father General and to his Belgian friends. As soon as he was able to get about, he began to prepare a three-thousand-dollar shipment for Oregon. But God called him to another scene of action. The Sioux, the tribe which he had dreamed of evangelizing for twenty years, and which had declared an implacable war against the whites, were to henceforth absorb his untiring efforts and bring him his greatest triumphs.

[14] Father Duerinck, born at St. Gilles-lez-Termonde, was Father De Smet's cousin. He was learned in the natural sciences, and refused a chair in the University of Cincinnati.   [15] To his brother, Feb. 26, 1864.
[16] To his brother, March 10, 1864.   [17] March 10, 1864.
[18] "When the legs creak, the heart is good." (Flemish proverb.)

CHAPTER XXI

THE REVOLT OF THE SIOUX—FATHER DE SMET'S JOURNEY OF PACIFICATION (1864)

Initial Troubles between the Whites and the Indians—War against the Redskins—Discovery of Gold Mines Long Known to Father De Smet—The Reservations—One Hundred Thousand Indians Disappear within Ten Years—The Uprising of the Sioux Tribes—The Minnesota Massacre—Generals Sibley and Sully Are Sent to Subdue the Rebels—Father De Smet's Journey—He Goes up the Missouri as Far as Fort Berthold—The Grosventres, Aricaras, and Mandans—Conference with the Sioux—They Accept Terms of Peace—General Sully's Mistake—Father De Smet Returns to St. Louis.

THE difficulties between the whites and the Indians dated back to the seventeenth century, when the English landed in America. Had all the colonists been as humane in their treatment of the Indians as Lord Baltimore and William Penn, friendly relations could easily have been maintained. More often, alas! the white man's injustice and cruelty made it evident to the Indian that he coveted his land, but desired no alliance with him.[1]

At the close of the eighteenth century the colonies threw off England's yoke, but continued to carry on a relentless war against the "red man." The white man's policy of exploiting the Indian's lands gradually drove him westward, and, finally, almost exterminated the original possessors of the soil.

---

[1] "When you first set foot on our lands," said an Iroquois sachem to some officials of New York, "you were destitute of food. We gave you our beans and wheat, and fed you with our fish: to-day you repay us by cutting our throats. The merchants your ships landed on our shores we loved as the apple of our eyes, and gave them our daughters as wives. Among the Indians you have massacred are children of your own blood." (Bancroft's "History of the United States," Vol. II, p. 564.)

"From that time the destruction of the Indians seems to have been such a fixed policy, that in some parts of the country, notably in Virginia, the law forbade making peace with them." (*Ibid.*, Vol. I, p. 204.)

The trappers and fur-trading companies [2] in their yearly journeys up the Missouri hunted the buffalo so relentlessly that it finally became extinct. The prairies became a desert, and the Indians' means of subsistence were destroyed.[3]

But killing their game was not enough: the Americans seized their lands. Behind the pioneers, the advance-guard, pressed the emigrant hordes, that not only populated the Atlantic coast, but, crossing the Alleghanies, overran the Mississippi valley, everywhere building cities, laying out farms, and starting manufactories. Before them, the Indians must either retire or perish.

In 1830 began a legal spoliation, when the Government drove the redskins across the Missouri. In 1854 a new seizure of land took place. A ridiculous treaty made between the tribes and the Government divided into three parts all the land situated west of the Missouri and extending to the foot of the Rocky Mountains. The two best tracts were taken by the Government, and formed the territories of Kansas and Nebraska; the land to the south remained in the possession of the Indians. In one year alone fifty thousand whites rushed to the new land grants, and terrible disorders disgraced the beginnings of the colonization.

We remember the emigrant invasion of California. In 1862 the discovery of gold in Idaho produced the same horrors and disorders in the Kootenais country, which the missionaries had evangelized.[4] One man had known for twenty years of the gold buried in the mountains, and that man was Father De Smet.[5] He could have become

[2] The principal ones were the Hudson Bay Company of Montreal, the American Fur Company, and the Rocky Mountain Fur Company, both of St. Louis.

[3] As early as 1846 Father De Smet predicted the day when the last buffalo would be contended for by the last survivors of these unhappy tribes. ("The Oregon Missions," p. 253.)

[4] "The treasures hidden in the heart of the mountains attract thousands of miners from every country. With them come blackguards, gamblers, drunkards, thieves, and assassins, the scum of society. Lately thirteen of these malefactors have been hung, and seventy-two others are condemned to the same end." (Letter to Charles De Smet, St. Louis, Feb. 27, 1864.)

[5] "In 1840 I scaled a high mountain several days' journey from Sacramento. The bed of the torrent that descended the mountainside seemed to me covered with golden sand, and so thickly packed that I could scarcely believe

famous, and enriched his Society; but he preferred to delay the discovery of gold, fearing it would mean ruin to the missions. He locked the momentous secret in his breast [6] and also swore the Indians to secrecy, predicting to them that if they revealed it they would be dispossessed of their lands.

The manner in which the Indians were defrauded of their lands is well known. The whites often obtained entire counties for a song. The Osages ceded twenty-nine million acres for an annual payment of a thousand dollars, a sum which would barely suffice to pay for the drinks used when the transaction was made.

In exchange for what they lost, the natives more often received lessons in lying and immorality. In speaking of the Kickapoos, an English traveler says: "They are completely demoralized by living near civilization. The men are given over to drunkenness, the women to impurity, and both sexes of all ages are royal beggars, whose principal vocation is horse-stealing." [7]

These facts explain the language used by the famous Chief Black Hawk in addressing the American agents:

"Like serpents, the whites have crept into our midst and taken possession of our homes; the opossum and deer have fled at their approach. We are dying of hunger and want. Contact with them has poisoned us." [8]

---

my eyes. I passed on without further examination. To-day I am convinced it was the precious metal." (Letter to Charles De Smet, St. Louis, April 26, 1849.) On another occasion, Father De Smet learned from a reliable Indian, that on one summit in the Black Hills the interstices of the rocks were filled with golden sand. (Chittenden-Richardson, p. 1522.)

[6] "You ask me to tell you about the gold lands, and to send you a map of the district if I am at liberty to do so. You must understand, dear friend, why I have kept silence up to the present. These reasons still exist, and I cannot in conscience deviate from my former line of conduct." (To V. H. Campbell, Sacramento River, Feb. 4, 1863.) However, when Father De Smet saw that the white invasion was an accomplished fact, he consented to speak. (See his letter to Major-General Pleasonton, Aug. 22, 1865. Chittenden-Richardson, p. 1521-1523.) Afterward, the name De Smet was given to one of the richest mines in the Black Hills.

[7] Burton. Cited by Marshall in "Christian Missions," Vol. II, p. 441.

[8] Cited by Father De Smet, Selected Letters, 1st Series, p. 286.

"The Americans in general were not a party to this injustice. The Secretary of the Interior, McClellan, in his report for 1856 says: 'Our conduct with regard to the destruction of a people which Providence has placed under our protection, is unworthy of our civilization, and outrages.

It is true that the Government from time to time sent commissioners to the West to pacify the country. These men, however, were less zealous in repressing the excesses of the whites, than in sanctioning, by treaties, the usur-

every feeling of humanity.'" (Quoted by Father De Smet, Selected Letters, 2d Series, p. 347.)

"Our nation must bear a heavier guilt than others. Its conduct with regard to the Indian is shameful. Every imaginable crime has been committed against them: unrelenting persecution, broken treaties, and confiscation of lands." (Rev. H. W. Beecher, in the *New York Evening Express*, Jan. 5, 1861.)

See also Helen Hunt Jackson, "A Century of Dishonor," p. 167; the protest of Bishop H. B. Whipple, Protestant Bishop of Minnesota; and, especially, the report of the commission appointed by President Grant to investigate the condition of the Indian tribes, p. 339.

Notwithstanding, many men of high intelligence furthered the destruction of the Indian race. "The red race has disappeared from the shores of the Atlantic; the tribes which resisted civilization have been destroyed. For my part, I cannot deplore what seems the result of a divine law. Nor can I regret that the wigwam has been replaced by the Capitol, the savages by Christians, the red squaw given way to the white woman, nor that such men as Washington, Franklin, and Jefferson have supplanted Powhatan, Opechanecanough, and other redskins, respectable, high-class Indians though they may have been. A people that finds itself in the white man's path has no other alternative than to become civilized or exterminated." (Quoted by G. Kurth, "Sitting Bull," Brussels, 1879, p. 7.)

"To civilize the Indians was the duty of the Americans, for in no other way could they justify the usurpation of their territory. If the tribes living almost exclusively upon the chase occupied a vast territory not commensurate with the number of inhabitants, if their right to hold lands whose richness they could not exploit could be contested: then the whites who seized these lands in order to develop them, were bound in justice to recompense the Indians, to instruct them, and to initiate them into agriculture and trade. It does not seem that the Yankees gave much thought to ameliorating the condition of those they dispossessed. They declared at the outset that the Indians resisted civilization, and coined the odious phrase, 'the only good Indian is a dead Indian.' Unquestionably, the Indians were idle, unreliable, vindictive, and cruel, and more given to imitating the white man's vices than his industry. Nevertheless, they were not inferior to the Hurons of Canada, nor the Guaranis of South America, and if the former became industrious farmers and the latter made the golden age of Christianity blossom again on the shores of the Paraná, what could not a great nation have accomplished under conditions infinitely more favorable than those in which the ancient civilizers found themselves?"

The results obtained by the missionaries in Kansas and Oregon show what the tribes in the United States were capable of. Only time was needed. "Imagine," writes Father De Smet, "two races brought into contact, the one keeping its barbarous habits, the other enjoying all the advantages of civilization. How many years must elapse before there is complete fusion between the two? Neither the second nor the third generation will witness that happy result." (To Madam Parmentier, St. Louis, Feb. 24, 1858.)

pations committed against the natives. Tracts of land called "reservations" were given exclusively to the Indians. An agent was stationed among them to keep peace, to punish the whites who injured the Indians, and to inform the Government at Washington of any untoward happenings. More often than not, the agent betrayed the confidence of the chief. His position being political, was obtained through favor, and held only so long as his party was in power. He also retained a large part of the indemnities paid the Indians.[9]

When the scandal became too open, and protests were made, the Government was forced to take action and the agent was asked to resign. But he departed with a well-filled purse and the assurance that he would not be prosecuted.

The Indians on the reservations were destined not to enjoy for very long their restricted domains, for valuable mines discovered on what was thought to be waste land attracted hordes of fortune-seekers to the country. The Indians resisted the invaders and exchanged shots. Then the Federal troops intervened, new treaties were imposed on the tribe, and again they were forced to retire to a new reservation, often far distant, and destined in turn to become the ground of similar disputes.[10]

He concludes it would be a fatal mistake to at once force learning and agriculture upon the Indian; he must first be made to recognize their benefits.

"But Americans do not know how to wait. The Indian cannot civilize himself. They have used him to further their own ends, and when he has rebelled, they have massacred him. 'The tyranny of the United States,' says an eminent economist, 'has rendered the Indian more lawless and less civilized than he was in his primitive condition. The physical and moral condition of these peoples has steadily declined, and they have become more savage as they have become more wretched.'" (De Tocqueville, "De la Démocratie en Amérique," Paris, 1840, Vol. II, p. 266.)

[9] In his vicinity, the Indians were often reduced to misery and poverty. "List shoes with paper soles and tin spades were distributed to them; they were fed on soups made of diseased animals. Squaws picked half-digested grain out of the cavalry horses' manure, and gave it to their children to keep them from dying of hunger." (Bishop Whipple of Minnesota, quoted by G. Kurth, "Sitting Bull," p. 152.)

[10] "The Creeks were forced twelve times to change their place of abode, and the whole tribe was finally wiped out by General Jackson, afterward President of the United States." (Marshall, "Christian Missions," Vol. II, p. 440.)

"In 1862 the Winnebagoes, heretofore on friendly terms with the whites, were driven from their reservation in Minnesota to the banks of the Mis-

"A tree too often transplanted perishes," says an Indian proverb. If to the steady invasion of a territory are added the methods of destruction above indicated, it can be understood how in ten years, from 1850 to 1860, the number of Indians in the United States fell from 400,000 to 300,000—a loss exceeding any heretofore recorded.

Father De Smet was an eye-witness of the events which transpired during these sad years, and writes in 1862: "Heaven will mete out justice to a country that permits such atrocities." [11] Then alluding to the grave crisis through which the country was passing, he adds: "The civil war is in my opinion a punishment, and alas, little is being done to propitiate heaven." [12]

Another war was about to bring America into conflict with the victims of its spoliation. The Sioux, numbering between thirty and forty thousand, resolved to guard their independence, so retired farther and farther into the wilds, and there lived by hunting. Their different tribes occupied a vast quadrilateral, bounded on the north by Canada, on the west by the Rocky Mountains, and on the east by the Sioux and Red rivers. The Missouri with its tributaries flowed through this desolate region.

Repelled by the aspect of the Bad Lands, the colonists sought a more fertile soil in the Far West. The Government had agreed to erect a certain number of forts along the river-front to protect the fur trade, and to assure its relations with the Indians.[13]

souri, to a barren desert devoid of game, and unfit for habitation. Many died of hunger. In vain the Indians tried to flee, hiding in bushes on the islands, but soldiers stationed along the river-front barred the way and forcibly compelled them to return to their desolate reservation." (Selected Letters, 3d Series, p. 195. Helen Hunt Jackson, "A Century of Dishonor," pp. 229-236, 393-395.)

[11] To his brother Francis, St. Louis, April 16, 1862.

[12] To the Mother Superior of the Sisters of St. Mary, March 1, 1862.

[13] The smallest incident sufficed to provoke bloody conflicts. "The Indians, to the number of two thousand, had repaired to the appointed spot at the time fixed by the Government agent to receive their annuities and presents. They waited several days for the Commissioner to arrive, and in the meantime they ran out of provisions. ·Then a Mormon wagon-train, on its way to the Territory of Utah, came peaceably by the Indian camp. One of the party was dragging after him a lame cow hardly able to walk. A famished savage, out of pity for his wife and children, and perhaps, also,

The conference held at Fort Laramie in 1851 had guaranteed to the Sioux tribes the undisturbed possession of their territory, on the condition that the highways should be left open and that forts should be built there. The United States agreed to pay the Indians an annuity of $50,000 for fifty years; but the Senate, without consulting the Indians, changed the provisions of the treaty and limited the payments to fifteen years.[14]

The rapidly increasing white colonies in the West began to invade the virgin solitudes of the central districts. Agricultural land was seized, and other tracts were overrun by gold-seekers. Towns sprang up, roads were made, and

from compassion for the suffering animal, killed the cow and offered the Mormon double value for it in a horse or a mule.

"Such an act with such an offer under such circumstances passes as very honest, very fair, and very polite in a wild country. Still the Mormon refused the proffered exchange and went and filed a complaint with the commandant of Fort Laramie, which is in the neighborhood. Like the wolf who leaped upon the lamb to devour it, crying: 'I know very well that you all hate me, and you shall pay for the rest,' the illustrious commandant straightway sent out a young officer with twenty soldiers armed to the teeth and with a cannon loaded with grapeshot. He was absolutely determined to capture the so-called robber, and make an example of him. The savages were astonished at the menacing turn that the affair of the cow, so frivolously begun, had taken; they begged the officer to take one, two, three horses in exchange—a hundred times the value of the cow, if necessary. They wished, at any price, to 'bury' the affair, as they express it; that is to arrange it peaceably and quietly, but without giving up to him their brother, innocent according to their code. The officer was inflexible, refused all offers; he must absolutely have his prisoner; and when the latter did not appear, he fired his cannon into the midst of the savages. The head chief, whom I knew well, the noblest heart of his nation, fell mortally wounded, and a number of braves beside him. At this unexpected massacre the Indians sprang to arms and, letting fly hundreds of arrows from all sides, they instantly annihilated the aggressors and provocators. Will you in Europe believe this tale of a cow? And yet such is the origin of a fresh war of extermination upon the Indians which is to be carried out in the course of the present year." (Chittenden-Richardson, pp. 1218, 1219.)

The American reprisals outrivaled the Indian methods, for during the following summer an army of about four thousand men, commanded by General Harney, penetrated into the desert. Upon the River Platte they came upon the Indians, who, knowing themselves inferior in numbers, asked for peace. While the chiefs were in conference with the General, the whites surrounded the Indians, cut off their retreat, and gave the signal to massacre. Eighty Sioux, among them women and children, were killed. An officer announcing the victory wrote: "It was the most splendid sight I ever beheld." (Quoted by Father De Smet in a letter to Father Terwecoren, Oct. 5, 1855.)

[14] Helen Hunt Jackson, "A Century of Dishonor," p. 75.

the Pacific Railway spanned the continent. The region of the Upper Missouri became part of the Republic, and formed the Territories of Dakota, Wyoming, and Montana.

With rage in their hearts, the Sioux watched the steady advance of the colonists and from day to day their complaints became more bitter: "Neither the buffalo nor antelope can subsist upon land trodden by the white man. We must not wait until the pale-face has exterminated the game that feeds our families; let us defend the desert: it is our property and our life!"

When hostilities broke out between the North and South, the Indians judged the moment propitious for repelling the invasion. England supported their cause, and sent them arms through the half-breed Canadians living on the border.[15] War-hatchets were unearthed, the tomahawk brandished, and the eagle feathers were brought forth.[16] The Sioux thirsted for the white man's blood; upon the Minnesota border in three days [17] they slew nearly a thousand victims and destroyed property valued at two million dollars.

Forthwith the United States sent an army against them, commanded by General Sibley, which engaged in several skirmishes, dispelled the enemy, and made many prisoners. Thirty-eight Sioux were condemned to the gallows. A priest visited them in prison, and all but five asked for baptism. A few were sufficiently instructed to make their first communion on Christmas day. As he saw them calm, almost joyful in the presence of death, the missionary was unable to restrain his emotions: "It is thus," he said, "that Christians of a day meet death." [18]

Learning of the fate of the prisoners, Father De Smet wrote to Washington to ask to have them kept as hostages, for he hoped in this way to save the lives of the whites who were still in the power of the Sioux.[19] His petition was refused, and before long came news of fresh atrocities.

[15] Chittenden-Richardson, p. 80.
[16] The number of eagle feathers a savage wore on his head indicated the number of enemies he had slain.
[17] From the 18th to the 20th of August, 1862. (See Helen Hunt Jackson, "A Century of Dishonor," p. 163.)
[18] See Annals of the Propagation of the Faith, Vol. XXXV, p. 239, *et seq.*
[19] This letter is cited by Chittenden-Richardson, p. 1510.

The Indians succeeded in blocking navigation on the Missouri. When they saw a boat approaching, they hid in the woods or behind rocks, and showered arrows and bullets upon the crew.[20]

It was necessary to send a second army against the Sioux under General Sully, who marched up the valley of the Missouri to join forces with General Sibley. Both armies had several engagements with the enemy, but the Indians at each attack offered but slight resistance and then retired. They appeared to have submitted; in reality they had only dispersed.

The most scientific strategy failed against six thousand warriors who were determined not to give battle until they had the advantage in numbers and position. Their wives and children were safe far from the scene of hostilities; they had no towns, forts, or arsenals to defend; no line of retreat to cover, and they were not encumbered with either baggage or beasts of burden. Mounted on fiery horses, they unceasingly harassed the enemy's troops and always escaped pursuit. Although in sight, they were never overtaken.

The campaign of 1862–1863 had cost the United States more than twenty million dollars, and yet the end was not in sight. It added a heavy weight to the strain of the Civil War. It was proposed that Father De Smet be appealed to as a mediator. Five years before he had accomplished the pacification of Oregon, and it was believed that he alone could induce the Missouri tribes to lay down their arms.

On his return from the mountain missions Father De Smet passed through Washington. The Secretary of the Interior and the Commissioner of Indian Affairs took advantage of his presence to request him to go to the Sioux, and in the name of the United States make proposals for peace. He was to act in concert with the commander-in-chief of the troops and the various Government agents. Moreover, the expense of the journey and a large financial compensation were offered him by the Government.

[20] During Father De Smet's last journey to the mountains he had experienced one of their attacks.

The proposition was in no way to Father De Smet's liking. "I fear to lose forever my prestige with the Indians," he writes. "Should I present myself to them as the representative of the 'Chief of the Big Knives' at Washington,[21] no longer their 'Great Father,' but now their mortal enemy, it would place me in rather an awkward situation. I have written to the Commissioner to say that if I undertake the mission, I will go on my own hook and without any remuneration. I will first visit the Sioux who have remained friends of the whites, and then, in their company, will try to reach their brothers in revolt. I will do my utmost to induce them to make peace and bring about an understanding between them and the General in command and the Government agents."[22]

The Government recognized the wisdom of Father De Smet's plan, accepted his terms, and the missionary began his preparations to depart. His Superior feared he was sending him to certain death, seeing him set out alone and unarmed to encounter the enraged tribes, drunk with carnage. But Father De Smet, although alive to the dangers of the enterprise, tranquilly wrote: "One thing reassures me: I go under obedience."[23]

Father De Smet took passage on a steamboat leaving for the Upper Missouri on April 20, 1864. The captain, Mr. Charles Chouteau, offered his former teacher the cabin de luxe, in which an altar had been prepared where he might daily celebrate Mass. The water was low and sand-bars numerous, so that after eight days they had advanced only a few miles. To pass the time, Father De Smet continued his study of the Missouri, "his river," he called it. "I observe the country, jog my memory, and consult well-informed travelers. Then I write."[24] He wrote to acquaint his friends in Europe with the varied and grand scenery of the river and the topography, fauna, and flora of this unexplored country.[25] In reading these pages one is reminded of the account written two centuries

[21] The Indians' name for the President of the United States, who was then Abraham Lincoln.
[22] Letter to Father Murphy, St. Louis, March 30, 1864.
[23] Letter to Father Terwecoren, St. Louis, April 16, 1864.
[24] Selected Letters, 3d Series, p. 189.
[25] Ibid., pp. 209–246.

before by another Jesuit, Father Marquette, when he first visited the Mississippi valley.[26]

Our missionary took advantage of these enforced stops to explore the surrounding forests and prairies, where he encountered many Indians he had baptized and who remembered him. They now begged him to marry them and baptize their children. Sometimes he came across a Canadian Catholic, whose instruction had been most superficial, to judge from the following: "I tried to give some much-needed advice to one of these men, and urged him always to be ready for God's call, saying it might come like a thief in the night, when least expected. What an irreparable misfortune it would be to appear unprepared before his Judge! Evidently my Canadian friend had understood nothing of my little sermon, as he was thinking only of encounters with the Sioux.

"'Father,' he replied, 'it is as you say; they come upon us unawares, riddling our bodies with bullets and with arrows. As for me, I am not at all prepared, for I am poor, and without means of defence. But now I shall have a better chance, for I have sold my wood to the boat and I can buy powder and lead. Let the devilish Sioux come: they will find me ready for them.'"[27]

The Sioux, as a matter of fact, continued to terrorize the country. On May 10th the news came that three thousand were armed and lying in wait to stop every steamboat they surprised on the river, and that they possessed two cannons, many guns, and an abundance of powder and bullets. "In a few days," writes Father De Smet, "we shall be able to judge of the truth of this information. I placed myself in God's hands, and under the protection of the holy Virgin, our good Mother. I came here under obedience, to carry words of peace. Of a truth the time is critical; but if God is with us, who can be against us?"[28]

Nor was his confidence betrayed. The steamboat advanced unimpeded, save for the sand-bars which several

---

[26] J. G. Shea, "Discovery and Exploration of the Mississippi Valley." New York, 1852; pp. 231–257. Alfred Hamy, "Au Mississippi. La Première exploration" (1673), Paris, 1903; pp. 222–255.

[27] Selected Letters, 3d Series, p. 200. [28] *Ibid.*, p. 198.

times obliged them to stop near the forts, in order to land
a portion of the cargo. At last, on June 9th, they reached
Fort Berthold, near the mouth of the Little Missouri.
Not far away there were living together in a single village,
the Grosventres, the Aricaras, and the Mandans. These
three nations had not entered into the revolt against the
whites, so Father De Smet decided to remain with them,
and await an opportunity of getting into relations with the
Sioux. On landing he sent a messenger to the chiefs,
announcing the object of his visit, and inviting them to a
conference, and while awaiting their arrival he preached
the word of God to the friendly tribes. A providential
event contributed largely to enhance the value of the
religion he taught.

The preceding year a long drought had destroyed the
crops. Not discouraged, the Indians had put under
cultivation a thousand acres of land with no implements
save hoes, broken spades, crooked sticks, and the shoulder-
blades of buffaloes. But again this year, a dry spring
threatened ruin to the crop. The distressed Indians had
recourse to Father De Smet. "'Black Robe,' they said,
'you who have such power, can you not also make a little
rain come?' I answered them that I had not that power,
that the Great Spirit alone is omnipotent. 'Let us implore Him together and offer him our hearts. I will say
the greatest of prayers [the Mass]!' The next day the
clouds gathered and rain fell for twenty-four hours. A
few days later, after renewed prayers, a heavier shower
followed, the fields became green, the grain formed in the
ears, and everything portended a rich harvest. These
favors from on high made a deep impression on the
Indians." They followed assiduously the missionary's instructions. Mothers brought their children by hundreds
to be baptized; the chiefs themselves undertook to erad-
icate vice and do away with superstition.

In the meantime the news of the great Black Robe's
arrival had reached the Sioux, and on July 8th they
encamped about three hundred strong on the opposite
side of the Missouri. Their presence terrified the whites
who were defending the fort. But Father De Smet went
out alone to meet them, crossed the river in a boat, and

was received with lively demonstrations of friendship. The warriors declared they had come for the express purpose of an interview with him. The conference lasted three hours. The chief seemed inclined to make peace and received favorably the proposals of the United States.

Two days later came a message from the Santees, a powerful tribe living on the Canadian border. This tribe had been the prime movers in the Minnesota massacre. They now wished strongly to see the Black Robe and learn from him the Government's communications. Father De Smet wished to go to them at once in the hope of inducing them to disarm, but he could not act without consulting General Sully, who, unfortunately, was burning to measure his strength with the Indians. He declared that this tribe should be punished before there could be question of peace. Such an attitude rendered Father De Smet's mission impossible, and rather than compromise his rôle of peacemaker with the Indians, he decided to return to St. Louis and communicate with the Government. Did Washington recognize Sully's mistake? The General was to learn that the words of a Jesuit were more powerful than armed force. A few months later he asked the Black Robe to intervene.

Although Father De Smet's official mission had failed, spiritually he had achieved a great success. Eight hundred baptisms, many marriage ceremonies, the Gospel preached to three or four nations, and a prospect of founding "reductions" upon the Upper Missouri—such were the fruits of his four months' journey.

CHAPTER XXII

A Bad Crossing—Father De Smet Assists in Rome at the Beatification
of Blessed Peter Canisius—Charles Rogier Manifests His Regard for
Father De Smet—He is Made a Knight of the Order of Leopold—Farewell to Belgium—Father De Smet Declines a Third Time the Honor
of the Episcopate—He Goes Up the Missouri as Far as Fort Benton
—He Confers Baptism on Hundreds of Children—The Yanktons—
Pananniapapi.

FATHER DE SMET had foreseen that he would soon
have to return to the Sioux, and was preparing to do
so, when an order came from the Provincial in October,
1864, to leave for Europe. Men were needed for both the
colleges and missions; moreover, the Civil War had
exhausted their resources, and another appeal must be
made to Belgium.

The missionary was happy at the thought of again seeing
his family. To them he writes, "This good news, I hope,
will be as agreeable to you as it is to me. Often in my
poor prayers, and when far off in the desert, I have asked
this favor of heaven." [1]

His crossing was stormy, and from that time dates the
malady which was to become fatal.[2] For weeks he suffered from insomnia, constant fever, and frequent hemorrhages. His suffering condition did not, however, prevent
him from starting for Rome as soon as he landed. The
Father General received him with cordiality and invited
him to attend the beatification of Blessed Peter Canisius
during November.

He tells us he suffered intensely from seasickness during
the journey from Marseilles to Civita Vecchia. "You

[1] To his brother Francis, St. Louis, Oct. 9, 1864.
[2] Bright's disease.

may not believe it, but the rolling and pitching of the ship acted as a remedy. Headache, blood-spitting, lack of appetite, etc., disappeared upon my arrival in Rome. The next day the fever was so slight that I was able to be present at the beatification of our illustrious saint. I shall never forget that ceremony, and I thank God for permitting me to witness it. The Holy Father declared in our presence that this beatification was the most glorious and the nearest to his heart of all those that had taken place during his pontificate.

"I have spoken to you about my fever, and now I will tell you how I got rid of it. I climbed to the dome of St. Peter's. The remedy, though most fatiguing, was salutary, and since then my pulse has not been so rapid." [3] The invalid possessed, undoubtedly, a robust constitution, but the preceding lines seem to have been written with the object of reassuring his friends.

Before leaving Rome he visited the celebrated basilicas and the places consecrated by the blood of the martyrs, and on the feast of St. Cecilia he descended into the catacombs. Several times he was received in audience by the Pope, who showed great affection for him and bestowed many favors on his missions. During his stay in Belgium he gave only a few days to his family, and set out in the depth of winter upon his arduous begging tour. Several times he was forced by illness to interrupt his travels—nevertheless he canvassed Holland, Luxemburg, England, Ireland, and his native country. The sight of this old missionary who had come from such a distance to ask for help, created a profound impression. Contributions flowed in, and many young men answered the call to the apostolate.

Such self-sacrificing devotion commanded the respect of even unbelievers. Charles Rogier, one of the ministers of Leopold I, and anything but clerical in his feelings and opinions, expressed great esteem for Father De Smet. He invited the missionary to his table and lent a willing ear to his discourses upon religion; he marveled that a man could travel such distances and suffer such fatigue and privation for what he called the salvation of souls. "If

[3] To his nephew Charles, Rome, Nov., 1864.

you should hear some day that I was on my death-bed
and that I had asked for you, would you cross the ocean
for that?" "I would not hesitate an instant," replied the
Jesuit; upon which Rogier threw himself upon the missionary's neck and embraced him before the assembled
guests. Several years later when the statesman felt his
end approaching, he called for a Jesuit [4] and was reconciled
with God. He, moreover, honored himself in making
Father De Smet a Knight of the Order of Leopold,[5] a distinction which the missionary received with his usual
modesty. At his family's insistence he consented to have
his portrait painted, wearing the distinguished decoration,
and after that nothing more was heard of it. To the last
he wore no other cross save that of the missionary, the
cross that had redeemed the world, and to which he owed
his best achievements.

The time for departure was drawing near. His labors
had borne abundant fruit. Besides great financial assistance and other gifts,[6] he had gained twelve new missionaries for America, of whom five were Belgians, four
Dutch, and three Irish. Four Sisters of Notre Dame de
Namur also accompanied him to the New World. Before
sailing he wrote the following lines: "Here I am once again
leaving my country, my family, friends, benefactors, and
brothers in religion. A fond farewell to all, perhaps forever, until the last meeting in heaven. This separation—
and why should I not admit it?—is for me a painful sacrifice;
but I hope to continue to work for God's glory and the
salvation of souls. It is a supernatural love that draws
me from Belgium and all that I love there. When I am
not with my dear Indians, I feel as if something was lacking,
and, despite the kind reception that I receive everywhere,
there is a void within me, until I get back to my beloved
Rocky Mountains. Only then am I satisfied and happy.
Hæc requies mea. I have spent the best part of my life
among the Indians and to them I wish to consecrate my
few remaining years; in their midst I wish to die." [7]

---

[4] Father Delcourt.
[5] The royal order was dated June 18, 1865.
[6] These gifts he owed to the generosity of the Dames de l'Œuvre des
Églises pauvres of Brussels.
[7] To the editor of *Précis Historiques*, Ostend, June 2, 1865.

Upon his return to America the missionary's name was again mentioned for episcopal honors. The Catholics were becoming so numerous in the West that the Archbishop of St. Louis asked the Sovereign Pontiff to create an apostolic vicariate in Montana, and, desiring that the incumbent be a Jesuit, proposed Father De Smet. The latter immediately wrote a letter to the Father General, which reveals his profound humility: "If, as the Reverend Father Provincial assures me, my name figures among those sent by Archbishop Kenrick, it is only, I imagine, to complete the list, which usually comprises three names. In the sincere belief that I possess neither the virtues nor ability that such an office demands, and not doubting that your Paternity will be consulted in regard to an affair of such importance, I am not uneasy. My sole desire is to live and die faithful to my vocation and to the obedience I owe my Superiors, and from this determination, thanks be to God, nothing can move me." [8]

Providence granted his wish, and Father De Smet was spared the burden he had feared would be imposed upon him. His mind now at ease, his great preoccupation was the distribution of the money and goods he had brought back from Europe.

On April 9, 1866, he left St. Louis to go by boat to Fort Benton, the post nearest to the mountain missions. This meant a journey of more than three thousand miles, through a country at war with the whites. But with his usual confidence and faith, he placed himself under the protection of the Blessed Virgin, and asked that a lamp should be kept burning day and night before her picture until he returned.

The spring thaw had brought about a sudden rise in the river: enormous blocks of ice crushed steamboats, trees were uprooted, and houses carried away. To breast the current, the captain had recourse to a windlass, but the cable broke and the boat swept along in the eddies until she crashed against a rock. She began to leak badly, but the deck-hands repaired the damage and the boat continued on her way.

As they were about to enter the Sioux country a cannon

[8] St. Louis, March, 1866.

was placed in the prow of the boat, pistols and guns were made ready, and every night sentinels stood guard—a needless precaution, as the enemy gave no sign of life. "Our arms," writes Father De Smet, "have been used only to kill game, which is served on our already abundant table." [9]

It was evident that Providence was caring for the travelers. "We have passed thirteen boats that started from ten to fifteen days ahead of us. We have been carried as on the wings of angels." [10] And yet our missionary's life was not wholly satisfactory. Far from his brothers in religion, and with little in common with the mercantile interests of the boat's passengers, he felt lonely, and often repeated the words of the Psalmist, "How good and how pleasant it is for brethren to dwell together in unity." [11]

He used his leisure to reread St. Francis Xavier's letters, his model in the apostolate. "This book fills my heart with consolation: two passages especially have touched me: 'Among other intercessions, I have recourse to the children I have baptized and whom God, in His infinite mercy, called to Himself before they had stained their baptismal robe. They number over a thousand, and I invoke them to obtain for me the grace to accomplish God's will in the way He wills it, upon this earth of exile and misery.' 'You can imagine what my life must be here, not understanding what is said to me, and unable to make myself understood. Yet I baptize new-born children, for which ceremony I need no interpreter, nor do I need one in my ministrations to the poor, who can make me understand their sufferings and misery.'" [12]

It is not surprising that Father De Smet should share the sentiments of this illustrious apostle, for his own life was a continual service of charity and devotion. Even upon the boat he found an opportunity to bring souls to God. He baptized a Protestant, and prepared several passengers to make their entrance into the Church. The Catholics attended Mass and received communion every Sunday.

[9] Selected Letters, 3d Series, p. 356.   [10] Ibid., p. 354.
[11] Psalms cxxxii, 1.
[12] Selected Letters, 3d Series, p. 400.

But the Indians were ever his special care. Now more than ever were they deserving of pity. In many places the whites had left them but barren lands, where even wild beasts could not exist. The annuities were not paid regularly, and the agents sometimes retained a part of them, or substituted barrels of whiskey or useless goods in place of the money. The winter was long and severe, and many families died of hunger; others, after they had killed their horses and dogs, lived on wild roots, and were happy when they could pick up the refuse from the soldiers' kitchen at Fort Sully, or rats that had been thrown over the stockade.[13]

Father De Smet relieved this misery as much as lay in his power. He spoke to them of the Great Spirit, of the future life and of the joys reserved for those who have shunned lies and injustice. He baptized nearly five hundred children, the greater number of whom he was persuaded would die before attaining the age of reason. "The regeneration of these poor little ones is for me a subject for rejoicing. I have a deep conviction that baptism has opened heaven to numberless souls whom I have had the happiness of meeting in my long sojourns among the Indian tribes."[14]

At last on June 7th, after a two months' journey, he arrived at Fort Benton, where, alas! he did not find his fellow-missionaries of St. Peter's Mission: the war between the whites and the Blackfeet had forced the Fathers to retire, for a time at least, to St. Ignatius' Mission. The church ornaments and sacred vessels which he had brought for the missions, he left for safe keeping with the officers at the Fort, and then returned to St. Louis.

This was Father De Smet's last journey up the Missouri to the Rocky Mountains. He was destined never again to see the Oregon tribes, nor the heroic missionaries who shared his first labors. His work there was firmly established; henceforth he would be able to labor for the other tribes.

In descending the river, he stopped several days with the

[13] Cf. Helen Hunt Jackson, "A Century of Dishonor," p. 166.
[14] Selected Letters, 3d Series, p. 401.

Yanktons, who were encamped near the mouth of the James River. Chief Pananniapapi, "the man that Strikes the Ree," was one of the noblest types of men of his race. He had met Father De Smet for the first time in 1844 and had attended his instructions, receiving from him the miraculous medal. From that time he had added the practice of admirable virtues to his invincible courage, and he professed toward the Blessed Virgin a touching piety. During the cholera epidemic he exposed his miraculous medal in the camp, and, following his example, the Yanktons, three thousand in number, assembled to venerate it. The same day the plague disappeared.

Time and again the Methodists who endeavored to penetrate to the tribe were kept at a distance by the chief, who said to them: "You wish to enrich your wives and children at our expense. The Black Robe has neither wife nor child; his heart is not divided; he lives only for God and the happiness of the people who surround his cabin." And the old man remained obdurate.

For twenty-two years he had looked forward to the day when he should receive baptism. The hour of grace had now struck. Father De Smet completed his instruction and received him into the Church. Once a Christian, Pananniapapi's only thought was to procure the same happiness for his people.

Thus the great missionary, in the twilight of his years, realized his life's dream, the evangelization of the Missouri tribes. A rich harvest was promised; not a single Indian refused to hear the word of God, not a wigwam remained closed. The Grosventres, Aricaras, and Mandans asked repeatedly for a Black Robe. The Yanktons offered to contribute two or three thousand dollars yearly to the support of the missions.

General Sully himself now asked for a missionary,[15] as he foresaw that the Sioux could only be conquered through the Gospel.

[15] Cf. Chittenden-Richardson, p. 1279.

CHAPTER XXIII

SECOND JOURNEY OF PACIFICATION (1867)

Age of Infirmities—The Whites Continue to Harass the Indians—The Massacre of Six Hundred Cheyennes—The Insurrection Spreads—Father De Smet is Sent upon a New Mission—A Journey through Iowa—"Major De Smet"—Generals Sully and Parker Join the Missionary—Conference with the Indians on the Borders of the Missouri—Iron Shield's Discourse—Father De Smet Pacifies the Tribes—Father De Smet Wishes to Meet the Tribes of the Interior—Fatigue Compels Him to Return to St. Louis.

FATHER DE SMET returned to St. Louis at the beginning of August. A torrid summer had followed a rigorous winter; the thermometer stood at 100° in the shade, and cholera was raging. The sudden change from pure, high mountain air to the stagnant air of a pest-ridden city seriously affected his health. For several months he suffered from overpowering fatigue, excruciating rheumatic pains, and, even worse, deafness threatened him.

Autumn, however, brought him some measure of relief. With his customary cheerfulness, he writes to one of his nephews: "My health, thank God, is fairly good now. I seldom consult a doctor or take medicine. For three months two little bottles, delicate attentions from the druggist, have been standing on my chimneypiece. Until now I have only looked at them, but I have taken the precaution to see that they do not evaporate, for they may be useful some day. I will soon enter upon my sixty-seventh year, an age when man's garments cover a multitude of infirmities. Yet I shall end by believing that I carry my years lightly, for every one tells me so, and people laugh when I say my end is drawing near." [1]

In the meantime the war against the tribes in revolt was still going on, and while Father De Smet, at the price of

[1] To Paul De Smet, Nov. 26, 1866.

unspeakable fatigue, labored to bring about peace, the Americans seemed to take pleasure in thwarting his efforts. Soldiers and colonists alike unceasingly exasperated the Indians.[2]

In November, 1864, an act of revolting barbarism had taken place in Colorado.   Six hundred Cheyennes, after refusing to join the warring tribes, sought refuge near Fort Lyon and begged protection of the whites.   Soon, however, Colonel Chivington, a former Methodist minister, arrived at the head of a thousand men to give chase to the Indians, and, despite their friendly assurances, the Cheyennes were massacred.   Not content with taking life, they subjected their victims to unspeakable outrages.   One lieutenant killed three women and five children with his own hands, and took savage pleasure in scalping them.[3]

When the news reached Washington, Congress demanded an investigation.   Numerous reports were submitted, then the affair was pigeonholed.   Justice was not meted out to the offenders; on the contrary, certain men were heard to applaud this odious butchery.   General Carleton, chief of a brigade in New Mexico, a cynical and cruel man, endeavored, through absurd theories, to justify his conduct

[2] The tribes in the neighborhood of Fort Berthold, as we know, remained friendly to the whites.   The Government, wishing to protect them against hostile bands, sent them troops; these were under no restraint and gave themselves up to brutality and libertinage.   "During the whole winter," writes Father De Smet, "the Indians have been the sport of the captain, whose sole object seemed to be to torture them.   When women with their starving children approached the Fort, to gather disgusting refuse from the soldiers' kitchen, they were chased away by having boiling water thrown on their ragged, emaciated bodies." (To Charles De Coster, St. Louis, Sept., 1867.)

"Preceded by the announcement to their agents that the military were able to chastise any tribes who should molest people crossing the plains, and that the Indians would be required to keep off the main lines of travel, a large expedition under General Hancock marched into their country. Some of the results of that expedition, as far as this office has been advised, were the destruction of a large village of Cheyennes and Sioux, the burning of its effects, and the dispersing of its terrified occupants.   The agents in charge of the Arapahoes, Cheyennes, Apaches, Comanches, and Kiowas insist that it cannot be shown that hostile demonstrations were made by any of them as tribes or bands, or by any considerable number of them, but that they should be regarded as peaceable, excepting the few uncontrollable and vicious, such as may be found in all communities." (Annual Report on Indian Affairs by the Acting Commissioner, Nov. 15, 1867.)

[3] For details of this massacre, see Helen Hunt Jackson, "A Century of Dishonor," p. 343, et seq.

and that of his colleagues. "God Almighty," said he, "brought this about, when He decreed that at a stated time one race should replace another. It is like a great circle traced visibly by Him; His reasons are too profound for us to be able to comprehend them. The mammoth and the mastodon have come and gone; the red man of America is passing and disappearing." [4]

But the Indians were not resigned to this idea of disappearing. Expelled from their own lands, tracked like beasts of prey, they felt justified in resorting to any measures against their oppressors. Several districts, notably Colorado, were ravished by pillage, massacre, and fire. [5]

The Indians in revolt numbered several thousand. Every day new tribes joined the coalition, and now that the Cheyennes and the Blackfeet had combined with the Sioux, it was imperative to check the progress of the insurrection. Again the Government appealed to Father De Smet. The Commissioner of Indian Affairs wrote him: "Your relations with the Indians and your marvelous influence over them are well-known facts. It is certain that

[4] Report to the Joint Congressional Committee on Indian Affairs, Jan., 1867. The following is the method by which the virtuous General assisted Providence in making the red man disappear: "You will make war on the Mescalaros and all the other Indians whom you find in the Mescalaros' country, until further orders. . . . Should the Indians ask to treat with you, tell them that you have no power to make peace, and that you are there to kill whoever you find." (To Colonel Carson, Oct. 12, 1862.)

"The troops must pursue the Indians in small groups, marching furtively in the direction of their haunts, waiting patiently for them. . . . A hunter in pursuit of a deer resorts to every kind of ruse to kill him at close range. The Indian is an animal of keener sight and deeper cunning than the deer." (To Colonel Riggs, Aug. 16, 1863.)

These and similar letters are quoted in the Report to the Peace Commissioners. *Appendix to the Doolittle Report*, p. 432, *et seq.*

[5] The news reached the Indians that a railway train was to pass through the forests, and their spies reported to them that one of the cars was full of powder. The redskins assembled, set fire to the trees, and, armed with scalping-knives, hid at a short distance and awaited their victims. Fortunately, part of their information was false, for the convoy contained no explosives. When the engineer beheld the flaming forest he was in a quandary. Should he advance, the locomotive, coaches, and passengers would be burned, but, on the other hand, should he stop the train, the Indians would fall upon the handful of whites and massacre them. Deeming that the situation called for extreme measures, he put on full steam and rushed through the forest. The strong current of air generated by the speed of the engine drove the flames back from the train, and the terrible furnace was traversed without damage to train or passengers.

your presence in their midst will obtain the best results. No special instructions will be given you and I leave you at liberty to take your own measures." [6]

Father De Smet accepted the commission on condition that he was to receive no personal remuneration. "I prefer," he said, "to be entirely independent in the matter of money: my sole desire is to be of service to the whites and above all to the poor Indians." [7]

As in 1864, his official mission gained prestige through the exercise of his apostolate.

Father De Smet left St. Louis April 12, 1867, not, however, without apprehension as to the result of his undertaking. "Shall I be received by those proud Indians, whose tomahawks are uplifted against the whites, from whose lances hundreds of scalps dangle, serving as decorations for the warriors and their steeds? The conviction that fervent prayers accompany me gives me courage. Knowing my own nothingness, I place myself unreservedly in God's hands and under the protection of our good Mother, the Immaculate Virgin." [8]

To avoid the dangers and delays of high water in the spring, Father De Smet journeyed overland to Sioux City by way of Chicago. This was the first time he had crossed the undulating plains of Iowa. "It looks like a troubled sea that had suddenly calmed. Day after day the scene is unchanged. Like waves, hills succeed valleys interminably; only here and there a clump of trees on the edge of a stream. In summer it is an ocean of verdure strewn with flowers; in autumn, fire burns everything, and the land is as if covered with a veil of mourning; then comes winter with its mantle of snow. Spring is just now beginning, and the snow that lay from two to four feet deep is melting and rapidly disappearing, and only a few glistening white patches are seen on the hillsides." [9]

At Sioux City the missionary, accompanied by Panan-

[6] Letter from Colonel Bogy, Washington, Feb. 13, 1867.
[7] To his brother Francis, St. Louis, March 29, 1867. While refusing all remuneration for his services to the Government, Father De Smet accepted sufficient money to cover the expense of his journey and that of his interpreter.
[8] To Father Terwecoren, Sioux City, April 30, 1867.
[9] Letter quoted.

niapapi, a small band of Yanktons, and a Sioux interpreter, went aboard a steamboat. Many soldiers journeying to different forts were passengers. In his capacity as envoy extraordinary, Father De Smet had been given the rank of Major—"A title singularly out of place for a Jesuit, nevertheless it gives me free access to the soldiers, many of whom are Catholics, and to them I devote much of my time, not in my capacity of officer, but of priest. It is like a little floating mission, and my days are spent in teaching the catechism or hearing confessions." [10]

But the soldiers were not the only ones to benefit by his zeal. At every landing he visited Indian villages or Canadian families, instructing them, performing marriage ceremonies, baptizing in all nine hundred children. On May 24th, the feast of Our Lady, Help of Christians, a rustic altar was erected in the open country, and under an azure sky, surrounded by his neophytes, he celebrated the Holy Sacrifice. As far as the eye could see, the prairies were starred with daisies and buttercups and a thousand other lovely flowers. After describing the scene in a letter, the old missionary with naïve piety invites his young friends in Europe to "come to the vast plains and gather exquisite bouquets to adorn the altars of the illustrious Queen of heaven." [11]

But his solicitude for the salvation of souls in no way interfered with the worldly object of his mission. The tribes along the river had not yet taken up arms, but a revolt was imminent. In concert with Pananniapapi, he endeavored to maintain their good relations with the whites, although the latter had committed crying injustices against the Indians. It was evident to these tribes that they could not long withstand the United States Army. The missionary argued to them that rather than make common cause with the hostile bands, it was wiser to assure themselves of the protection of the Government, which engaged itself to do what was right and admit all just claims.

Everywhere Father De Smet heard the same story: "The Government agents visit us frequently. They are

[10] Selected Letters, 4th Series, p. 21.
[11] Letter to Emile de Meren, St. Louis, Oct., 1867.

amiable and prodigal of words and promises, but why do such professions come to nothing?" The Indians would then enumerate the evils of which they were the victims. "Notwithstanding, we still hope that our appeals will reach the ear of the Great Father and touch his heart, and that he will take pity on us. The Black Robe's words to-day strengthen our hope." [12]

The meeting between Father De Smet and Generals Sully and Parker, the peace Commissioners appointed to investigate the grievances of the Indians, took place near Fort Peter. They decided to travel with him as far as the mouth of the Yellowstone, as they realized what great services Father De Smet could render them. General Sully, who had formerly refused the Jesuit's mediation, now deemed himself fortunate to be able to approach the Indians under his protection.

Then began a peace campaign which affirmed in a striking degree the prestige of the Black Robe. Father De Smet, the Generals, and the faithful Yanktons stopped at Forts Sully, Rice, Berthold, and Union, and wherever they found a group of lodges they sought out in each place the chief, and asked him to convoke a council. When the warriors had assembled, and the calumet had been passed around, the priest would address the gathering, declaring the object of his mission and making known the advantages of an agreement with the whites. Then pointing out the Commissioners, he explained: "Your Great Father desires to know your grievances in order to remedy them." The Generals in turn invited the chiefs to speak openly, telling them that their complaints, formulated in council, would be sent to Washington and submitted to the President.

Ranged in a circle, the warriors listened in silence. Then arose a chief of gigantic stature, proud of mien, and of stately tread, his head ornamented with eagle feathers, and his feet encased in rich moccasins. Placing himself in front of the Commissioners, with a quick gesture he threw back the Indian blanket that served as his mantle, and, lifting his hand, called for attention. "When the Great Father," said he, "sends honest men to my country I am

[12] Selected Letters, 4th Series, p. 11.

glad to speak with them. Among you is one known to me, a man of God: I and my people love him. You tell me that the Great Father loves his red-skinned children, that he wishes to be just to them and make them happy. Formerly we were happy, because the whites who came to us to hold council did not deceive the Indians. If the Great Father really loves us, why has he sent agents into our country who lie to us? Since the coming of these men all is changed, prosperity and goodness have disappeared. Even the climate, which before was pleasant, has become bad.

"We have never troubled your lands, and you come to ours to sow unhappiness. Why do you do this? You have built four railroads through our country and driven away the wild animals. You refuse us powder and bullets, and why? The game has become so shy that my bow and arrow are useless. I now need powder and lead.

"Since the white man has come here and deceived us we cannot live in contact with him. I am ashamed to put my foot in a white man's lodge or to receive him in mine. Also, the soldiers have treated us badly. If the Great Father would recall them and leave us only the traders whom we need, happiness would return and the climate would again become good. He must also do away with all the railroads built on our lands. This is my country; it does not belong to you, and we have no intention of surrendering it. We do not wish to inhabit the lands you offer; we wish to live here, and I and my warriors choose rather to fight and die in defending our rights than leave our country and die of starvation. Moreover, we swear to scalp every white man that falls into our hands, if the Great Father does not withdraw the soldiers and restore to us our lands. I have spoken."[13]

The Indians remained defiant. Father De Smet alone had any influence over them, and that through private counsels rather than by haranguing them. He finally succeeded in calming them, assured them of the sincerity of the Commissioners, and restored their confidence in the good intentions of the Government. To defend a cause in many respects an unjust one, was a difficult task for the

[13] This speech was made by Iron Shield, chief of the Miniconjous.

missionary, but he declared his belief that the Indians' resistance would finally be their undoing.   Moreover, the Government had formally stated its terms; both Presidents Lincoln and Johnson had sent the tribes assurances of their friendship.   Was it not to remedy the evils that they were now investigating their grievances?   Why should they imagine that such agreements would remain a dead letter?

The Indians never wavered in their loyalty to Father De Smet nor did they think he could ever betray their cause.   He was always "the white man whose tongue does not lie."   His sympathies were for them; they knew him and fully trusted him.   "If all would speak and act as you do, Black Robe, the sun of peace would not be eclipsed."

After some weeks of deliberation the tribes living in the vicinity of Missouri renewed to Generals Sully and Parker their assurances of a good understanding.   Even the hostile tribes agreed to make peace.   Sa-tanka, or Sitting Bull, great chief of the Kiowas, was known as the most formidable enemy of the white man, and on his head the Governor of Colorado had more than once put a price.   Hence, great was the surprise of the Commissioners when this fierce chief came to ask their friendship.

"We have made war on the whites, but only because they forced us to take up arms.   We thank the Great Spirit that our troubles are drawing to an end, and that peace and union are before us.   We come to you as friends; you have listened to our complaints, and we have given you our hearts.   Henceforth the grass of the prairie will no longer be stained with the white man's blood.   Your people shall be our people, and peace shall be our common heritage.

"I am an old man and shall soon go to join my brothers; but those who come after me will remember this day. The memory of it will go with them to their graves; they will transmit it to their children as a sacred tradition, and it will be handed down to their grandchildren's children. Farewell.   Perhaps we may never meet again, but do not forget Sa-tanka, the friend of the whites."

Encouraged by these successes, Father De Smet longed to penetrate into the interior of the country, which was

23

occupied by rebellious tribes. Several chiefs had expressed a desire to see him, and he hoped to induce them to lay down their arms, but the fatigue of a four months' journey had so exhausted him that he was obliged to return to St. Louis. He had, however, amply fulfilled his mission; over fifteen thousand Indians had sworn to keep peace.

"It is my candid opinion, should due regard be paid to the just complaints of the Indians, should their annuities be delivered in due and proper time, and implements of agriculture be supplied to them; should they be dealt with honestly and kindly by agents and other persons in the employ of the Government, the bands mentioned will be kept friendly to the whites, and the warrior bands in the Upper Missouri plains will soon cease their depredations." [14]

Such views were too wise, at least in principle, not to be accepted by the Government, and the Secretary of the Interior expressed to Father De Smet his great satisfaction. But the missionary attributed his success to the prayers of his friends, especially those of the little children.

[14] To the Commissioner of Indian Affairs, St. Louis, Sept., 1867.

CHAPTER XXIV

SITTING BULL'S CAMP (1868)

A Commission of Five Generals is Sent by the Government to Subdue the Indians—The Commission Asks Father De Smet to Intervene—Conference with the Indians on the Shores of the Platte—Father De Smet's Offer to Go to the Hostile Bands—En Route for the Hunkpapas' Camp—Father De Smet is Received by Sitting Bull—The Great Council—Father De Smet's Discourse—Black Moon's Reply—The Banner of Peace — The Hunkpapas' Deputies Accompany Father De Smet to Fort Rice—The Complete Success of the Conference—Generals Harney, Sanborn, and Terry Express Their Gratitude and Appreciation to Father De Smet.

FATHER DE SMET returned to St. Louis in the month of August and suffered from the intense heat, as in the preceding year. "More and more I feel the weight of years. My strength is failing and I am getting thin. I still hope to spend a year or two with the Indians, especially those who are at enmity with the whites. A large number of chiefs have invited me to visit them and seem disposed to make peace, but the winter is too far advanced and I am too weak to undertake the journey of over three thousand miles. I must put it off until next spring."[1] When spring came he was able to carry out his intentions, however.

Generals Sully and Parker were of the opinion that an understanding could be arrived at with the hostile tribes. On the other hand, the complete submission of the Indians, if obtained by force of arms, would cost the country five hundred million dollars.[2] It was deemed wiser to continue negotiations.

A new commission was empowered to conclude a lasting peace; it was composed of the most distinguished officers of the United States Army: Generals Sherman, Harney,

[1] To Father Terwecoren, St. Louis, Sept. 21, 1867.
[2] General Sherman's estimate.

Sanborn, Terry, and Sheridan. It is noteworthy that these men, who had just brought the Civil War to a close, now asked the aid of a missionary to induce a few thousand Indians to lay down their arms.[3]

Father De Smet gladly placed his services at the disposal of the Commission.[4] He had full confidence in their integrity and wrote of them: "I do not hesitate to say that the gentlemen composing the Commission are all animated with the best of feelings toward the Indian tribes and to provide for their future welfare. Resistance on the part of the Indians will finally be overcome and bring great misery among them."[5]

On March 30, 1868, the missionary left St. Louis in his sixty-eighth year and in broken health, to embark on the most perilous undertaking of his life. He joined the Commission, which traveled by way of Chicago and Omaha. The first council with the Indians was held on the borders of the Platte River; the results were satisfactory, but news was brought that certain tribes, notably the Hunkpapas and Ogallalas, had refused to treat with the whites. So long as these tribes, two of the most powerful in the plains, refused to disarm, peace could not be assured.

It was evident that Father De Smet alone could triumph over their fierce animosity, so he offered to go in person to invite them to a conference that would take place three months later at Fort Rice. Deeming it wiser to advance ahead of the Commission, he traveled up the Missouri alone. A Black Robe in the midst of military uniforms would be unseemly to the Indians and far from agreeable.

After thirty-three days of difficult navigation he reached

[3] This peaceful disposition on the part of the Commissioners denoted a remarkable change of opinion. In 1866, General Sherman had written in his "Indian Views": "We must pursue the Sioux until they are exterminated, men, women, and children. No other method will get at the bottom of the question."

[4] "When occasions present themselves at Fort Rice, please let the Indians of the interior know of my coming and let them be well and fully persuaded that nothing is nearer and dearer to my heart than their welfare and happiness. I pray daily to the Lord that peace and quiet might be restored and reign again through the land. It would be my greatest consolation should I be able to do anything to bring it about." (Letter to Mr. Galpin, St. Louis, Feb. 22, 1868.)

[5] Letter to Mr. F. F. Gerard, St. Louis, Feb. 25, 1868.

the fort situated near the mouth of the Cannonball River, where hundreds of Indians were gathered to attend "the great peace council." Learning that he had arrived, they rushed to the river and gave him a warm ovation; then they conducted him to the lodge that had been prepared for him, where the great chiefs were anxiously waiting to learn the Government's intentions toward them. He assured them of the Government's peaceful attitude, but declared he could not conclude any negotiations before the arrival of the Commissioners. The following days he devoted to instructing the Indians, and six hundred children received baptism. He also prepared the soldiers in the garrison to receive the Sacraments on the day of Pentecost.

On June 1st the missionary announced that he was going to seek the hostile tribes, in order to induce the chiefs to attend the conference. The Indians were astounded at such audacity, and wished to dissuade him. "Black Robe," they said, "it will cost you your scalp." But the missionary replied: "Before a picture of the Blessed Virgin, Mother and Protector of all nations, six lamps are burning day and night during my absence, and before these lamps more than a thousand children implore heaven's protection for me." Then the Indians lifted their hands to heaven, exclaiming: "How wonderful! How splendid! We want to accompany you. When will you start?" "To-morrow at sunrise."

The missionary accepted, however, only an escort of twenty-four men, and for interpreter chose an old trapper named Galpin, who had lived for thirty years among the Sioux.

The moment of his departure was a solemn one. Surrounded by the Indian chiefs and soldiers from the fort, the Father placed his journey under the protection of the Great Spirit, and recommended himself to the prayers of his friends, many of whom never expected to see him again.

The Indians whom he wished to reconcile with the whites were nursing their hatred on the far side of the Bad Lands, an immense, sterile plain, furrowed with deep undulations.

Numbering over five thousand, they roamed about with the uneasiness and restlessness of wild beasts. They were pagans, and knew of the Catholic religion only through the prestige attached to the Black Robe.

Taking a westerly course, the missionary's caravan traveled for days without coming upon any traces of the white man, and only now and then encountered the remains of some Indian warrior, supported on four poles. The Indians would then halt, smoke the calumet, and celebrate in song the bravery of the dead.

> "Thou hast preceded us to the land of souls;
> To-day at thy tomb we admire thy lofty deeds.
> Thy death has been avenged by thy brothers in arms.
> Repose in peace, illustrious warrior!"

As they advanced vegetation became sparse; they had only stagnant, greenish water to drink, and even game was becoming scarce. Despite these hardships, Father De Smet's cheerfulness kept up the courage of his companions.

One evening one of the men of his escort, who had formerly been a great enemy to the whites, entered his tent. "Black Robe," said the Indian, extending his hand, "ever since our departure I have observed you and am more than ever convinced you are a great and brave man. As I have always admired the brave, it rejoices my heart to see you." He then conversed at length with the missionary upon the means to bring about peace.[6]

June 9th, Father De Smet dispatched four men to seek the enemy's camp and provisioned each with a quantity of tobacco. "The gift of tobacco is equivalent to an invitation or signifies the desire for a conference upon an important affair. If the tobacco is accepted, you can present yourself; if not, access to the camp is forbidden you."[7]

Six days later a band of Indians appeared upon the horizon. These were scouts, and were followed by a deputation of eighteen warriors, who had come to shake hands with the missionary and smoke the calumet of

---

[6] This and other information is taken from Mr. Galpin's unpublished diary.

[7] Selected Letters, 4th Series, p. 75.

peace. "Black Robe," they said, "your tobacco has been accepted. The chiefs and warriors are eager to know the object of your visit; but entrance to our camp is accorded to you alone: no other white man could come out of it with his scalp."

The camp was three days' journey away, in the valley of the Yellowstone near the confluence of the Powder River. On June 19th they reached the hills that overlook the river, and from there Father De Smet beheld a detachment of five hundred warriors coming across the plain to meet him. "I immediately unfurled my standard of peace, which was a banner with the holy name of Jesus on one side, and on the other a picture of the Blessed Virgin surrounded with a halo of stars. Believing it the United States flag, the Indians halted, and appeared to be holding a consultation. The four chiefs rode up at full gallop and hovered about the banner. But as soon as they learned what it represented, they shook hands with me and signaled to their warriors to approach. They all drew themselves up in a single line and we did the same. Then the two lines approached each other. On both sides rose cries and shouts of joy. I was moved to tears by the reception these pagan sons of the desert gave me." [8]

Then followed, according to their custom, the exchange of presents; afterward they started, with the banner at their head, for the camp only a few miles distant. There Father De Smet found the Hunkpapas, the Ogallalas, the Blackfeet, the Miniconjous, and others. The great chief, Four Horns, shared his authority with Black Moon, No Neck, and Sitting Bull. The last named was soon to become famous.[9] His courage, his eloquence, and his prestige made him the most formidable of the redskins. Eight years later he was to successfully lead the final resistance of his expiring people.[10] It was this fierce chief who received Father De Smet; he had prepared for him a large lodge in the center of the camp, where a guard of his faithful warriors stood watch day and night.

[8] Selected Letters, 4th Series, p. 78.
[9] On the day of his birth a buffalo came and seated itself a few feet from the tent in which he first saw the light of day. Hence his name.
[10] G. Kurth, "Sitting Bull," Brussels, 1879.

Exhausted by his sixteen days' march, the missionary asked that he might be allowed to rest, and although surrounded by four thousand Indians, sworn enemies of the whites, he tranquilly fell asleep in the full assurance of the good faith of Indian hospitality; until he awakened, his guard kept watch over the venerable white man, wrapped in his Jesuit cloak.

When he opened his eyes the four chiefs were standing before him, and, in the name of his tribe, Sitting Bull addressed him:

"Black Robe, I hardly sustain myself beneath the weight of white men's blood I have shed. The whites provoked the war; their injustices, their indignities to our families, the cruel, unheard-of and wholly unprovoked massacre at Fort Lyon [where Chivington commanded] of six or seven hundred women, children, and old men, shook all the veins which bind and support me. I rose, tomahawk in hand, and I have done all the hurt to the whites that I could. To-day thou art among us, and in thy presence my hands fall to the ground as if dead. I will listen to thy good words, and as bad as I have been to the whites just so good am I ready to become toward them."

Complying with Father De Smet's request, the chiefs convoked a great council for the next day, when the Black Robe would inform them of the Government's proposals, and the warriors would decide if they should send a deputation to Fort Rice to treat for peace with the Commissioners.

Early on the morning of June 20th men and women began preparing the place for the conference; this space covered nearly a half acre, and was surrounded by a series of tepees or Indian lodges, composed of twenty-four buffalo skins each, which were suspended on long pine poles. The banner of the Holy Virgin rose from the center, and on one side a seat covered with fine buffalo skins was prepared for the Black Robe. When all the Indians, at the appointed hour, had taken their places, ranged in a circle, Father De Smet was solemnly introduced by the two head chiefs, Four Horns and Black Moon. The council was opened with songs and dances, noisy and joyful, in which the warriors alone took part. Then Four Horns lighted his

calumet of peace; he presented it first solemnly to the
Great Spirit, imploring His light and favor, and then to the
four cardinal points, and to the sun and earth, as witnesses
to the action of the council. Then he himself passed the
calumet from mouth to mouth, commencing with Father
De Smet. When the ceremony of the calumet was finished,
the head chief addressed the missionary, saying:

"Speak, Black Robe, my ears are open to hear your
words."

All this was done with the greatest gravity and amid a
profound silence.

Then the Father rose to his feet and raising his hands to
heaven implored guidance from on high. For almost an
hour he laid before them the disinterested motives that
had brought him among them, which could only tend to
their happiness. He spoke especially of the dangers with
which they were surrounded, and of their weakness beside
the great strength of the whites, if the Great Father were
forced to use it against them. The harm done by the war
had been terrible, and the crimes committed on both sides
atrocious. The Great Father desired that all should be forgotten and buried. To-day his hand was ready to aid
them, to give them agricultural implements, domestic
animals, men to teach them field-work, and teachers of both
sexes to instruct their children, and all this was offered
them without the least remuneration or cession of lands on
their part.

"And now," said Father De Smet in conclusion, "in the
name of the Great Spirit, and in the presence of your chiefs
and braves here assembled, I conjure you to bury all resentment and accept the hand that is generously offered to
you. The banner before you is the sacred emblem of peace,
and never before has it been carried such a distance. I
will leave it with your chiefs as a guarantee of my sincerity,
and as a continual reminder of my wishes for the happiness
of the Sioux tribes."

No one interrupted the orator, and when he was done,
Black Moon arose.

"Black Robe, your words are plain and good, and filled
with truth. I shall lay them up in my memory. Still, our
hearts are sore. They have received deep wounds. These

wounds are yet to be healed. A cruel war has desolated and impoverished our country; the desolating torch of war was not kindled by us; it was the Sioux east of us and the Cheyennes south of us who raised the war first, to revenge themselves for the white man's cruelties and injustice. We have been forced to take part, for we are victims of their rapacity and wrong doing. To-day, when we ride over our plains, we find them spotted here and there with blood; these are not the blood-stains of buffalo and deer killed in the chase, but those of our own comrades or of white men, sacrificed to vengeance. The buffalo, the elk, the antelope, the bighorn, and the deer have quitted our immense plains; we hardly find them any more, except at intervals, and always less numerous. May it not be the odor of human blood that puts them to flight?

"I will say further—against our will, the whites are cutting up our country with their highways; they build forts and arm them with thunderers. They kill our animals, and more than they need. They cut down our forests without paying us their value. Not content with ruining us, they maltreat and massacre our people.

"We are opposed to having these big roads, which drive the buffalo away from our country. The soil is ours, and we are determined not to yield an inch of it. Here our fathers were born and buried. We desire, like them, to live here, and to be buried in this same soil. We have been forced to hate the whites. Let them treat us like brothers and the war will cease. Let them stay at home; we will never go to trouble them. To see them come in and build their cabins revolts us, and we are determined to resist or die. Thou, Messenger of Peace, thou hast given us a glimpse of a better future. Very well; so be it; let us hope. Let us throw a veil over the past, and let it be forgotten. I have only a word more to say; in the presence of all my people, I express to you here my thanks for the good news that you have announced and for all your good counsel and advice. We accept your tobacco. Some of our warriors will go with you to Fort Rice to hear the words and propositions of the Great Father's commissioners. If their words are acceptable, peace shall be made." Then he took his seat.

All applauded the words of Black Moon. The other chiefs followed and touched on the same matters and pronounced in favor of peace. Sitting Bull only named three conditions for the peace: the whites should abandon their forts; no more land should be ceded to them; lastly, they must respect the trees, especially the oaks, which the Indians almost worshiped. "They have resisted the storms of winter and the heat of summer," he said, "and like ourselves, they seem to draw from them new vigor."

A standard-bearer was chosen for the sacred banner. The honor fell to a warrior covered with scars and distinguished for his exploits. "I expressed the wish," writes Father De Smet, "that this banner on which were embroidered the name of Jesus and the image of the Blessed Virgin might be for all a pledge of happiness and safety. For a last time I recommended the tribe to the protection of Mary, *auxilium et refugium Indianorum*, as she was anciently in Paraguay, in Canada, everywhere and forevermore." [11]

The council lasted four hours. It ended with a song that roused the echoes of the hills, and a dance that made the ground tremble. Upon his return to his lodge, the missionary found it invaded by a clamoring crowd of mothers with their babies in their arms, and followed by their other children. He at once came forth to them, and they crowded around him with a rare trustfulness, very unusual among Indian children, to offer him their little hands. The mothers were not satisfied until he laid his hands upon the heads of all the babies and little ones, when they withdrew contented and happy. To contemplate the reflection of pure souls in the innocent glance of these children was a solace and repose after his arduous labors.

The next morning before daybreak, Father De Smet set off on his return journey to the fort, where the Commissioners were anxiously awaiting the result of his interview. Repeating the ceremony of his arrival, the chiefs escorted him, and did not leave him until he had crossed the Powder River. Eight deputies chosen by the council and several warriors accompanied him back, among them a venerable

[11] Selected Letters, 4th Series, p. 89.

old man, a worthy emulator of the virtues of Pananniapapi, who had come to the camp to shake the missionary's hand and to express his happiness at seeing him again. On his breast he wore a copper cross, old and worn. This was the only religious token Father De Smet had seen in all the camp, and it filled him with joy and emotion. He questioned the old man to know from whom he had received this cross. "It was you, Black Robe, who gave me this cross. I have not laid it aside for twenty-six snows. The cross has raised me to the clouds among my people. If I still walk the earth, it is to the cross that I owe it, and the Great Spirit has blessed my numerous family."

The Father asked him to explain further, and he continued: "When I was younger, I loved whiskey to madness, and at every chance I would get drunk and commit excesses It is now twenty-six snows since my last wild orgy. I was stupid and sick from it. Just then I had the good fortune to meet you, and you made known to me that my behavior was against the will of the Master of life and offended Him grievously. Since then I have often had opportunities; my friends have sometimes sought to induce me to join them in their illicit enjoyments, but each time this cross has come to my help. I would take it between my hands and would recall your words and invoke the Great Spirit. Ever since we first met I have renounced drink, and have never touched a drop."

Struck by this heroic perseverance, Father De Smet wanted to baptize the old man, but there was not time to instruct him. The intrepid neophyte at once proposed to join the caravan, happy in the thought that when they camped he could receive instructions from the Black Robe. At the end of eight days he was made a Christian, and with a soul overflowing with joy, returned to his tribe.

Two days later Father De Smet arrived at Fort Rice. News of his success had reached the officers and soldiers, who had prepared a triumphal reception for him. Hundreds of Indians, proudly wrapped in their mantles, their heads ornamented with feathers and ribbons, and their faces daubed with vermilion, came to meet him. The air rang with cries of joy, in which the deputies from the Hunkpapas took part. "The warriors formed a long file and marched with true military precision. It was a really remarkable spectacle, though little in accord with the tastes of the good Father, who does not love the sound of trumpets and the glare of parades," an eye-witness reported.[12]

On July 2d the great peace council was held, in which fifty thousand Indians were represented. Not in half a century had there been such an assembly on the Missouri. The presiding Generals made solemn promises to the Indians that if they would lay aside their arms, the Government would respect their rights, provide for their livelihood, and treat them as friends. Then the representatives of the tribes spoke in turn, beginning with the standard-bearer of the Hunkpapas, whose discourse was a faithful repetition of the speeches Black Moon and Sitting Bull had made to Father De Smet. When the Hunkpapas consented to make peace, the assent of the other tribes was assured. On condition of an adequate indemnity, the Sioux were to cede to the United States their reservations in Kansas and Nebraska, but they were to demand the exclusive possession of the lands north of the Niobrara.

Upon these conditions the treaty was signed. The Commissioners distributed presents to the Indians, who then dispersed, each one rejoicing over a reconciliation which he believed to be lasting.

"I am persuaded," writes Major-General Stanley, "that this is the most complete and the wisest of all the treaties thus far concluded with the Indians of this country. Without doubt the fulfilment of the provisions of this treaty will assure peace with the Sioux. But whatever may be the result, we can never forget, nor shall we ever cease to admire the disinterested devotion of the Rev. Father De Smet, who, at the age of sixty-eight years, did not hesitate, in the midst of the heat of summer, to undertake a long and perilous journey across the burning plains, destitute of trees and even of grass; having none but corrupted and unwholesome water, constantly exposed to scalping by the Indians, and this without seeking either honors or remuneration of any sort; but solely to arrest

[12] Major-General Stanley's letter to Bishop Purcell, Fort Sully, July 12, 1868.

the shedding of blood, to save, if it might be, some lives, and preserve some habitations to these savage children of the desert." [13]

The Generals who negotiated the peace wished at once to acknowledge their debt of gratitude, and immediately after the signing of the treaty they presented an address to Father De Smet, enumerating the eminent services he had rendered the United States. "We are satisfied that but for your long and painful journey into the heart of the hostile country, and but for the influence over even the most hostile of the tribes which your years of labor among them have given you, the results which we have reached here could not have been accomplished. We are well aware that our thanks can be but of little worth to you, and that you will find true reward for your labors and for the dangers and privations which you have encountered in the consciousness that you have done much to promote peace on earth and good will to men; but we should do injustice to our own feelings were we not to render to you our thanks and express our deep sense of the obligations under which you have laid us." [14]

The humble missionary did not tarry long to listen to such praise. On July 4th he started for St. Louis. He also believed that peace was assured, and so it would have been had not the cupidity of the whites overruled the good faith of the treaty.

[13] Letter quoted.

[14] The address is dated at Fort Rice, July 3, 1868, and signed by Generals Harney, Sanborn, and Terry.

CHAPTER XXV

FATHER DE SMET'S LAST LABORS—GRANT'S PEACE POLICY
(1869–1872)

Father De Smet's Eighth Visit to Belgium—Two Journeys Made in the
Autumn—Project to Found a Mission on the Upper Missouri—Indian
Peace Policy—Father De Smet is Given the Right to Appoint Catholic
Agents—Nearly All the Agencies are Given to Protestant Function-
aries—Injustice Done to the Catholic Indians—Father De Smet's
Unsuccessful Efforts—He Resigns—Courageous Fidelity of the Catholic
Indians—"Give Me the Value of My Soul"—Fervor of the Cœur
d'Alènes—Letter to the Sovereign Pontiff—Reply of Pius IX.

FATHER DE SMET regarded the pacification of the
Sioux as but the prelude to their conversion. For
twenty years he had held the belief that despite their
savagery they would listen to the teaching of the Gospel.
"Their conversion," he said, "will be a miracle of grace,
but with God's help we will succeed. In my intercourse
with the Indians I have always found them respectful,
diligent, and attentive to the words of the missionary,
manifesting a strong desire to see their children instructed
in the truths of religion, and nowhere have I encountered a
spirit of opposition."[1]

Time and again the Sioux had clamored for Black Robes,
and now they came to Fort Rice to renew their entreaties.
The head chief of the Yanktons, Two Bears, said in his
speech: "When we are settled down sowing grain, raising
cattle, and living in houses, we want Father De Smet to
come and live with us, and to bring us other Black Robes
to live among us also. We will listen to their words, and
the Great Spirit will love and bless us." Father De Smet's
Superiors approved his project for founding a mission for
the Sioux,[2] but men and money were lacking. Hence it

[1] Selected Letters, 4th Series, p. 143.
[2] The Father General, on Nov. 16, 1867, wrote the following to Father
De Smet: "Accepi et magna cum jucunditate legi Revæ Væ carissimas

was necessary that he undertake another journey to Europe.

The health of the old missionary demanded that he should rest after his recent journey to the wilderness. He writes: "This letter may well be my last. My health is very much undermined in consequence of my late painful journey of about six thousand miles, but still more by the shocking heat that we have suffered for three months past. In proportion as I advance in age, heat becomes more and more insupportable to me. Very often one would say that I resemble a man whose end is at hand."[3] For three years he had been threatened with loss of hearing and Father Coosemans, his Provincial, wished him to consult "some good old Belgian doctor." So, on November 25, 1868, he sailed for Europe.

This voyage was destined to add another burden to his infirmities. Before arriving at Liverpool, the boat ran into a violent storm, during which Father De Smet fell on deck and broke two of his ribs, not receiving proper attention until he landed several days later. In spite of this he set out almost immediately upon his begging tour through Belgium, France, and Holland,[4] and the following June he returned to America. The energy and activity of a man of his years are truly amazing: in sixteen months he had traveled fifteen thousand miles. On his return to St. Louis he was obliged to keep to his room for several weeks, and alas! abandon his journey to the Sioux.

The following autumn, however, he managed to make "two good trips," one of 1,200 miles, the other of 800 miles. He accompanied as far as Omaha six Sisters of Charity who were going to the Blackfeet, and arranged that they

litteras, et plurimas gratias ago pro notitiis super tribubus Indorum et in specie Jantonum. Profecto ea quae scribit de tanto desiderio tribus istius, et de iteratis tot annis supplicationibus pro obtinendo sacerdote, valde me commovent, et plane cupio ut, si quid fiere possit a Provincia vestra, fiat. . . . Scripsi Patri Provinciali commendans Revæ Væ desideria, et aliunde jam novi ipsum serio idem cupere, velleque omnino, quam primum possit, manus operi admovere."

[3] To Father Terwecoren, St. Louis, Aug. 28, 1868.

[4] During this visit the missionary had the happiness of performing the marriage ceremony of his nephew, Paul De Smet and Mlle. Augusta Vercruysse, and of being present at the first communion of his grandniece, Maria Cornet, now Mme. Liénart.

should travel in comfort the rest of their journey, himself paying most of their expenses.

Then he visited the Potawatomies of Kansas; the Indians and missionaries received him as a father, but it pained him to see there, as elsewhere, the demoralizing influence of the whites upon the Indians. "If the missionaries," he writes, "are to effect real good among the savages, under the present circumstances, they will need a profound humility, a truly disinterested zeal, and above all a sovereign scorn for the judgments of men."[5]

But with all this, he did not forget the Indians of the Upper Missouri, his most cherished mission. Never had he so desired a foundation, and his correspondence from 1864 reveals his constant preoccupation with this project.[6] At last he felt strong enough to take the journey to that region, and departed from St. Louis on June 1, 1870. Out of solicitude for the missionary's safety and comfort in his advanced age, his Superiors sent Father Panken, a Hollander, whom Father De Smet had gained for the apostolate in 1857, to accompany him. This was Father De Smet's last visit to "his children of the desert." How many times in the past thirty years he had gone up the Missouri, a crucifix in one hand, the olive branch in the other! Every wigwam brought back consoling memories: thousands of children baptized, enemies reconciled, suffering relieved, and souls enlightened in the mysteries of faith. Moreover, he could see the beneficent results of the peace negotiated two years before by himself. The Sioux were living on most friendly terms with the soldiers at the fort; in the reservations they tilled the soil, were clothed by the Government, and received weekly rations of flour, meat, coffee, and sugar. From all directions the Indians flocked to greet "the great Black Robe," and declared their desire to remain faithful to the Fort Rice conventions.

On the banks of the Grand River was a large reservation inhabited by Indians of different tribes. Its central position would render the spread of the Gospel easy through Dakota, and its proximity to the forts would enable the missionaries to visit the soldiers often, of whom the greater

---

[5] Selected Letters, 4th Series, p. 199.
[6] Cf. Chittenden-Richardson, pp. 1279–1299.

part were Catholics. It was here he wished to build a new foundation.

During this journey he visited about twenty thousand Sioux, and administered baptism to four hundred. His resolutions were made, a mission should be opened the next spring. In August, fatigue compelled Father De Smet to return to St. Louis.

On March 20, 1871, he wrote his relatives in Belgium: "To-day I begin my annual retreat as a preparation for a long journey to the Indian tribes of the Far West. Two Fathers will accompany me, and we intend to establish a mission for the Sioux. The head chiefs of the tribe are expecting me, and I have just written to inform them of my plans and to ask them to prepare a cabin for us in their camp. I send you the names of these chiefs; they are my intimate friends, and you, too, will love them for my sake, I am sure, and will pray for their conversion." [7]

But the long-cherished project was destined never to be realized. His failing strength was not equal to the labor involved, and, moreover, the time was not propitious for a foundation. A recent decision of the Government endangered the future of the existing missions, namely, Grant's Indian Peace Policy. The conqueror of Richmond, elected to the Presidency in 1868, had rallied all parties, and inaugurated a "peace policy" in the United States. He proclaimed that he wished equally to bring about a good understanding between the whites and Indians, and to accomplish this two factors were necessary: the agent and the missionary.

On December 5, 1870, the President informed Congress in a message that "Indian agencies being civil offices, I determined to give all the agencies to such religious denominations as had heretofore established missionaries among the Indians, and perhaps to some other denominations who would undertake the work on the same terms, i.e., as missionary work." Representatives of the different denominations designated in the order would henceforth enjoy the privilege of naming the agents in the reservations

[7] To Felix and Elmira Cornet-De Smet.

where they had missions, upon the sole condition of submitting their choice for the approval of the President.

This seemed to be a triumph for faith and civilization. The Indians would no longer be imposed upon by functionaries who enriched themselves at their expense. Acting in concert, the missionary and the agent would both gain in authority, and more abundant resources would enable them to increase the number of schools.

The Catholic Church, especially, could congratulate itself upon President Grant's rulings, since the greater number of the agencies had been evangelized by its missionaries,[8] and which numbered over a hundred thousand neophytes among the Indians. The Protestant sects numbered less than fifteen thousand adherents. Great was the astonishment three days later to learn that a Jew had been appointed Superintendent of Indian Affairs in Oregon. From that instant Catholics knew what to expect from promises of the Government.

In January, 1871, Secretary of the Interior Delano consulted the episcopacy upon the choice of a representative to nominate Catholic agents. Father De Smet was proposed by the Archbishops of Baltimore, New York, Cincinnati, and St. Louis. Called to Washington, the veteran missionary found himself in the company of about thirty ministers of the reformed church, likewise summoned to give their advice on the means of civilizing the tribes. They claimed the lion's share in the partitioning of the agencies. "Neither my presence, nor my demands in behalf of the Catholic missions, produced any effect. The plan for civilizing and evangelizing the Indians had already been decided upon by the President and approved by the Senate."[9]

Afterward it was learned that instead of forty nominations to which the Catholics were entitled, only eight had been accorded to them,[10] the remainder being divided

[8] Besides the Jesuit missions, there were missions established by the Franciscans, Oblates, and secular priests.

[9] Account addressed to Dr. Linton.

[10] These agencies were the Tulalip and Colville agencies in Washington; the Grande Ronde and Umatilla agencies in Oregon; those of the Flatheads in Montana; those of the Papagos in Arizona, and those of Grand River and Devil's Lake in Dakota.

among the different sects. The President favored especially his coreligionists, the Methodists, in granting to them a third of the agencies.

The Superintendent of Indian Affairs began the discharge of his new functions by making over the Catholic schools and churches to his Protestant friends, and, in the case of the Yakimas, forbade Catholic missionaries to enter the reservation. At one stroke, eighty thousand Indians, without being consulted, found themselves torn from the Church or exposed to apostasy. But this was not all. Large sums of money due the Indians in exchange for their lands were held by the Government, and the interest on this was used for the upkeep of the schools. Henceforth this money would be expended on the salaries of Methodist, Presbyterian, and Quaker school-teachers, employed to teach the children of Catholic Indians. In this manner did the Government repay the services rendered their country by the Catholic missionaries.

"If it be true," writes a journalist, "that the Indians are condemned to annihilation, should they not at least be allowed to choose the faith in which they wish to die? Baptized and instructed as Catholics, the Indians have been divided between the various denominations, and the missionaries, who collected money in Europe for evangelizing these poor savages, are now expelled from the missions they founded. Incredible as this seems, documentary proofs of this condition of things are now in the hands of General Grant. It is horrible to think that these Indians, who have immortal souls as well as the negroes lately set free, are divided into bands and placed under ministers of every denomination, regardless of their own wishes and convictions." [11]

Nor were Father De Smet's missions spared. In the Rocky Mountains the Flatheads were the only tribe that had a Catholic agent. The missionary in charge had to cover a distance of ninety miles to visit his flock. The Quakers established themselves in the Kansas "reductions," and were guilty of shameful extortions. "One can scarcely believe that such a state of things could exist in the republic of the United States, so much vaunted for

[11] *New York Freeman's Journal*, Dec. 14, 1872.

its liberty." With touching confidence which nothing could shake, he adds, "We pray and hope that justice will be done." [12]

Not content with praying, the intrepid veteran re-doubled his efforts; he exerted himself to obtain men of recognized integrity for the posts at his disposal,[13] and fully informed himself through the missionaries upon conditions in each reservation and upon the relations existing between the agents and the Indians.

On March 27, 1871, he addressed to General Parker, Commissioner of Indian Affairs, a long account of the situation, notably in Montana, Idaho, and Washington territories. The Nez Percés, a tribe almost exclusively Catholic, were handed over to the Presbyterians. The chief of the Spokanes was threatened with imprisonment for having tried to restrain the licentiousness of his tribe. The Catholic agent among the Blackfeet had been replaced by a sectarian as debauched as he was malicious. In Dakota, where the Sioux clamored for Black Robes, all the agencies but two had been given to Protestants.

Recalling the services rendered by his fellow-missionaries, Father De Smet demanded for them the right to pursue their apostolate unhindered: "For thirty years we have labored among the benighted tribes of the Far West with only the view of promoting the knowledge of God among them and adding to their temporal welfare. We have divided with them the little means placed at our disposal, and often have we joyfully shared their poverty and privations."

Four years before General Parker had owed the success of his office among the Sioux to Father De Smet, and common justice required that he now should accede to the priest's request. But for the moment the Indians were quiet, so why consider a priest whose services were no longer necessary? The letter remained unanswered. For a year Father De Smet repeated his requests at Washington. He could not resign himself to see his neophytes become Methodists and free-thinkers. He wrote the Secretary of

---

[12] St. Louis, May 3, 1871, Cf. Letters and Notices, 1871, p. 329.

[13] Father De Smet had Major O'Connor appointed to the agency at Grand River, and Major Jones to the agency among the Flatheads, both of whom were exemplary Catholics.

the Interior: "All that the Catholic bishops and missionaries aim at, in this country of religious liberty, is to be
allowed their rights, in accordance with their call from
above, to evangelize the Indians who have received them
with joy, and not to be turned out of the missions where
they have labored for years with zeal and fervor for the
welfare and salvation of the Indians, as has been the case
in several sections." [14]

Like his colleague on Indian Affairs, the Secretary of
the Interior did not deign to reply to the grievances of a
Jesuit.   Wearied at last with fruitless protestations, and
in the knowledge that the right to appoint agents depended for each diocese upon the Bishop, Father De Smet
sent in his resignation as representative.

The Indians found it difficult to get along with their new
masters, and felt like orphans since the departure of the
Black Robes.   They sent frequent messages to the Great
Father at Washington, entreating him to give them back
their Catholic agents, their priests, and their Catholic
schools.   Such petitions received scant recognition at the
White House, the religious convictions of the Indians being
of as little importance in the eyes of the Government as
their lives and property.

Without the slightest provocation, the soldiers gave
themselves over to fearful massacres.[15]   Then came the
revolt of Sitting Bull and the bloody death of Custer,
slaughtered together with his regiment,[16] which opened the

[14] St. Louis, June 19, 1872.
[15] "Had it not been for the influence exercised by the missionaries, the
injustice inflicted on the Flatheads and Pend d'Oreilles would long ago
have made them revolt." (Report of the Commissioner of Indian Affairs
to the Secretary of the Interior, 1869, p. 254.)
   "The whites to-day occupy Idaho and Montana territories to the great
detriment of the Indians.   American soldiers have lately committed fresh
massacres in which one hundred and seventy-three Indians, mostly women
and children, have perished." (Letter from Father De Smet to G. Van
Kerckhove, St. Louis, March 8, 1870.)
   On April 30, 1871, about five hundred Apaches were put to death near
Camp Grant in Arizona.   Cf. Helen Hunt Jackson, "A Century of Dishonor," p. 325, et seq.
[16] It will be remembered that in 1868, at Fort Rice, the United States
guaranteed to the Sioux possession of the Bad Lands north of the Niobrara.
Some years later gold was discovered in the Black Hills, and miners overran the country and took complete possession of it.   Again and again
the Indians appealed to Washington without redress.   This occupation

eyes of legislators to the state of things. But Father De Smet was not there to repair the faults and mistakes made by the American Government, and to bring about peace when the burdens of war had made it too heavy to continue.

Despite persecutions, the Catholic Indians with but few exceptions remained faithful to the Church.

A Methodist minister who for some time had labored to turn Ignace, the chief of the Yakimas, from his faith, asked him one day how much he would want for changing to Protestantism.

"A big price," the chief answered him.

"Two hundred dollars?"

"More than that."

"Then how much? Five hundred, six hundred dollars?"

"Oh, more than that!"

"Indeed! State your price."

"The price of my soul." [17]

It was thus that the Christian spirit, united to Indian pride, made these primitive natures admirable types of nobility and fidelity.

But of all the tribes, the Cœur d'Alènes were distinguished for their devotion to the Church. "During the fifteen years I have known them," writes Father Joset, "never has their faith been so ardent as now. I am convinced that if we had sufficient means, these Indians would outrival the Paraguay missions." [18] Learning in 1871 of the Pope's situation and that the Italian Government had seized Rome, the Cœur d'Alènes immediately addressed to Pius IX the assurance of their filial attachment:

"Most merciful Father, it is not temerity, but love which moves us to write to you. We are, it is true, the most humble of all the Indian tribes, while you are the greatest among living men. But you were the first to cast a look of pity upon us. Yes, Father, thirty winters ago we were

of land, added to the villainy of the agents, provoked an uprising of the tribes in 1876. Sitting Bull, in the valley of the Little Big Horn, surprised General Custer, who perished with seventeen officers and more than three hundred soldiers. The maddened victors mutilated the bodies in a shocking manner.

[17] Letter from Father Grassi to *Catholic Missions*, 1873, p. 15.

[18] Letter from Father De Smet to the *Catholic Review*, Aug. 9, 1872.

a savage people, miserable in both body and soul until you sent us the great Black Robe, Father De Smet, to make us children of God through baptism. We were blind, and you sent him to open our eyes. Many of us were still in darkness when Father De Smet left us; then you sent us another Black Robe, our good Father Nicholas,[19] who came and lived with us and awakened us, directing us in the path that leads to heaven. And how many other Fathers have you not given us to teach us and our children the law of God and make us better Christians.

"Hence, Father, hearing that you are in affliction, we wish to thank you for your charity, and express to you our great love and deep sorrow in learning that some of your wicked children continue to cause you suffering after having robbed you of your house.

"Although we are only poor Indians, ignorant of the amenities of life, we regard such conduct as a crime. Only fifty years ago, we ourselves were still savages, but we would not have dared to act thus had we known that the dignity and power of the Pope come from Christ. For this reason we have prayed and will continue to pray with all the ardor poor Indians are capable of, for thee, Father, and for the entire Church. Moreover, having come from our various camps to assemble in the mission church, we have for nine days said many prayers and performed acts of virtue which we offer to the Heart of Jesus for thee. This morning we counted our acts and devotions and found they numbered 120,527. Judging this insufficient, we offered our own hearts for our excellent Father, the Pope, in the assured belief that this offering will not be rejected.

"We have a number of soldiers, not trained for war, but to keep order in our camp. If these men can be of service to the Pope, we offer them joyfully, and they will esteem themselves fortunate in being able to spill their blood and give their lives for our good Father Pius IX.

"And now may we tell you our fears and misgivings? The sellers of whiskey are daily drawing nearer. We fear to betray our Saviour in taking back the hearts we have given Him. Help us, and strengthen us by thy

[19] Father Nicholas Point.

prayers! But our dear children are still more to be pitied, because they are more exposed; not so much our sons, who have real fathers in the Black Robes, but our daughters, who as yet have no kind mothers to look after them. We have often asked for Black Robes of their sex, but our voices are too weak to be heard, and we are too poor to do more than ask. Who will send us good mothers to instruct our daughters and strengthen them against the enemy that draws near, if not thou, who hast always had compassion on us, even when we were pagans?

"These are the sentiments of our hearts, but as we poor Indians attach little value to expressions of feeling unless they are accompanied by material gifts, we have collected dollars and small coins, that we may give you, so to speak, a piece of our own flesh, as a measure of our sincerity. Notwithstanding our poverty, to our great surprise we have been able to collect $110.

"And now, Father, once again allow us to open our hearts. Oh, how happy we would be, despite our unworthiness, could we receive a word from your lips, a word that will help us and our wives and children to find an entry into the Heart of Jesus!

"VINCENT, of the Stellam family.
"ANDREW SELTIS, of the family of Emote."

If we reflect that the Cœur d'Alènes formerly passed for the most ferocious of the mountain tribes, we shall see in their naïve and generous piety an extraordinary fruit of grace. The Father General presented the letter to Pius IX, who in reading it forgot for the moment the misery of his captivity. If old Europe repudiated the Faith, the Church now beheld new sons coming to her from the other side of the ocean, their fresh souls ignorant of falsehood and opposed to vice and error with a fidelity worthy of the early Christians.

The Holy Father's reply reads:

"BELOVED SONS, *salutation and apostolic benediction!*

"The devoted sentiments which you, in the simplicity of your hearts express, have caused us great joy. Your sorrow over the attacks made against the Church, as well as your devotion and filial love for the Holy See, is a striking proof of the faith and charity that fill your hearts, attaching you firmly to the center of unity. For this reason we feel certain that your prayers and supplications which rise unceasingly to God will be efficacious for us and for the Church, and we accept with deep feelings of gratitude the offering of your generous charity. The hand of God protects those who seek Him sincerely, and we believe that your good words will obtain the grace to resist the dangers of corruption that threaten you, and the spiritual help which you desire for your daughters. We beg God to complete in you the work of grace, and to fill you with His choicest blessings. As a presage of this and a token of our gratitude and paternal favor, we give you from our heart the apostolic benediction.

"Given at Rome, near St. Peter's, July 31, 1871, in the twenty-sixth year of our Pontificate.

"Pius IX, Pope." [20]

In transmitting to Father De Smet these encouraging words, the Father General writes: "This is the first brief that has ever been addressed to an Indian chief by the Sovereign Pontiff." It was on August 15, 1872, that the reply of Pius IX was communicated to the Cœur d'Alènes. Father Cataldo had convoked an assembly of several mountain tribes, each one of which was represented by a large delegation. At the appointed hour they formed in procession, headed by twelve acolytes in surplices with

---

[20] "Dilecti Filii, *salutem et apostolicam benedictionem!*

"Iis devotionis sensibus, quos in simplicitate cordis vestri Nobis significastis, Dilecti Filii, non mediocriter delectati sumus, cum in dolore a vobis concepto ob insectationes Ecclesiæ, non minus quam in filiali erga hanc Sanctam Sedem obsequio et amore, splendescere viderimus fidem illam et caritatem, quæ diffusa est in cordibus vestris, quæque, vos huic Unitatis centro arctius obstringit. Quocirca, sicuti non dubitamus quin orationes et obsecrationes vestræ, fidenter et instanter elatæ ad Deum, suffragaturæ sint Ecclesiæ et Nobis, sic stipem a vobis tanto corrogatam amore pretiosissimam ducimus. Et quoniam manus Domini est super omnes quærentes eum in bonitate, confidimus pia opera vestra conciliatura quoque vobis esse, cum auxilium adversus curruptionis, pericula quæ timetis, tum spiritualia subsidia quæ pro filiabus vestris concupiscitis. Nos certe Deum rogamus ut gratiæ suæ opus in vobis plenius semper perficiat, vosque suis omnibus ditet muneribus. Horum autem auspicem, et grati animi Nostri acpaternæ benevolentiæ pignus, apostolicam benedictionem vobis peramanter impertimus.

"Datum Romæ apud S. Petrum, die 31 julii, anno 1871, Pontificatus Nostri anno vicesimo sexto.

"Pius P. P. IX."

tapers in their hands. Then came the missionaries in copes and dalmatics, preceding a statue of the Blessed Virgin, placed on a dais ornamented with flowers and garlands and carried by the four head chiefs. To the right and left of the statue walked two lines of Indian soldiers in full dress and armed. Then followed an immense concourse in serried ranks, reciting the rosary and chanting litanies.

The procession stopped before the improvised altar. High Mass was said in the open and many neophytes received holy communion. The ceremony over, one of the missionaries read in Latin the pontifical letter and it was then translated into the dialects of the Cœur d'Alènes, Kalispels, Kettles, Nez Percés, and Yakimas. Every head was bowed to receive the Holy Father's benediction, and from that time the redskins felt themselves ennobled. The brief that they had just heard read was their charter of admittance into the fold of Christ.

As for Father De Smet, he found in the Holy Father's benevolence and in the neophytes' fervor the greatest recompense for his labors.

CHAPTER XXVI

FATHER DE SMET'S LAST VOYAGE TO EUROPE—HIS RETREAT
IN ST. LOUIS—HIS RELIGIOUS VIRTUES—HIS DEATH
(1872–1873)

Father De Smet's Serious Illness in Brussels—He Thinks of Living in
Belgium and Opening a School There for Apostolic Work—His Jubilee
as a Jesuit—His Retreat—New Edition of the "Letters"—He Begins
the History of the Origin of the Missouri Province—Father De Smet's
Intercourse with His Fellow-Jesuits—He is Esteemed by Outsiders—
Dr. Linton—The "Linton Album"—The Missionary Traveled Nearly
261,000 Miles—Father De Smet's Spirit of Faith—His Love of the
Religious Life—How He Practiced Poverty and Obedience—His
Piety—His Devotion to the Blessed Virgin, St. Anthony, the Souls in
Purgatory—Last Illness—Farewell to the Indians—His Last Letter
to His Family—His Death—His Funeral—Bishop Ryan's Panegyric—
The Grief of the Indians—How Father De Smet's Work Lives After
Him.

ON July 1, 1871, Father De Smet sailed from New York
on his last journey to Belgium in search of men and
money for his missions. After visiting his native country
he spent the rest of the year in traveling through Holland,
Luxemburg, the north of France, England, and Ireland.
Never had he displayed more zeal nor obtained greater
success.

"What are the principal obstacles to the conversion of
the savages?" he was asked. "There is only one," he
replied, "the scarcity of priests. If we had enough priests
to instruct the Indians they would all become Catholics."

New apostles presented themselves, attracted by the
hope of a rich harvest of souls, and nine were accepted to
return to America with the eminent missionary.[1] In
Brussels, Antwerp, Ghent, Tournai, and Bruges charitable
and generous women gave quantities of ornaments and
sacred vessels for the mission churches.

[1] Father Guidi, then in his third year at Tronchiennes, was of this number.

In January, Father De Smet was forced to interrupt his travels and give up the conferences he usually made with young college students. "I am so weak," he writes, "that even a short conversation tires me. The doctor orders complete rest and forbids all work or preoccupation for the missions."[2]

On February 12th, at the college in Brussels, he was suddenly seized with a violent attack of nephritis, accompanied by frequent hemorrhages. It was thought necessary to bleed him, an operation very repugnant to the invalid; he resigned himself to it only by submission to the rule of St. Ignatius which enjoins obedience to the physician. His condition improved after a few days, but his strength returned so slowly that Dr. Cranincx, his old schoolmate at Mechlin, did not disguise his anxiety.

During the past two or three years, when it had seemed likely he would not be able to continue his missionary work, he had thought of returning to Belgium to live, founding there a training-school for apostolic work. A proof that he seriously contemplated this step is found in the following lines written by his brother-in-law, Mr. Charles Van Mossevelde: "During Father De Smet's stay in Termonde, we often went to my country-place, Saint-Gilles, and there in the garden we chose a spot for the chapel and the institution which he proposed to erect with the consent of his Superiors, to be opened as a novitiate for the American missions of the Society of Jesus. This was to have been built at my expense.

"Although ill and enfeebled after his last crossing, he could not be persuaded to rest. Ever confiding in God's help, he hoped to regain his strength sufficiently to return to his dear Indians. 'Oh,' said he, and it slipped out through excess of devotion to his missions, for he loved us too much to dispel our hopes of having him with us in his declining years, 'if I must die soon, I trust God will let me die in the midst of my Indians.'"[3]

[2] To Charles Van Mossevelde, Antwerp, Jan. 30, 1872.
[3] To Father Deynoodt, Termonde, Dec. 8, 1873.
More than once Father De Smet himself made illusion in his letters to this project: "Dear Rosalie, our conversations often return to the subject of erecting a chapel at Boomwijck, an agreeable perspective for me, now that I am nearing my seventieth year with the infirmities that usually ac-

In November, 1872, Father Boeteman opened an apostolic school at Turnhout, next to Mr. De Nef's old college, which had been prospering for forty years. Father De Smet took pleasure in encouraging this new work; he interested generously-disposed people in the cause, and sent them promising young men.[4]

After a sojourn of nine months in Europe, the missionary longed to return to his neophytes, but his friends tried to dissuade him from taking the long journey, telling him that even if he survived the voyage he would languish in a state of invalidism, for the malady from which he suffered was incurable. All that was human in him said: Stay! But a voice stronger than that of nature, the voice of zeal and charity, cried out: Go! You may still, in that far-off country, accomplish much good. Go to your beloved Indians; take them once more the fruit of your labors, your last words, and if need be, your last sigh!

And the old man went, tearing himself from his beloved family and friends. On April 7, 1872, he sailed from Antwerp with nine other missionaries, arriving eighteen days later at St. Louis, never to leave it again.

On October, 10, 1871, St. Louis University was the scene of a solemn and affecting ceremony, when Fathers Van Assche and Verreydt celebrated the fiftieth anniversary of their entrance into the novitiate at Whitemarsh. They, with Father De Smet, were the last surviving members of Father Nerinckx's little band.[5] From all parts of Missouri came the Jesuits to offer their congratulations to the pioneers of the Gospel, who with Father Van Quickenborne,

company this age, and from which I am not exempt. We all cherish illusions at times, and this is permissible when one leaves all in God's hands in perfect submission to His holy will." (To Charles and Rosalie Van Mossevelde, St. Louis, April 21, 1870.)

[4] "In helping this institution you are rendering a great service to the cause of Catholicism. From Turnhout will go forth in time young apostles, who, after the example of the first twelve, shall spread throughout the world the gracious light of the Gospel; in which work you will share through your zeal, help, and prayers." (To Mlle. Athalie Werbrouck, St. Louis, Nov. 8, 1872.)

[5] Father Verhaegen died at St. Charles in 1868, after having filled the office of Rector of the University and Provincial of the Missouri and Maryland Provinces. Father Van Assche died at Florissant in 1877; Father Verreydt at Cincinnati in 1883.

upon the hill overlooking the village of Florissant, had laid the cradle of the Province.

Detained in Europe, Father De Smet was unable to take part in this happy celebration. He was compensated in a measure, however, by the tokens of sympathy that came to him from all parts; the missionaries promised to say many Masses for him in gratitude for all he had done for them; the children of St. Ignatius' Mission sent to St. Louis a list of communions, prayers, and rosaries offered for "their good Father," on the occasion of his jubilee.

Nine years had passed since Father De Smet's last visit to the Rocky Mountains. One day the Cœur d'Alènes came to Father Cataldo, saying: "We wish to invite the great Black Robe to come once more to visit us." "Father De Smet is an old man," replied the missionary, "it will be difficult for him to make such a journey." "Be it so. But at least it will give him pleasure to hear that the Cœur d'Alènes keep him ever in grateful remembrance." [6]

The Flatheads and Kalispels professed the same attachment, and also pleaded for a visit from the beloved missionary. "Gladly would I undertake the journey did my health permit. It may be possible in the spring, but I must tell you the doctor gives me little hope and says I am *un oiseau pour le chat*," he was forced to reply. Then alluding to the wrongs suffered by the Flatheads,[7] he says, in a letter to Father Giorda, "I share in their sufferings and pray daily for their happiness and that they may persevere in the Faith. I ask the same grace for the Pend d'Oreilles, the Cœur d'Alènes, the Kootenais, etc. I am firmly convinced that their good Fathers will not abandon them." [8]

[6] The Annals of the Propagation of the Faith, 1874, p. 352.

[7] From 1870 the Government unceasingly urged the Flatheads to leave the Bitter Root Mountains, and, with the Kalispels, go north to the Jocko reservation near Missoula. In the summer of 1872 a convention was drawn up, by which the Indians were to give up their lands to the United States. "Witnesses present on the occasion, among them General Garfield himself, state that Charlot, chief of the Flatheads, opposed the convention, and refused to sign it. The original copy preserved at the Department of the Interior at Washington proves the truth of this statement. The act submitted to and approved by Congress nevertheless bears the name of Charlot as first signatory. Who was guilty of this flagrant violation of the rights of the tribes?" (Palladino, "Indian and White in the Northwest," p. 66.)   [8] St. Louis, Oct. 27, 1872.

Having been relieved of all his active duties, Father De Smet continued to serve the missions through his pen. He wrote articles of interest for the Catholic magazines in America and England, and in Belgium published a new edition of his "Letters,"[9] with some notices of the principal Missouri missionaries. "I wish, as far as in my power, to save them from oblivion, and at the same time give pleasure to their families."[10]

For his fellow-priests he began a history of the origin of the Province, but death arrested the work hardly begun. It is with deep emotion that we read these pages yellow with age, upon which the old missionary wrote the account of his first journey and his recollections of his novitiate.

During his sojourn at the University, the St. Louis Jesuits learned to appreciate the charm of Father De Smet's society, and the quality of his virtues. Their testimony enables us to throw in relief the distinguishing traits of this exceptional and noble figure. In community life he was noted for his amiability. Years had rendered even more indulgent his natural kindliness, and far from demanding consideration for himself, he sought the last place and permitted the younger members to joke and make merry with him.[11]

He was much sought after by outsiders. The prestige of his name and labors, his dignified and simple manners, his amiability, and the charm of his conversation, opened every circle to him. He was listened to for hours, less from deference to his person than for the charm of his recitals.[12]

"I can truthfully state," writes one of the St. Louis Fathers, "that there does not exist a priest, nay, not even a bishop, in the United States so well known and esteemed

[9] This edition in six volumes was published in Brussels (1873-1878) through the efforts of Father Deynoodt.

[10] Letter to Father Deynoodt, St. Louis, 1872.

[11] A few months before his death he wrote to one of the Belgian Fathers: "I am very grateful to you for the interest you take in the new edition of my 'Letters,' and I thank you for the good opinion you express about me. Your Reverence honors me in thinking that I am so popular, but this is far from being the case. In any case, should I become so, it will not be because I merit popularity." (To Father Deynoodt. Quoted at the beginning of his Selected Letters, 4th Series, pp. viii and ix.)

[12] The Woodstock Letters, 1874, p. 62.

as Father De Smet. He is the glory of the University, the idol of Americans. I know a man who traveled a great distance for the sole pleasure of seeing him; another told me he would give almost anything to hear him preach." [13]

He seldom preached, however, but he waxed eloquent in conversation when speaking about the unjust treatment of the Indians. On one occasion he was asked: "How could you take pleasure in being with those terrible savages?" "Terrible savages!" he replied. "You do not know what you are saying. You do not know these simple, good people. I have met many more savages in the great cities of America and Europe than in the plains and deserts of the West. Why is it astonishing that the Indians attach so little value to the blessings and advantages of civilization? They judge them by the vices which the whites practice under their eyes. And what have they seen to appreciate in the conduct of the American agents, who have often robbed them?" [14]

This frankness never offended any one; Protestants and Catholics alike, officers and statesmen, professed great esteem for the missionary. One of his greatest friends was Dr. Linton, a Presbyterian convert, for thirty years a professor at the St. Louis University. A remarkably gifted man, he was not only a physician, but a poet and an orator; he was deeply attached to the Society of Jesus,[15] and to him we owe one of the most precious souvenirs of Father De Smet, namely, the "Linton Album," a richly-bound volume replete with photographs and drawings, in which the missionary year by year inscribed his itinerary.[16] On his return from every journey he found his friend's

[13] Letter from Father Busschots to Father Deynoodt, St. Louis, Good Friday, 1875.

[14] Cf. Bishop Ryan's sermon at Father De Smet's funeral, in the *Western Watchman*, St. Louis, May 31, 1873.

[15] "*Ad majorem Dei gloriam!* Who devised this motto? I should like to know. Nothing is more sublime; nothing more profound is to be found in human language than these four words. They embrace heaven and earth, and apply equally to the most august hierarchies that surround the throne of God and the humblest dwellers on earth. They contain what is greatest in poetry and eloquence; they signify what is holiest, most worthy, and best in time and eternity." (Extract from a farewell letter written by Dr. Linton to the St. Louis Jesuits a fortnight before his death. Cf. W. Hill, "Historical Sketch of the St. Louis University," p. 112.)

[16] The Linton Album is now the property of the St. Louis University.

25

book lying open on his table; he would then take his pen and in his clear, firm handwriting add a page to the account of his expeditions. No doubt it was an immense satisfaction to sum up the number of miles he had traveled. From 1821 to 1872 it amounted to 260,929 miles, nearly nine times the distance around the earth.[17] Many explorers and travelers have won fame for much less.

Through his high connections, Father De Smet could have furthered his personal ambitions, but never did he profit by them save in behalf of the Indians. Nor did he sacrifice for popularity the interest of souls or his priestly duties. Such was his reputation for integrity that even the worst enemies of the Church and the Society of Jesus were constrained to exclaim: "If only he was one of us!"[18]

The motive power of his life was the spirit of faith; this gave him the courage to face the hardships of his prodigious labors. He tells us this himself in a letter written in 1849, after his first journey to the Sioux: "To those who have passed their days amid the joys of family life, and been blessed with prosperity, a journey across the desert appears a forbidding experience of human suffering and misery. But he who lifts his thoughts above the passing things of the world to consider truth, which all nature speaks, and desires the salvation of the many souls who would love and serve their Creator if they but knew Him—he sees in the privations of the desert and in the dangers and perils one encounters there, but slight inconveniences, far preferable to the sweets of indolence and the dangers of riches. Such a man meditates on the words of the Saviour: 'The kingdom of heaven suffereth violence, and the violent carry it away.' He recalls the sufferings and trials of God, made man, 'who being without sin, yet bore all sufferings.' Through tribulation and dangers, through cold and

---

[17] It is possible that this number is somewhat exaggerated, as Father De Smet, in his first journeys, was often forced to roughly estimate distances.

[18] Long ago Father De Smet had learned how little men's favor counts. "All is vanity on this earth and nothing wholly satisfies the human heart. Many times have I realized this truth in my travels, when I have conversed with men of all religions, of every shade of opinion, and of all classes of society. The happiest are the believers, I mean, the children of the Church, and among them also are found those who make others happy." (Selected Letters, 3d Series, p. 262.)

heat, through blood and death, did Christ enter into the kingdom of His Father; along this path must he travel who wishes to live and die under His noble standard." [19]

The spirit of faith also explains Father De Smet's calm assurance in adversity, which was so much admired by those around him. "I lived with him for some time," writes Father Gazzoli, "and more than once accompanied him on laborious journeys over bad roads, through bad weather and countless other difficulties, and what always struck me was his unalterable cheerfulness and equanimity of temper." [20]

Refusing nothing to the Master he served, he counted always on His providence, and abandoned himself to it with a simplicity that recalls the naïve confidence of the saints. He was sincerely attached to his vocation and declared he had found in it the hundredfold promise: "In the course of my long peregrinations through the world, it is in community life that I have found the greatest happiness to which man can aspire here below." [21] He knew, moreover, that to fully enjoy the advantages and rewards of this state, one must accept its obligations.

"Poverty for him was not an empty word; he loved to see it put into practice. Those who lived with him knew how he disliked to see a priest too elegant and fastidious in his dress, which he contended impaired his prestige with the faithful, and shocked them not less than excessive negligence. He was most careful and exact in his own expenditures, and although he administered the finances of the Province for many years, he never spent the smallest sum upon himself without asking permission." [22]

[19] To Gustave Van Kerckhove, St. Louis, May 1, 1849.
[20] To Father Deynoodt, Cœur d'Alènes Mission, Aug. 2, 1879. In another letter Father Gazzoli relates the following fact, told him by an old Iroquois, one of Father De Smet's former guides: "During one of his journeys, the missionary, overcome with fatigue, gave the order to camp. His traveling companions protested, saying there was no water in that locality, but, as he insisted, they gave way. The Father, who had never traveled through this country before, assured them they would find water and indicated the spot. They went and found enough water for the caravan. Every member of the party attributed the find to the prayers of the missionary." (To Father Deynoodt, Jan. 6, 1881.)
[21] To the Superior of the Servants of Mary, at Erps-Querbs, Brussels, Dec. 3, 1856.
[22] The Woodstock Letters, 1874. "Father De Smet. His Services to the

380 THE LIFE OF FATHER DE SMET, S. J.

Yet still more remarkable was his obedience. Father Coosemans, for nine years his Superior, speaks of it in the following words: "Father De Smet valued and practiced obedience to a degree that astonished outsiders, who marveled to see an old, white-haired man as obedient as a little child. He never undertook the shortest journey without the sanction of his Superior. If the affair in question was important, approbation was not sufficient; he wished an express order. Then and then only did he confidently set off, sure of heaven's protection, to brave gladly the dangers and hardships inseparable from his journeys. In community life he observed faithfully and strictly the rules of the house; although strangers often came to visit him during the evening recreation, he somehow managed always to be present at the Litanies.[23] It sometimes happened he was unable to get rid of his visitor, when he would beg to be excused to attend evening prayers."[24] Such virtue as his found its nourishment in a sincere and tender piety. From 1827 on Father De Smet offered daily and with lively faith the Holy Sacrifice of the Mass. Even during his long journeys he omitted it only on rare occasions through force of circumstances.

We have often spoken of his devotion to the Blessed Virgin. During his dangerous voyages he invoked the protection of her who, though gloriously enthroned in heaven, still keeps the heart of a mother, the all-powerful Mother of Him who rules the waves.[25] The rosary he wore in his girdle and which he recited daily, was the means of many conversions.[26]

After the example of Father Marquette, who centuries before had consecrated the valley of the Mississippi to the

Society, and his Religious Life," p. 63. Article by Rev. R. Meyer, later Provincial of Missouri, and assistant of England.

[23] In Jesuit houses it is the custom to recite the Litany of the Saints in the evening.

[24] Letter to Father Deynoodt, Chicago, April 26, 1876.

[25] Itinerary, 1856.

[26] This rosary, worn thin by the missionary's fingers, is to-day the property of one of his nieces, Madam Liénart of Tournai. She tells us, "One of my cousins, ill with typhoid fever, was *in extremis*. Father De Smet's rosary was put under her pillow, and immediately her condition improved and she finally recovered. I was at that time very delicate and my mother hung the precious rosary near my bed, where it has remained for thirty years." (Tournai, Nov. 3, 1910.)

Immaculate Virgin, he gave the name of St. Mary to the first mountain mission. He loved to associate the happiest memories of his life with the feasts of the Virgin. "After Him who is the Author of all good," he said, "let us render thanks to Her whom the Church permits us to call *our life, our sweetness,* and *our hope,* since it has pleased divine goodness that great favors should be accorded us on the feasts in which she is especially honored." [27]

All Father De Smet's friends knew of the confidence he reposed in St. Anthony. On more than one occasion the great wonder-worker had found things for him, seemingly lost beyond reclaim. He himself loved to tell of instances: "You have perhaps heard that I had on board the *Humboldt* [28] a case filled with silver chalices and monstrances. For five months I believed they were at the bottom of the sea; I made a novena to St. Anthony—rather late, you will say. But not so, for a month afterward the case was returned to me in as good condition as when it left the shop." [29]

Another distinguishing trait of piety was his touching devotion to the souls in purgatory. "Every time," writes Father Coosemans, "that he returned from a long journey, either from Europe or across the plains from the Far West, we knew he would ask Masses for his dear souls. In fact, whenever a serious difficulty arose, or he found himself facing danger, he asked the help of the souls in purgatory. In return he promised them many Masses, more even than he could himself say, but he counted on the charity of his fellow-priests, who willingly helped him discharge his debt." [30]

The hour of reward for the heroic missionary was approaching. Scarcely had he returned to St. Louis when the kidney trouble from which he had suffered at Brussels reappeared in an exaggerated form. "As regards my health," he writes on June 21st, "the machine is completely out of order. For two months I have been confined

[27] Letter to the Carmelites of Termonde, Bitter Root, Oct. 26, 1841. ("Journeys in the Rocky Mountains," 2d Edition, p. 214.)
[28] In regard to the shipwreck of the *Humboldt*, see p. 297.
[29] Letter to Mr. J. Key, a ship-owner at Antwerp, St. Louis, Sept. 12, 1854.
[30] Letter quoted.

to my room by order of the doctor, and I have to follow a very strict and, for me, quite new régime. My mantel-piece looks like a drug-shop and the very sight of it takes away my appetite. I am extremely feeble. Nevertheless, I am not without hope, for I am convalescing. May God's will be done."[31]

In this weakened state of health he depended more and more upon the affection of his family, and he thanked them effusively for a pilgrimage they made to Lourdes for his recovery. "Your kind and dear letter," he writes, "was a most agreeable surprise. It is always a day of rejoicing when I hear from my family, and I will always be grateful to those who write to me and remember me. I pray especially for them each time I have the happiness of ascending to the altar. Encourage them all to write often, if only a few lines."[32]

One of his nieces sent him a chasuble, "whose beautiful handwork was much admired by the whole community." To her husband he wrote, "Dear Gustave, please give Marie my best thanks. This chasuble is a souvenir which, with my Superior's permission, I will keep to the end of my days. I promise you to wear it on all the feasts of the Blessed Virgin, when I will offer the Holy Sacrifice for the pious donor's intention, for the welfare and happiness of her husband and dear children, for her esteemed parents, and for all those whose intentions she wishes to join to hers."[33] In return he sent "Indian curiosities" and holy pictures for the children, and "a big kiss for dear little Paul and Etienne."[34]

The year 1872 in the United States was marked by the presidential campaign which preceded Grant's reelection. Father De Smet, however, took little interest in politics,[35]

---

[31] To Father Deynoodt.

[32] To his nephew Emile de Meren, Sept. 6, 1872.

[33] To Gustave Van Kerckhove, Sept. 11, 1872.

[34] Paul and Etienne De Smet, grandsons of Francis, the brother of the missionary.

[35] "To a disinterested spectator, the campaign is amusing. The whole city is decorated, either for Greeley or Grant. Every night bands of music march through the streets with banners, followed by thousands shouting to wake the dead and burning an enormous amount of fireworks. It is unbearable, yet one gets accustomed to it. The world must go on in its own way, and after all there is no harm in working for either Greeley or Grant;

the progress of Catholicism being his sole occupation. "When we first came to St. Louis the town boasted of 4,000 inhabitants and possessed but one church. To-day its population numbers 450,000 and next Sunday the Bishop will bless the thirty-sixth church. Our first establishment in Missouri was composed of two Fathers, seven novices, and three lay Brothers. We now number two hundred and seventy-five; we possess three large colleges and a dozen houses with prosperous missions." [36]

It had always been a trial for the ardent apostle not to be able to share the labors of his fellow-priests. However, in 1870, when an eight-day retreat brought together an immense congregation in the college church in St. Louis, Father De Smet gave the Benediction of the Blessed Sacrament every evening. On the last day of the retreat he celebrated Mass and helped two other priests distribute two thousand communions. He wept for joy.

Some months before his death he devoted himself to an aged infidel, and with untiring patience and goodness taught him the elements of religion. Upon the feast of the Immaculate Conception he had the joy of conferring baptism upon him.

This was his last apostolic act. Two days later he writes: "I feel very weak; my left eye is totally paralyzed, and the sight is gone. The winter has been a severe one; never have we had such weather since I first came to St. Louis; fogs, snows, and unprecedented cold. Old and full of infirmities, I await with resignation my last hour. *Expecto donec veniat immutatio mea.*" [37] He was so low at one

one is as good as the other. You say that in Europe you wonder which will be victorious. The individual majority favor Greeley, but Grant's party has the money, which is used unstintingly to assure his reelection. You can count upon his victory as assured; and once in it will be difficult to get him out of the White House. Grant is a Methodist, a man of no particular merit, the tool and humble servant of the radical party—just as William of Prussia is the tool of Bismarck." (To Emile de Meren, St. Louis, Sept. 6, 1872.)

In regard to Grant's sectarian policy, see Claudio Jannet, "Les Etats-Unis Contemporains," Paris, 1877, Vol. II, p. 66.

[36] To Leon Van Mossevelde.

The Province of Missouri to-day numbers nearly 900 religious. It possesses a dozen colleges, eight residences, and a mission in British Honduras.

[37] To Father Deynoodt, Dec. 10, 1872.

time that the Last Sacraments were administered, but the crisis passed and he once more took hope.

For two years the Sioux had been expecting him to come and found a mission, and in October a deputation of chiefs arrived to remind him of his promise. On February 18th he wrote to the Catholic agent at Grand River, "I hope the approaching spring may be of some service in regaining my lost strength and general health. In regard to my prospects of seeing the Indians in the spring later, it is difficult to determine beforehand and under my present dispositions. Should there be any prospect on my part, I shall certainly inform you in due time." A month later he wrote him again: "Captain La Barge's boat (*De Smet*) is advertised for Benton, and will leave St. Louis on the 12th of April. My room is kept ready and at my disposal. Should my health permit I shall gladly undertake the trip. I had of late a very severe attack of sickness. I am again convalescent and in good hope."[38]

Those who saw the old man daily did not share his illusions. He could scarcely get out of a carriage, and himself acknowledged "that since his return from Belgium he had aged ten years."[39] He soon realized he must abandon all hope of leaving St. Louis. His heart was crushed with disappointment, and in the following words he assures the Sioux of his prayers and that he will always keep them in mind. To their agent he wrote: "I sympathize sincerely with my good Indian friends, who have been very severely visited by sickness this last winter and lost many of their dear children. I pray for them daily that the Lord may have pity on them and take them under His holy protection." It was the old missionary's last farewell to those he had loved so dearly.

The spring that year was backward. In the middle of May a succession of hurricanes and thunder-storms battered the windows of the University; torrents of rain and hail fell from a lowering sky. The cold was so intense that in many places travelers perished from it. Such weather was very trying for the invalid. "For seven months," he writes his family, "I have been sitting in the

[38] To Major O'Connor, March 24, 1873.
[39] To Charles and Rosalie Van Mosseveldé, Feb. 14, 1873.

chimney-corner, and I find my fire an agreeable companion. Since all things change in this world, I still hope for fine weather, and I shall enjoy it when it comes. The next time I write I hope to give you more reassuring news." [40]

But this letter, alas! was the last news he gave his family. It seemed as though he had a presentiment that this was his farewell, for he had never been more affectionate. "The devoted and fraternal sentiments you constantly express in your letters have touched me deeply. I am most grateful. Let me now speak openly. In my present condition the great project which was often the subject of our conversation continues to allure me; [41] but I fear it is but a *château en Espagne*, for the reason that I am not equal to the journey. In the meanwhile ask God that His holy will, and that alone, may be accomplished." Then alluding to a stanza that his sister Rosalie, then seventy-six years of age, had sent him, he essayed a reply in rhyme. This innocent badinage shows at least with what serenity he saw the close of his life approaching.

A last act of kindness and consideration for others precipitated his end. His intimate friend, Captain La Barge, was about to launch a new steamboat on the Missouri, and asked Father De Smet to bless it. Not wishing to refuse the request of one who had so often obliged him in his visits to the Indians, he accepted, and the ceremony took place on May 13th. That evening he felt much worse. The next day, after saying Mass, he said to the server: "This is the end. I shall never again ascend the altar."

The last attack was of unusual severity. Finally a painful operation was performed. It gave relief, but his weakness increased daily. On the 20th he asked for the Last Sacraments and received them once more with touching piety and perfect resignation. From that time, we are told, [42] he seemed oblivious of earth and thought only of eternity.

"During his life he was not exempt from the fear of

[40] To Charles and Rosalie Van Mossevelde, May 4, 1873.
[41] The project referred to was the institution M. Van Mossevelde thought of founding at his country-place, Saint-Gilles. See p. 373.
[42] Fathers O'Neil and De Blieck.

death; but at the end his fears vanished."[43] If he ceased praying it was but to speak of God's goodness and infinite mercy. He found consolation in the thought of the hundreds of little children he had baptized, who were now praying for him in heaven.

"When I saw Father De Smet last, on Wednesday, the 21st of May, two days before his death," said Bishop Ryan, Coadjutor of St. Louis, "I found him full of courage and hope. He said to me: 'I have served the good God for many years; I am going to come before Him pretty soon, and my heart is very full of confidence and real consolation. I have the greatest hope,' he said further, 'in the efficacy of the prayers of all to whom the Lord sent me in times past; I count especially on the merits of Jesus Christ, poor sinner that I am, and I love to think that the Lord will have pity on me in my hour of agony.'"[44]

During the nights of the 22d and 23d it was evident that the end was at hand, and final absolution was given with plenary indulgence *in articulo mortis*. Up to the last moment he retained full use of his faculties, and he was calm and seemed not to suffer. At a quarter past two on the morning of the feast of the Ascension he rendered up his soul to Him whom he had ardently loved and for whose glory he had labored for fifty years.

The news of his death caused universal sorrow. Newspapers of every shade of opinion outrivaled each other in praise of the missionary. The *Missouri Republican* said: "In him the world loses one of the most intrepid pioneers of Christian civilization. If he did not accomplish all that he believed possible, he at least gave an example of what a profound conviction can do in the struggle against insurmountable obstacles."[45]

The funeral took place on May 24th in St. Francis Xavier's church. In the center of the nave stood the catafalque, draped in black and covered with flowers. The upper part of the body could be seen through the coffin lid; over his head had been placed a wreath of white

[43] Father Coosemans' letter to M. Van Mossevelde, Chicago, June 1, 1873.
[44] Funeral Oration over Father De Smet.
[45] Issue of May 24, 1873.

roses. From early morning, crowds pressed around the precious remains, eager to look for the last time on the apostle of the Indians, who even in death wore his kindly smile.

What a striking contrast to the life of this humble man was his funeral, worthy of a prince of the Church! The aged Archbishop of St. Louis, Mgr. Kenrick, assisted by his coadjutor, presided. With the clergy from the different parishes mingled secular and regular priests, come from Chicago and Cincinnati to attend. The army was represented by three generals, General Harney being one, and by a large number of other officers. After the solemn High Mass celebrated by Father Van Assche, Bishop Ryan gave the absolution, and mounting the pulpit preached the funeral oration over the departed missionary.

Comparing Father De Smet to the great priest Onias, he applied to him the words of the sacred book of Machabees: "That truly good and gentle man, so modest in his countenance, so regular and moderate in his ways, so agreeable in his speech and who had practiced all kinds of virtues from his youth up.[46] Such were the eminent qualities of that Onias, high priest of Judea, whom the Jews so bitterly bewailed and whose loss was regretted by even Antiochus himself, mindful of the amenity of character of the great priest and of the upright life he had led. These words, my brethren, are admirably suited to the apostolic man whose mortal remains are here exposed to your view before the holy altar.

"Despite the luster which his apostolic labors shed over his person, and all the meritorious work which marked his life, this man of God displayed in all his conduct the simplicity of a child; he was kindly, candid, modest, and even showed the timidity of tender years, and the language of Tertullian may be applied to him, which he was wont to use in speaking of the old servants of Christ in his time: 'They are old men, but at the same time they have the graces and simplicity of youth. The purity of their lives and the cleanliness and uprightness of their souls enable

---

[46] "*Virum bonum et benignum, verecundum visu, modestum moribus, et eloquio decorum, et qui a puero in virtutibus exercitatus sit.*" (2 *Mach. xv. 12.*)

them to preserve to the close of their lives the springtime freshness of their earlier years.' Such was our regretted and venerable friend; he was at the evening of his life what he had been at the dawn of his career and at the noonday of manhood. It was his rare qualities of rectitude and simplicity that won him the confidence of so many friends, and it was the support of this confidence, with God's help, that enabled him to effect such great things." [47]

After recalling thus Father De Smet's characteristic virtues, Bishop Ryan spoke at length of his love for the Indians and his devotion to their cause. Although hastily prepared, his discourse vibrated with emotion and profoundly impressed his audience. Sobs resounded through the church and sorrow bowed every head.

The remains were taken to Florissant for burial in a modest enclosure where Fathers Van Quickenborne, De Theux, Elet, Van de Velde, Smedts, and Verhaegen were sleeping their last sleep. After so many years of arduous travel, the heroic old missionary had come to seek his long rest near his novitiate, beside those who had been his Superiors, his friends, and his fellow-workers.

A few days later, the new steamboat that Father De Smet had blessed shortly before his death sailed up the Missouri. When the *De Smet* arrived in the Indian country, the redskins, having learned of the Black Robe's death, flocked to the landings, emitting wails of grief, and covering their heads with dust. "Not only the Christians," writes Father Guidi, "but pagans as well wept over the loss of their beloved Father, and many Indians regard his loss as a calamity to their tribe, which alas! is but too true!" [48]

But great as was his loss, Father De Smet's work was still to survive. Without counting the Franciscans, Oblates, and secular missionaries, thirty Jesuits were in charge of seven flourishing foundations in the Rocky Mountains.[49]

---

[47] Chittenden-Richardson.
[48] To Father Adolph Petit, rector of Tronchiennes, Colville, Oct., 1873.
[49] The following is a list of the foundations:
St. Mary's Mission among the Flatheads. This mission, founded in 1841, was attached to St. Ignatius' Mission in 1891.

Twenty years later in Montana alone the Catholics resident in the nine missions numbered seven thousand. If lately, progress has been less marked, it is because the race, being more and more confined to restricted reservations, has declined. The Cœur d'Alènes, now reduced to a few hundreds, have remained a saintly tribe, among whom a priest can hear confessions for years without ever having to absolve a single mortal sin. The Sioux, for whose conversion Father De Smet labored twenty-five years, have several missions in South Dakota, and have become as strong Christians as they were formerly terrifying warriors. Even in Alaska the Indians have received the Gospel, and among those who have been attracted to this fruitful apostolate, many have acknowledged that Father De Smet's example decided their vocation.

Thus the missionary's work lives after him,[50] and although he was powerless to prevent the extermination of

St. Ignatius' Mission among the Pend d'Oreilles or Kalispels.
The Sacred Heart Mission among the Cœur d'Alénes.
The St. Paul Mission at Colville on the Columbia.
St. Peter's Mission among the Blackfeet on the Upper Missouri.
St. Joseph's Mission among the Yakimas, in the State of Oregon.
The Mission of the Sacred Hearts of Jesus and Mary, at Helena.
To these missions were attached other less important posts established among the different tribes, notably those for the Spokanes and Kootenais. In 1884, Senator George Vest informed the Senate in full session of the growing prosperity of these missions: "I can assert that nowhere in the United States have such satisfactory results been obtained as in the Jesuit Missions. . . . The girls are taught needlework; they are taught to sew and teach; they are taught music; they are taught to keep house. The young men are taught to work upon the farm, to herd cattle, to be blacksmiths, carpenters, and millwrights. . . . I do not speak with any sort of denominational prejudice in favor of the Jesuits. I was taught to abhor the whole sect. I was raised in that good, old-school Presbyterian church that looked upon a Jesuit as very much akin to the devil, . . . but I defy any one to find me a single tribe of Indians on the plains—blanket Indians—that approximate, in civilization, to the Flatheads, who have been under the control of the Jesuits for fifty years. I say that out of eleven tribes that I saw, and I say this as a Protestant—where they had had Protestant missionaries, they had not made a single solitary advance toward civilization, not one; yet among the Flatheads, where there were two Jesuit Missions, you find farms, you find civilization, you find Christianity, you find the relation of husband and wife and of father and child scrupulously observed." (Speech of George Vest before the Senate of the United States, May 12, 1884.)
[50] The Rocky Mountain Missions, with those of Dakota and southern Alaska, form to-day a part of the California Province, founded in 1909. Of the four hundred members composing the Province, over one hundred devote their lives to the apostolate of the Indians.

the Western tribes in the United States, he procured for
the Indians in the bosom of the Catholic Church the
assurance of a better life and of a kingdom that could not
be taken from them through the injustice of men.[51]

[51] At Termonde on Sept. 23, 1878, was unveiled a statue erected by the
Belgians to the apostle of the Rocky Mountains. Many civil and ecclesiastical notables were present. Father Charles Verbeke of the Society of
Jesus pronounced an eloquent panegyric, followed by a cantata, the work
of the illustrious composer, Edgar Tinel. (See the *Précis Historiques*,
1878, p. 699, *et seq.*)

This monument stands in the center of a square beside Notre Dame College. The sculptor, Fraikin, has represented the missionary holding in
one hand a crucifix and in the other an olive branch. On the pedestal is
the following inscription:

PETRUS · JOHANNES · DE   SMET

E · SOCIETATE · JESU

PERPETUITATE · LAUDIS · VIVET

QUOD · XXX · ANNORUM · LABORIBUS

INDOS · ULTRA · MONTES · SAXOSOS

A · BARBARIE · AD · RELIGIONEM · CIVILEMQUE · CULTUM

TRADUXIT

INDEX